TESTIMONY

TAKEN IN

AN INVESTIGATION

BEFORE A JOINT COMMITTEE OF THE

MICHIGAN LEGISLATURE OF 1875,

Touching the Administration of the Affairs of the

STATE PRISON AT JACKSON.

BY AUTHORITY.

LANSING:
W. S. GEORGE & CO., STATE PRINTERS AND BINDERS.
1875.

STATE PRISON INVESTIGATION.

PRELIMINARY PROCEEDINGS IN THE HOUSE AND SENATE.

On March 29th, 1875, the following preamble and concurrent resolution were introduced into the Senate by Senator Redfield and adopted. It was concurred in by the House March 31:

Whereas, The Daily Press, a newspaper printed and published in the city of Adrian, Lenawee county, in this State, charges in its daily edition of the 27th and 29th instant that John Morris and his subordinates in charge of the State Prison at Jackson have practiced extreme cruelty upon the convicts in said prison; " that about nine months since a convict therein received 100 lashes upon the bare back;" " that another convict was strung up by the thumbs for 24 hours, and in consequence thereof is now a cripple for life;" " that another convict was taken out into the yard and plunged into cold water, and died before they got him out;" "that on Friday, the 19th instant, a convict over the age of sixty years was stripped and strung up to a post and received 25 lashes upon his bare back, from which he is now in the hospital of said prison;" therefore,

Resolved (the House concurring), That the committees of the Senate and House upon the State Prison be instructed to investigate the said charges, and that they have power and authority to send for persons and papers, and report the result of said investigation; and that such investigation shall be conducted without secrecy and with doors open to the public.

On April 7, 1875, the following concurrent resolution was introduced into the Senate by Senator Warren and adopted. It was concurred in by the House April 8:

Resolved, By the Senate (the House concurring), That Hon. Wm. L. Webber, Senator from the 25th District, be added to the committee of the two Houses for the purpose of investigating charges made against the Agent of the State Prison, as directed by concurrent resolution of the 29th ultimo.

On April 8, 1875, the following concurrent resolution was introduced into the Senate by Senator Nelson and adopted. It was concurred in by the House April 9:

Resolved, By the Senate (the House concurring), That the powers of the joint committee on examination of the charges against the management of the State Prison at Jackson be enlarged so as to embrace the general administration of the prison during the time Mr. Morris has been acting as agent of the prison.

The members from the Senate consisted of Messrs. Nelson, Jones, Mellen, and Webber; and from the House, Messrs. Livingstone, Eggleston, Morse, Bartow, and Keyes. Mr. Bartow was chosen chairman.

TESTIMONY TAKEN.

WM. S. WILCOX SWORN.

Examined by Senator Webber :

Q. Mr. Wilcox, you are one of the inspectors of the State prison at Jackson?
A. Yes, sir.
Q. How long have you been acting as such inspector?
A. Six years.
Q. Where is your residence?
A. Adrian.
Q. During the six years that you have been inspector, how often have you visited the State prison at Jackson?
A. I think I visited it every month, and sometimes oftener.
Q. And when you visit it, state, if you please, generally, what duties you perform at the prison—what examination you make as to its conduct?
A. We examine the monthly statement, the financial statement for the month; we, during our visit there, either separately as inspectors, or in company with each other, go through the prison, through the workshops, and through the insane asylum. We decide upon the good time to be taken from the prisoners, upon record of the infractions of the rules, and of the punishments therefor, as read before the inspectors at every monthly meeting, and we have that record to judge from in deciding upon the good time to be taken from or allowed the convicts. One of the items of business of the board is to give any convict an opportunity to come before us and make any complaint he may have of any treatment that is not satisfactory to him, or the officers of the prison, and in deciding their good time, if it is an important case, where the convict has committed a good many infractions of the rules, and it looks as though he were going to lose all his time, as a rule give him an opportunity to make a statement before the board.

Q In making these examinations, is it usual for the three inspectors to be and act together, or do they go separately?
A. In making the examinations of the prison and books, accounts, etc., as a rule we keep together.
Q. Have you any set time in the month for making these examinations?
A. Yes; the law provides the first Wednesday in the month. I may be mistaken as to the law providing it, but this is the rule.
Q. That is the time you go?
A. Yes; the time we go together.
Q. Now, in making these examinations, how much time does the board of inspectors occupy at the prison each visit, say?
A. Well, two days, sometimes three days or parts of the third day. There have been instances where we have used more time, but this is very rare.
Q. When convicts are allowed an opportunity to come before the inspectors and make a statement, is the agent present?

EXPLANATION.

It is due to Mr. Wilcox to say that some of the questions and answers were not taken in full, and that in a few instances he is made to say sentences in a manner and with a meaning different from what he wished to convey.

A. He is sometimes and sometimes he is not. If the convict notifies us that he wishes to see us we give him an opportunity to do it in the absence of the agent. If we send for him not feeling fully satisfied, in order to make good time or take from him, the agent is present if he wishes to be.

Q. You have adopted rules and regulations for the discipline and government of the prison?

A. Yes, sir.

Q. (Handing witness a copy of book.) Is this a copy of those rules?

A. I suppose that it is; I have never read this copy. We adopted rules and they were printed, and I have no doubt but this is a copy of the rules.

Q. This appears to have been revised the 4th of February, 1873?

A. Yes, sir.

Q. Have you made any material changes in the rules and regulations since that date?

A. I do not now recollect of any.

Q. At the time of this revision was there any material changes from the rules in force before this date?

A. Yes, sir.

Q. Have you a copy of the rules which were in force before February 4, 1874?

A. No, sir.

Q. What discretion has the agent given him by the inspectors as to inflicting punishment upon convicts?

A. I do not now recollect of any definite regulation upon that point, only the general feeling and views of the board, as made known to him from time to time. Almost every session we talk,—when he reads over the convict record,—we talk about it and give him our general views. We never set an exacting mode upon him. We never specify that he shall specify in this direction so much and no more, or in any other direction.

Q. State whether the inspectors have ever adopted any rules and regulations providing the character of the punishment to be inflicted, or the offense for which punishment shall be inflicted by the agent.

A. I would like to answer that question yes or no, but would like to explain.

Q. Answer it just as you choose, so that it is just as it is.

A. Yes, I think you will get the facts in the case in that way. When I first went to the prison we conferred together in regard to the discipline and decided that the punishments were entirely too severe, especially such as had been represented to have been administered there, and we requested if there were any convicts who required punishment that they be put in the cell and wait until we could decide. That was the work for some time. When Mr. Morris came into the prison it was the understanding of the board of inspectors and Mr. Morris, that we dispense with the severe punishment entirely, and proposed or talked of an entire abandonment of the lash. It is understood by the Inspectors, or the Agent understands from the Inspectors, that we expect discipline there.

[Witness handed a copy of report of inspectors to the Governor.] Reads several rules. We have never said to Mr. Morris, "You shall administer so many lashes." From the reports of Mr. Morris, and from the character of the convicts he had punished, the inspectors were led to believe that it was safe to leave this matter largely in his hands, and there has been no specific number of lashes—no limit.

Q. And no offense for which lashes shall be inflicted?

A. Yes, sir; the lashes have been inflicted.

Q. In what way, when offenses for which the agent should be at liberty to inflict?

A. I think this I shall read is endorsed by the the board.

Q. I speak now of written rules and regulations in the statute.

A. I don't recollect that there is a written rule. [Witness reads from 6 and 7 pages of prison rules for 1874.] Now, I want to add to this, that about twenty months ago we ordered the lash out of the prison ; and if Mr. Morris will show me the substitute, I will let you see what we use.

By Mr. Barlow:

Q. How long since was that?

A. About twenty months. We have no record of the use of the lash before the Board of Inspectors for the last about twenty months. [Witness shows substitute : a leather strap some two feet long, and perhaps one and one-half inches wide, with short wooden handle.] This instrument was adopted as a substitute for the lash. This was the only thing we have to punish a man with. I mean that we inflict a punishment with, and this is termed a " strap." You can call it anything you are a mind to. We punish with the strap. It is understood by the Inspectors that that will not draw blood in the hands of the most brutal man inside the prison. If we thought it would we should make it thinner, or if it made black places under it where it strikes. It will make a red place.

Q. State whether you have ever been present to witness the punishment of any convicts either by the lash, strap, or otherwise?

A. I have never seen a man showered ; have never seen a man whipped. I have seen a man on what we called the " cross."

Q. Describe, if you please, this weapon you have called the cross—the instrument and the manner of applying it.

A. There is an upright standard with a cross upon it which can be adjusted to the height of a man. The convicts stand up to the cross, and it is placed across his shoulders. On either end of this cross is a strap. One strap goes once round the wrist, the other goes over and comes around twice and buckles back. 1 think the strap was drawn through the slat on this cross instead of being nailed on ; it was reported it was nailed on. I came into the prison from early breakfast from the outside gate, as I have done a great many times, at any and all hours before any of the officers of the prison knew I was there, and wandered round among the prisoners. I had an aversion to this cross from the commencement, not from its cruelty, but from the associations that the public would connect with it. I went into that room ; I have been in a good many times, but this was the only instance I ever found a man on the cross. One arm was on the cross and the other fastened ; one arm was loose. This was the only man I ever saw on the cross there. He had been on for about an hour then. Just before I went to dinner (I generally leave about two o'clock) I slipped out there and slipped up again to see how the man was getting along, and he was gone. That is all the punishment that I have ever witnessed.

Q. State whether this convict was made fast to this cross in any other manner than by the wrists, as you speak of ?

A. He was not.

Q. Do you know whether it has been the practice in the prison to make them fast otherwise than by the wrists?

A. I do not know it from my own personal knowledge.

Q Have you had any information from Mr. Morris, since he has been acting as Agent, on that point ?

A. I had information from some one, that there was an arrangement made so. They were in the habit of carrying this cross away with them. A strong man could carry it about, and an arrangement was made so that they could not get a hitch upon the cross and lift it away.

Q. You said a short time ago, that it was the rule for some time, to abolish the use of the lash. State whether that was a written rule, or merely oral instruction to the Agent?

A. That was oral instruction to Mr. Bingham.

Q. How long has Mr. Morris been acting as Agent at the Prison?

A. Four years.

Q. Who were the Inspectors beside yourself?

A. L. W. Lovell of Climax, and A. A. Bliss of Jackson.

Q. How long has Mr. Lovell been acting as Inspector?

A. It must be either three or four years.

Q. How long has Mr. Bliss been acting as Inspector?

A. Over a year; I don't know but two years; time passes with me very rapidly.

Q. What instruction, and state whether oral or written, has the Agent received, as to offenses for which he should be at liberty to inflict corporal punishment?

A. It is understood that a freeman, a keeper, or a foreman (all these contractors have to be foremen), must not be meddled with by prisoners. That is considered a very grave offense. We could not maintain the discipline of the prison without this rule. If we find a prisoner with a knife, that was evidently prepared for mischief, we regard that as a very grave offense. If we find a prisoner,—well, there was another grave offense that we didn't take much exception upon,—when a man called the guard at night to his cell door, and dashed the contents of his bucket into his face, we regarded that as a very grave offense. Some of those very grave offenses I do not think the board would have criticised Mr. Morris very severely, if he had given them a reasonable punishment. It has been understood that we do not wish the skin of any man broken; that we do not wish any man punished so as to draw blood; that we do not want any cruel punishment. That has been the rule, it has been the talk, it has been constant. But for these offenses we have left it,—I think we understand it,—the other Inspectors may not understand it as I do,—I think we left it to the judgment of Mr. Morris, after six months; after he had been there six months we came to feel that he did not like to punish.

Q. Do you know by whom these punishments were inflicted, whether by Mr. Morris or the keepers?

A. Not by the keepers; all the responsibility of the punishments are upon Mr. Morris. If the deputy keeper inflicts any punishment it is under his direction, and we expect it is under his eye.

Q. Do you know whether the practice has been for *all* the punishments to be inflicted under his eye?

A. We so understand it; we do not know to the contrary.

Q. Describe the manner in which the punishment of showering is inflicted.

A. Well, a man that puts the hose onto a man can describe it better than I can.

Q. As you received it from Mr. Morris would be competent.

A. I understand that a man, if it is a pretty severe case, that he is stripped and placed in a position so he cannot run away, and that they stand off from eight to twelve feet, and commence playing upon his feet, and the representation to us is, that when the man yields, they turn the hose off,—the screw is turned off. But if there is any apprehension of an excessive punishment, it is stopped, and the man is talked with; that he never puts it on, or intends to put it on (that is his representation to us) to exceed ten minutes in all. I understood him to say that he had never put on a continuous stream for more than about five minutes.

Q. What is the size of the stream?
A. I never saw the stream; I believe it's about three-eighths of an inch.
Q. You have seen the nozzle through which it is played?
A. I cannot say to a certainty.
Q. Do you know under what pressure the water is forced?
A. No, but I should say strong; I cannot state exactly.
Q. Is there any one of your board charged with any more duty in regard to the supervision of the prison than others?
A. I'm not aware that there is; we divide the responsibility. If we differ upon any point the majority run the institution.
Q. Are there any other corporeal punishments inflicted, other than you have mentioned—the lash, strap, showering, and cross.
A. Well, the cross has been abandoned for at least two years or more.
Q. That has been abandoned?
A. Yes, sir. There were but few records of the cross. That was an experiment of Mr. Morris as a substitute for the whip—not as a substitute on his part, but he came in there with the full belief that he could keep discipline in that prison without the use of the lash. But as it was an experiment, we never gave any specific orders, to my recollection, about it. I simply recall it. I did not like to hear a record of it; didn't like the association; I was afraid it would be misunderstood.
Q. This strap, do I understand you, was a substitute?
A. Yes; the strap came in vogue as soon as it was abandoned. They may have always had this strap for mild punishment. I cannot say as to that.
Q. Was there ever any punishment by suspending convicts by the arms or thumbs or wrists.
A. I do not believe there was.
Q. There has never been any such authorized by the inspectors?
A. No, sir; there never has been a record of anything of the kind.
Q. Have there ever been any punishments there, authorized by the inspectors, of placing persons in cold water?
A. No, sir, only from the hose.
Q. In that case they didn't stand in the water?
A. No, sir. Perhaps we might say that this is an experiment, as well as the cross.
Q. I understand you then, Mr. Wilcox, that there is no corporeal punishment inflicted, other than such as you have named.
A. I do not know of any other.

By Mr. Bartow:
Q. How do the inspectors give the convicts to understand that they have a right to make a complaint?
A. The convict understands that he can say to his keeper that he wishes to see the inspector. He gives him that information.
Q. They have it in the main from whom?
A. From the agent. There's not a convict in that prison that does not understand that this is his right; at least, I don't think there is. He gives that notice

to his keeper, his keeper gives it to the deputy, and when we come together we have the names of the convicts. We have established a rule, I don't know that we have referred to the rule there. I have not read over those rules since we met, and of course I could not remember distinctly. But I would not be surprised if you find the rule there—in fact, it is a rule that each keeper carry a book.

Q. If every keeper carries a book in which he is to make a memorandum of the name of any convict that wishes to see the board, if an instance should come to the knowledge of the board that any keeper had neglected to hand in the name of such convict, would that cause his dismissal?

A. I think they understand that distinctly. The convicts have been told it repeatedly, and I think it is one of the rules; but I do not recollect. [Witness reads rule eight.]

Q. Yes; I understand in your examination, when Mr. Webber was questioning, that that was understood, but my theory was: How the prisoners were informed that, how they know their right in regard to it?

A. This [showing a card of printed rules] hangs in their cells, and every prisoner has one of these; at least, that is our instruction.

Q. Well now, you stated in the examination that you talked, soon after Mr. Morris became agent there, about the abandonment of the lash altogether?

A. Yes; we talked about it.

Q. When did the Board of Inspectors determine to abolish that as a punishment?

A. There has been no—I don't think there will appear any record of the kind; it is oral instruction to the Agent.

Q. Well, you gave such instruction to the Agent, did you,—the Board of Inspectors,—to abolish the lash?

A. About twenty months ago the whip was abandoned, but there was no positive orders, it was because of our views upon the use of the lash that carried it out of the prison. Perhaps more largely Mr. Morris' language contributed to this result, but I understand inspectors to be generally opposed to the lash, as stated in our report.

Q. What was this lash—what was it made of?

A. In the first place it was a piece of wood braided together—what we would call a sort of stallion whip. If I were selling whips, and a man were to come in and ask for a stallion whip, I should hand him out one like that. It was covered with leather, and on the end of it was a lash—a good fair whip to handle a team with.

Q. What was the lash—a leather lash?

A. I guess the lash was called buckskin and made out of sheepskin.

Q. No wires braided in the lash?

A. I never saw a lash that had wires braided in it, either in a prison or outside.

Q. Now tell us a little more about that cross. When a man was fastened on that cross, so far as your knowledge or observation goes, could he stand upon his feet?

A. Right square upon his feet.

Q. Do you know of your own knowledge, or from reliable information, anything about a man who was shot there while trying to escape, or after he had escaped from prison?

STATE PRISON INVESTIGATION.

A. I only know from reading. I did not see him.
Q. Do you know who attended him?
A. I know who was the prison physician at the time.
Q. Well, do you know whether it was the prison physician who extracted the shot?
A. I Didn't see him do it, or learn that he did it.
Q. Did you learn from any source that he did it?
A. Only from the testimony that came before the Board of Inspectors.

By Mr. Morris:
Q. Didn't you get it in monthly report at the end of the month?
A. He has inquired about the physician that extracted the ball; that I only knew from the prison records, but that would not tell who extracted the ball; that I don't know only from evidence that came out before the Board of Inspectors.
Q. My first question was, whether you knew from your own knowledge, or from reliable information, anything about the man being shot?
A. I only know from the prison records.
Q. Now, Mr. Wilcox, when a man is whipped, or punished with this strap, is he fastened in any way during the flogging, or applying of the lash or strap?
A. Yes, sir?
Q How are they fastened?
A. With their hands back there in this way [showing,] and raised.
Q. Standing up, somewhere?
A. Yes, sir.
Q. Have you ever seen the men punished by this "improved method" of punishment?
A. No, sir. I only know this from the description I got from others. I never saw it as stated.
Q. I see here the 14th prison rule in regard to the Agent [reads rule.] Now, is that all of the rules that you know of in regard to giving him plenary powers in regard to punishment?
A. I don't know of anything further.
Q. And you don't know of any restriction further than that, or do you?
A. Well, I know of the restrictions I have stated here.
Q. No more?
A. I know what the rules were.
Q. Do you know, Mr. Wilcox, whether, or is it understood there, that a record is made of all the punishments inflicted?
A. We expect a record of every punishment.

By Mr. Webber:
Q. Have you any rule absolutely requiring it?
A. I would like to read these rules over. If we ain't we ought to have one—it is the law, the statute law.

By Mr. Bartow:
Q. That a record must be kept of all punishments?
A. Every one; yes, sir.
Q. Have any cases come to your knowledge where the punishment has been inflicted without a record being made?
A. There was one during the investigation that came to our knowledge, that we had no record of. There was one punishment inflicted there that we didn't

STATE PRISON INVESTIGATION. 11

require a record of. The reason that was not recorded was there was no blame on the part of the prisoner The blame was on the part of the keeper. Had the prison board gone out and a man's time expired, if there were a record of the infraction of rules, the convict would have taken from him some good time, and we did not feel that it would have been just to have the convict lose any good time if there was no blame attached to him. He was led into the difficulties that he got into by the keeper.

By Mr. Webber:
Q. Is this a record of punishments?
A. It is one of them.
Q. Look at it please, and see if you can identify it?
A. Yes, sir, this is the first, commencing January first, 1874.
Q. You spoke of one punishment that was not recorded. State what information you have on that subject, in regard to that one punishment that was not recorded.
A. There was Mr. Martin testified that they put a man upon the cross on a certain day in July, and I have not seen anything of it in the record.
Q. Do you know how often this book is written up?
A. Once a month. We understand it to be the deputy's business to keep a memorandum of all these infractions of the rules, and from this memorandum the deputy reads and the Agent writes them out. But the fact that Deputy Martin could not write up the record, Mr. Bingham used to write them.
Q. The report then is not written up close every month?
A. I don't know when it is written up; it is presented to us once a month.
Q. I understand that the usage is, as you understand it, that the deputy keeps a memorandum of the record?
A. Of the time of the infraction of the rule and of the punishment and its manner.
Q. And he passes that over to the Agent, who writes it up afterwards?
A. This is written up by the Agent, or it is his handwriting, and the other man keeps a memorandum.
Q. Now, when the Inspectors meet monthly, is this read over by the whole board?
A. Yes; it is read to us in session; to all of us.
Q. Read to you?
A. Yes, sir, all of us, and sometimes commented upon. Every case of severity is talked over and investigated as thoroughly as we can, to see whether the Agent is justified in administering the punishment or not.
Q. There are two handwritings; whose is this on the right hand side of the page?
A. I don't know whose this is.
Q. What explanation do you make of that one on your right hand, "cancelled by order of Agent?" I notice several others that were marked as errors and crossed off. State how it occurs that they were recorded and then marked out.
A. This is the one that I referred to as cancelled for the benefit of the convicts, because we did not want it to stand against them and take their good time.
Q. This cancellation then is done?
A. This cancellation is for the benefit of the convict. I know all about that; I have the history of the whole transaction in my pocket if you want to hear it.

Q I don't want to hear it, but only asked for an explanation of this part marked as cancelled.

A. It was marked as cancelled against the convict.

Q. Do you understand it as one of the rules that any breach of discipline subjects a convict to these corporeal punishments?

A. No, sir; not when not an aggravated case.

Q. Well, suppose a man should whistle in his cell, would that, according to the rules of the Inspectors, justify the Agent in inflicting punishment by showering or the strap?

A. No, sir.

Q. Suppose a man should be talking in his cell on Sunday afternoon, would that be sufficient to justify it?

A. No, sir; there might be circumstances, you know, connected with it. A man might be talking so he would be heard in the gallery, where others were trying to read, and he might be asked to stop, and if he refused to stop, he might receive some slight punishment. So if a man should persist in whistling, and keep whistling, so as to demoralize the discipline of the prison, it might be taken notice of; but if a man was to stop whistling and say it whistled itself, he would not be likely to get any punishment or any reproof that was at all severe.

Q. Here is one I find on February 15th, 1874, "James Donahue, for talking with Martin Robinson, in bare cell, and also receiving tobacco from him, watered;" was that within the discretion which the Inspectors understood the Agent to have?

A. The tobacco question has been a very serious one with us. We have a contractor there who was making cigars, and he claims they are stealing him poor, that we must cancel his contract or do something with them; and we have said to the Agent "You must commence on this, and if you cannot stop this grand stealing of tobacco and cigars, the contract would have to be abandoned." We have also said to the Agent that we were more exposed than formerly, in tearing down the center building. The past year, and the year before, there has been no time but what a half-dozen convicts could have gone out there, and we felt that we were in danger, and we have said to him that we must arrange the discipline closer if we had to build up again. We have had men work around with freeman, and it is wonderful how a freeman will come there and begin to demoralize the convicts, and we have had to restrict with rules, and draw the lines closer than formerly.

Q Can't you impose rules on these freemen that will prevent them injuring the discipline of the prison?

A. We have done it, and in every instance they speak against the prison. We cannot punish the freemen if we would.

A. I notice under January 25th, a case of punishment for talking in gallery: "cold water on feet." Was that punishment allowed by the Inspectors without criticism on the Agent?

A. We talked about the effect of cold water on the feet a good many times, and having a physician on the board, we never had become very much alarmed about injuring the convict to wash his feet.

Q. The question which I asked was, whether watering as it is called, was permitted simply for these minor offenses, like talking in the cell?

A. Our understanding of the application of water is that it can be put on as mildly as any other punishment.

Q. But when applied, it was applied as a punishment, and not simply as a washing?

A. No, sir; it is to scare them.

Q. I find under date of January 8, 1874, three names, "O'Neil, O'Leary, and Bailey, for talking in cell, watered on feet."

A. Yes, sir; I will state it. We're obliged to prevent their talking in cells, and a severe punishment would not be justified by the Board. You've probably had an explanation of that, Mr. Webber, at the time, and it was not an ordinary disturbance.

Q. When punishments were inflicted by a whip, either with a lash or with a strap, did you require the record to show the number of blows inflicted.

A. We expected it to exactly. We may say we require it. We expect it to a blow. We expect to know just how the convicts are punished.

Q. In reading this record did you ever find a case where the record is insufficient, in your judgment, to be satisfactory to the inspectors?

A. We have talked about the record being written up more fully, that we could judge more fairly of the nature of the offense, in judging upon the good time of the man, whether we were justified in taking all his good time away, whether the offense would be of sufficient magnitude, whether there was not something in connection with it that would justify the convict.

Q. I notice this record under date of Sept. 25, 1874 (see case of James Fairfax, page 56, of prison record.) Do you remember whether the prison inspectors criticised that entry or the punishments inflicted in that case.

A. I do not now recollect that special case. [Witness shown another book commenced June 1, 1870, and ending Dec. 31, 1873.]

Q. Look at that, and state if that is the record used prior to the time we have been talking about?

A. Yes, sir, I think it is.

Q. Do you recollect any record of the punishment of a prisoner by the name of Thurston?

A. Yes, sir.

Q. Do you remember when,—what year it was in?

A. I will have to go back to find the record. I cannot place it in my mind now. I might have to look the book clear through, but I recollect Thurston's punishment. [Witness shown entry under date of June 3, 1873, page 132.]

Q. What control has the contractors over the convicts?

A. None, nothing more than they are to have the use of them so much.

Q. What is the manner of intercourse between the contractors and the convicts,—is it done through the agents and keepers, or direct by the contractors in giving directions to the prisoners?

A. We understand it is done through the officers of the prison.

Q. Have you been there sufficiently so you can speak of your own observation what the practice is?

A. Well, make it definite.

Q. The general manner. I'm not speaking of any particular case. The general manner when prisoners working for contractors, and the wishes of contractors in regard to work they should perform were observed; whether there was any criticism on the work being done; how that is conveyed from the contractors to the convicts; whether through the keepers or direct?

A. The convict was put upon the work, and the contractors have a foreman, and if they have any complaint to make of prisoners, they make it to the deputy, and the deputy makes it to the keeper, and the keeper makes it to the Agent. They make it to the keeper, and the keeper makes it to the deputy agent, and the deputy agent makes it to the Agent. The report comes from the keeper.

Q. I'm not speaking of complaints but only of the general directions as to the manner and time of work.

A. Oh, the general directions and manner in which the work is to be done are given by the foreman direct to the convict.

Q. So, then, the foremen of these contractors, are allowed to hold conversation with the prisoners?

A. Yes, sir.

Q. Well, are there any others acting with the contractors, or any other employes, allowed to hold intercourse in the way mentioned, except the foremen?

A. No, sir, none except the foremen and the contractors and their employes.

Q. That's what I want to get at. Their employes are allowed to talk with the contractor about the business the convicts are at work at?

A. Yes, sir.

Q. About the business they are doing?

A. Yes, sir.

Q. Now what motives have these contractors, aside from other foremen who work about the prison, to have this daily intercourse with the prisoners?

A. Oh, I could not tell you probably. The wagon contract, for instance, would have to have a skilled foreman of the room, that looks over each department of the wagon. In the tool contract they have one general manager that looks after the machinery, and in each department they have to have at least one foreman to instruct the convict how to do the work.

Q. You have now mentioned only foremen, you spoke before of employes, and not foremen.

A. What I meant by that was that a contractor might have an hundred and fifty men there, and they might be divided into four or five departments, and they would require four or five employes in each department. There may be same foremen about the shop in a different capacity; but I don't now recollect of any.

By Mr. Bartow:

Q. Mr. Wilcox, was your attention ever directed to this record, before your investigation at the prison?

A. I recollect distinctly when the record was first read to me. It was the first meeting after the date of it.

Q. Did you then notice the dates endorsed upon it?

A. It was read to me; I did not read it.

Q. Did you then notice the record, a record purporting to be made June 3rd, the next one June 13th, and then the last record being made June 3d, the day the first record was made.

A. I recollect the discussion that came up upon the desperate man Thurston, and we had considerable conversation with Mr. Morris previous to that about this man, about the trouble they had had in the prison to manage him, and the conversation settled down upon that more particularly, perhaps, than anything else. I have not read it. This is all the recollection I have of it. It may be in print now; if so, I have not taken the pains to read it. I have never read it myself, but heard it read at the time.

Q. Did you notice the dates at the time, so that you know the record was then in that shape. Just look at the record on the previous page. It purports to be written June 3d, and on this page June 13th, and then the former page again.

A. This record would be made June 3d. We all have to be there the first Wednesday in June. Our record would reach about the 31st day of May, the record that would be read before us in June; and then in July we would get the record of this. The first of July up to July, we would get it.

Q. For June?

A. Yes, sir. Now if a man had, during the month, two or three punishments whether they would be coupled together, I do not know,

Q. My idea is this, Mr. Wilcox; perhaps I did not ask so you understood me. Did you at the time you were there at the prison, making the examination, did you notice that the dates of the record to which your attention has been called, were in the shape they are now?

A. I do not recollect thinking of it at the time. Perhaps some of the other Inspectors might remember. I do not now recollect more than the general character of the man, and the general character of the punishment?

Q. Well, now, that record, Mr. Wilcox, reads that he received not less than fifty lashes. Do you remember having made any inquiries about how many lashes he did receive at the time?

A. My understanding of it was, that that was about the number.

By Mr. Morris:

Q. Mr. Wilcox, you said in the early part of your testimony, that the convicts in the prison appeared to know that it was their right to see the board in the absence of the Agent?

A. Yes, sir,

Q. Mr. Wilcox, will you tell us how you know it? Have you ever heard a convict say that I had proclaimed it frequently in the dining room?

A. I have heard them say that you had proclaimed it, and I have proclaimed it myself.

Q. Do they often ask to see the board alone?

A. Yes; hardly a morning but what they have some conversation.

Q. I mean alone?

A. Yes, sir, in the absence of the Agent. Not often; there have been instances where they have.

Q. Do they often make complaints against their treatment, or of their treatment?

A. I do not now recollect an instance where a convict wanted to see the board to make any complaint about his treatment. Ordinarily they want to see us about their good time, to make some apology for their committing infractions of rules, or to appeal to our sympathies not to shorten up their good time; to get home to their friends, urging the necessities of their friends, etc.

Q. Did you ever see a convict manifest any fear of punishment when coming before you?

A. I never did on account of the present Agent.

Q. Is it a common thing for the Agent to intercede in behalf of men who are liable to lose good time?

A. His intercessions in behalf of convicts who are liable to lose good time are very creditable to his heart.

Q. What disposition has he generally shown to men who have come to him in their troubles.

STATE PRISON INVESTIGATION.

A. I do not now recollect of any instance where you have manifested any disposition (hesitating),—I was hunting for a word,—to follow a man up after he had treated you bad, and you had punished him and treated him bad.

Q. I will instance one case, Mr. Wilcox, the case of Thurston. It was a matter of considerable inquiry how Thurston became entitled to any good time after his terrible conduct. Did the Agent ask you with reference to his conduct after his punishment?

A. I think he stated that since the last punishment he had been a good convict and wanted the Board to be merciful to him and take no more notice than it was obliged to.

Q. Did you meet Thurston at any time after the latter part of his confinement in prison? Did you ever meet him, or have any conversation with him in regard to his conduct?

A. Yes, sir; several times.

Q. Do you know how he felt in regard to the punishments he had received, and how he afterwards behaved himself?

A. He thought he had made a mistake; that it would have been better if he had obeyed the rules of the prison and been a good convict instead of being a bad one.

Q. Is it a common thing for the Agent to consult the board in regard to the handling of bad men?

A. Yes, sir.

Q. In your conversation with Thurston at any time, did he ever seem to feel as if he had demurred to the penalties he had received in the prison?

A. Mr. Thurston intimated to me one time that he had had it in his heart to let his knife into the guts of the Agent, but he had made up his mind that he would have done a very foolish thing if he had, and was glad that he didn't. I'm using his language; that's the reason I answer the question in the manner I do.

Q. Do you think I liked the lash at any time?

A. You mean applied to you?

Q. Yes, sir.

A. I don't think you would like it.

Q. My question was pretty short; I mean in regard to convicts.

A. I never thought Mr. Morris really delighted in punishing convicts, but that it was one of the most unpleasant duties he had to perform in the prison.

Q. I think you have stated very clearly that in the beginning of my administration I didn't use the lash.

A. I think that you thought that you could maintain discipline without it; I think that you tried to.

Q. You stated that the nozzle of the hose was perhaps, three-eighths of an inch?

A. I didn't state definitely; I think it was about that, but cannot tell.

Q. Will you state the size of the hose?

A. It is an inch rubber hose.

Q. Have you ever had any reason to think that I was disposed to be precipitate in my decisions as to how I should punish a man in serious cases, where the offense was a flagrant one?

A. I do not know that I have; I know that it has been the understanding that a man should not be punished the day that he committed an infraction of the rule; that you should wait until both got cool before you come together.

STATE PRISON INVESTIGATION. 17

Q. Is that a general rule, or simply your wish, or is it my rule generally in handling convicts?

A. I rather think as a general thing it is your rule in handling the men; there may be exceptions to it.

Q. Have I been a frequent correspondent of yours since I came to the prison?

A. Kept me constantly informed of the running of the prison, almost every week, and sometimes two or three times a week.

Q. What has been the general tone and character of my letters?

A. The general tone of your letters was a sort of exulting tone when you had run through a week without having any infliction, or serious things in the way of discipline to contend with.

Q. Mr. Webber noticed on the records two instances where the water was applied for seemingly light offenses, for talking by Burgen, on the gallery. Do you recollect Burgen?

A. No, sir.

Q. Do you recollect the man who stabbed (?) the keeper in the upper wood-polishing shop?

A. Yes, sir; I recollect it.

Q. Might not talking upon the gallery be a dangerous offence?

A. Oh, yes; there might be instances when talking on the gallery might bring together a squad of men and lead to bad results.

Q. Have I often alluded to the importance of a full memorandum from my deputies of all the details?

Q. In the reading of the record, monthly, you have said, as well as the board, that they ought to be more full.

Q. Would it be possible for an agent to be cognizant of all that was going on about the yards and shops, and still attend to his other duties in the office, and looking up supplies for prisoners up town?

A. It might not be possible for him to know everything that was going on there, but he could keep a pretty good share of it.

Q. What I want to bring out is, whether it is the duty of the deputy to keep these memorandums. Have you any idea how these two dates, June 3d and 13th, are in succession, concerning offenses and punishments of Thurston?

A. No, I have not; hadn't thought of it at all; hadn't observed it.

Q. Would it be considered any impropriety to put two dates in succession, to put one date after another, in case he had been punished twice during the month?

A. No, sir, not if each offense was described. Why, I can account for that. In copying from your memorandum books you copy the record of the 3d, and knowing this report of the 13th to be in the same month, you put the two together so they would be read together.

Q. That's all there was to it.

A. Perhaps I've not understood what the question was. I don't see any mistake about it.

A. Have you any idea of the character of the men I have always sought to aid me in taking care of the prison?

A. Do you mean as keepers?

Q. Yes, sir.

A. You've claimed always to be seeking for good men.

Q. What qualities do you think I admire in a man?

A. I think you would rather object to a man that was arbitrary and vindictive.

18   STATE PRISON INVESTIGATION.

Q. Have I not always said in talking about men who have been proposed as candidates for positions in the prison, that I desired well poised men, men of education, men who were kind, etc.

A. Yes, sir ; that has been the understanding that that was the kind of men you were seeking.

By Mr. Webber:

Q. Mr. Wilcox, how long have you been personally acquainted with Mr. Morris, the Agent?

A. About twelve years. I met Mr. Morris at the prison, I believe, in 1865. I was chairman of the prison committee of the House. I won't be positive, but I know he was one of the Inspectors, and I think I met him there then. Mr. Morris thinks it was earlier. My first acquaintance with him was as prison Inspector.

Q. That was when you was Inspector?

A. When he was Inspector.

Q. State whether from your knowledge of him, his temper is uniform and constant, or whether it is variable, depending on moods?

A. Well, I could not say that he was a very moody man, and I could not say that he was a very even tempered man. Somewhat like the rest of us: no marked feature about it.

By Mr. Morris:

Q. Has the gratuity of more good time to convicts than is now allowed by law been a prominent idea with me for some time past, say a year or two years?

A. The Agent has regarded the good time laws one of the best instrumentalities for keeping good discipline in the prison, and has been anxious that it should be increased.

Q. Have I sought to introduce it to do away with more severe punishment?

A. Well, couldn't tell what your motive was.

Q. I think I mentioned that as a motive.

By Mr. Eggleston:

Q. Tell us whether the Inspectors ever found any fault with Mr. Morris for punishments he had inflicted on the prisoners?

A. The way that I have found fault, (let the other Inspectors speak for themselves), has been that when he would read over the reports, I would say, "Now, I was in hopes that we should strike this month without a single record." Instead of finding fault with the punishments I have remarked that his conduct accorded well with my own ideas as to the best manner of getting them to work in the prison. Not under Mr. Morris but under Mr. Bingham, in no instance where they have left the matter to me, have I punished the men, and they have behaved themselves, as well, I think, as though they had been punished.

By Mr. Mellen:

Q. I think you said that Thurston had it in his heart to strike some one with a knife ; was this before or after his punishment?

A. It was before he was punished that he was going to use the knife.

MR. L. W. LOVELL SWORN.

By Mr. Webber:

Q. Your residence, Mr. Lovell?

A. Kalamazoo county, town of Climax.

Q. How long have you been acting as inspector?

A. About four years.

Q. State whether the inspectors have any rules and regulations in regard to the government and discipline other than these?
A. Not that I know of.
Q. State to us, Mr. Lovell, generally, as to your knowledge as an inspector, either alone or in connection with other inspectors, as to the supervision, management, and discipline of the prison since you have been on the board, commencing and giving it in detail so that it will not be necessary to follow it with further questions?
A. You mean our usual routine of business.
Q. The usual routine of business, and the manner in which it has been done, so that we can see what supervision you have exercised?
A. The general business at our monthly meetings is to examine the financial condition of the institution; the examining of the good time record of the convicts who will be discharged that month, that is, whose time would expire that month if there were no charges against them; the reading of the infractions of the rules by the agent, and comments made upon it; listening to complaints of prisoners, if there are any; going through the shops; visiting the hospital; insane asylum; inspecting the cells in regard to clothing, bedding, etc.; and examining the food—is the general business of the monthly meeting.
Q. What specific attention, if any, did you give at your meetings to the discipline of the prison?
A. In the reading of the infractions of rules, the question comes up in regard to the punishments for such infractions.
Q. State whether the inspectors, singly or together, without being attended by the agent or keepers, are in the habit of mingling with the prisoners and conversing with them.
A. Yes, sir; together and singly; frequently passing through singly, and frequently together, unaccompanied by the Agent.
Q. State what your understanding was as to the character of the offenses for which the Agent was at liberty to inflict corporeal punishment.
A. I supposed he was at liberty to inflict corporeal punishment for attacks upon any of the employes of the prison, personal violence. We regard that as a flagrant offense.
Q. What others?
A. If a person should refuse to work, I think that he would be justified. I think the inspectors would justify his inflicting moderate punishment,—I mean refusing to work without cause.
Q. Suppose one of the convicts should furnish a freeman with money, and he should buy some tobacco outside and furnish it to him, would the procuring of tobacco in that way be esteemed an offense for which punishment should be inflicted?
A. I think he would not be punished severely; I think he would be justified in inflicting some punishment.
Q Would he be justified, in the judgment of the inspectors, in inflicting the water punishment.
A. Well, we regard the water punishment,—as the record has been read here, watering on the feet and showering upon the feet,—now, the showering means, as I understand it, playing upon them with this little hose. We regard this showering of the feet as a light punishment.
Q. Did you ever give attention enough to this showering to know the diameter of the nozzle?

A. I have seen it.
Q. What is its diameter?
A. Well, the testimony taken said about a three-eighths nozzle; that is my impression, that it was about three-eighths of an inch.
Q. Now, what attention have you given to the pressure that the water has?
A. I think I have seen it playing, but no further than that. I never saw it play upon a prisoner. I have seen it play.
Q. Have you ever seen any of this punishment inflicted in the prison?
A. Never any at all.
Q. Have you ever had occasion to examine any of the prisoners after the punishment?
A. I never have.
Q. Have complaints ever been made to you upon the severity of the punishments by any of the prisoners?
A. Never, never.
Q. Have you ever had reason to believe, from your observation about the prison, that the prisoners were deterred from making complaints to you, fearing they might be punished or deprived of some liberty if they made complaints?
A. I never have; prisoners have frequently spoken to me when I have been passing through the shops, and have asked to see the inspectors upon some other subject.
Q. When you have passed through the shops and mingled with the prisoners, do they generally understand that you are one of the inspectors?
A. Yes, sir. They have often spoken to me about seeing the inspectors in regard to their good time, and they have sometimes wanted to see the inspectors in regard to labor,—the place that they were put to work,—wanting to be changed from one place to another.
Q. Until these recent changes have been made, since Mr. Morris has been agent, have you or the board ever examined into the question of punishment inflicted in the prison?
A. Made inquiry?
Q. In regard to the liberty exercised?
A. No, sir; I don't think I ever made inquiry in regard to any liberty exercised. This case of Thurston was regarded as a severe case of punishment, this case that has been referred to as the man that was shot. I recollect my attention was called to him the first time I passed through the yard. I did not examine his wound. I saw the man in the yard at work. I inquired into the circumstances as they occurred.
Q. Have the board ever tried the punishment of confining convicts in their cells, either without food or on bread and water, to see if that would have as good an effect in the way of subduing them as punishment with the whip, or water, or strap?
A. They have been confined.
Q. With what result usually?
A. Well, I think this mode of punishment is usually effective; some men have to be confined a long time. I think now of one man who was stubborn, and I think he was confined several days, with very light food, before he would yield at all; I don't recollect his name.
Q. Have you not had cases in the prison where, after the lash had been tried and failed, the prison authorities have been obliged to resort to those means of punishment to subdue them?

A. I don't recollect of any.

Q. Did the board ever give any further attention to this record of punishment than simply to hear it read over.

A. You mean investigate?

Q. Yes, consider the particular cases, or did they simply go through with it rather as a formal matter?

A. Well, we were in the habit of discussing and considering whether the punishment was justified by the circumstances of the case. A great many cases occur where there is no particular consideration, but in case of a severe punishment we discuss it, and inquire into the circumstances under which it is inflicted, the character, amount, &c.

Q. Have the board, or you, as a member of it, ever taken any pains to ascertain whether these records were full and accurate?

A. There have been frequent complaints that they were not sufficiently full, and it was thought after the present board of inspectors were superseded, that the succeeding board would not be able to determine in regard to the good time; that they were not sufficiently full. As, for instance, a man is reported for insolence. That we regard as a little indefinite; that is, it might be a slight offense, or it might be a very severe one, and we think the record should contain the word used.

Q. Well, have you ever made a rule requiring that done?

A. I don't think we have any written rule to that effect; I understand it to be the statute law, that we keep a record of the offense and the cause of it.

Q. Have you ever considered the object of requiring a record to be made out, immediately after the punishment had been inflicted?

A. We understand that it is made at the time, immediately after the punishment.

Q. His memorandum, but not this record?

A. Yes, sir; it is transcribed from the record kept at the time. It is transcribed into this book.

Q. When the board met was the punishment read from this book?

A. Yes, sir.

Q. Did you examine the original?

A. I think we have at some time. I know we have.

Q. What form is the original in; a book or memorandum?

A. A book.

P. A little memorandum book?

A. Yes, sir; a diary generally; at any rate I have seen it kept in that way. I think that is the usual way; in fact, at sometimes I don't see the originals, but at times I have seen them copying from that book into this.

Q. Have you ever examined one of those books?

A. I have.

Q Did the board ever, to your knowledge, examine this to see whether it is as full as that, whether it was all copied?

A. I have seen them writing from that, and I know it was an exact copy of the memorandum that I saw.

Q. I see these entries are all checked off. What's the meaning of that pencil check mark at each entry?

A. My impression is that it was used to indicate that the record had been examined to determine as to the good time—it would be a guess though.

Q. I see that to place convicts in a bare cell was adopted as a punishment. Did you ever look into one of those bare cells?
A. Yes, sir.
Q. What are they, a blank wall without any furniture?
A. Yes, sir.
Q. What is the floor?
A. Sometimes it is board, sometimes stone.
Q. Has it been found that the health of the convicts was impaired by placing them on the bare stone floor?
A. I don't know.
Q. Have you ever inquired into it to see if that effect followed?
A. I have inquired of the physician, in regard to the effects of different kinds of punishments.
Q. Now, here is an entry under date of Sept. 18th, 1873 (reads from record, p. 157, case of a man punished for refusing to pile brick). Now let me ask whether the board took note of an entry of that nature?
A. I don't recollect that particular case.
Q. What I wish to get at is, whether the board passed entries of that nature without criticism, or whether they would require the Agent to be more specific in the statement of his punishment?
A. We would frequently inquire what he meant by such expressions.
Q. Here is another entry under date of Sept. 10th, "Wm. Robinson, by Keeper Fay.(?) Bare cell over night, and light shower bath in the morning." (p. 157.) Any especial criticism on that character of entries by the board?
A. I don't think there would be.

By Mr. Morris:

Q. Are you satisfied in your own mind that you have correct ideas of the general management of the prison; that is, are you satisfied yourself?
A. Of the way it is managed; yes, I think I know how the prison is managed. Perhaps I do not understand your question.
Q. You might have misgivings in regard to its management, whether your ideas were correct or not?
A. Perhaps I didn't understand your question.
Q. Yes, you did. Have your visits to the prison ever happened without the free knowledge of the agent or other officers. For instance, I will instance just to illustrate the point I have in view. The first Wednesday in the month required by law, do you often come on Tuesday?
A. Frequently.
Q. Do you go to the agent's office or to the front gate, or do you go around by the back way and get into the yard?
A. I frequently go into the yard without going into the office at all. But they know I am there.
Q. Under the contracts made for the labor of the convicts' work in the prison, has the agent any power to dictate what kind of work a strong and healthy man shall do on a contract; for instance, a man is well adapted to business physically, can I say anything as to where he should work—put him on a grind-stone or polishing belt?
A. I do not understand that the authorities exercise any authority over the men further than is necessary for their well being. If a man was put in a place that you thought he was not competent to fill, you would have him assigned to another place.

Q. The question was asked, what is the most prominent objection to confining men in bare cells; for instance, over night in a bare cell, without food. I think there was some objection mentioned?
A. What is the objection to locking them up, etc.
Q. Yes, in a bare cell, in preference to punishing by some other method, as in the case of Calkins (?), who before fifty men swore he would not wheel another brick that day. Would you have made him wheel brick that day or wait until he got ready?
A. If the offense was of that nature there should be punishment; that is, such refusal in the presence of a large number of convicts would be regarded as an offense, and it would be necessary to the discipline of the prison that the punishment should be such that the convicts will generally be impressed that they are punished for such infractions.

By Mr. Webber:
Q. Are these punishments inflicted publicly before all the convicts?
A. No, sir; still they understand it is inflicted. [Mr. Morris here gave it as his opinion that many of the convicts would rather go to a bare cell and lay there all day than labor.]

By Mr. Morris:
Q Is there any objection to the use of a bare cell in certain instances?
A. I think not in some instances, if I get your idea correctly.
Q. The idea I meant to convey is, where a man takes a position it is his own choice.
A. The authorities, of course, exercise their discretion in regard to the punishment necessary to inflict. He might make up his mind that he had rather go to the cell than to work if we would give him his choice.
Q. One word in regard to the record not being full. Do you know that I have made it a prominent point with my men, for instance, in cases of insolence, it might be a look or word, have I wanted the language given every time?
A. That has been the point with you, that the keepers in making the reports of offenses were not sufficiently accurate. Of course the offenses were committed in the presence of the keepers, and you would insist on their being reported more fully than they made them to you or to the deputy.
Q. Is it a general rule for you to visit the hospital every time you come to the prison.
A. I usually visit the hospital every time I go to the prison.
Q. Do you usually converse with the patients when you go there?
A. I do.
Q. Did you ever find a man lying there suffering from any punishment?
A. I never did.
Q. Did you ever find a man in the hospital that you thought was deceiving us; complaining of illness that did not ail him?
A. I've seen men in the hospital who claimed to be unable to work, when I didn't see any external manifestation of disease about them.

By Mr. Webber:
Q. In deciding what amount of punishment should be inflicted for misconduct in the prison, is the question of the economy of the convict's time ever taken into consideration to settle the point?
A. No, sir, not with us.
Q. Have you ever inquired whether the Agent of the prison decides on showering; that is, the water punishment, instead of shutting in a cell, with a view

to saving so much of the convict's time, as would otherwise be expended in the cell.

A. I don't think he does. I know complaints have sometimes been made from other parties, that we were sacrificing the time of the men by shutting them up, instead of punishing them in some other way.

Q. You say you don't think he does. Have you ever inquired into it, so that you could know that this was the case?

A. Of course I don't know anything beyond his statement; I have his word for it.

Q. Now Mr. Morris asks you, if he has not complained that his deputies and keepers did not make their reports full. Is it not in the power of the Agent, before inflicting a punishment, or permitting one to be inflicted, to procure as full a report as he desired?

A. Well, this was generally in cases that were not punished with a whip nor showered, but were simply sent to the cell for a few hours.

Q. Well, it is in the power of the Agent, is it not, to procure as full reports as he may need?

A. Yes, sir.

Q. Now what examination have you made as an inspector, or has the board, to your knowledge, to learn whether the reports of these offenses, insolence and other minor offenses, made by the keepers to the Agent, or to the deputy and he to the Agent, whether they were true?

A. We have frequently called men in, that is, men have come in at almost every meeting and wanted to see the inspectors in regard to their good time, and they have been called in and asked to give an explanation in regard to offenses, with which they were charged, and we judged by that, of the record.

Q. Suppose they deny the charge, what do you do to ascertain the truth of it?

A. I don't recollect that there has ever any man done that; I don't recollect that any man has made complaint that he was charged with anything that he was not guilty of.

Q. Has it ever occurred that the insolent language of the convict, was given in reply to harsh language from the keeper?

A. I think there may have been instances of that kind given as an excuse; there don't now occur to me any particular instance.

Q. Has it ever come to your knowledge that any of the keepers had any particular feelings against any of the convicts, and treated them differently on account of having that feeling?

A. No such case ever came to my knowledge. I don't think there has ever been any complaint of that kind.

WILLARD STEARNS SWORN.

By Mr. Webber:

Q. Where do you reside, Mr. Stearns?
A. Adrian.
Q. Your occupation?
A. Attorney-at-law.
Q. You sometimes act as a correspondent for newspapers?
A. Yes, sir; have for the last five years.
Q. State whether you are the writer of the article which appeared in the Adrian Press on the 29th of March last?

A. Relative to the State Prison?

Q. Relative to the State Prison, relative to certain charges against its management?

A. Yes, sir.

Q. Now, without specific questions, will you give us generally the knowledge on which you made those charges?

A. They were made from statements given to me by Capt. H. N. King of our city.

Q. You had no other information?

A. No other.

Q. At what time did he give you this information?

A. Twice; once in the forenoon of the day when he related to me the particulars, the different cases of cruel treatment, and the other in the afternoon along somewhere about five o'clock, I apprehend, when I went to him to get more specific information in the way of names and dates. He mentioned several cases of cruelty, and gave the name of Hinckley at that time as the man who administered the punishment.

Q. What authority did he assume to have for the statements he made to you?

A. He claimed to have seen the punishment of the old man, as I understood him to say; he witnessed the punishment, had talked with the man himself, had seen his wounds, and that the old man was in the hospital to be seen the day before when he came out. The rest, I understood, was given to him, but portions of it he had seen. He mentioned Mr. Donough as having seen some things there, but whether any of these things he had spoken to me about, I can't be positive; I understood it that way, but won't be certain.

Q. What authority did he assume to state on which you based the charge, that about nine months since a convict in the State Prison received one hundred lashes upon the bare back?

A. Why, he gave me the bare fact that one man had received a hundred lashes, and that his body was so cut up that there was no spot upon his back where you could lay your finger without laying it on a scar. He did not state any particular authority. As to the date, I was not positive, and went down a second time to see when the punishment was inflicted, and I asked the day that punishment took place, and he said he did not exactly recollect, but believed last summer, didn't say positively. He gave no time when the other punishments were inflicted,—in fact, that question was left undecided in my mind, whether it had occurred under Mr. Morris' administration or that of some one else.

Q. Which of these was it that he claimed to have witnessed?

A. The one that was the most horrible,—that of the old man, by Capt. Hinckley.

Q. Did you make any inquiry as to the source of his information, as to any of the other cases?

A. No, sir, I didn't ask him, I think, as to that. As I said, there was something said about what Mr. Donough had seen, but as to his having seen any of these, I couldn't say that he did say so. I know neither Mr. Morris, Mr. Holt(?) nor Mr. Donough; Mr. Donough was a resident of Adrian, of whom I had heard but did not know.

Q. On what day did you receive this information?

A. On Friday, the day before I published it, or the day before I wrote it.

Q. And you had no other information?
A. No other except that.

HENRY N. KING SWORN.

By Mr. Webber:
Q. You reside at Adrian?
A. Yes, sir.
Q. You are the Mr. King that the last witness spoke of?
A. Yes, sir; I am the gentleman he had reference to.
Q. Will you state to us whether you have any knowledge on which you based the statements you made to him, and if so, what that knowledge is?
A. Well, I would like to answer that question as it would naturally occur to me. The only knowledge,—will I be permitted to give an explanation?
Q. Explain, as long as you are substantially answering the question, in such form as best pleases you.
A. Mr. Stearns came to my office on business; I think it was on Friday, and wanted I should speak of prison improvements and the management, and I related to him the punishment of a man on Friday,—no,—yes, Friday, the 19th of March. I told him that there was an old man punished who, I was informed, was sixty years old; that I saw a man going with Capt. Hinckley towards the prison hospital pointed out to me as being the man that was punished; that the prisoners informed me,—one of the prisoners who was working in the same room with me,—informed me that he received twenty-five lashes. I asked him how they managed to punish a prisoner,—how they fixed him. He said they done it by tying his hands together so [showing], and fastening him with a rope and putting the rope up over a railing of the second tier cell. The testimony in regard to his saying that I informed him that I had talked with this man: I never spoke with the old man, never talked with him, and have no recollection that there was any such word ever passed between him and I.
Q. Had you any knowledge concerning the punishment of that old man, further than what you have stated?
A. No, sir; no further than as I had information from the prisoners. He asked me where the punishment was done, and I told him it was done way out there to the west end of the cell wing.
Q. Did you inform him that about nine months since a convict in the prison received one hundred lashes on the bare back, or did you give him any such information in substance?
A. I may have said to him that I had been told by some who had been to see the convicts, that some of them had been punished severely; but as to stating one hundred lashes—I have no recollection of stating to him that any convict had received a hundred lashes. I criticised corporeal punishment very severely, because I didn't believe in it.
Q. Did you assume to have any information further than what was told you? Do you know the name of the person who spoke about a convict having been severely punished by lashes?
A. No, sir.
Q. Did you give any information about a convict being tied up by the thumbs?
A. No, sir; I never heard the words "tied up by the thumbs" until I saw it in the Press.
Q. Did you give him any information concerning any person being tied up in any way?

A. The exact language that I used? Now, this is all that I ever said to him, and it was based upon prison rumors and what I had heard in and outside the prison. I was talking in a social way, not supposing that any thing was going to be published or repeated. I think I told him that I had heard of men being bound to a cross; I think I have some recollection of it, but the exact language that I used I am not positive about; but I stated no date and said "I know of no facts or date." I said "I have no data to go from, and all that I say to you is based upon prison rumors and rumors that I hear in prison and out of prison; that I make no charges."

Q. Did you, in that conversation, call his attention to punishments by plunging in cold water?

A. No, sir.

Q. Any punishments by water?

A. No, sir; I don't think I did; still, I may have mentioned the shower bath, but I have no recollection of it. It is possible I may have said it; I would not be positive as to that.

Q. How long had you worked at the prison?

A. I had been there about eight days at that time.

Q. Inside the walls?

A. Yes; I was inside the walls, next to the guard room, near the upright part of the prison.

Q. What were you doing there?

A. I was putting up a flight of stairs.

Q. Were the convicts working with you?

A. There was one convict working with me; the other convicts I saw passing through the rooms with mortar and other material.

Q. While you were there, did you converse with the convicts freely?

A. No, sir; there was but one man that I conversed with, and that was the man I was at work with.

Q. While you were at work were you and him at liberty to converse together as though he had not been a convict.

A. I have understood since that it was an infraction of the rule, but I didn't know it at that time. I did converse with him some about our work, and also asked him why he was there.

Q. Who employed you there?

A. Mr. Donough. I was putting up the stair work, subject, I suppose, to the approval of the board.

Q. Was Mr. Donough a contractor?

A. No, sir; as I understood it, he is superintendent of prison repairs.

Q. And when you was at your contract, nothing was said to you about its being an infraction of the rules to converse with convicts?

A. No, sir; there was nothing said about that. All Mr Donough said, was, "You will have to look out for your tools and coat, because the prisoners are liable to take them, and give us trouble." So I kept my chest locked except when I was in the room.

Q. Then all the information you had concerning it was what you got from that convict that was working with you?

A. I don't know the convict that gave me the information. The way I got the information about the old man, there was three or four convicts in the room at the time that I heard the outcries of the man. I spoke up and asked what they were doing, and one of them spoke up and said. "They are flogging a man."

That is, one of the convicts in the room. I wanted to know who it was, and he gave a name, but I don't recollect the name. It was but a moment after that I stood looking out of the window, and he said "There goes the man with Capt. Hinckley," and I looked out and saw the man going out. I saw a man going with Capt. Hinckley down to the hospital.

Q. You knew and recognized Capt. Hinckley?
A. Yes, sir.
Q. Was there any other keeper there in charge of those convicts in the rooms?
A. I saw no one. Still there might have been in the other room. The convicts were going in and out, and sometimes they were taking work up the elevator, and in that case they would be in the upper room.
Q. From what convicts did you get the information concerning punishments in the prison?
A. I didn't get it from any one, only as I heard them talking.
Q. As they were talking among themselves?
A. Yes, sir.
Q. While you were there were the convicts conversing with each other without restraint whilst at work?
A. I would hear them talking once in awhile. All I could see was there was a grate and door between them and where the stairs were going up. This was —well, I couldn't say whether it was among the convicts or the freemen doing the plastering.

By Mr. Bartow:
Q. Have you ever worked in the prison more than that one time?
A. No, sir, never was in the prison before. That was the only time I ever done any work inside prison walls.
Q. Well, is what you have related all that you know about punishments there?
A. Yes, sir, all that I know about it. I have seen nothing of the punishments there before or since. I had an idea that corporeal punishment was entirely abandoned, and when I heard the outcries of this man it made me terribly excited.
Q. You never saw anybody punished?
A. No, sir; not as an eye witness—never saw anybody struck a blow.

By Mr. Webber:
Q. I would like to ask how long those cries continued?
A. I could not answer that with any degree of certainty.
Q. Well, you could tell whether it was one minute or fifteen.
A. Well, when a man was excited he couldn't come any where's near to the time. I couldn't tell.

By Mr. Bartow:
Q. Did any of these convicts, at any time, tell you they had seen men who had been punished there with marks upon them?
A. I don't recollect of a convict telling me that he had seen them.

By Mr. Nelson:
Q. Will you state how far you was from the convict at the time he was being punished?
A. I don't know the length of the cell wing. I was in the guard room, right off the southeast corner of the guard room, and that is right at the east end of the cell wing, and I should judge that cell wing to be 250 to 300 feet long, judging from distance, but not knowing the distance.
Q. This convict, in going to the hospital with Hinckley, was able to walk by himself?

A. Yes, sir.
Q. Was he dressed in his ordinary clothes?
A. Yes, he had his clothes on.
By Mr. Jones:
Q. Were the outcries loud?
A. Yes, sir; I should judge that they could have been heard outside the walls.
By Mr. Nelson:
Q. What length of time would you judge it was from the time you first heard the outcry until you saw the man going out in the yard?
A. I couldn't answer that. I was that excited at the time, it seemed to me a great deal longer than it was; it seemed to me a long while; it seemed to fill me with such horror that I don't really know—I can't describe my feelings.
Q. Did you hear any of the blows struck?
A. I don't think that I did hear the blows. I won't swear that I did, won't pretend to.
By Mr. Jones:
Q. Was there anything about the convict walking with Capt. Hinckley, to give you to understand, from his appearance that he had been punished.
A. Nothing, except that he was stooping over. He was a spare man, and I should think past the middle age of life,—the man that I saw, but I have no other means of knowing it was the man. He seemed to stoop over a little, and looked like a feeble man to me.
Q. How far were you from this man when he passed with Captain Hinckley?
A. Well, I don't know the exact distance from the window to the walk, but I should think it was two or three hundred feet; it might be more than that.
By Mr. Nelson:
Q. Would you think this man had time to put on his clothes from the time you heard him until you saw him pass along the yard?
A. Well, that is something I didn't think of at the time. I should judge,— still I couldn't think positively, and I really don't know how long it would take a convict to dress. He might have had time enough to have got on his clothes and got there.
By Mr. Jones:
Q. What was the name of this convict that worked with you?
A. My impression is his name was Cole. He was from Grand Rapids, in for man-slaughter. I asked him why he was there, and he told me he was there for man-slaughter; and I had a curiosity to know how he took his first downward step, if liquor wasn't the cause of it, and he told me it was, and bad associations. But the man who told me about this old man, he was a thick-set person. He seemed to be a man that went about the prison to look after and procure towels and one thing and another. I saw him one Saturday going through the prison and taking up the towels and issuing clean towels.
By Mr. Morris:
Q. Captain, I would like to ask you if you saw the man who was punished?
A. No, sir; I have no positive idea at all. I have no idea only as I was informed by that convict. That was the only information I had as to the number of lashes.
Q. What do you think about it to-day?
A. Well, I think now that was not the man.
Q. Why do you think so?
A. Well, I think it was not the man because I heard no punishment—no out-

cries before I was at work there; and when I was before the Board of Inspectors there was a prisoner brought forward who had been punished, and swore that he was punished on Friday, March 19th, and he was a dark-complexioned, thick-set man, and round featured.

Q. A colored man you mean?
A. No, sir; but dark-complexioned. I could not call him a colored man, but a very dark man, and a man of low intellect.

By Mr. Webber:
Q. What age would you suppose the man to be who was punished on Friday?
A. I should think he was a man of 32 or 33 years of age. As I stated before the board, I had no positive knowledge of any kind only as I had related, and that was not positive personal knowledge.

EVENING SESSION, APRIL 7.

MR. GEORGE COOK SWORN.

By Mr. Webber:
Q. Mr. Cook, where do you reside?
A. Grand Rapids.
Q. Have you ever been employed in the State Prison at Jackson?
A. I have.
Q. When did that employment commence?
A. December 2d, 1872.
Q. And how long did it continue?
A. Until April 10, 1874.
Q. In what capacity were you employed?
A. Hall keeper.
Q. What opportunity had you to observe the treatment of the convicts while you were there?
A. My opportunity, I presume, was as good as that of any one employed in the prison. I was inside the building.
Q. Did you ever witness any punishing of convicts while you were there?
A. Yes, sir.
Q. State the kinds of punishment that you witnessed.
A. Showers, flogging, and locking in the bare cell.
Q. State whether you ever saw any instances of severe punishment?
A. I have, several.
Q. Name such as occur to you as the most severe, and give dates and names as near as you can.
A. You mean you want the names of those who were flogged?
Q. Yes.
A. I couldn't mention all of the names of those who were flogged.
Q. Mention any that you have seen,—any particular case.
A. One was Thurston.
Q. When was that?
A. It was in June, I think, 1873. I saw him flogged.
Q. Who inflicted the punishment?

A. Mr. Morris, the Agent.
Q. What was he flogged with?
A. Flogged with a whip.
Q. Describe the whip?
A. Well, it was a common horse whip. I think there was a lash, and the end of the lash was part buckskin, or calfskin braided on the lash.
Q. Describe the manner in which the punishment was inflicted. How was the convict; what shape was he in?
A. The first time that he was flogged his hands were tied together, and he was tied up, drawn up to a railing to the first gallery,—the railing that runs round the first gallery.
Q. State whether he was stripped?
A. Yes, he was stripped.
Q. Describe the manner of the punishment?
A. He was whipped,—flogged with a whip.
Q. Well, on what part of his person was it applied?
A. I think the most of the flogging was about his breast and shoulders the first time that he was flogged, perhaps some down as low as his body.
Q. Was he whipped from the front, whipped on the front part of his person, or back part?
A. Round his person. He was tied up, so there was nothing to prevent his being whipped round his person.
Q. Do you know how many lashes he received the first whipping?
A. I do.
Q. How many?
A. Seventy-four.
Q. State whether it cut his person much; describe the particular effects of the whipping.
A. I don't recollect that he was cut up much. He might have started the blood in some places.
Q. You speak of this as the first whipping. Did he have another?
A. Yes, sir.
Q. How long afterwards?
A. I couldn't state the exact time,—a week or more.
Q. Who inflicted the second whipping
A. The Agent, Mr. Morris.
Q. Was he prepared to receive it in the same way, by being stripped and tied up?
A. He was tied up the second time to a post out in one of the shops; taken out to one of the shops and tied up to a post. Instead of being tied up so the whip would go clear round him, he was tied up to the side of the post.
A. Do you know how many blows he received the last time?
A. I don't know exactly. I counted over ninety, and he talked to him after that, and I couldn't say how many. There was considerable talk among the keepers as to how many; some thought he struck him over a hundred, some thought less.
Q. You are sure you counted ninety?
A. I counted ninety.
Q. What effect had these lashes upon his person?
A. Well, they cut him pretty bad in places.
Q. State whether you saw blood.

A. I did.

Q. Do you know of any other instances of severe punishment while you were there?

A. I have seen some pretty severe ones from showering.

Q. Describe some of the more severe ones.

A. Well, among the first after I went there was the showering of an old man by the name of McEvoy, a man I should say about sixty years of age.

Q. What offense was he showered for?

A. He was reported by one of the guards as having smoked in his cell,—reported that he saw smoke coming out of his cell, and he was showered for denying it.

Q. Describe that punishment by showering. State the manner in which the convict was placed to receive it, and how long it continued, and how severe it was, and the effect of it upon him.

A. He was showered, I should think, about twenty minutes to half an hour. It was among the first I had witnessed, and although I didn't time it, it seemed a long time to me; it seemed over that. But after that I had occasion to time the punishments, and my impression is now that he was not showered over twenty to twenty-five minutes.

Q. Showered from the hose?

A. Yes, sir.

Q. State whether he was stripped to receive this showering.

A. He was not stripped.

Q. What was the effect upon the person of this convict?

A. Well, the old man was so cold and chilly that he could hardly walk—barely get to the stove.

Q. What time of the year was this?

A. In December. I think it was in December or the fore part of January. It was the first one that I witnessed after I went there. It was in December, 1872, or the fore part of January, 1873. He told me in less than half an hour after he was showered that he lied about it. It was the only way he could stop the showering; that he had never smoked in his cell. He said that was the the only way he could stop it, so admitted that he did.

Q. What other instances of severe punishment did you witness there?

A. I saw one man flogged. I thought it was rather severe for the offense, though he was only given ten lashes, I believe, with the whip.

Q. Do you recollect the name of this convict?

A. His name was McMartin—John McMartin, I think.

Q. Can you tell when that was?

A. I think that was in June or July, 1873.

Q. What was the offense with which he was charged?

A. One of the other convicts had got into a little trouble with the guard, and endeavored to strike the guard, who was at work on the appropriations, and McMartin left his work and came into the hall.

Q. Who inflicted that punishment?

A. Mr. Morris.

Q. State any other instances.

A. I saw quite a number of them flogged there at one time for making keys.

Q. Making keys?

A. Yes, sir.

Q. By whom were they flogged?

STATE PRISON INVESTIGATION. 33

A. Mr. Morris.
Q. Do you know how many lashes they each received?
A. I don't, to say the exact number. I know that one of them received over thirty before he would admit that he made the keys.
Q. Do you know whether these punishments were put on the records of the prison?
A. I do not.
Q. Did you have access to the prison record of punishments?
A. I had access, if I requested. I never looked at the prison records, except once in the absence of the deputy, when I had his book, and was making records in his place.
Q. Did any instance ever occur, to your knowledge, where the records did not state the facts truly in regard to the punishment and offense.
A. There have been instances. There was one instance where there was a punishment there was no record made of at all; when I put it on the deputy's book in his absence; it don't appear on the prison record. I was shown the prison record last week, and didn't find it there.
Q. What case was that?
A. A case of showering two boys.
Q. Do you remember when?
A. February 4, 1874.
Q. Who inflicted the punishment?
A. Mr. Morris.
Q. Did you ever witness any punishments in the prison except by Mr. Morris?
A. Yes, sir.
Q. By whom?
A. By Capt. Winans.
Q. What was his position in the prison.
A. He was deputy; also Col. Van Arsdale, when I went there.
Q. State, if you know, what punishments inflicted by the deputy were by Mr. Morris' direction or otherwise.
A. They were by his direction, I suppose.
Q. State whether he was present.
A. Not always; sometimes he was absent.
Q. Describe Mr. Morris' general treatment of the prisoners as to whether it was kind or otherwise.
A. At times it was very kind; it would seem at times that he could hardly treat a prisoner well enough; at other times in a fit of passion, I have seen him ill treat them, punish them when I thought they didn't deserve it.
Q. When Mr. Morris inflicted punishment, as a rule, state whether it was done in anger or how otherwise?
A. It was very frequently done in anger.
Q. What induced you to think it was done in anger?
A. That was the general appearance at the time.
Q. Did you hear him use any language to prisoners which indicated the condition of his mind?
A. I have seen him, when they were endeavoring to make some explanation, strike them with his hand in the face and tell them to shut up, and not allow them to make an explanation.
Q. Can you give instances of that kind?

A. I could not give the particular names.
Q. State whether you ever saw that on more than one occasion.
A. I have.
Q. How many can you state confidently you have seen it?
A. Oh, I couldn't state positively, how many I have seen; as many as three or four; perhaps more.
Q. When convicts were brought before him for punishment, state what his custom was as to giving them an opportunity to explain.
A. It was his general custom to give them an opportunity for explanation; that was the custom, but there were quite a number of cases where he did not.
Q. Can you mention any other instances where he exhibited a violent temper or anger?
A. I remember particularly one instance, on Sunday, of his pulling a convict out of the ranks and cuffing his ears before an audience of Jackson people, probably 25 or 30, in the dining room.
Q. For what offense?
A. Well, the convict was looking towards Mr. Morris and grinning, I believe. He was a kind of half crazy man any way,—a man I believe, who had spent two years at the Asylum, at Kalamazoo.
Q. Describe the manner in which he boxed his ears?
A. Well, he pulled him out of the ranks, boxed his ears, and made him sit down on the stage until the convicts were marched out.
Q. Was the strap in use as an instrument of punishment while you were in the prison?
A. It was not; I left there in April, 1874.
Q. Where was the water taken from that was used in showering?
A. It was taken from the hydrant, in the lower hall of the central building,—Holly water works.
Q. Holly water works?
A. Yes, sir.
Q. Do you know what pressure was generally applied?
A. I do not.
Q. Do you know the size of the nozzle through which they generally apply it?
A. I think it was about half an inch.
Q. Did they use more than one?
A. Yes, they had two nozzles there; I think one of them got a little out of repair some way, and they used the smaller one I think most, when the larger one got out of repair.
Q. What was the temperature of the water applied?
A. That depended on the season of the year, somewhat; I couldn't say what the temperature was.
Q. Well, was it the same as it would be from the weather—water from the outside, out of doors?
A. Yes, sir; it was about a mile, I think, from the prison to the mill pond, where the water was taken from.
Q. What distance from the nozzle was the convict usually placed, when applying this punishment?
A. From four inches to eight feet.
Q. Upon what part of the body was the stream directed?
A. All parts—the face and all parts of the body.
Q. Was this water applied in the room, or out of doors?

A. It was applied in the room; in what we called the center hall of the main building.

Q. In what condition were the convicts, ordinarily, as to being clothed?

A. They were generally stripped and tied up to an iron door.

Q. Stripped entirely naked?

A. Yes, sir; after the first two months that I was there—I think the first two months—there wasn't any one stripped, but they were showered with their clothes on.

Q State whether you ever saw Mr. Morris use any violence upon any of the convicts, other than what you have already stated?

A. I saw him strike one man with a cane.

Q. With a cane?

Q. Where did he hit him?

A. On the head.

Q. What was the offense?

A. He was ordered to go into a room and strip for a shower bath. He stepped in there and seemed to be looking around for something to defend himself with, and Morris knocked him down.

Q. Any other instances?

A. I don't know that I ever saw him strike any one else with a cane. I don't remember that I did.

Q What proof of guilt was furnished or required before convicts were punished?

A. Well, sometimes it was a report from the guard of some offense during the night, sometimes from the keepers of the shops. I think I have seen them punished on a report from another convict.

Q. When they were called up to make their explanation, if they denied the charge, state whether any further inquiry was made, to ascertain the truth of it.

A. Sometimes there was further inquiry, and sometimes they were punished until they would admit the charge.

Q. Did you ever mention any of these severe punishments to the Inspectors?

A. I did not.

Q. Why not?

A. I didn't find anything in the prison rules requiring me to report the Agent to the Inspectors.

Q. What opportunities, while you were there, had convicts to converse with what are called freemen—other workmen that were about there?

A. They had, during the last year that I was there, they had a good many opportunities. There were a great many freemen going in to work on the appropriations, and they worked with the convicts without an overseer directly over them.

Q. Was there any regulation of the prison, either of the Inspectors or the Agent, which prohibited freemen from conversing with the convicts they were working with?

A. I think there was. I think the prison rules required freemen not to converse with convicts, except in regard to their duties as foremen—explaining to them about their work.

Q. Was that rule violated?

A. I think it was?

Q. State whether the Agent knew of the violations?

A. I think he did.

Q. Well, what induced you to think so.

A. We had several conversations in regard to the men who were in there— that we thought they were saying things that they had no right to say to the convicts.

Q. You say you and the Agent had?

A. Yes, sir.

Q. What measures were taken, if any, to put a stop to the practice?

A. There were several men, I think in the fall of 1873, shut out of the yard —several freemen—at different times, for tampering with convicts

Q. While you were there how frequent an occurrence was it for punishment to be inflicted on convicts?

A. During the summer of 1873 it was a very frequent occurrence.

Q. Well, state whether once a week or oftener?

A. Yes, sir; on an average, I should say, once a day from the time I went there until December 2d—until May 2d or 3d I think there was no flogging done; I think that May 3d was the first flogging that I witnessed in the prison; and, in fact, I didn't witness that, I got there just after the flogging was over; I heard the blows, but didn't see the man flogged; he was lying on the flagstones when I got there, on his back.

Q. Why was he lying there?

A. He appeared to be faint. He looked very pale and appeared to be faint.

Q. You say that was in May, 1873?

A. The second or third of May, 1873.

Q. Did you observe any difference in the treatment of prisoners by Mr. Morris, as to whether any of them were treated with more regard than others—whether he made any distinction?

A. I think of one instance where I thought he did make quite a distinction.

Q. State that instance.

A. The instance was where one Benjamin Thomas was detected stealing cigars; some of the cigars were found in his pocket; he was working in the cigar shop; he was punished for a long time to make him tell who he gave the cigars to, or who he was getting them for; he accused a man by the name of Kingen; (?) Mr. Morris punished him sometime after he had accused this man thought it was not possible that this man had taken the cigars; finally he sent for him; Thomas couldn't give the man's name, but he showed us his cell where he was locked; they sent for the man and brought him in; he admitted —denied it on the start, but finally admitted that he had taken forty-five cigars from Thomas; Thomas stated that he had given him a hundred and fifty through the week; and he was sent back and shut up without any punishment; I thought at the time that that was quite a distinction.

Q. State what offense Thurston was charged with for which the first punishment was inflicted by whipping?

A. He was ordered to go to a bare cell and be locked in, and refused to go till a revolver was produced; I think he used some bad language while he was locked in the cell,—some threats towards Mr. Morris.

Q. And for that refusal, and for those threats he was flogged?

A. Yes, sir; he was showered in the first place, from the large hose on the hydrant in the yard.

Q. You say the large hose,—state its size?

A. I should say from the best of my knowldge, it was a two and a half or three inch hose.

STATE PRISON INVESTIGATION. 37

Q. And the size of the nozzle?
A. The length was probably five feet, and the mouth of the nozzle, probably an inch; it might not have been quite as large.
Q. You say he was showered from that first?
A. Yes, sir.
Q How long a time was he showered?
A. Ffteen minutes, I presume.
Q. And then taken out?
A. And then taken out.
Q. And flogged?
A. Yes, sir.
Q. What was he punished for on the second occasion?
A. On the second occasion he was punished for having a dirk.
By Mr. Bartow:
Q. Can you describe the whip that was used. What kind of handle did it have; what was it composed of; was it what was commonly denominated a black whip?
A No, not what I understand was a black whip. The handle was more like a common buggy whip, rattan or whalebone.
Q. Was it a whip that would be denominated by men who use them, a stallion whip?
A. Sir, I don't know as I understand what that would be.
Q. Well, I don't know myself. The reason I asked the question was on account of some previous testimony. You think it was a sort of ratan or whalebone, with a lash attached, do you?
A. I should say it was, to the best of my knowledge. I wouldn't be positive about the material of the whip.
Q About what was Mr. Thurston's age?
A. I should say he was a man about thirty.
Q. Now, at what time was this McMartin whipped,—about what time did that whipping occur?
A. I think that was in June or July, 1873.
Q What was he whipped with?
A. He was whipped with the same whip. It was on a new staff.
Q. Was the whip used as an instrument of punishment all the time during your stay there, or was the leather strap substituted for it?
A. The leather was not substituted for it while I was there. As far as my observation went there was very little whipping done during the winter months.
Q. Now I want to ask the witness what is Mr. Morris' temperament, as to being even or uneven?
A. I think it is quite uneven.
Q. Did he sometimes, when inflicting punishment, appear cool and calm, and at other times act exasperated and in a rage?
A. He did.
Q. Now, during your observation there of punishment, what seemed to be the most effectual in subduing the prisoners? Have you made any observation?
A. As far as my observation goes, I think that locking in a bare cell was the most effectual.
Q. You think it would subdue them more?
A. Yes, unless it was in some extreme cases of insubordination.

Q. Was you there at the time the convict escaped and was pursued and shot?
A. I was.
Q. Who was that convict?
A. John Driscoll.
Q. About what time was that?
A. That, I think, was in May or June of 1873; I won't be positive which.
Q. Did you see the man before he was brought into the prison after the shooting?
A. I did not.
Q Did you see him after he was brought in? Did you see the wound?
A. I did.
Q. Where was that?
A The wound?
Q. Yes, sir.
A It was in his back.
Q. What was he shot with?
A. Shot with a navy revolver.
Q. I mean whether it was ball or shot?
A. It was a conical ball, generally known as a Minie ball.
Q. Did you see the ball extracted?
A. I saw the doctor when he was probing the wound for the ball, and saw the ball after it was extracted. I have it somewhere in my possession, but haven't it here.
Q. Was Mr. Morris present when the wound was being probed and the ball extracted?
A. I don't remember if he was.
Q. Did you hear any conversation between Mr. Morris and the convict about what occurred at the time he was pursued and shot?
A. I didn't between Mr. Morris and the convict. I had some conversation with Mr. Morris.
Q. About the affair?
A. Yes, sir.
Q. State what that conversation was between you and him about it.
A. Mr. Morris said the prisoner said "My God! what did you shoot me for without speaking?"
Q. Well, what further did Mr. Morris state the prisoner said?
A. He didn't say he made any reply to that.
Q. Did you hear Mr Morris say during that conversation that he demanded the man to surrender, or demanded him to stop?
A. He said he didn't; he saw him rising out of the bushes and fired at once.
Q Have you now related all the instances of severe punishment that you remember of?
A. I don't recollect of any others in particular. There were several punishments that I couldn't name the convicts or tell what they were punished for.
Q. Was you in the prison at the time a punishment occurred on some convict,—I can't call his name now,—when Capt. Winans struck the convict after he was down,—knocked down?
A. I was.
Q. When was that?

A. That, I think, was in March, 1874, about a month, I should say, before I left there; it might have been in February.
Q. State the circumstances under which that occurred.
A. The circumstances were that a convict who had refused to work in the wagon shop was brought into the hall and Mr. Morris came in and ordered him to go into a room,—an old cellar,—and strip for a shower bath. He went in there, and instead of stripping, he was looking about as though looking for some way to escape, or some weapon to defend himself with. Mr. Morris struck him and knocked him down, and Capt. Winans struck him while he was down. He was lying down on his knees, with his head about a foot from the floor. He was asking them to stop and he would comply with their wishes.
Q. Did he say he would stop before he was struck by Capt. Winans?
A. Yes, sir.
Q. Mr. Morris was present all the time?
A. Yes, sir.
Q. Do you know whether Mr. Morris, the agent, did anything to Captain Winans, or reported him, for striking the convict after he was down?
A. He didn't at the time.
Q. Do you know whether he did afterwards or not?
A. I do not.
Q. Mr. Cook, have you ever seen the prison record of the punishment of Thurston?
A. I haven't seen it; I have seen the newspaper report of it.
Q. You didn't see the report itself?
A. I did not.
[Witness was shown prison record of June 3, p. 133: "Drayton Thurston for several months past has been under lock and key fully half the time," was vomiting, etc.]
Q. State whether you discover anything in that reading?
A. That vomiting—I never discovered anything of the kind; he was spitting blood all through the winter previous to that; he was in the hospital for quite a while, and was afterwards locked in his cell; I have seen him spit apparently fresh blood, at other times it would be clotted; we asked the surgeon's opinion about it several times, where the blood came from, and he gave it as his impression that in the first place he picked his teeth till he made them bleed, but he never seemed to be thoroughly satisfied where the blood came from; I never saw him vomit. There is another thing there in regard to his saying, after he was tied, that he would let a knife into Mr. Morris' bowels; he may have made some such threat as that in his cell; he didn't make any such threat as that after he was tied; I remember Mr. Morris striking him after he was tied—taking him out of the shop and striking him over the head.
Q. What with?
A. With a whip handle.
By Mr. Bartow:
Q. What was this man knocked down with at the time Capt. Winans tied him?
A. Knocked down with a medium-sized cane.
By Mr. Webber:
Q. Did you know of any case where a couple of convicts were inquired of about some checks, by parties from Detroit?
A. Yes, sir.

Q. Give the details of that.

A. There was a couple of colored boys, Fairfax and Jacobs, that were sent from Detroit—one for five, I think, and the other for six years, in the early part of January, 1874. On the 4th day of February a detective came there from Detroit, and asked Mr. Morris for an interview with those two convicts. Mr. Morris sent for them. One of them was already working in the shop, the other one, I believe, was in his cell. He was sent there about that time. I don't think Fairfax had been assigned to the shop. They were questioned by Mr. Morris, and by the detective, in regard to some bond check they had found in a satchel. I think the satchel belonged to Jacobs when they were arrested. Mr. Morris afterwards had them stripped and showered them.

Q. Because their answers were not satisfactory?

A. Yes, sir.

Q. How severely were they showered?

A. Oh, not very severely; not over ten minutes. One of them was sent to the bare cell afterwards for five or six hours.

Q. You gave the date of that?

A. February 4, 1874. [Mr. Webber looks at record.]

[Mr. Morris.] It is not on the records.

By Mr. Webber:

Q. At the time Mr. Morris was telling you about shooting Driscoll, did he tell you how far Driscoll was from him at the time he fired?

A. I don't know that he told me exactly—somewhere from fifteen to twenty feet I think it, or about that distance. I don't remember positively. I won't be positive as he said the exact distance. He told me at the time about how far it was. I had got the impression that he was about a rod from him.

By Mr. Morris:

Q. Mr. Cook, how came you to go to the prison at all?

A. Mr. John R. Stewart of Grand Rapids came to me and stated that they were raising the devil at the prison. Said that two of the keepers had resigned; that Mr. Morris had written two letters to him asking him to send some man down from Grand Rapids, that he had no faith in the Jackson people—they were all down on him—and he asked me if I would go down there, and I told him, after consulting with my family, that I would go down there the next day and look the prison over and see what could be done, what the duties were, and what the pay was, and if I concluded it was enough, I would stay there if they wanted me. I went down on the day before Thanksgiving. Had a talk with you. You expressed yourself as very glad to have some one there from Grand Rapids, and offered me the hall-keeper's place. I told you I would come down on the following Monday, and did so.

Q. What was Mr. Stewart's position in connection with the prison?

A. He was one of the inspectors.

Q. How long?

A. How long was he inspector?

Q. Yes, How long had he been on the board?

A. I don't know that I could say exactly how long he had been on the board —perhaps three or six months.

Q. Three or six months?

A. Yes, about a year I should think.

Q. What sort of a place did he say he thought the prison would be for you?

STATE PRISON INVESTIGATION. 41

A. I don't know as I recollect exactly. He thought perhaps I would fill the place.

Q. Did he say anything about the management of the prison?

A. Yes, I think he did.

Q. Will you state it?

A. Well, I remember his saying in particular that he thought the deputy and hall keeper were trying to injure you all they could.

Q. When they was endeavoring to get the appointment?

A. I don't know that I heard Mr. Stewart say in what way.

Q. How did Mr. Stewart, as inspector, regard the management of the prison,—good, bad, or indifferent?

A. Good; I never heard him say anything against the management of the prison.

Q. What was there about it that pleased him?

A. I don't know that I ever heard him mention any one thing in particular, unless it was the improvement in the feed; and, perhaps, the opportunities for reading that you had given them.

Q. The feed of what,—mules or convicts?

A. Feed of convicts.

Q. That was the only thing?

A. I don't recollect of any other thing, particularly. I never had any conversation with him in regard to the discipline.

Q. Did you ever write him after you left the prison?

A. I never.

Q. What did you say to him about the prison?

A. I don't remember.

Q. Did you write to your acquaintances in Grand Rapids,—business men and others, you knew there, what you thought about it.

A. I don't remember writing to any one in particular, at Grand Rapids, about it?

Q. Well, anywhere.

A. I remember writing to some here at Lansing,—one in particular.

Q. Who was it?

A. Senator Crosby.

Q. What did you say to Senator Crosby?

A. I don't recollect all that I said.

Q. Did you tell him that you saw me give Thurston seventy-four lashes?

A. No, sir.

Q. Did you take an oath when you went into prison?

A. I took one soon after.

Q. Well, when you commenced your duties? What was the nature of that oath?

A. It was an ordinary oath of office.

Q. Well, what was it.

A. To perform the duties of assistant keeper in the State prison.

Q. What are the duties of a keeper there?

A. Well there are different duties,—it depends on where they are placed.

Q. Have they got any other duties besides serving the Agent?

A. Yes, sir.

Q. Will you state what the duties are; talk right along freely; you talked freely before.

A. Well, duties to the convicts, I believe, are to see that they are kept at work, and the keepers in general; the duties of the keepers in the shops are to see that the convicts are kept at work.

Q. You was not in the shop?

A. No, sir; not as a general thing, unless it was for a short time.

Q. Well, Mr. Cook, will you please define what you regarded as your duties as a sworn officer of the prison?

A. My duties were those of hall keeper.

Q. Had you any moral duties?

A. I thought I had.

Q. Was it your duty to stay there and keep your mouth still when you saw the Inspectors every month, and knew that men were being cruelly punished there?

A. I should have left six months before I did. I think that would have been my moral duty.

Q. I told you so when I discharged you. I have a copy of the letter now. Could you have told the board without my knowing where the information came from?

A. I don't know whether I could or not.

Q. Yes you do know. Did you ever have any conversation with the board during your service there concerning the management of the prison?

A. I presume I did, Mr. Morris.

Q. How did you express yourself?

A. I don't recollect. I don't recollect having any conversation with the members of the board respecting the management of the prison. I may have had.

Q. Do you recollect of any conversation within a few weeks before you left?

A. I remember having a conversation with Mr. Wilcox, but not with regard to the management of the prison.

Q. Did you want to stay?

A. I don't know whether I expressed any such desire to him. It was with regard to the application I had sent to the Board of Inspectors.

Q. How many pages were there in it?

A. I couldn't say positively; three or four, perhaps.

Q. Did you hint at any thing like wrong treatment of the men there, before you left?

A. I think possibly I might, before I left.

Q. To any one connected with the prison now, that had any authority or influence there.

A. No, sir.

Q. Did you join the church while you were at the prison?

A. I did.

Q. Did you have any different convictions after that?

A. I don't know, Mr. Morris, as that has any thing to do with it.

Q. Yes, it is right on the point.

A. I don't know that I did.

By Mr. Barlow:

Q. Mr. Cook, while you were at the prison did you witness any punishment that was called the cross?

A. I did not, sir.

STATE PRISON INVESTIGATION. 43

B. W. CHASE SWORN.

By Mr. Webber:
Q. Where do you reside, Mr. Chase?
A. Jackson.
Q. How long have you resided there?
A. About four years—between three and four.
Q. In what business are you engaged?
A. Blacksmith and wagon business—carry on business there.
Q. Have you been in the same business at the same place since you have been living at Jackson?
A. No, sir.
Q. State whether your business is in connection with the prison.
A. Not at all, at the present.
Q. How far from the prison is your present place of business located?
A. My opinion would be that it is in the neighborhood of half a mile now. It may not be quite, and it may be half a mile.
Q. Have you at any time been connected with the work at the prison?
A. Two years and six months, I think.
Q. From what time to what time?
A. I think I went there in April or the first of May, in 1870, and stayed there until the first day of December, 1873.
Q. The business in which you are engaged now has no connection with the prison or any of its contractors?
A. With none of the contractors except that I work for them—some work for the State.
Q. While you were at the prison where did your duty call you?
A. My duty called me as foreman to the blacksmith shop, in the wagon contract.
Q. That is in the prison?
A. In the prison.
Q. How many men were employed in that shop?
A. At the time I went there, I think the books showed about fifty-two men; at the time I left the contract expired. We took a new contract, and there was in the neighborhood of from sixteen to eighteen checked in the book of that shop.
Q. What was your relation to those men?
A. My relation? I was overseer of the works. My business was to superintend the ironing department of the wagons.
Q. What had you to do with the men? Anything with the care or direction of the convicts?
A. I had to do with the quality and quantity of the work.
Q. State whether any keeper was with them.
A. Yes, sir; two most of the time.
Q. In the same shops?
A. Yes, sir; in the same shops. Well, I will alter that a little. I think there was about half the time two keepers, a part of the time only; perhaps two-thirds of the time two keepers.
Q. Were you there constantly during this time?
A. I was absent at one time three weeks on account of sickness. I think I was absent three days besides that.
Q. What were the hours of labor?

A. The hours of labor when I first went there, was about eight and a half to nine, in the winter season—short days. In long days it was ten hours about half the time, and the balance it was an average of about ten hours a day for a year, amounting to an average, I think, of about ten hours a day for the last year.

Q. Did you have any direction or control of the convicts, further than to instruct them in their work?

A. I had control of the convicts; the foreman is supposed to exercise control as regards the work, and how the men shall work, if it is under the control of the Agent or others, unless it be to take a man outside the jurisdiction of the keeper, then he has to have special permit.

Q. Were you free to converse with the convicts as you would with other laborers in their places?

A. Anything about their work—anything pertaining to their work.

Q. And they conversed with you equally free?

A. Yes, sir; that was so more particularly the latter part of the time that I was there; I didn't see any difference in conversing with convicts and any body outside. They had the same facilities for knowing anything that happened outside, and would converse among themselves and with others. I didn't know of any difference at the time.

Q. Were there any other freemen beside yourself that worked in the shop?

A. Yes, sir.

Q. How many?

A. One man was at work in the shop with me, beside the keeper.

Q. And did he converse with the convicts equally free with yourself?

A. I know nothing to the contrary, sir.

Q. You suppose he did?

A. I suppose he did,—in fact, I've heard him talk before convicts, and I presume it was his habit.

Q. And with them?

A. Yes, sir.

Q. Was this considered contrary to the practice in the prison?

A. I don't think it's a habit, in my experience in the prison, of there being any difference.

Q. In conversing with the convicts or freemen?

A. Only in the discipline of the prison it was not allowed at all. What I am speaking of would be politics and natural occurrences.

Q. Were they prohibited from speaking to the convicts, except in the presence of the keepers and in their hearing.

A. No, sir; not that I have heard of.

Q. While you were there, did you ever have any opportunity to observe the manner in which the convicts were punished for any offenses?

A. I did in one or two instances.

Q. What punishments did you see inflicted?

A. In one or two instances I saw men showered.

Q. Showering was done in the room?

A. It was.

Q. How far was that room from the place in which you were engaged?

A. I cannot tell exactly; I should think it was perhaps twenty rods from the shops. I think both times I was going to get shaved at the barber shop, and passing through the room saw some showering?

STATE PRISON INVESTIGATION.

Q. Do you know of any other punishments except those two instances?
A. Well, I knew of its being done, but didn't see it done myself.
Q. Did you know of any flogging being done there?
A. Yes, sir; that is, I knew the convicts and saw some of them. I did not go to see it done. Never saw a man flogged.
Q. Did you know of any punishment by being tied on the cross?
A. I saw one man on the cross.
Q. Do you know what he was put there for?
A. I don't; I didn't know at the time and ask no questions.
Q. Do you know how long he was there?
A. I do not; I was merely passing by a solitary cell. A friend of mine was there, and he asked to see a solitary cell, and I asked permission of the hall-keeper, Mr. Lane, to see a solitary cell, and, as it happened, I opened the door where the cross was in, and there was a man at the time on the cross, and we closed the door and came away.
Q. How often did you see Mr. Morris while you were there?
A. I don't know; I do not think I could tell upon an average. Sometimes I saw him every day, sometimes not for two or three days. Sometimes I would talk with him for two or three days, and sometimes not for a week.
Q. What opportunity had you to observe the general treatment of the convicts?
A. What opportunities I had was in regard to reporting men to the keepers, in regard to the kind and quality of the work, and I always knew in what way a man was punished, as did most of the foremen in the shop.
Q. Describe the practice in that regard—what you regarded as offenses that you would report to the keeper?
A. I would report to the keeper any infraction of the rules, the same as I would of a child; and if a convict knew of any infractions of the rules by others, it was my duty to report that.
Q. On your complaining to the keeper were there any instances where the convicts were not punished?
A. I know of two or three instances where the convicts were not punished, when they were reported.
Q. How common an occurrence was it for you to make such report?
A. There was no average. Sometimes we would report a man once in thirty days, sometimes every day, sometimes once or twice a day, just as the discipline of the prison happened to be at the time, or as the weather had to do with the discipline of the man.
Q. In what way did the weather affect them?
A. Well, you take men in a shop of a hot day, they certainly cannot work as easily and conveniently as of a cool day, and sometimes the weather would have that effect—make men peevish in that way.
Q. And in such cases reports would come oftener?
A. In such cases reports would come oftener; as I say, it was the feelings of the convicts.
Q. It was your duty under the regulations, as I understand you, to report every breach of discipline?
A. Yes, sir, and I never calculated to let one slip. I would report to the keeper, he would send for the deputy, and the matter would be reported to the deputy. Sometimes the deputy would take the man in at the time; sometimes

he would report the case to Mr. Morris, and the man would be taken in at night after his day's work.

Q. Were you ever called before Mr. Morris to verify any of these charges?

A. I was, once.

Q. But once?

A. But once, I think.

Q. Do you recollect the instance; what the man was charged with?

A. I was reporting a man by the name of Stewart. I was grinding an axe, a hand axe; he came into my shop; he was a man that worked in the wood shop, and he came and took the hand axe, and was holding it on the face and cutting out the stone, and I went to him and told him not to hold the axe on in that way. He said it was none of my business; that another foreman had told him to hold the axe in that way, and I told him I did not want he should do it. We had some words, and I saw that he would not desist, and I reported him to the keeper for the offense, and the keeper reported him to Mr. Morris, and the next morning I was called in; Mr. Morris sent for me to come in. The convict, I think, was sitting in the window. Mr. Morris says, "Chase, take a seat here, on the other side of me," and says "Stewart, tell your story," and turned around to me after he had heard Stewart's story, and said, "Now Chase, tell your story." It appears that the convict, after I reported him, complained that I swore at him, and told him to go away from the stone or I would break his head, or something of that kind; that I used an oath about it.

Q. Was he punished?

A. I will tell you. Mr. Morris, after he heard the story through, made a remark as though it was a clear case that the stories were in contradiction to each other. I told him that I had told my story. He said, "It is queer that you tell one story and the convict another, and I don't know which to believe." Upon that I went back to my shop, and I don't know whether he was punished or not. My impression is that he was not.

Q. While you were there did you hear any foreman or freemen using any profane or violent language to any of the convicts?

A. I don't know that I ever did.

Q. Did you ever hear any keepers or agents, or any others, use any violent language?

A. I don't know that I ever heard any man having charge of the convicts use profane or violent language towards them.

Q. Did you ever hear them use threatening language?

A. Well, not what you would call threatening language. It is quite a common occurrence, in giving a man a task, to tell him what they want him to do. It would be quite a common occurrence for either keepers or foremen to say, "If you don't do it I shall report you." In cases of that kind, if it be threatening,—if that is what you call threatening,—that is what would be often said to them. I have heard keepers say it, and I have said it to them myself; have told them they'd better do it, and not get themselves into trouble.

Q. Was it common to say this before they had absolutely refused?

A. No, sir; I never heard it.

Q. Was not the refusal itself a breach of the rules?

A. It was a breach of the rules, yes, sir. If they would totally refuse to do it, the case would be reported at once; at least, it would be the foreman's duty to report it to the keepers at once.

STATE PRISON INVESTIGATION.   47

Q. In conversation with the convicts, did any of them ever speak to you of the manner in which they were treated by the agent and keepers?
A. Yes, sir; I have heard them speak of their manner of treatment.
Q. I speak now of times when you and they were conversing together,—have you talked with them about that question?
A. Yes, sir.
Q. That was not one of the subjects that was prohibited?
A. In talking about the discipline of the prison, I did'nt argue with a man.
Q. Was it customary to punish a man if he did not get out in season?
A. I think they had what they call "chalking" the men. The keeper will make a cross check on his cell—the night keepers—and after the guards are changed in the morning, and the day guards come on, those cells are not unlocked. The cases I refer to went to the deputy or agent, usually to the deputy, for investigation, and it was discretionary with the agent or deputy, at that time, whether they would be punished and sent to the shop, or sent to the shop without punishment. That is what I mean by getting out late. They have always to be in time unless they are sick.
Q. What offenses do they commit for which they are chalked in?
A. I have never been keeper, only heard or learned.
Q. From Mr. Morris?
A. Only, and from knowing what his duties were.
Q. I understand that you have stated all the instances that you ever saw of punishment?
A. I say these are the only instances that I ever witnessed.
Q. Did you ever discover any indications of violence or anger on the part of Mr. Morris in the management or treatment of any of the convicts?
A. Do I understand you to ask if I have seen him use any violence on the convicts in an angry manner, or when appearing angry?
Q. Yes.
A. I think I did at one time,—one instance that occurs to me now.
Q. Give the particulars of it.
A. The instance was that of a man who was in the hospital, and said he was sick, and they didn't know, and the hospital keeper, I believe, claimed that he was trying to play off,—to get rid of work by feigning sickness. He had been there several days in the same position. At that time he was hallooing, making a loud noise, and I believe the keeper said he had been for a day or two. I had occasion to go into the hospital to see the keeper. As I went in Mr. Morris was turning water on this man, on the couch. The man was lying on the couch and he was turning water on him. My impression was, that it was from a can, like,—something of that sort. It might have held probably a pail full, or a little more.
Q. Turning it from a hose or from a spout?
A. Turning it on the man as he was lying on the bed,—on the couch; turning water out of a can onto him to make him stop his hallooing, I believe; but the man did not stop hallooing, and said,—he was hallooing, I think, "Jesus! Oh, Jesus!"
Q. How did he halloo; that he wanted to see his Jesus?
A. I believe these were the words he used; and Mr. Morris, as I said, was pouring water onto him, and seemed to be excited. I judge from his appearance and what he said at the time.
Q. What remarks did you hear Mr. Morris make at the time?

A. He asked him if he wanted—I wont be positive whether he asked him if he wanted to see his Jesus now, or wanted to halloo that he wanted to see his Jesus.

Q. How long did this continue?

A. He was pouring water on him when I went into the hospital, about ten minutes, and was turning it on when I went away; he was not turning it on constantly, but would stop when he would quit hallooing, and talk to him.

Q. Was that the only instance in which you witnessed any exhibition of anger on the part of Mr. Morris towards convicts?

A. There was one other time; that was the case of Thomas Betts—that was the name he was known by there; he was whipped the same afternoon that David Smith was whipped, and David Smith was the first man whipped under Mr. Morris' administration.

Q. Go on and give us the particulars of it.

A. Betts was working on tire; he had made the authorities a great deal of trouble, he and two or three others in the shop, and this time Mr. Morris came out; Mr. Morris and I stood in the yard, talking—stood right near where they have the arrangment made for setting tire; talking at the time about Smith's being punished; Mr. Morris made the remark that unless some of them began to obey, to live up to discipline, there would be more; at that time Betts was straightening tire, and he looked up at Mr. Morris—I wouldn't swear that he was looking at Mr. Morris, but at all events he laughed as Mr. Morris looked up, and I don't know but he was making some remarks about Mr. Morris; we couldn't hear from where we sat; he was laughing any way as he looked up.

Q. Go on.

A. And Mr. Morris said something to him; I can't quote his words now at all, but he gave them a warning; said something as though he had stood his insolence as long as he would, or something of that kind. Mr. Morris went into the hall, and a spell after that they sent for Betts. Betts went inside; came back I should think in about twenty minutes to half an hour, and came to me and says "I have got it." I says "Got what?" He says "Got ten or fifteen lashes," and he turned round and showed me his shirt, and I could see the prints of the leather or whatever it was. In the afternoon I saw him pull up his shirt and show his back to some men, and I should think there was some ten or twelve ridges on it. It is my impression there were as many as that; I didn't count them, and I asked him what he was punished for. He made the remark that he didn't know, and said he supposed it was for laughing at Mr. Morris, or laughing when Mr. Morris was looking at him. He said that Mr. Morris told him that he hadn't whipped him so much for the offense committed that morning as that he wished to square up his account to date.

Q. Do you recall any other instances, Mr. Chase, of Mr. Morris' manifesting anger?

A. These were the only exhibitions of temper, and I think the deed manifested more temper than the remarks or his appearance. I don't know, would not swear that he was passionate either time. I didn't see him punish the man. All I judge from was that the man was punished for that offense.

Cross-examined by Mr. Bartow:

Q. Do you know what this man was charged with that you saw upon the cross?

A. I do not, sir.

Q. What was his position upon the cross when you saw him?

A. He was standing upon the cross, one of his arms stretched out. His feet were not tied. He was standing up with his arms stretched out like that [indicating].

Q. From your observation there of Mr. Morris, what would you consider his temperament to be, even or uneven; whether he is a man of even temperament, or whether he is given to fits of passion?

A. At times I thought Mr. Morris was rather remarkable for his seeming disposition to put up with a great deal rather than punish, and then again at times the men seemed to act as though they were bound to be punished, and it would seem that he was equally willing to punish a man and give them what they deserved.

Q. Was you there at the time a man who escaped had been shot?

A. The man Driscoll? if that was the same man. I saw him before and after he was shot. I didn't see the wound, but I saw him after he came up into the shop.

Q. How long was he disabled or detained from work on account of treatment?

A. Well, he got away, escaped. He was loading in hubs and went out the first wagon that went out in the morning. He was in the shop before noon, but after noon,—my memory doesn't serve me whether he was in the shop after noon; I wouldn't swear whether he was or not.

Q. Did you have any conversation with Mr. Morris about the capture of the man?

A. No, sir; I don't know that the man was ever mentioned.

Q. Do you know any thing more about the affair than what you know from hearsay?

A. About the affair of what?

Q. About the shooting affair of Driscoll.

A. I didn't know any thing about the shooting affair of Driscoll, except as to his reputation before that.

Q. What was that?

A. It was very bad; one of the worst in the yard. Several times, some of my men came to me and told me that Driscoll was trying to work up a plan for escape.

Q. When you say he was one of the worst in the yard, what have you reference to; his general conduct, or his efforts to escape?

A. His conduct towards the discipline; the principle of inciting insurrection, and trying to escape. That is, I got this from other convicts. The convicts would come to me and tell me as a freeman; when any thing of that kind happened they would go to some freeman and tell it,—tell me that they were trying to escape, and Driscoll was aiding the movement.

Q. At the time you was there were there any female convicts confined in the prison?

A. There was, part of the time.

Q. Up to what time?

A. My impression is, for a year; it might have been longer than that, but it is my impression, about a year.

Q. About how many?

A. It is my impression there was not far from eight, or nine, but I don't know; I have seen them out at church; I don't know that I ever counted them, but that is my impression.

Q. They continued there about a year after you went there?

A. To the best of my impression, it is about a year; I couldn't swear definitely as to the time.

Q. Now, when punishment was inflicted, was it usually inflicted when the convicts were alone, or in the presence of other convicts?

A. I had no way of knowing that.

Q. Well, in those cases that you witnessed?

A. In the cases I saw there was other convicts punished; in the case of the man on the cross there was no one around that I know of, that is, no one in the room with him; there was other men around.

By Mr. Webber:

Q. I would like to ask you if you knew what became of the man that you saw being showered in the hospital?

A. I don't know what became of him; I have heard, but can't swear to anything positively that I know anything about it; I was told by the hospital keeper at that time; I think he said he went into a saw-mill, and worked ten days after that, and they concluded that he was deranged, and they put him into the asylum.

Q. Do you recollect about the date of this punishment of Thomas Betts that you speak of?

A. I can't tell you the date—I have no way of knowing the date, only that it was the same morning that Smith was punished, and Thomas Betts was flogged the same forenoon, because Mr. Morris was the man who whipped him.

Q. Here is a record of July 17th, of David Smith being put on the cross, and closes up with "thirty lashes, the first refreshment of the kind this season," is the way the record reads, and then, immediately under it, is the following record : "Thomas Betts had been reported for various offenses of a serious character for several months; showed little disposition to amend. Was told on this very morning, by the Agent or deputy, that a whip had been purchased, and that it was brought into the prison for the benefit of two or three of his class; that he had better be on the alert and keep within the rules, or he would be the next subject ; on the same day keeper Hall detected him in passing a letter to another convict; he received ten lashes on general account." You don't recollect of his being punished more than once on that day?

A. I do not.

Q. Did you know of any one dying in the hospital while you was there?

A. No, sir; that is, I never heard of any one's dying there that died from the effects of any punishment received there. Some died after they were punished, for most of them have been punished.

By Mr. Morris:

Q. State when you came to the prison?

A. I think I went there in May, last of April or first of May. It is my impression that I went there in 1870. I know it was about two months after you went there as agent.

Q. In 1870 or 1871?

A. I was there two years and six months. I hadn't thought of the time. I left there in December, 1873, or November, last day of November.

Q. Have you ever read the prison rules?

A. Yes, sir; I have seen them.

Q. I understood you to say the rules of the prison didn't prohibit freemen from any ordinary conversation with convicts outside the work.

A. I didn't swear that; didn't wish to be understood that the rules didn't prohibit it, but that the custom. He didn't ask in regard to the rules.
Q. You say it was the custom?
A. I never knew but it was.
Q. Do you know whether it was in the shops or not? Where did you work most of the time?
A. I worked in the blacksmith shop.
Q. Did you work outside of the shop?
A. No, sir.
Q. Did your men work outside?
A. Some of them worked out of doors.
Q. Every other day?
A. Every day, with few exceptions.
Q. How many tires were they setting there, the first season in 1871?
A. They were setting from eight to thirty set a day.
Q. What do you mean by "set?"
A. There are four tires to a set, you know.
Q. Do men outside the shop have more liberties to talk than men in the shop?
A. They have more liberty than the men in the shop.
Q. Are men ever reported for talking in the shop?
A. Yes, sir.
Q. Did you sometimes stand and talk with the prisoners in reference to the Beecher trial?
A. There was no such trial then; but I don't know but the convicts know as much about that as I do.
Q. Could you stand and talk upon any ordinary subject, outside the walls to any prisoner if the keeper knew you were talking to the convicts?
A. Do you mean to ask the question was it customary to talk about common occurrences outside?
Q. Yes, anything,—a horse-race for instance?
A. Yes; I never knew anything to the contrary.
Q. Did you ever talk to a convict outside the prison?
A. I have talked to the keeper.
By Mr. Bartow:
Q. I understand him to ask whether you could talk to the convicts about ordinary business, within the hearing of the keeper?
A. Not as a rule; there may have been exceptions.
By Mr. Morris:
Q. You thought that I seemed excited, or perplexed, or angry at something. You thought that I showed some unusual mood in the case of the man Smith, in the hospital.
A. I didn't know the man's name. I said from your language and your appearance at the time—I thought it was a queer question to ask at the time—that was why I thought of it as I did. I thought you seemed in anger when you asked him the question or you wouldn't probably have used that language to a convict.
Q. Are convicts always what they appear to be?
A. Convicts? No, sir.
Q. Do they ever deceive anybody?

A. I never knew anybody to have anything to do with them that they didn't deceive.

Q. Did you ever know an instance where they were playing off?

A. Yes, sir, or I supposed they were.

Q. Do you suppose they ever went out to work of their own accord?

A. No, sir, I have no idea they did.

Q. Can you tell how much water I poured on the convict's face when he was hallooing for Jesus?

A. I don't know; I know you was pouring water on him. Well, you must have poured a pot full, because the clothes on the bed were wet as well as his clothes. I judge from the couch and the floor under it that you must have poured as much as that, and more too.

Q. Where would it run to?

A. I don't know, unless the man drank it.

Q. Well, I will ask you another question, Mr. Chase, in the best humor; is it possible for a man to get punished and not get on to the records, do you think?

A. Do I think it possible for a man to be punished and not get on to the records?

Q. Yes; do you think that case would have gone on to the records?

A. I don't know, sir; I never saw your records, and don't know whether you put the case on to the records.

Q. Did you think it was put on?

A. I didn't know.

Q. Would you, as foreman of the shop, have much chance to know about the discipline of the prison? Has it a discipline?

A. Yes, sir.

Q. Did you have much interest in it any way?

A. Yes, sir; I would have as much interest in it as any man would have to have.

Q. Would you be likely to have as much interest in it as an agent or officer?

A. Perhaps not, because not having such men under my control.

Q. You have control of work, and no control of men whatever?

A. You asked me the question if I would have as much interest as an agent.

Q. Suppose I would test a case, I would'nt understand whether the case was real or deceptive, I might try him a little while with water or something, and make up my mind in ten or twenty minutes that it was a real case, and send him to the asylum?

A. I shouldn't suppose such a thing would happen in twenty minutes.

Q. In regard to Betts—you said Betts was punished in July?

A. I didn't say he was punished in July.

Q. You said he was punished the same day that Smith was?

A. Yes, sir.

Q. Had you any idea what his conduct was previous to that time; and how did you regard it?

A. I regarded his conduct as very mischievous and troublesome as a convict.

Q. Had you known of him committing any violence before that, in the case of Shumway or Mr. Bingham?

A. That was before I was there. I understood that he was one of the leaders in that arrangement.

STATE PRISON INVESTIGATION. 53

Q. You intimated that there was strong indications of a revolt on the west side shops Did you regard it as necessary to take any unusual precautions in that direction?
A. I think there was.
Q. Do you think you had a worse set of men than any other shop?
A. As a body they were reported to be the worst men in the shop.
Q. Well, what was your opinion? Did you think they were?
A. I wouldn't be a competent judge, Mr. Morris.
Q. Were they a class that you would call strong, burly men?
A. They were usually chosen on the contract; the stoutest, best men on the contract, were put into the blacksmith shop. The best men were men of long sentences.
Q. Did the fact of their sentences being long indicate that they were bad men?
A. Nothing more than as indicating the crimes they had committed.
Q. Did you know men there who had thrown cars from the track, been caught committing burglaries, etc.
A. Several cases.
Q. What was Driscoll's general reputation?
A. Very bad.
Q. Did you think that I had any occasion for fears in regard to him?
A. Well, I considered him a dangerous man, one that would get up a revolt if he could, and even lead it.
Q. Do you remember as to Driscoll's appearance when he was returned to the shops?
A. I remember there was blood on the side of his ear, where he had hurt his ear or something.
Q. Did he look as though he had been in the river?
A. He looked as though he had been in the mud somewhere.
Q. How soon after he escaped before you saw him in the shop again?
A. I think he was returned to the shop the same day.

THURSDAY, APRIL 8, 1875.

MR. RANSOM THORNE SWORN.

By Mr. Webber:

Q. Mr. Thorne, state your residence?
A. I reside in Jackson.
Q. How long have you resided in Jackson, Mr. Thorne?
A. Somewhere about twelve years, or thirteen years, I think.
Q. In what business have you been engaged?
A. The most of the time I have been engaged at the prison.
Q. Are you engaged there now?
A. I am not, no sir.
Q How long since you have been?
A. I left there on the 7th or 8th, I think it was, of April last, a year ago.
Q. About a year ago now?

A. Yes, sir, I am not positive about the date.

Q. What position did you occupy at the prison while you was there?

A. Well, I occupied different positions.

Q. State the different positions.

A. When I first went there I went as a guard. After that I was keeper; after that I was foreman, and then I was keeper again.

Q. What position did you occupy, at the time Mr. Morris entered upon the administration of the prison as agent?

A. I have forgotten. I don't know whether I was foreman before he came there or whether it was after. I think though it was before. I think I was foreman at the time he came there.

Q. Of what department were you foreman?

A. The wagon contract and paint shop.

Q. State whether you were employed by the contractors or in behalf of the State?

A. While I was foreman, I was employed by the contractors.

Q. How long after Mr. Morris came there did you continue as foreman?

A. Something over a year, I think.

Q. And then what department did you take?

A. I had charge of the dining room when I was at work for the State,—the dining room and kitchen,—furnishing the dining room department,—the provision department.

Q. What title?

A. As keeper.

Q. And how long did you continue in that particular department?

A. I think I was something over a year at that.

Q. And after leaving that, what department did you go into?

A. I was at the entrance gate,—the small gate, or in other words, what would be called the guard room gate.

Q. In what capacity?

A. Well, that would be gate keeper, or his substitute rather. I was put in the place of the regular gate keeper.

Q. How long did you remain in that capacity?

A. I can't state exactly, but think it was somewhere about three months,— two or three months.

Q. And then what department did you take?

A. I think that was about the time I resigned, or shortly after that at least; I may have staid a few days afterwards; I don't remember particularly.

Q. At the time you were at the prison, and after Mr. Morris became Agent, state whether you knew of any severe punishments being inflicted on convicts?

A. Well, I have heard of some punishing.

Q. State what character of punishments you have witnessed.

A. Well, I have seen them do some showering,—what they called showering, with the hose; also flogging. I didn't see but one man flogged,—don't remember that I did.

Q. Do you remember the name of the party flogged?

A. I saw this man Thurston flogged once. Suppose it to be the last time that he was flogged. Whether it was the last I don't know. I saw him flogged once.

Q. Did you ever see any other kind of punishment, except the flogging you speak of, and which one?

A. I don't think I did except putting in the bare cells. I have seen them put in the bare cells.

STATE PRISON INVESTIGATION.

Q. That is under Mr. Morris' administration?
A. Yes, sir; while he was acting as Agent.
Q. As keeper, state whether you had occasion to make any reports of convicts for breach of discipline?
A. Yes, sir, sometimes I have done such things.
Q. How were your reports made?
A. They were usually made to the deputy.
Q. In writing or orally.
A. Orally.
Q. When not made to the deputy, how were they made?
A. To the Agent, or sometimes to the deputy's substitute,—but that would be a deputy.
Q. Did your opportunities enable you to judge what action was taken upon your reports?
A. Well, not at all times; sometimes they did, sometimes not. They usually did.
Q. What was the character of the offenses you were called upon to report?
A. I don't think I had any very serious ones. They were mostly in regard to work or some little breach of discipline.
Q. Do you know whether any of the cases reported by you were punished or not?
A. I think they were; yes, sir.
Q. Can you remember any particular case?
A. I don't bring to mind now any particular case.
Q. After Mr. Morris became Agent, what opportunity had you of observing the treatment of convicts?
A. Well, I had some considerable opportunity. I was back and forth through the hall more or less; being connected with the dining-room, my business called me backwards and forwards through the middle hall quite often.
Q. State the manner in which the convicts were treated by Mr. Morris usually, as to whether kindly or harshly, or how otherwise?
A. Well, generally speaking I didn't think it was very harshly, what I had observed myself.
Q. State whether you ever heard him speak to the convicts angrily.
A. I have somewhat, yes.
Q. Can you recall any particular instances?
A. I don't know that I can particularly, unless it be in the case of Thurston.
Q. Was his treatment of convicts uniform? that is, was his temper uniform, even, so that he would be the same every day, or was he variable in his disposition and treatment of the convicts?
A. Well, sir, to speak just as I think about it, I think he didn't balance himself just as he ought to at all times.
Q. Now, will you please state to us the particulars wherein you thought he was lacking in that regard?
A. Well, I haven't any particular instance that I call to mind to refer you to.
Q. Do you remember any expressions of his to the convicts from which you judged that he had angry moods?
A. I couldn't tell any particular expressions that he used,—only his way,—because I didn't bear them in mind.
Q. Did you ever hear him indulge in profanity?
A. Not that I know of.

Q. State whether you ever saw him strike a convict, except the convict was called up for formal punishment.

A. Not to my knowledge.

Q. While you were there, did you observe any discrimination as between convicts, whether he treated some more leniently than others?

A. Not that I know of; I don't think I have any knowledge of anything of the kind.

Q. How often did you observe the inspectors at the prison?

A. They would usually get around there about once a month.

Q. How long time did they usually remain there?

A. One, two, or three days, I think.

Q. What examination did they make of the prison while they were there?

A. Well, the most that I saw of them was when they were passing through the shops; we would see them pass through the shops every time they came.

Q. State whether their custom was to go through the shops by themselves, or whether the Agent or some people was with them?

A. Well, they were by themselves usually, I think.

Q. What opportunity had the convicts to converse with the inspectors privately?

A. The rules were that if they had any reports to make to the Board of Inspectors to do so through the keepers.

Q. Were the convicts at liberty, under the usages of the prison, to apply directly to the Inspectors when they were on their examination?

A. That I couldn't say; do not know.

Q. State whether you know of any instances where convicts requested of the keepers an opportunity to speak with the Inspectors when it was denied them.

A. I don't know of any, sir.

By Mr. Seager:

Q. Mr. Thorne, did you know of the administration of the prison six or seven years prior to Mr. Morris' administration?

A. Yes, sir.

Q. How did Mr. Morris' administration compare in point of severity with that of previous administrations?

A. In regard to punishment?

Q. Yes, sir.

A. Well, sir, I think it was fully as lenient in regard to punishment as former administrations.

A. A. BLISS, SWORN.

Examined by Senator Webber:

Q. You reside at Jackson, Mr. Bliss?

A. I do, sir.

Q. You are acting as one of the inspectors of the State prison?

A. Yes, sir.

Q. How long have you been engaged as inspector?

A. Since about the middle of August, 1873.

Q. Before being appointed as inspector, had you any particular familiarity with the workings of the prison?

A. No, sir; no more than any other citizen.

Q. Since your appointment, will you tell us about what opportunities you have had to observe the workings of the prison?

A. Well, I think I have had every opportunity that one could have to observe the general workings of the prison. As far as punishments are concerned, I have not seen any; I am not present when any thing of that kind is done, but so far as the general management of the prison is concerned, its sanitary condition, its neatness, and the disposition of the convicts' work and duty, I have had opportunities; I have been in the prison on an average as often as four times a week for the last year. Some reasons why I have been at the prison at particular times have not had reference to the general management of the prison, but to notice the improvements that were going on; I have had considerable to do with them.

Q. The new buildings and repairs?

A. Yes, sir; the new buildings.

Q. Describe to the committee, if you please, Mr. Bliss, the manner in which you exercise a supervision, and how you obtained your knowledge of the discipline of the convicts in the prison.

A. The only way that I exercise or influence the supervision, is to look through the prison in all its departments; whenever a prisoner wanted to converse with me to give him a chance to do so. and to have an eye generally upon the thing in that way. I have also had frequent conversations with Mr. Morris in reference to discipline, punishment, &c.

Q. State whether the convicts generally are at liberty, and understand that they are at liberty to make direct personal application to the inspectors?

A. I supposed, sir, that they did ; I didn't know that there was any rule to the contrary, and I supposed they understood they had the privilege at any time; and if they wished to meet the board in session, I supposed they could indicate it to the keepers, and through them come before the board; but in passing through the shops I have understood that it was the custom they could speak to me or any other inspector at any time, as has frequently been the case.

Q. You have been spoken to by the convicts, directly, without the intervention of the keeper?

A. Oh, yes.

Q. Have you ever been applied to directly, by convicts, with complaints against the treatment of the Agent?

A. I don't recollect any cases of that kind at all. The general causes of application were for some trifling favor. Since tobacco has been abolished in the prison a good many have wanted tobacco, and have applied to me that I might restore it again. Others speak to me in reference to time and ask if they could not get a pardon so they could go home to their friends. They have spoken to me freely about these things, and I to them, but I don't remember now any case where a prisoner has ever complained to me of severe punishment at all. It doesn't follow, as a matter of course, that a prisoner has not been punished, but it has not been brought to my attention.

Q. Have you ever given special attention to the point as to whether convicts were restrained from making such complaints, from fear of future rigorous treatment from the Agent or keepers?

A. No, I don't know that I have given particular attention to this question, but I suppose it was well understood from various circumstances.

Q. State whether, during your acting as inspector, any punishments have been inflicted, which the inspectors felt called upon to inquire into, in order to pass their own judgment as to the propriety of the punishment, and its quantity.

A. I don't recollect now of any case of that kind since I have been on the board. There may have been cases when the question was brought up. Mr. Morris has at several different times spoken to me individually in reference to punishing in particular cases, stating the fact of the punishment, and the reasons given for it, but I don't remember now any case before the board, where special complaint has been made since I have been on the board.

Q. Has the subject of punishment been under consideration by the board as to the kind of punishment, or the offenses for which it should be inflicted.

A. The subject of punishment generally has been talked of a good deal by the Board; it has been a great problem with us to know what was best in the premises; what sort of punishment was best, and whether any particular kind of punishment was cruel or otherwise in its nature; the general opinion of the Board has always been—and we have always understood Mr. Morris to coincide with us in that—that the punishments should be just as few and just as light as it was possible to have them and maintain discipline; we felt that it was important that discipline should be maintained; I think we were agreed on this point, that sometimes it was absolutely necessary to inflict punishment.

Q. Was there ever any discussion in the board particularly as to the limit of discretion to be given the agent as to the infliction of punishment, or as to offenses for which it should be inflicted?

A. I don't know whether there has been any particular discussion on that point as to whether there should be any particular limit. Of course it has been understood that the Agent must have some discretion, but he never should abuse the power he has in any case.

Q. Are you aware of any rule ever having been made by the Inspectors, or being in force since you have been Inspector, that would prescribe any limit to the discretion of the Agent, either as to the offense for which punishment should be inflicted, or the nature and extent of the punishment?

A. I do not know of any such rule.

Q. I understand you that since you have been Inspector there has never been any inquiry on the part of the board as to whether this discretion as to punishment has been abused by the Agent?

A. There never has been what might be called an official inquiry; we have talked about the matter informally, and talked with Mr. Morris about it, but we never have gone into any formal investigation in any particular case to ascertain whther the power he has has been abused or not.

Q. Have the board or any of its members ever inquired of other parties than the agent to this punishment?

A. I don't know that there has been any inquiry except of the agent and the officers of the prison.

Q. What supervision has been exercised by you or the other inspectors, to your knowledge, as to breaches of discipline being reported and entered upon the prison records, and what pains taken to see whether the records were correctly made up in accordance with the facts?

A. There has been no investigation for the purpose of ascertaining positively whether those records are correct. The rule is, as I understand it, for the keeper or whoever has charge of the men, to report any infractions of the rules to the deputy, who shall make a record, and that record shall be taken to the office and entered upon the book, and the inference is as we look every month at this book that it is properly made. There is no way to judge except from the record itself.

Q. At what time is the record kept by the deputy written up?
A. I can't tell you whether it is written up daily, or whether he makes the records on his pass book for three or four days and it is brought in and all written up at a time; I don't know about that.
Q. Have the inspectors ever made inquiry as to the time when the record should be written up?
A. No, sir.
Q. State whether it has been the usage for the inspectors to examine the record kept by the deputy—the book of original entries I mean?
A. I don't think it has.
Q. What means have the Board of Inspectors of knowing whether the record written up by the agent from the deputy's minutes is a correct transcript?
A. They have no means of knowing that I know of.
Q. What is the rule of the prison about conversation between convicts and freemen who are employed to work in the same shops with convicts?
A. The rule, as I understand it, is that there shall be no conversation except on matters of business in which they are mutually interested. If a man is at work under a foreman, of course he must converse more or less with him, but generally conversation is prohibited by the rules. The rules are printed and hung up in the shop. I cannot now repeat all the rules.
Q. What proportion of the prisoners are unable to read?
A. That I can't tell you sir.
Q. Are there any?
A. I presume there are sir, but can't tell. I never investigated that matter among the prisoners; whether there is any thing of that kind in the Regent's report, I do not remember.
Q. Has your observation been such as to enable you to state positively whether the rule prohibiting conversation between convicts and freemen in the shops, is observed in all cases?
A. Well, sir, I don't believe it is observed in all cases; I think that has been one of those things which has been very difficult to enforce thoroughly. I don't know that I can say that I know that from any observation, but from an impression we have formed.
Q. Do any difficulties grow up in the way of enforcement of discipline by reason of the breach of that rule, that has come to the notice of the Inspectors, or any of them?
A. Well, I do not now remember any particular cases, but my impression is that it is a question that has involved difficulty in the management of the prison. The directors have been spoken to on the subject.
Q. How long since the use of tobacco by the convicts has been prohibited?
A. Can't tell you, sir; that was before I came onto the board.
Q. State, if you know, how long the manufacture of cigars has been carried on in the prison?
A. Well, sir, I can't state that, but quite a number of years.
Q. Since before you came on the board?
A. Yes, sir.
Q. What further breaches of discipline, in your judgment, since you have been on the board, have grown out of difficulties arising in the cigar shop?
A. Well, sir, I am not able to give an opinion on that subject; I should think a good many had, but what proportion I don't know.
Q. How many men are employed in the cigar shops?

STATE PRISON INVESTIGATION.

A. One hundred and twenty-five, I think, is what the contract calls for.

Q. Is tobacco manufactured in the prison in any other manner than in the form of cigars?

A. Nothing else.

Q. Has the question ever arisen in the Board as to the propriety of discontinuing the manufacture of cigars in the prison?

A. The question has been, I think, informally talked of, but I never supposed anything was to be done, because the contract was there; it has been—I don't know that what I am about to say is proper to be said here at all; I will simply say, it has been my impression that it was not the best kind of contract for the prison; in some respects it is a good contract, because we have men there who are not able to work at anything else, and this furnishes them with work; but there are probably more difficulties growing out of the manufacture of tobacco in the prison than are offset by any advantages.

Q. How long have you been acquainted with Mr. Morris personally?

A. I have been acquainted with him casually for several years before he came to Jackson; I can't say that I was ever intimately acquainted with him; I have seen him in Charlotte and in Jackson a good many times.

Q. What opportunities have you had to observe his manner towards the convicts in their treatment since you have been on the Board?

A. Well, I don't know whether I have had what would be called a first-rate opportunity or not; I have been with him frequently in the presence of the convicts; have occasionally attended church at the prison, and have been around with him sometimes through the shops, very often alone, and in that way have had some opportunity to observe his manner; I don't know whether that would be called a good opportunity or not.

Q. State whether you have ever observed anything to lead you to believe that his conduct in the treatment of convicts was not uniform?

A. I can't say that I have ever seen anything of that kind at all; I have heard rumors of that kind, but never anything tangible, or any complaints from any of the prisoners or any party in the prison; I don't think this matter has ever been brought before the Board for the purpose of examination or investigation.

Q. Have you ever taken any special pains to inquire concerning the foundation of these rumors to which you allude?

A. I don't know that I have. I don't think it would be proper to go around and inquire of prisoners with reference to that matter, as a general thing; although there are cases where it might be proper to inquire of the prisoners, especially when they come before the board with a statement of grievances, but, ordinarily, it would not be proper. Every prisoner who has spoken to me has taken particular pains to state how well treated they have been since I have been there. Whether they had a motive is not for me to say. I simply state the fact.

Q. Have you ever had reason to believe that convicts might have a motive for making favorable representations concerning the Agent?

A. Why, from what we all understand of human nature, we might suppose that a convict might think, that in some indefinite way it would benefit his condition; that is all. I don't know of any special advantage he would conceive it to be to him; but being in the power of the authorities, he might think to get favored in this way,—that is all.

STATE PRISON INVESTIGATION.   61

Q. Do you know whether, since you have been inspector, any convicts have been punished by the "cross," as it has been called.

A. I don't think there has.

Q. Do you know whether, since you have been Inspector, the punishment by flogging has ever been resorted to?

A. I don't know that the whip has ever been used at all since I have been on the Board. If at all, it must have been about the time I came on. After that, as I understand, the strap was substituted whenever it was deemed necessary to inflict punishment of that kind, in place of the whip.

Q. At the monthly meetings of the Inspectors state whether their attention was more particularly directed to the business of the prison or to its discipline?

A. Well, in the first place we would look after the business interests of the prison; that would be attended to at any rate; that was the first thing to be attended to, and when through with that, or had any time, the general management of the prison has been strictly under consideration. This included the examination of the different departments as to cleanliness, the food, and clothing of the convicts. All these things have been talked about at our meetings. I understand it to be the duty of an Inspector to exercise a general supervision over these things.

Q. When the Inspectors have had the subject of discipline under consideration, what is the primary object thought to be attained by discipline by the Board?

A. Well, that question involves a great deal. I will say this, it is one object of prison discipline, if possible, to reform the party. It is another object to induce him, if he can't be induced in other way than by punishment, to comply with the rules of the prison. The discipline of the prison is considered absolutely essential to the safety of all. It is true, a great many men go to prison who are not bad men in the general acceptation of the term. They are not vicious men; they are men who have been overcome by their passions at particular times, and have committed crimes that they ever after regretted. They are well-behaved men, and are never subjected to discipline. They conform to the rules and are the best men in the prison. There are others, men who have committed few crimes, who have been suddenly overcome by temptation. When they come there they see the folly of their course and have no disposition to disregard the rules. There is another class who get there because it is their business to commit crime. They are defiant towards the authorities and determined to have their own way. When their sentence is out they will go out and commit crime the first opportunity they have. That is the class of men that make nearly all the trouble in the prison. Now, as to what is best to do with those men. Before I went onto the board I thought it possible to get along in the prison without any considerable punishment of any kind. I will say further, that the more I have seen of prisoners the more I have been convinced that there is a class of convicts who cannot be governed in any other way than by some sort of punishment of that kind.

Q. Speaking with reference to the reformatory feature had in view in inflicting punishments, has the board ever considered the question of the kind of punishment best adapted to secure that end.

A. Well, that is a question that has been talked about. We don't know what kind of punishment is best. This question of punishing by showering with the hose, has been talked about a good deal. It has been a question whether that was the best. We know that punishment by that method, unless it is carried to excess, is comparatively light. It has no particular effect upon the individual, and in general, I don't think they care much about it. The flogging, or whipping by the strap, we have understood, should be resorted to only in cases of last resort, when nothing else will answer the purpose. I am inclined to think there are a good many men in prison, that nothing but fear of punishment will keep within the rules. Their moral sense seems to be perfectly dead. We can appeal to them in no other way than by punishment. In this case of Thurston, though I know nothing about it, I know the result of the punishment,—that Mr. Thurston, from having been one of the worst men in the prison,—a man who had for months lived in defiance of the laws, after that became one of the best men in the prison, and gained a large amount of good time, and made the remark (which is in evidence before the inspectors at Jackson), to the man under whom he was working, on the appropriations, that he intended now to behave himself, and did behave himself from that time on. I think there are men flogged in prison, just as I think there are boys flogged at school, and children at home,—although it goes hard at the time, but I think it is the best discipline for them; and if they feel,—that is after the thing is done,—that they deserved it, it is a benefit to them, and they do better afterwards; further, I will say this, that punishment is exceedingly repugnant to our feelings, and I have long felt that if it were possible to substitute anything else for it, and the discipline of the prison be preserved, it would meet my hearty approval.

J. Has the system of punishment by solitary confinement, either with or without rations, been resorted to, to any considerable extent?

A. I think it has never been resorted to except for slight offenses, and for a temporary purpose. For slight infractions they have been put into solitary cells for three or four hours, sometimes for a day or two, but not with a view to doing away with other punishments.

Q. From your observation of Mr. Morris, state whether he is subject to fits of passion, or whether his temper is uniform?

A. I couldn't give any answer to that question; I have never seen him in a fit of passion at all.

Q. Do the employes of the prison other than the Agent, hold their appointment under him and subject to his will, or subject to the Inspectors, and subject only to their will?

A. The employes, keepers, and guards, as I understand the law to be, are appointed by the Agent, and hold their office at the pleasure of the board. That, I think, is what the law says; but practically, it has always been understood that Mr. Morris, being the responsible Agent of the prison, must have it in his power to discharge men if he thinks they are not doing their duty as they should be, or from any motive that would govern him in such cases, presuming such motive to be a proper one. Whenever such action has been brought before the board, I do not know of any case where the board has not confirmed it.

Q. Has any case arisen since you have been on the board, where he has discharged men and they have appealed to the board, and a hearing has been granted them as between them and the Agent, to see whether the discharge was warranted or otherwise; in other words, have the Board ever inquired into the cases of discharge, to see whether the discretion vested in the Agent was properly or improperly exercised.

A. Well, perhaps I should answer that there has not. The board in such cases have thought that the Agent was the proper man to decide who was best fitted to fill the place, and much better qualified than the board could be.

STATE PRISON INVESTIGATION.

Q. So far as the discipline of the prison is concerned, then, as to the employment and discharge of keepers and guards, and as to the treatment of the convicts, the entire matter rests in the discretion of the Agent?

A. Practically, I should say it was so—it must necessarily be so.

Q. Is it the opinion of the board that it is impracticable to prescribe rules for the government of the agent as to the offenses for which punishment should be inflicted by the agent, and as to the extent of the punishment for each class of offenses?

A. I don't think that particular phase of the thing has been discussed by the board; I don't remember that it has.

Q. Can you state about the time of the abandonment of the lash?

A. I cannot, but I think it was before I came on the board.

Q. Do you know of any instance where the lash has been used since you have been a member of the board?

A. I do not.

Q. In the reading of the record of punishments at your monthly meetings, have you any recollection of observing any records of punishment by the lash?

A. I have not. I don't wish to say positively that it has not been so, but I do not now remember, and I think I should remember if there had been anything of the kind.

Cross-examined by Mr. Bartow:

Q. Did you understand that the lash had been abolished before you became a member of the board?

A. No, I didn't understand anything about it particularly.

Q. Now, there was some testimony in regard to the punishment of Thurston. Was you a member of the board when he was punished?

A. Now, I can't tell you when Mr. Thurston was punished. If he was punished after I came in—it was about that time.

Q. I understood you to say in your examination you knew he was a better man after the punishment than before?

A. My statement was from the information of those who came in contact with him; of myself I know nothing about it. It was the testimony of all concerned, and particularly of the man who had him charge, that he was a good man after that, and Thurston himself stated to him that he intended now to behave himself.

Q. That testimony was the evidence you speak of that he was a better man afterwards?

A. Yes, and the fact that he gained good time. Such matters always come before the board. That showed that he complied with the rules strictly after that; otherwise he would not have been allowed good time.

Q. Do you know from observation that Thurston was punished after you became a member of the board?

A. No, sir, I cannot tell you now whether I was or not. By referring to the books I could find out very easy, but cannot now remember.

By Mr. Webber:

Q. Here is an entry under date of September 10, 1873. [Reads from record about the punishment of a prisoner with ten lashes, which "brought him down beautifully."]

A. That was within a month after I came there. I don't remember anything about the case at all.

[Another case was here read from record under date of September 26, 1873; —a case of three men being punished by having to wear wire caps.]

Q. What are these punishments by wire caps?

A. I don't know, sir, that I can describe them. They are a cap made of wire, with the meshes, perhaps, half an inch apart, and there is a band round the bottom, and that opens and is put around the neck loosely, and locked, and this covers the whole head. It is so they work in it, can do anything in it. I talked to one of the prisoners about it one time particularly, and he said it was no trouble, except in sleeping nights; it was dificult for them to sleep nights as well. I don't know how long this punishment has been inflicted. I suppose it is more to distinguish those who have been violating rules than for anything else.

By Mr. Bartow:

Q. Were there any cases that came under your observation or knowledge where you considered the punishment severe for the offense?

A. Well, sir, I must say that I have never seen any punishment whatever; I simply know of the severity of the punishments from what I have heard; and in cases where I have heard of punishments being inflicted, and heard all the circumstances, and the reasons for it, it has not seemed to me that the punishments have been unusually severe; there is this thing to be considered; if a prisoner suffers very severe punishment, by the strap, or in any other way, he would be himself responsible for it; if he shows the spirit that he ought to show, is sorry for what he has done, and promises to do better in future, the punishment ceases at once; if he is flagrant in his violation of the rules, and shows contempt of all the rules of the prison and its officers, I don't know—it is a question how far he might be properly punished; of course, there has got to be proper discretion used in the punishment of such a case; but I never heard of a case where a prisoner didn't, in a short time, promise to do as he ought to do; and I never heard of a case where he didn't do very much better afterwards; and in such cases I felt that the punishment was actually deserved. I have never seen the punishment. I don't know how I should feel if I should see it myself.

Q. When you speak of punishment being deserved, do you mean to be understood that it has a reformatory influence, or that it is simply a penalty due to the offense?

A. I don't know that in using the term deserve I have any particular reference to that one way or the other; but simply that he has committed such an act that, by the rules of the Prison, he is liable to be punished.

Q. Well, now, let me ask you if there is any rule of the Prison that indicates to the convict the character of the punishment he will receive for any breach of discipline?

A. Nothing, except that if the breach is an aggravated one, showing a direct defiance of the authorities, refusing to conform to the rules in any respect, I suppose it would be absolutely necessary to bring such a prisoner to conform to the rules; otherwise there would be anarchy in the prison. I suppose the particular character of the punishment should be left largely to the discretion of the Agent.

Q. Has the question ever been considered whether it would have a better effect on discipline if the convicts understood that certain fixed punishments would follow certain breaches of discipline, than to leave it entirely to the discretion of the Agent?

A. I don't know as that question has ever been discussed; it would be an almost impossible thing under our rules to define every infraction of the laws, but still, I don't know but it might be done; I don't think the matter has ever been seriously discussed in reference to fixing anything of that kind.

Q. I find a punishment recorded of riding a wooden horse,—two men face to face. Do you know how that punishment is inflicted?

A. I don't know anything about it, sir.

Q. Do you know whether punishment is ever inflicted in the Prison as a means of inducing confession?

A. I never heard of such a case until this case came up.

[Witness' attention was here called to a case recorded December 7, 1873, being the punishment of James Keyes for writing to another convict, but had no recollection of it.]

By Mr. Bartow:

Q. Have the board of inspectors ever inquired about punishment any further than those shown by the record and the statements of the Agent?

A. Well, I don't know that—in general terms, perhaps, I may say they have not—still the conversation with reference to punishment has been often before the board, but we have taken the record and the statement of the Agent with regard to the punishments. There has no person ever come before us with any complaint in reference to punishment at all, and I don't know how we could get at it in any other way. If any case of punishment should come before us, or any one of us, that seemed in its nature to be unusual or severe, we should certainly have the question brought up at the next meeting of the board and examined into, but I don't remember any case of that kind.

By Senator Nelson:

Q. Do you know whether the prison rules are made known to the prisoners in any other way than by being posted in their cells?

A. No, sir, I don't; but I think that if a person were inside the prison yard a short time he would find that everything that one prisoner knows pretty much all know in a very short time.

Q. Is it not customary for the rules to be read to the prisoners at stated times?

A. I don't believe that I can state about that, but my impression is that these rules have been read to the prisoners by the Agent when they were congregated in the dining-room or chapel; I don't know, but that is my impression.

Q. [To the Agent.] Is that the fact, Mr. Morris?

[Mr. Morris.] I will state very clearly, Mr. Nelson, that that is a matter that has been neglected, and I can see to day why it is an evil. I don't recollect ever reading the rules to the men in a body. It is a frequent custom with the hall master or his deputy to talk with every man that comes into the prison, to try to make up their acquaintance, and to give them a general idea as to the management of the prison, and how they should do, but of the rules there I have not read them. There is a feature in the bill relating to that subject that I admire very much, but it hadn't occurred to me before.

By Senator Nelson:

Q. Do the keepers read these rules to the convicts at any time?

[Mr. Morris.] The keepers talk to them about all the rules of the prison, perhaps almost every hour of the day. They are right with them and talk to them every hour and keep them posted every day. We have quite a number of Germans in the prison, perhaps fifty or sixty, and it is hard work to converse with them.

Q. The rules are not printed in any language but the English?

A. No, sir; but I don't know of a man being punished to any extent at all when he pleaded ignorance as an excuse; I should hesitate to punish him at all.

By Mr. Seager:

Q. Mr. Bliss, have you ever had any reason to doubt the correctness of the record, as made by the Agent, of the different punishments inflicted?

A. No, sir; that is a question that has not been brought up; they are presumed to be correct; we have never had an examination to find out whether the record was right or wrong, and I don't think this question has been spoken of at all in the meetings of the Board with reference to that, one way or the other; I knew the record should be read, and presumed it was correct.

Q. From your own observation and familiarity with the prison, have you, directly or indirectly, learned of any case that was not reported upon the record —any case of punishment?

A. I never until this investigation came up.

Q. I mean prior to this time; of your own observation?

A. No, sir.

Q. Has there ever been any conflict, any difference of opinion between the Board of Inspectors and the Agent on this subject of punishments?

A. No, sir; I don't think there has. It has been a principle of the Board, assuming that punishments were necessary, that the Agent should get along with as few as possible, and as light as possible; and it has been the representation of the Agent that this has been the case, and I don't think there has been any controversy on the subject.

Q. How often is this record submitted to the Board?

A. Every month; the first Wednesday in every month is the regular meeting of the Board.

By Mr. Webber:

Q. I find, under date of June 22, 1874, this entry: "Geo. McIntosh, Edward Hudson, John Welsh, and John Stevenson, all reported for talking in the ranks and dining room. All suspended by hands for one hour. Suspending is done by placing the cord around wrists loosely and drawing them up." State if you knew of this punishment being inflicted.

A. I don't know anything about it at all.

Q. When this record was read, do you remember whether it excited any comment?

A. I don't remember anything about it at all. The presumption is, it was read; but I do not now remember anything about the case.

By Senator Nelson:

Q. I would like to ask the last previous witness whether he has known the rules to be read to the convicts by the keeper?

Mr. Thorne:

A. Yes, sir, I do.

Q. Is it a common thing for the keepers to read the rules?

A. Not particularly to read them.

Q. Or to inform them of the rules?

A. Yes, sir. It is customary, I guess, when a convict first comes into the shop to inform him with regard to the rules.

Q. Is that repeated at different times, or once a month?

STATE PRISON INVESTIGATION. 67

A. No, sir, there is nothing regular about it, still it is frequently done.
By Senator Nelson:
Q. It is customary for all prisoners to be made acquainted with the rules when they enter?
A. Yes, sir, it is.

GEORGE WINANS SWORN.

Examined by Mr. Webber:
Q. Mr. Winans, you reside at Jackson?
A. No, sir, in Shiawassee county.
Q. At what place?
A. Between Ovid and Owosso.
Q. Near the village of Ovid, is it?
A. Four miles.
Q. Have you ever been employed at or about the State prison?
A. Yes, sir.
Q. In what capacity?
A. As Deputy Keeper.
Q. At what time did the employment commence?
A. In March, 1872.
Q. At what time did it end?
A. In October, 1874.
Q. Mr. Morris was Agent during all the time you were employed there?
A. Yes, sir.
Q. State what your duties were in that employment?
A. My duties were to have general supervision of the yard, including all the work-shops, having charge of the men at the dining-room, and a general supervision of the yard.
Q. During what hours?
A. All hours.
Q. Day and night?
A. Except night. At night I have been called up when there was any thing the matter with the men.
Q. During the time you were there were there any cases of convicts being punished, that you know of?
A. Yes, sir.
Q. Did you have any thing to do with the keeping of the prison record?
A. Yes, sir.
Q. What duties did you have in that regard?
A. I kept the report, the copy that Mr. Morris copied.
Q. What kind of a book did you keep this on?
A. A small book.
Q. A memorandum-book, that you carried in your pocket?
A. Yes, sir.
Q. When did you make the entries in it?
A. I made the entries at the time of the punishment.
Q. Was it a part of your duty to be present at all punishments?
A. No, sir.
Q. From what information did you make the entries as to the punishments inflicted?
A. When I was not there I used to take it from the Agent.

Q. When you was not present at the punishment?
A. Yes, sir.
Q. What proportion of the punishments did you witness?
A. Well, I should say I witnessed the most of them.
Q. When you received information from the agent, how early after the punishment was the information communicated to you?
A. Well, if a man was punished to-day, I would always get the report before night.
Q. From the Agent?
A. Yes, sir.
Q. Did it come to you direct from him, or through others?
A. Direct from him.
Q. Then you made the entry in your memorandum-book?
A. Yes, sir.
Q. After making the entry did you read it over to him, to see whether you had it correctly written?
A. No, sir; I did not.
Q. When you were present at the punishment by showering, did you time it, to see how long the showering continued?
A. No, sir; I did not.
Q. I notice the reports of punishment by showering usually state how long the showering continued?
A. Yes, sir.
Q. How was that time determined?
A. The Agent would hold his watch sometimes—usually.
Q. Was punishment ever inflicted by showering, in your presence, when no time was kept?
A. Yes, sir.
Q. How frequent an occurrence was that?
A. I don't know that I can say; it was usually done.
Q. It was usual to take the time?
A. Yes, sir.
Q. When the punishing was done, was the Agent present and held the nozzle?
A. Sometimes he did, sometimes I did.
Q. Was the water taken from the Holly water works?
A. Yes, sir.
Q. What was the diameter of the nozzle through which the stream was played?
A. Well, I should think it was about three-eighths of an inch.
Q. Do you know the pressure of the water?
A. No, sir; I do not.
Q. Do you know the temperature?
A. No, sir.
Q. What distance would this nozzle be held from the prisoner on whom the water was being played?
A. From six to twelve feet.
Q. State whether it was usual to strip convicts to receive this punishment.
A. Yes, sir.
Q. Entirely naked?
A. Yes, sir.

Q. How were the prisoners confined during the infliction of this punishment?
A. Tied with their hands on their back, their arms.
Q. And they made fast to what?
A. Made fast to an iron door.
Q. How were they fastened to the door?
A. Tied with a rope around their arms.
Q. What was the diameter of the rope used for that purpose?
A. Well, I think it was a half inch rope.
Q. How long a time was the longest ever used in showering?
A. Well, I don't remember; I should say twenty minutes.
Q. On what part of the person was the showering applied?
A. All over.
Q. Were the convicts usually tied so the showering was applied in front of the person?
A. Yes, sir.
Q. What other punishments did you witness while you were there except showering?
A. I have seen men whipped, and locked in a bare cell, and tied up by the hands.
Q. Explain this punishment of being tied up by the hands. How was it inflicted?
A. The hands were drawn together and tied up in that way [showing].
Q. How high were the arms drawn, that is, how tight was the cord, so they could stand square on their feet, or drawn up tip-toe?
A. No, sir; they could stand square on their feet—stand down.
Q. How frequent was that punishment resorted to?
A. That was not a very frequent punishment.
Q. How long did you ever know it to be continued?
A. How long were they tied up?
Q. Yes, sir.
A. I think I knew a party tied up two hours at one time.
Q. What was his condition when he was taken down?
A. He went to his shop.
Q. Was he able to go immediately to work?
A. Yes, sir.
Q. For what offense was he tied up?
A. I cannot say now.
Q. Do you remember his name?
A No, sir.
Q. What rule in inflicting punishment for offenses was adopted by the Agent; in other words was there any rule other than his discretion at the time?
A. Well, I think there was not.
Q. Up to what period was the lash used as a punishment?
A. I think some time in July, 1873.
Q. How came the use of the lash to be abandoned?
A. The Inspectors and Agent thought they could govern the prison without the use of it.
Q. What did they adopt as a substitute?
A. They used a strap,—that you had here yesterday.
Q. State whether the strap was more or less severe than the lash.

A. Well, about being severe, I don't know that I could say. It didn't mark a man as bad as the lash did.
Q. Didn't mark him as bad?
A. No, sir.
Q. Was it more dreaded than the lash, or less?
A. I thought it was less dreaded than the lash.
Q. For what offense was the lash used, while it was used, and the strap afterwards?
A. I don't know that I can say now for what offenses.
Q. What other punishments did you know of being used there, other than those you have named?
A. Not any, I think.
Q. Did you ever know punishments by riding the wooden horse?
A. Yes, I did know that.
Q. Describe that punishment.
A. The wooden horse was seven feet high, and a person set on that. It was made out of 4x4 scantling.
Q. And how was it prepared; state whether it was round on the top?
A. No, sir.
Q. It was square,—the corners were square?
A. Yes, sir.
Q. State how the convicts were made fast to the horse.
A. Not any way; simply set on it.
Q. State whether he was at liberty to set on it in any way he pleased.
A. Sometimes he was, and sometimes not.
Q. When he was not at liberty in what position was he placed?
A. He was usually placed astraddle the horse and set in that manner.
Q. Were they ever made fast to it in any way?
A. No, sir.
Q. How long time did you ever know a man to be punished in that way?
A. I knew one man to be kept there two hours.
Q. What were the offenses for which that punishment was used?
A. Well, I disremember now.
Q. Did you ever know the punishments by the use of wire caps?
A. Yes, sir.
Q. Describe those caps?
A. It was a wire cap with four wires set up over their heads crossing each other in this way [showing] and covering the entire head.
Q. And made fast to the neck?
A. Yes, sir.
Q. How were they fastened on?
A. They were locked on.
Q. What was the size of the wire?
A. I think it was the sixteenth of an inch.
Q. How long were those wire caps usually kept on for punishment?
A. I have known them to be kept on thirty days, I think.
Q. Continually, night and day?
A. Yes, sir.
Q. What was the character of the offenses for which that punishment was inflicted?
A. I remember one instance it was put on two men who broke out?

Q. Do you recollect any other offenses for which that punishment was used?
A. I do not now.
Q. State whether it was frequently resorted to?
A. It was quite frequent.
Q. No other kinds of punishment that you now remember other than stated?
A. I don't now remember others, except locking in the bare cell.
Q. Was the punishment of locking in the bare cell without food ever resorted to?
A. It was.
Q. How long were they kept in the bare cell without food?
A. I remember one man being kept there for four days.
Q. What was his offense?
A. Well, he refused to tell something, but what it was I can't remember; I can't think.
Q. Do you remember his name?
A. No, sir.
Q. Do you remember about the time?
A. It was the first summer I was there.
Q. It must have been in 1872, then?
A. Yes, sir.
Q. You went there in March, 1872?
A. I was there nearly two years.
Q. Was it the first summer you were there?
A. Yes, sir.
Q. Then it was in 1872?
A. Yes, sir.
Q. Did you make a record of that punishment?
A. Yes, sir.
Q. Did you ever examine to see whether the record you made of the punishment was correctly recorded?
A. No, sir, I don't think I ever did.
Q. Were the records kept by you compared with the copy of the record kept by the Agent, to your knowledge?
A. I read from my book and Mr. Morris copied.
Q. That is the way the record was made up?
A. Yes, sir.

By Mr. Morris:

Q. Was it ever customary for me to read my records after you had given yours?
A. Yes, sir.
Q. Most always?
A. Yes, sir, very customary.

AFTERNOON SESSION.

EXAMINATION OF CAPT. WINANS, CONTINUED.

By Mr. Webber:

Q. In making the record of punishment, what instructions had you as to recording the extent of the punishment?

A. My instructions were to record the full extent of the punishment.
Q. Were you ever criticised for not making the record full?
A. Yes, sir.
Q. By whom?
A. By Mr. Morris.
Q. And was the deficiency supplied in those cases?
A. Yes, sir.
Q. Was it usual, while you were in the prison, to whip men to make them confess?
A. No, sir; it was not a usual thing to whip for that purpose.
Q. Was it sometimes done?
A. Yes, I think it was; I am not certain of it.
Q. Did you know of any instance of severe whipping or other severe punishment to induce confession?
A. I know an instance of what I would call hard whipping.
Q. State it, please.
A. His name was Thurston.
Q. Thurston?
A. Yes, sir.
Q. Do you know how many lashes Thurston received?
A. I counted sixty-two.
Q. First or second punishment?
A. First punishment; I was not there at the time of the second punishment.
Q. You counted sixty-two at the first?
A. Yes, sir.
Q. Who administered the blows?
A. Mr. Morris.
Q. Describe the whip used on that occasion.
A. I don't know that I can exactly do so. If my memory serves me right it was a whalebone whip, with a lash on it.
Q. About how long a lash?
A. I should think about three or four feet,—three feet, perhaps.
Q. And how heavy a lash?
A. Well, it wasn't a heavy lash; it was medium size.
Q. Do you recollect what the lash was made of?
A. I am not positive about that, but I think it was buckskin.
Q. Braided?
A. Yes, sir.
Q. How long was the stock to which the lash was attached?
A. I should judge about three feet perhaps.
Q. How far from the convict did Mr. Morris stand while whipping him?
A. About three feet, or perhaps four.
Q. Was Thurston stripped?
A. Yes; his shirt was taken off.
Q. His pants also?
A. No, sir; I think not.
Q. On what parts of his person were the blows applied?
A. Around the arms and under the arms.
Q. From the middle up to the chest?
A. Yes, sir.
Q. Did Mr. Morris stand behind or in front of the convict, when whipping?

STATE PRISON INVESTIGATION. 73

A. Well, I can't say as to that matter.
Q. Did you see any breaks in the skin from that whipping?
A. Yes, sir.
Q. More than one?
A. Yes, sir.
Q. How many?
A. I can't say,—I didn't count them.
Q. Well, quite a number?
A. Yes, quite a number, I should think.
B. On what part of the body was the skin broken?
A. It was broken across the chest and across the back.
Q. Did you notice any place where the skin was broken across the abdomen?
A. No, sir; I didn't.
Q. Were there any blows given on the abdomen?
A. I think there was.
Q. What was Thurston punished for?
A. He was punished for sauce and ugliness to Mr. Morris.
Q. Now let me read you this record of May 16, 1873: "Joseph Coveyear, John Welsh, and Napoleon La Mountain, had been observed by keeper Wood, of the upper cabinet shop, to be in some mischief, for several weeks, by frequent sly interchanges of notes, on paper, blocks, &c. La Mountain and Welsh locked on the east wing, Coveyear on the west. Coveyear and La Mountain came from Detroit together on the same charge. Proof, ample and positive, that they were making keys and dirks, came into possession of the Agent, for several days previously,—in fact, their whole plot to escape was clearly reported and understood every day; but before it had culminated in any harm, the three men were each brought in, separately, stripped to the hide, and whipped until they admitted everything clearly and fully, producing keys, knives, &c." Now, was an entry which recorded a whipping in that manner approved?
A. Was it approved by whom?
Q. By the Agent
A, Yes, sir.
Q. It was not required that you should state in the entry the number of lashes?
A. No, sir, at the time those men were whipped I was not present.
Q. You were not present at this whipping?
A. No, sir, I didn't make this record, but I made a record that that was taken from.
Q. You made it from information given you by Mr. Morris.
A. Yes, sir, partially, and partially from what I found out from the convicts themselves. I was present at the time Mr. Morris was whipping one of those men; the other time I was after the other men.
Q. Do you know how many blows these men received?
A. No, sir.
Q. Now, were these men whipped at that time to make them confess their plot?
A. Yes, sir.
Q. Do you remember how many blows the one received that was whipped when you were present?
A. I don't remember exactly,—I think fifteen.
Q. Were you present at the meetings of the inspectors with the Agent?

A. No, sir.

Q. Were you ever criticised for not specifying particularly the quantity of punishment in your record?

A. I think that I was not.

Q. Did you ever see Mr. Morris, in his intercourse with any of the convicts, appear to be angry?

A. Yes, sir.

Q. Can you give any instances where you have seen him exhibit anger to convicts?

A. I thought he showed anger towards Thurston that time.

Q. Any other instances?

A. I don't remember any other.

Q. Did you ever see him strike a convict except when he was brought out for formal punishment?

A. I have seen him,—well, I can't say now who it was reported to him,—and he hit him a slap with his hand.

Q. Where did he strike him with his hand?

A. In the face.

Q. State whether that was a common occurrence.

A. No, sir; it was not a common occurrence.

Q. In striking in the face, state whether he did it angrily, or how otherwise?

A. Well, I couldn't say that he was angry; he didn't show anger.

Q. Were they running the cigar shop when you was there?

A. Yes, sir.

Q. What proportions of punishment arose from the tobacco question, and stealing tobacco and using it?

A. Well, I don't know exactly; I should think nearly one-half.

Q. Were any of the convicts in the prison allowed to use tobacco at all?

A. Yes, sir.

Q. How much tobacco was furnished them?

A. I think there were seventy-four men in the prison that used tobacco.

Q. Well, were they furnished it?

A. Yes, sir.

Q. How much?

A. I don't know exactly how much; they were furnished a ration of tobacco.

Q. Well, how often?

A. Once a month, I think.

Q. In what manner were they allowed to use it?

A. Allowed to chew it.

Q. Was smoking allowed?

A. No, sir.

Q. While you were there was there any difficulty arising from conversation between freemen and the convicts?

A. There has been at times.

Q. What precautions, if any, were taken to prevent that practice?

A. The freemen were notified that they must not talk so much with convicts.

Q. Any other precautions?

A. No more than I took precaution to see if I could catch them talking, or something like that.

Q. What was the regulation in case they were detected in talking?

A. Mr. Morris told them if they didn't stop talking he would shut them out of the yard.

STATE PRISON INVESTIGATION. 75

Q. Was there any rule or regulation of the prison to that effect?
A. Yes, sir.
Q. Did you ever see any body knocked down with a cane while you were there?
A. Yes, sir.
Q. Who had a cane?
A. Who had a cane? I had, and Mr. Morris.
Q. Who did the striking?
A. Mr. Morris, I think.
Q. What was the name of the convict struck?
A. Wilson.
Q. Relate the circumstances.
A. Wilson was put to work on the wagon contract. He said he would not work, and came in. Was asked by Mr. Morris if he was going to work. He replied he would not. Was told to go into the other room and take his coat off and shirt,—I guess take his pants off,—for a showering. In a few moments Mr. Morris stepped to the door. As he passed in, Wilson ran for the back side of his room. Mr. Morris went for him, and I also.
Q. Well, what induced Mr. Morris and you to use violence upon him at that time?
A. He was making as fast as he could to a lot of rubbish,—broken bedsteads, etc.,—and we thought he was going to get a broken bedstead, or something.
Q. You anticipated resistance?
A. Yes, sir.
Q. Was this convict a desperate character?
A. Yes, sir.
Q. What was he in prison for?
A. He was there for fifteen years; he was taken from Detroit, and in being arrested he was shot twice, I think, and he shot the officer that arrested him twice. The charge that he was there on I don't know that I can tell.
Q. He was a fifteen years convict?
A. Yes, sir.
Q. Can you give the name of that convict who was placed on that wooden horse for two hours?
A. Beckhold,—I think that's the name,—I am not certain.
Q. Can you give the date?
A. No, sir.
Q. Do you know anything about the shooting of Driscoll? And can you give the year in which that man was there two hours, and the season, so we can find it on the record?
A. It was the fall of 1873, I think.
Q. What about the Driscoll case? Give us the particulars as you recollect them.
A. He got out, rode out in a load of hubs, raised up after he got out to the back side of the wall, broke a way up through the hubs, jumped out and ran. The man,—I forget his name now,—who was with the load of hubs came and told Mr. Morris that "Silver Jack" had got out.
Q. Did you go with Mr. Morris when he went after him?
A. No, sir.
Q. How long was Mr. Morris gone?
A. I should think about an hour.

Q. Did he bring him back?
A. Yes, sir.
Q. How was he brought back?
A. Bucked.
Q. State whether he was wounded.
A. He was.
Q. Where?
A. In the shoulder, in his right shoulder, I think.
Q. Shot in the back?
A. Shot in the side, right here [indicating].
Q. Bleeding much?
A. No, sir.
Q. Were you present when the wound was examined?
A. I didn't go into the hospital with him.
Q. How long after after he was brought back before he was whipped?
A. Well, some of the keepers told me he was whipped the next morning, but I have forgotten entirely about his being whipped.
Q. Do you recollect his being showered after he was brought back?
A. No, sir.
Q. You don't remember being present at that whipping?
A. No, sir, I might have been present, but I don't remember anything of his being whipped.
Q. Did you know any instance where persons assumed to be,—acted as though they were crazy?
A. Yes, sir.
Q. What was Mr. Morris' practice in the treatment of such cases?
A. He would usually take them to the asylum.
Q. What means did he resort to to test the question whether they were really insane, or were merely shamming.
A. Never anything that I remember of, more than when a man was crazy, or appeared to be crazy, he was taken to the asylum and locked up.
Q. You mean an asylum connected with the prison?
A. Yes, sir.
Q. Was that also in Mr. Morris' charge?
A. What?
Q. The lunatic asylum connected with the prison?
A. Yes, sir.
Q. He had the same control of that as of the other portions of the prison?
A. Yes, sir.
Q. And when they were placed there, state whether they were in separate cells or how they were kept?
A. They were; all those in the lunatic asylum were in separate cells; sometimes they might have been crowded, but was in separate cells.
Q. Do you remember how many there were at any time in the lunatic asylum while you were there?
A. I may not be correct, but my idea is there were six cells—twelve cells, six on a side.
Q. Were they full?
A. Yes, sir.
Q. Were any sent away from prison, to Kalamazoo, while you were there?
A. No, sir.

Q. Did you observe inequalities in the temper of Mr. Morris, as Agent, in his treatment of the convicts—difference in times and in temperaments—whether he would be pleasanter on some occasions than on others?
A. Yes, sir.
Q. Well, how frequently, and to what extent did these extremes go?
A. Well, they wouldn't go to any great extent; I have seen him some days he would see the convicts and be good natured with them, and other days he would say nothing to them at all; and on other days he would see them doing something they hadn't ought to be, and give them a raking about it.
Q. I understand that on some occasions he would censure convicts and speak harshly to them, when, on other occasions he might see the same thing and pass it by without notice?
A. Yes, sir.
Q. Did you ever discover any evidence of favoritism in his treatment of the convicts?
A. I don't know that I ever did.
Q. Did you ever see anything that indicated the existence of such favoritism?
A. No, sir.

By Senator Nelson:
Q. Was tobacco given to all who wished it in the prison?
A. No, sir.

By Senator Jones:
Q. What was the reason for giving it to a part, and refusing it to others?
A. It was refused to long time men that were there at that time. There was an arrangement with the convicts and Agent to give tobacco to certain men; men who came in after that time were to receive none; if they wanted tobacco, they was to have it. In the forepart of my testimony I made a mistake. I was not about the prison until 1873, in the spring.
Q. Then you were there until the fall of 1874,—about 18 months?
A. Yes, sir.

By Mr. Seager:
Q. In this punishment by showering, how is it inflicted,—is it continuous?
A. Yes, sir.
Q. In the case you spoke of, showering for twenty minutes, was there any intermission, or was the showering continuous?
A. I think there was.
Q. You think there was what?
A. An intermission.
Q. What for?
A. For nothing, more than the Agent stopped to give him a rest.
Q. What man was it that was showered twenty minutes.
A. I forget who that man was now.
Q. Do you remember his offense?
A. No, sir.
Q. Did you time him?
A. I didn't hold my watch on him.
Q. You refer to an instance of striking in the face; was there more than one such case?
A. Yes, I think there was two or three.
Q. Do you remember what the offense was?
A. No, sir, I do not.

Q. What was the blow with, the fist?
A. No, sir; with his hand.
Q. A slap or light blow?
A. A slap.
Q. I understand you to say you don't remember what the offense was?
A. Yes, sir.
Q. When the punishment was inflicted on Beckhold, do you remember what his offense was?
A. I do not; I think it was some trouble with the men; I think he and one of the other men had some struggle, and he was going to fight him, or something like that.
Q. When was that?
A. In the spring of 1874, I think.
Q. What was Thurston punished for?
A. Thurston was punished for,—I brought him,—he was punished for his insolent language to me and for attempting to go to work.
Q. Attempting to go to work?
A. Yes; I brought him in and told him he must go to a bare cell, and he got his coat off and swore he wouldn't go to work.
Q. What was the reason he was ordered to a bare cell? What had he done?
A. Well, I disremember now. He was reported by Donough, and I brought him in.
Q. Do you know how long he had been at work out of doors?
A. I think he had been there about a week.
Q. Where was he working before that?
A. I disremember where he was before that.
Q. What was the general character and behavior of this man?
A. Very bad.
Q. Was he a dangerous man?
A. Yes, sir, he was considered so.
Q. What was he in prison for?
A. I don't remember.
Q. What was his term?
A. Five years, I think.
Q. Do you know anything about his pretending to be sick?
A. He pretended to be sick at the time before this. I talked with him; he pretended to be sick at that time.
Q. In what way and what did he take?
A. Pretended that he spit blood,—pretended that it came from his lungs.
Q. Do you know anything about his vomiting?
A. I think he did vomit blood.
Q. What was the general build of the man? Was he a weakly man, or strong?
A. No, sir; a very strong man.
Q. A very strong man?
A. Yes, sir.
Q. Did you think he was shamming?
A. Yes, sir.
Q. Did you have any doubt about it?
A. No, I didn't.
Q. How did you get him into the bare cell?

A. Put him in front of a revolver.
Q. Who did you get the revolver from?
A. From Mr. Burkhart at the gate.
Q. Was Mr. Morris present?
A. No, sir.
Q. After he was put in the bare cell did any one go near him again that day?
A. No, sir, I think not.
Q. When was he punished?
A. The next day,—the next forenoon.
Q. Was any water taken to him in the cell,—I mean was he showered in the cell?
A. Yes, sir.
Q. Was it thrown so it hit him, or did he conceal himself?
A. He concealed himself and held a bucket up in front of his face.
Q. Did he stand behind the door?
A. Yes, sir.
Q. Did the water hit him at all?
A. No, sir, it didn't hit him; it didn't hit his face or hit him around the head, or anything like that; because he held the bucket.
J. What was it far that he was showered?
A. I think Mr. Morris told him to come out of his cell, and he said if he come out he would fix him.
Q. If he came out of his cell?
A. Yes, sir,
Q. Do you know anything about this man Thurston making a weapon about the shop, or having one in his possession,—a slung-shot?
A. No, sir.
Q. On the cabinet contract when you was first there?
A. I can remember something about it, but it is not distinct.
Q. A slung-shot that he called a mason's plumb bob.
A. I think he had such a weapon, but I wouldn't swear positively.
Q. Do you know of his ever threatening your life, or that of Mr. Morris.
A. Yes, sir.
Q. What way, and how many times?
A. Well, I don't know in what way; but he said, perhaps half a dozen times, perhaps a dozen times,—that he would fix me, and would fix Mr. Morris when he got out of prison.
Q. Did he say anything about taking your hearts out?
H. I didn't hear him say anything about taking my heart out, but he said he would take Mr. Morris' heart out.
Q. How soon, when?
A. Well, it is my impression that he was going to right off.
Q. Had other punishments been tried with this man before he was whipped?
A. I think there had. I was not there but a short time before. I went to the prison in March, and I think this was in May.
Q. Did you recommend the whipping when you reported him?
A. Yes, sir.
Q. Do you know about his threatening any one else besides yourself and Mr. Morris?
A. Yes, I think he also threatened the conductor and Mr. Donough.
Q. Were these threats that you speak of previous to this punishment?

A. No, sir, I think not, not as far as I was concerned; I had done nothing to have him threaten me for. Other keepers told me that he had threatened Mr. Morris before I went there.

Q. This first punishment, if I understand you from the dates here, was but a little while after you came inside the prison?

A. About two months, I think.

Q. I think you have already stated that you were present and saw the sixty lashes inflicted?

A. Yes, sir.

Q. What did the man say while receiving this punishment; did he make any threats after he was tied up?

A. Yes, sir.

Q. What were they?

A. To the effect that he would fix the man that whipped him.

Q. That was while he was being punished?

A. Yes, sir.

Q. Was the punishment continued after the man gave up?

A. No, sir.

Q. Only while he was obstinate, and threatening?

A. That is all.

Q. Where was he placed after being punished?

A. In the cell.

Q. What was his subsequent behavior, as compared with that prior to the punishment?

A. Well, his behavior was better after the thirteenth of April, after he got that flogging; I think he never was reported but once after that.

Q. After he was placed in the cell, after the first flogging, how did he conduct himself in the cell—dance and sing?

A. Well, if I remember right, I left the next day and went home.

Q. Were you there at the second whipping?

A. I was not.

Q. You were back there after the second whipping, were you not?

A. Yes, sir.

Q. Were you there from that time up to the time he was discharged?

A. Yes, sir.

Q. What was his behavior after the second whipping until the time he was discharged?

A. It was good; I think he was not up more than once after that; that was for stealing tobacco, I think.

Q. Do you know anything about the knife spoken of before?

A. I saw the knife, but didn't see it with him.

Q. Do you know anything about his having a false key to his cell?

A. I know about his having a key that was in process of being made.

Q. When was it; I mean with reference to this whipping?

A. My impression is that it was after this whipping.

Q. After his second whipping, or between the two?

A. Between the two.

Q. Was that the knife? [Showing witness knife.]

A. That is the knife, I think.

Q. Was that the key? [Showing key.]

A. I don't know.

Q. Do you know who made it?
A. No, sir; I suppose Thurston made it; it was given to me by a man by the name of Simmons, of the wagon contract.
Q. What is the knife?
A. A putty knife.
Q. A putty knife ground down?
H. Yes, sir.
Q. Where did he get the knife from, probably; I mean where were such knives used?
A. They were used on the wagon contract.
Q. Coming now to the case of this man Wilson—"Silver Jack," I think they called him; please state fully what the general character and conduct of that man was prior to his punishment?
A. Wilson's?
Q. Yes, sir.
A. It was very bad, sir.
Q. In what way?
A. In every way that a man could be,—revolutionary.
Q. Insubordinate?
A. Yes, sir.
Q How much time did he work as compared with the time he wes locked up?
A. Well, he did n't work but a very small part of the time. He was nearly all the time locked in his cell.
Q. What was his general build,—was he a large or small man?
A. He was a man of about five feet four or five inches tall, I should think, would weigh 160,—may be more, may be less.
Q. A muscular man?
A. Yes, sir.
Q. Especially so?
A. Yes, sir.
Q. A very strong man?
A. Yes, sir.
Q. Had he been a man of threatening character?
A. Yes, sir.
Q. Well, in what way?
A. Well, he had been a man that always done as he was a mind to,—so the keepers told me,—a man that had always worked when he was a mind to, and played when he was a mind to.
Q. Were the keepers afraid of him?
A. Yes, sir.
Q. What did he threaten?
A. Threatened to take the life of anybody that interfered with him, so the keepers told me.
Q. How long had he been there when you came?
A. I don't know. I am inclined to think he has about six or seven years yet, if he misses all his good time.
Q. Do you know anything about this knife? [Showing witness a knife.]
A. No, sir; I don't think I ever saw it before.
Q. Do you know of a knife ever being taken away from Wilson?
A. No, sir; I don't know as I do.
Q. Where did Wilson work?

A. On the shop contract until it expired, and after that on the wagon contract.

Q. This man Wilson is the man you say you saw knocked down.

A. Yes, sir.

Q. When he was making towards a pile of broken bed-steads?

A. Yes, sir.

Q. What more was done than knocking him down? Was he pounded?

A. No, sir.

Q. Who did the knocking down?

A. I don't know whether Mr. Morris knocked him down or whether I knocked him down; both rushed for him at the same time.

Q. Was he struck after being down?

B. I think not.

Q. What was done with him then?

A. He was taken out and showered.

Q. Do you remember whether when he was ordered into the other room to take off his coat he took it off or buttoned it up?

A. No, sir; he buttoned it up.

Q Didn't undress himself at all, but started for this pile of rubbish?

A. Yes, sir.

Q. How did he behave after that?

A. Behaved very nicely.

Q. As a rule in these cases of punishment, was or was not the punishment continued after the convicts gave up?

A. No, sir.

Q. Only while he was resisting?

A. That's all.

Q. Was it so in Wilson's case?

A. Yes, sir.

Q. Coming now to this man Driscoll, what was his general character while in prison? One moment, allow me to go back. [Reads from the record, page 22.] "Wm. Wilson," etc. "No better man in the yard."

Q. Was this record made up from minutes furnished by you?

A. I don't know whether I wrote the records or not. I presume I did not. I presume I put his name down in the book and then it was copied by Mr. Morris.

Q Are the facts as here stated in regard to the conduct of the man before the punishment was inflicted?

A. Yes, sir; with one exception. That book doesn't state that I struck him, at all. I did strike him.

Q. That is one of the two blows he got was from you?

A. One of those two blows was from the Agent; but I struck him one and I don't know but two.

Q. What was the character and conduct of this Driscoll?

A. It was bad.

Q. In what way?

A. Well, I think he never had been reported to me, but was considered a bad man. If my memory serves me right he went there in the winter that I went there in the spring, the winter of 1873.

Q. Where did he come from?

A. Saginaw.

STATE PRISON INVESTIGATION. 83

Q. What was he convicted of?
A. I don't know.
Q. Do you remember what his sentence was?
A. He was sentenced for five years, I think.
Q. Was he a troublesome man?
A. He had never given any trouble in the shops.
Q. A man that you were suspicious of?
A. Yes, sir.
Q. Why?
A. Well, he was a long time man, and he was a large, strong man, and a man that we knew would take chances if there was any chances.

By Senator Mellen:
Q. In showering, was it usual to apply the water to the face?
A. No, sir, I think it was not usual to apply the water on a man's face, though I have seen it done often.

By Senator Webber:
Q. In the case of Wilson, when he was knocked down, I understand you that he yielded, and begged and promised to go right back to work, yet, before being permitted to go back to work, he was taken out and showered?
A. Yes, sir.
Q. Do you know how long he was showered?
A. Well, he might have been showered ten, fifteen or twenty minutes, I can't tell you exactly.
Q. Who did that showering?
A. Mr. Morris.
Q. Were you present?
A. Yes, sir.
Q. The record of that case says that when he went into the room he pushed the door to after him or pulled it to?
A. It was a slide door — a door that slides back.
Q. Did you notice that he closed the door after him as he went in?
A. Yes, sir.
Q. The record is correct in that particular?
A. Yes, sir.
Q. I understood you to say in your cross-examination that a prisoner was never punished after he yielded?
A. Yes, after a man gives up he is not punished.
Q. Well, in this case of Wilson, was he not punished after he gave up?
A. Well, I don't think he gave up.
Q. I understood you that he begged, and promised to go right back to work?
A. No, sir; I didn't understand the question.
Q. Well, state what he did after being knocked down.
A. He says, "Hold on, and I will do anything you want me to," or something like that.
Q. Well, was n't that regarded as satisfactory?
A. No, sir, it was not. We ordered him to take off his clothes.
Q. Did he do it?
A. Yes, sir.
Q. Then what was the occasion of further punishment?
A. He was punished for trying to get hold of something to knock us down, and also for refusing to work.

Q. Then it was not always the case that as soon as they yielded, and promised obedience, that you considered it satisfactory, and further punishment was sometimes inflicted?
A. No, sir.
Q. I don't understand how you account, in this particular case, for punishing him after he had yielded and promised to do as you wanted him to.
A. No, sir, he did not promise to do as we wanted him to. He says, "hold on," or something to that effect, "and I will do as you tell me to." Mr. Morris told him to take off his coat, shirt, and pants. He pulled them off; I tied him up, and he was watered.
Q. Now, do I understand you that, in all cases while you were there, the punishment was resorted to simply to subdue a refractory prisoner until he would yield obedience?
A. Usually, I think, that was the case.
Q. Well, was it always so?
A. I think it was, always.
Q. And it was never resorted to as a punishment for past offenses?
A. Past offenses was what they were punished for.
Q. If punishment was resorted to only to subdue the refractory convict, how can you say that it was inflicted for past offenses?
A. Well, we couldn't punish a man for something he hadn't done; it must be for something he had done.
Q. Well, why couldn't you punish a man for something he hadn't done?
A. We could, I suppose, if we wanted to, but we didn't want to.
Q. Were men never punished when they begged to be permitted to go to duty and promised obedience?
A. No, sir; I think not.
Q. I understand you, then, that men were not punished at the prison except as a means of subduing them to obedience; were any prisoners ever punished for attempting to escape?
A. I think there was; I am not certain about it, but I think there was.
Q. You say that when Thurston was punished you counted sixty-two lashes?
A. Yes, sir.
Q. Why didn't the record show the number of lashes given, instead of saying "not less than fifty?"
A. I don't know.
Q. Did the record which you made show the number of lashes?
A. I think it did; I am not positive, but I think it did; a whipping of that kind was so uncommon that I may have just written his name in my book.
Q. Well, was it not customary for you to write the minutes in full?
A. Yes, it was customary.
Q. Did you ever hear anything about the showering of McEvoy?
A. No, sir.
Q. Don't remember any such case while you were there?
A. No, sir.
Q. Do you remember such convict?
A. Yes, sir.
Q. You spoke of taking a man (Thurston, I think), into his cell before a revolver?
A. Yes, sir.
Q. Was the revolver in your hands?

A. I am not certain ; I think it was in the hands of Mr. Burkhart.
Q. Was it cocked?
A. I don't know; I think not.
Q. And presented at the convict?
A. It was presented, but, I think, was not cocked.
Q. Was any threat used that if he didn't obey he would be shot?
A. Yes, sir.
Q. Have you ever known a convict to be fired upon in the prison?
A. No, sir.
Q. Is it the usual custom to present revolvers to convicts to enforce obedience?
A. No, sir.
Q. When he went into his cell and the hose was turned on him, what sized hose was it?
A. I think it was a 2½-inch hose.
Q. And what was the size of the nozzle in that case?
A. I should say about an inch.
Q. How long was it played on him?
A. Well, I should think about half an hour. It was played on him some time before I got there.
Q. How far was the nozzle held from the convict?
A. About a foot and a half or two feet.
Q. And it could strike any part of his person except his face which he kept covered with the bucket?
A. No, sir; he was up in a corner of the wall, and not fully exposed.
Q. How much of his person could it strike?
A. I should think about one-half.
Q. State whether he said anything while this was being played on him.
A. Yes, sir.
Q. What did he say?
A. Well, he wanted us to quit.
Q. How long did he profess a willingness to quit before the showering was stopped?
A. He didn't profess a willingness to quit; he wanted that we should quit.
Q. Quit playing on him.
A. Yes, sir.
Q. Was he screaming?
A. Yes, sir; hallooing and swearing.
Q. Well, how came you to stop playing on him?
A. Mr. Morris came to the conclusion that there was no use, for he had a bucket held up over his face, and he was playing into the bucket.
Q. And quit playing for that reason?
A. Yes, sir; quit playing for that reason.
Q. Did he keep on his talking?
A. No, sir.
Q. Who was he talking to?
A. To Mr. Morris.
Q. Well, what was he saying to Mr. Morris?
A. He remarked to him that if he didn't stop showering him he would kill him.
Q. Did he change the character of his conversation?

A. He did after he went down to the lower end of the hall.
Q. Not before?
A. No, sir.
Q. Were you there when Thurston was showered?
A. This was Thurston.
Q. How did he go down to the other end of the hall?
A. Went down with his hands behind him and a rope around them. Mr. Cook led him down.
Q. Who went into the cell and took him out after you quit playing on him?
A. He came out himself.
Q. By order?
A. He came out after being ordered by Mr. Morris probably the third or fourth time with a revolver drawn on him. Mr. Morris sent for the revolver and drawed it on him and told him to come out, and he then came out.
Q. Had Thurston any weapon in the cell?
A. I think not. Yes; I won't say. He had something, I think, after he was showered, while he was being taken to his cell. I won't say what it was. I think, though, it was a knife.
Q. What severe punishments besides the one you have mentioned did you witness while you were in the prison?
A. I saw men showered.
Q. Anything else?
A. I saw men flogged.
Q. Severely?
A. No, I didn't think they were severely.
Q. Did you ever see a man showered until he was exhausted?
A. I have seen them showered until they were black.
Q. Have seen them showered until they were black?
A. Their skin looked black the next day, not at the time.
Q. Did you ever see one punished by whipping until he was exhausted?
A. No, sir.
Q. I think I asked you if the cross was resorted to while you were there?
A. It was not.
Q. Do you know the name of the man who was showered and turned black the next day?
A. I can't think of his name. He was out painting on the cabinet contract— painting and varnishing. [Witness refers to Mr. Morris and learns that the man's name was Spaulding].
Q. What was the offense?
A. I don't remember now.

By Mr. Seager:
Q. What kind of man was this Spaulding?
A. A very bad man.
Q. Was he a man that was frequently reported?
A. Yes, sir.
Q. How frequently was he reported?
A. Well, there was a time that I used to make two or three records against him a month.

By Mr. Webber:
Q. What were your records made for?
A. I don't know that I can tell you what one of them was made for.

Q You say that Thurston was only reported once, you think, after that showering?
A. I think that was all.
Q. I find him reported December 10, 1873, for insolent talk to keeper Bedford, and when told to stop said, "I can't, and report me if you want to." That is not the case you alluded to as a subsequent report. He was punished then by bare cell one day. Then he was reported again January 5, 1874, for stealing cigars.
A. That is the report.
Q. That is the one you have reference to?
A. Yes, sir.
Q. I want to ask you whether in showering convicts, when they were stripped naked it was usual to direct the stream upon their private parts?
A. No, sir.
Q. Was it ever done continuously for any length of time?
A. No, sir; I think not.
Q. Well, was it done at all?
A. I think not, more than in passing the water up and down it might strike the private parts.
Q. It was never directed steadily?
A. No, sir.

By Mr. Seager:
Q. Spaulding, you say, was showered till his skin was black the next day; do mean by that black and blue?
A. Yes, sir.
Q. All over his person?
A. No, sir; in spots.

ELISHA VAN SANDT SWORN.

Examined by Senator Webber:
Q. Where do you reside, Mr. Van Sandt?
A. Adrian.
Q. Have you ever been employed about the prison, at Jackson?
A. I have.
Q. In what capacity?
A. As a foreman in charge of the brick and mortar department, under Mr. Donough.
Q. What is Mr. Donough's first name?
A. I don't recollect now.
Q. How long were you employed there?
A. From May 12, 1873, until January 14, 1874.
Q. Was Mr. Donough a contractor?
A. No; he was superintending improvements there.
Q. For the State?
A. Yes, sir.
Q. How many men did you have working under you?
A. Well, there was from thirty to forty, part of the time?
Q. How many of them were convicts?
A. All.
Q. All engaged in what?
A. Well, they were making mortar, wheeling brick and stone, and unloading lumber and brick outside, a great part of the time.

Q. What opportunities did you have to observe the discipline of the prison while you were there?

A. Well, I had some; I had, after I had been there some two or three weeks, to look in the first place, to see that the men worked, delivered the mortar and stone, something like that. Probably three weeks after I went there, I was asked by the deputy to take charge of the men, and march them into their meals and out to breakfast.

Q. Now tell me whether you observed any thing in regard to the discipline there, which attracted your attention particularly?

A. I did.

Q. State whether you saw any prisoners punished severely, or any other conduct on the part of the prison officials which seemed tyrannical or unjust?

A. The first case I didn't see; I didn't see the punishment; but there was a man by the name of Thurston, that Mr. Morris brought out to the mortar bed and asked me to take charge of him, and keep him at work. He brought him out there and left him and said he would like for me to take him and look after him and keep him at work. I put him immediately to work stirring mortar, or tempering mortar, I forgot which, and after a little bit he sat down; I told him he must get up and go to work; he said that he was in such pain that he couldn't work. I asked him what the matter was. He said he had been flogged. He got up and commenced stirring the mortar again; after a bit he sat down again, and I said to him again, "I want you to be at work," and he said "Probably you don't believe how bad I am flogged;" and then he unbuttoned his pants and pulled up his shirt and showed me his bowels and thighs where he had been whipped.

Q. Well, describe the appearance of his person.

A. Well, in his person he was a large man and tolerably full, and he was cut; it appeared from the gashes that he had been whipped from the right side. There was probably twenty-five or thirty, may be more, on his bowels and thighs of those marks.

Q. Well, state how deep they were.

A. Well, there was a number of them, especially one right here [indicating diagonally across the abdomen] seemed to be cut through,—what you would call cutting through the skin; the balance of them was what I would call gashes not cut through, that was the greater portion of them.

Q. Did you discover any injury on his private parts?

A. There was one. His left testicle was cut with a gash an inch or an inch and a quarter long, and looked as if it had been done with a whip.

Q. Do you remember when this was?

A. Some time in June.

Q. 1873?

A. Yes, sir.

Q. Anything else that you discovered about the management or discipline of the prison that attracted your attention?

A. Well, I have seen two or three pretty severe showerings in the wing.

Q. Were you permitted to be present to see the showering?

A. It was accidental. I was coming through the outside gate on business of Mr. Donough, I think, and both times I saw the showering. One was a small man, the other a large colored man.

Q. Who was showering them?

A. I think the deputy was showering one of them and Mr. Morris the other time.

STATE PRISON INVESTIGATION. 89

Q. Do you know how long the water was applied?
A. No, I don't; I stood perhaps two or three minutes looking to see how it was done.
Q. Do you know whether any serious results followed?
A. I don't know of those two.
Q. Do you know of any case where punishment was so severe as to result in long continued injury to the individual?
A. Yes; there was the case of a young man under me who was taken and showered,—he said he was, I did n't see him. When he came back, after he had been reported and came back, his head was wet. I said to him, "Where have you been?" I knew he had been taken to the hall; and he said he had been showered, and I told him to go to work. We was then whitewashing over the blacksmith shop, and painting the walls over-head,—some ten or a dozen men in there. He took hold of the brush and commenced work, and he was all in a shiver, and could n't work, and his hands were blue, and his nails were very dark,—under the nails,—and I several times urged him to work, and he shook there until he let the brush go; and finally he sat down. He went to the hall that night, and I did n't see him again.
Q. Any other cases that you observed of severe punishment?
A. There was one case of kicking a man that I thought pretty severe.
Q. What?
A. Kicking.
Q. Describe that.
A. I was standing in the new dining-hall door, and I heard a voice out by the entrance, and there was a man just stepping up out of the entrance,—a prisoner. Mr. Morris spoke to him to stop, and the man did n't stop, but walked on at a slow gait. Morris came in and caught him by the arm, and kicked him three times, apparently very severe.
Q. You observe no other provocation than that one?
A. No, sir.
Q. Do you know the name of that convict?
A. No, sir; but he was a man that would probably weigh about 125, or 130 or more.
Q. Can you tell when that occurred?
A. I think it occurred in the fore part of October or the first of November. It was when I was plastering the dining hall. I was plastering at that time.
Q. On what parts of his person was he kicked?
A. He was kicked right behind twice, right in the bottom, the first two kicks, and the third kick was on his side. The man, when he kicked him on his side, he wilted down. He was very lame, and Mr. Morris helped him to the hall,— he could hardly get to the hall, apparently from the lameness.
Q. Now, state whether you ever observed any other instances of violence?
A. Well, I saw two men put on a wooden horse in November, a very cold day.
Q. How long were they kept there?
A. They were put on in the morning,—I forget whether it was when the men marched out to go to their breakfast, or after, I think after,—and they were kept on till noon.
Q. Well, how long were they there to your knowledge?
A. Well, I should think they were there five hours probably. The horse was

90   STATE PRISON INVESTIGATION.

made (the one they had at that time) of 2½ inch stuff, and 8 inches the other way; and the place they sat on wouldn't exceed 2½ or three inches.
Q. The widest way of the plank was up and down?
A. Yes, sir.
Q. Were the corners square?
A. Yes, sir.
Q. State whether they were tied on.
A. No, sir; they were not.
Q. How were they sitting, astride?
A. Yes, sir.
Q. Do you know the names of those two men?
A. I don't.
Q. Any other case that you noticed?
A. I noticed once that the deputy punished a man two or three times pretty severe with a cane.
Q. For what offense?
A. I don't know what the offense was. The man was walking ahead of him and walked rather slow. He was taking him in to be punished, I suppose, and Mr. Winans, the deputy, punched him two or three times pretty severely with his cane, that he had in his hand.
Q. Do you know for what offense these two men were placed upon the horse?
A. I am not sure, but I was told—
Q. No matter about that; you were not told by any of the officers of the prison?
A. Not that I know of.
Q. Any other instances you recollect?
A. Well, the instance of the men being marched in from the cigar shop when they were searching that and taking tobacco from them, as I saw and understood it, I thought it very severe.
Q. Describe it?
A. It was on Saturday, I think, in September or October; the men were searched as they very often had been, to see if they had tobacco with them. One of the men was found with tobacco in his pocket. I think Mr. Morris took it out; and I understood Mr. Morris to say to him "eat," but I won't be sure. The piece was about four inches long, and perhaps as thick as my finger, and he ordered him to eat, as I understood him. The prisoner seemed to bite off a piece, and chew and swallow; from the distance I was, I thought he chewed and swallowed it. I was about four or five rods from the place at the time.
Q. Were any others on that occasion required to eat tobacco?
A. No, sir, not that I knew of. There was a number of them that tobacco was taken from at the same time.
Q. Did you ever discover any other instances of severe or unusual punishment?
A. No, not that I recollect of.
Q. What was Mr. Morris' manner in speaking to a convict?
A. Sometimes he was quite pleasant, and at other times he was the reverse
Q. What do you mean by the reverse?
A. That he could speak short and prompt.
Q. Did you discover any evidence of discrimination, while you were there, as in favor of one prisoner or set of prisoners, as against another prisoner or set of prisoners?

A. No, I don't know as I did.

Q. Did you notice any thing which led you to believe that there was any favoritism showed to any of the prisoners?

A. Well, there was not with the men in the gang that I had. I think not to my knowledge.

Q. Is there any other fact within your knowledge connected with the discipline of the prison that would tend to show improper conduct on the part of officers or keepers?

A. Well, I don't know that there is.

Q. Let me ask what opportunities had convicts and freemen to converse together when they were working in the same shop?

A. Well, I don't know much about it in the shops, for I scarcely was ever in the shops.

Q. Well, outside in the yard?

A. Well, there was some talking. There were carpenters working with convicts and freemen, some half dozen together, and I have seen them standing and talking, what about I didn't know, whether about the work or what they were talking about.

Q. Well, at the time this man Thurston came back to you and showed you his wounds, was the keeper inside?

A. No, sir.

Q. Were the men you were working working with the keeper?

A. I was the only keeper.

Q. How many men did you have under you?

A. I should think there were about thirty or forty, making brick and stone wall, carrying mortar, etc.

Q. And you was allowed to talk with them as much as you pleased.

A. I never saw a prison rule while I was there. My business was to keep the masons in stone, mortar, and brick, and keep them at work.

Q. Did you ever see a case where a convict was struck on the head with a cane, or any thing else, after he had been whipped?

A. No; I think not.

Mr. Eggleston:

Q. Do you know the name of the man who punched the convict with the cane in the yard?

A. Capt. Winans.

Q. Do you know the name of the convict?

A. No, I don't.

By Mr. Webber:

Q. When you saw Thurston's wounds, from their appearance, how long should you judge it had been since the punishment was inflicted?

A. Well, I should suppose, from the looks of them, it had probably been fifteen or twenty hours.

Cross-examined by Mr. Seager:

Q. It was the next day after the punishment, the next morning, that you saw the wounds.

Q. Did you use the term gashes as applied to these wounds?

A. Yes, sir.

Q. Do you mean that the skin was broken, or that there were marks?

A. I mean that the skin was broken.

Q. When you said the skin was broken you spoke of one wound here [across the breast].
A. Yes, sir.
Q. At the time of this kicking referred to, was any one else in sight?
A. I think not.
Q. No one present but Mr. Morris, yourself, and the prisoner?
A. I don't recollect seeing any one at all. I don't think there was.
Q. Where was the man coming from?
A. He came out of the main entrance hall, and I was about 30 feet from Mr. Morris when he overtook him.
Q. What was done with the man afterwards?
A. I don't know what was done afterwards. Mr. Morris took him into the hall with him.
Q. Can you fix the date when this was?
A. It was in November. It was when we were plastering the dining room, and we plastered that in November.
Q. Did you see the man afterwards?
A. Not that I know of.
Q. Have you ever seen him since that you know of?
A. Not that I know of.
Q. Do you know Mr. Wilcox, one of the inspectors?
A. Yes, sir, I do.
Q. You reside in Adrian, do you not?
A. Yes, sir.
Q. Were you and Mr. Wilcox intimate?
A. Pretty much so.
Q. Do you know the other Inspectors?
A. I know them by sight, and reputation,—never was introduced to them, I believe.
Q. Did you see them there at the prison, frequently?
A. Yes, sir.
Q. Did you ever know of any complaints being made to the Inspectors?
A. I did not.
Q. Did you have any trouble with Mr. Morris while you were there?
A. No, sir, none.
Q. Were you not reprimanded for negligence in handling the men?
A. No, sir.
Q. By no one?
A. Not to my knowledge.
Q Were you not shut out of the yard, ultimately.
A. No, sir.
Q. Can you fix the day these men were placed on the horse you spoke of?
A. It was in November, I should think about the middle of November, as near as I can recollect.
Q. 1872, or '73?
A. November, 1873; I know it was a very cold day for November.
Q. Do you know by whose order it was done?
A. I don't know. I know Mr. Winans ordered them to go out there.
Q. Were you in sight when they were placed there?
A. Yes, sir.
Q. Where did this horse stand?

A. It stood in the prison yard. Here is the cabinet shop, and here is the walk leading to the cigar factory. It is right in this corner, probably 20 feet from the walk, where the horse was.

Q. Where you were working, and had charge of the men?

A. In the same square. I was on the walk, and my business called me to see the men passing back and forth a good many times through the day.

Q. When was it you saw them placed on there?

A. Well, I think it was after breakfast.

Q. How long after breakfast?

A. I think it was right away. I think they put them onto the horse just after breakfast, as I was marching my men from the dining-room.

Q. When were they taken off?

A. When I came out from the dining-room at noon they were off.

Q. Were they on when you went into the dining-room?

A. Yes, sir.

Q. Were they compelled to remain in one position or allowed to shift position, that is, as much as they could on that?

A. I don't know whether they were compelled to or not; they seemed to be in one position every time I saw them,—a number of times that day.

Q. Any body near them?

A. I think not.

Q. Then they were at liberty to move round as much as they could on there?

A. I don't know what the orders were, but they seemed to be sitting astride when I took notice of them.

Q. And nobody with them?

A. No, sir.

Q. How long did the men work in November?

A. How long did the men work?

Q. Yes, what was the time?

A. I think about 8½ or 9 hours.

CAPT. WINANS RECALLED.

Examined by Mr. Seager:

Q. Mr. Winans, do you remember anything about the two men being punished by placing them on a wooden horse, as testified by the last witness?

A. I remember two men put on the horse. One of them was Beckholt; the other man I disremember his name, and my impression is it was about 10 o'clock. These are the only two men I remember being on the horse.

Q. Those two men were put on together?

A. Yes, sir, put on together.

Q. How long were they kept on?

A. My impression is, about two hours.

Q. What was it for?

A. I don't remember, but it is my impression it was caused by Beckholt and the other man getting into a fight.

Q. Was that the only instance of that kind of punishment while you were there?

A. That is all the instance I can remember.

Q. Did Mr. Morris order it?

A. Yes, he ordered them up on the horse. I went to the shop and brought them in, and went to the office and reported the matter to him, and he ordered them up on the horse.

Q. In that punishment by sitting on the horse, is the man compelled to sit astride all the time, or can he change his position?
A. He can put himself in any position he chooses.
Q. Can sit sideways or astride, or in any position he can?
A. Yes, sir.

By Mr. Bartow:
Q. Mr. Winans, were you in the prison at the time a man was in the hospital who was afterwards found to be crazy, and water was being poured on him?
A. No, sir; I don't know anything about that.

By Mr. Jones:
Q. You have heard of the case?
A. Yes; I heard it spoken of yesterday. I think that was before I went there, on the 7th of May.

FRIDAY, APRIL 9.

DAVID R. STROUD SWORN.

Examined by Mr. Webber:
Q. Were you ever connected with the prison at Jackson?
A. Yes, sir.
Q. At what time and how long were you there?
A. I went there in the fore part of April, 1871; I can't give the exact day.
Q. What position did you hold there?
A. I was keeper at the middle gate, at the main entrance.
Q. How long did you remain there?
A. Until a year from the next fall; my memory is not clear as to the exact time I left, but I think it was in October or November.
Q. What opportunities had you for knowing, during that time, the general management of the prison and the treatment of the convicts?
A. Well, sir, while my position was at the gate, as gate-keeper, I often relieved Col. Van Arsdale, the conductor, and I would show visitors through the prison for him. He was in ill health. At other times when there was no business Mr. Morris gave me liberty to pass on the inside of the prison, and to go through the various shops.
Q. During that time did you ever know any instances of severe punishment?
A. I saw some punishments while I was there.
Q. Any instances of undue severity?
A. I don't think at any time that there were any punishments beyond what the circumstances of the case demanded.
Q. Did you ever see any partiality exhibited towards the different prisoners?
A. I don't know as I did. They were all treated alike as regards discipline, but of course there were some prisoners who had certain privileges granted them as a result of good behavior.
Q. Was that uniformly the case?
A. Yes, sir.
Q. Did you ever know of any man being struck, except when called up for punishment?
A. No, sir.

Q. Did you see Thurston punished?
A. I did not, sir; that was after I left.
Q. Did you frequently see men punished?
A. I saw several flogged.
Q. At the time you were there was the lash or strap used?
A. The lash.
Q. What were the classes of offenses for which men were flogged?
A. The first man I saw flogged was one named Smith, David Smith, I think.
Q. What was the offense?
A. He was the man who emptied the contents of the night bucket onto the guard Lewis. Smith signaled the guard for water, and when it was brought he said he did not want it. Lewis went away and Smith called again for water. Lewis told him he would let him wait, and Smith dashed the contents of his night bucket on him. I think this was the first time the lash was used after I went there.
Q. What was the most severe punishment you saw while there?
A. Well, sir, I don't know as there was much difference between that and one other instance of flogging.
Q. How many lashes did Smith receive?
A. My impression is that Smith received 30 lashes.
Q. Did you ever know of any convict being punished in such a manner that it rendered him unable to work?
A. No, sir; I did not.
Q. What was the rule as to men getting good time?
A. I think the rule is sixty days in a year.
Q. What date did you enter into the employ of the prison?
A. The fore part of April, 1871.
Q. At what time did you leave?
A. In October or November, 1872.
Q. While you were there was there any rule which prescribed any particular punishment for a particular offense?
A. I did not so understand it.
Q. Was there any rule for inflicting punishments for offenses other than the Agent's discretion?
A. No, sir; I don't know of any.
Q. You spoke of privileges granted for good behavior. Were these privileges granted by printed rules, or was it left to the discretion of the Agent?
A. No, sir; they were oral, and given by him, if I understand it.
Q. Was there any rule for good behavior other than the discretion of the Agent?
A. No, sir; they had the general rules.
Q. All the general rules were printed or written, were they not?
A. I don't know that I ever saw a printed rule in regard to writing.
Q. Was it understood among employes that there were any rules of the prison other than on paper?
A. I don't know as there was, sir.
Q. What punishments have you known to be inflicted in prison?
A. Well, I have seen them use the lash, I have seen them on the cross, I have seen them in their cells, and I have seen others wearing a sort of a clog, or iron, from the ankle.
Q. Did you ever know of any convicts being showered?

A. No, sir.
Q. Did you ever know them to wear wire caps?
A. No, sir.
Q. Did you ever know them to be punished by riding a wooden horse, or tied up by the wrists?
A. No, sir.
Q. If these punishments had been in use while you were there, you would have known it?
A. I think I should, sir.
Q. Were the punishments inflicted openly, or in a certain part of the prison?
A. Well, the punishments by the lash were in one place at the end of the hall,—the cell hall.
Q. Was it the usage to inflict punishments openly where the employes and convicts could witness it, or privately, where no one but those giving or receiving the punishment were present?
A. They were not openly exposed; only those in the end of the hall could see the punishment.
Q. Describe the whip that was used in the punishment of David Smith.
A. I should think the stalk was about three feet long, with a short lash upon it. And the stalk was covered.
Q. Describe the lash.
A. I think, perhaps, it was 10 or 12 inches long,—I never measured it,—made out of some kind of leather, either buck-skin or sheep-skin, or it might have been horse-hide. It was the same as an ordinary covered whip.
Q. In inflicting that punishment, was the skin broken?
A. I think not, excepting in one instance. My impression now is that in the first instance it was.
Q. On what part of the person were these lash punishments inflicted?
A. When the Deputy inflicted punishments he stood partly to the left side of a man, and struck around the body, or over the shoulders, probably.
Q. So that the lash came around in front?
A. Probably.
Q. Did Mr. Morris, in his treatment of the convicts, exhibit uniform equanimity of temper while you were there?
A. Well, sir, I should think about as the average of human nature develops itself.
Q. The answer is indefinite, please be more specific?
A. Well, sir, I couldn't say that he was at all times even in his treatment.
Q. Did you ever see him exhibit anger in his intercourse with the convicts?
A. I don't know but I have.
Q. Describe this punishment of having the clog fastened to the foot?
A. Well, sir, it consists of two straps of iron, formed in such a manner that there is a cavity between them, so that it comes around the limb above the ankle, in such a shape that a man can walk with them.
Q. How heavy are they?
A. I couldn't tell you, as I never lifted one of them.
Q. State whether they are made round to fit the limb, or whether they have sharp corners which come in contact with the limb?
A. They are made round.
Q. For how long a time have you known any one convict to be punished by wearing these clogs continuously?

A. I couldn't tell you exactly the length of time. For some specific cases they may perhaps wear them from two to four weeks.
Q. Were convicts required to labor while these were upon their feet?
A. Yes, sir.
Q. Can you give any estimate of their weight?
A. I couldn't come within four or five pounds, and that would be simply a guess.
Q. Did you ever have any thing to do with keeping the record?
A. No, sir.
Q. Did you know of your own knowledge whether all punishments were recorded?
A. I had no means of knowing.
Q. Did you have an opportunity to observe whether convicts and free men, working in the same shop, conversed together freely?
A. I have seen them talking together frequently, but I did not know whether they were talking particularly about the work or not.
Q. Was there a code of printed rules for the government of prisoners and officers, and in force while you were there?
A. Yes, sir.
Q. Did you have a copy of these?
A. Yes, sir, I did.
Q. How often did you read these rules?
A. I kept a copy lying on my table and read them as opportunity afforded.
Q. Did you look to these rules to prescribe your duties, or did you look to the oral instructions of the agent?
A. As keeper I looked for my instructions from the rules.
Q. Did you ever receive any instructions from him conflicting with the prescribed rules?
A. I do not know as I did, sir.

By Mr. Bartow:

Q. About this whip you have described. Was it such a whip as we generally denominate a stallion whip?
A. My impression is that it was covered with leather.
Q. Was it such a one as is generally termed a black whip?
A. No, sir, I did not understand it to be that kind of a whip. This whip was about three feet long; it was more like a braided carriage whip. I don't know what was inside of it. It was one of those whips which a teamster would use in driving a team, and my impression is that it was covered with leather.
Q. [Addressed to Mr. Wilcox, one of the Inspectors.] Do you remember about that, Mr. Wilcox, whether it was of leather?
A. Yes, sir, the reason why I called it a stallion whip is because it is a little shorter than the ordinary farmers' whip. I sell whips in my store, and when farmers come to buy these shorter whips they call them stallion whips. I understood it, I suppose I know it, to be a solid handle of wood covered with russet leather, with a short lash braided on to that.

Mr. Stroud cross-examined by Mr. Seoger:

Q. Please state what was the rule in regard to correspondence while you were in the prison?
A. When I went there I think a convict had the privilege of writing to his friends once in three months, and at a subsequent time it was reduced to two months, from that to six weeks, and finally it was reduced to one month.

Q. Was that the uniform rule, or was it only allowed as a reward to certain convicts?

A. I understood that it was a uniform rule which all could avail themselves of unless they violated that rule by smuggling letters.

By Mr. Conely:

Q. State whether the convicts did not understand that if they behaved themselves that they could avail themselves of this privilege. Your answer to Mr. Webber left the matter in doubt as to whether this privilege applied to all.

A. I could not answer, sir.

Q. Then what do you mean by saying it was a uniform rule. Couldn't every convict avail himself of this rule if he did not violate the privilege?

A. Yes, sir, I think that all understood they were entitled to the privilege if they did not violate it by smuggling letters.

Q. The punishments were inflicted largely in the west wing, that is, farthest removed from public observation?

A. I think they were sir.

Re-direct examination by Mr. Webber:

Q. You say the convicts understood the privileges granted them; how do you know this?

A. I know it because Mr. Morris told them in the dining-room; the Agent generally, on Sabbath morning, talked with them a few minutes when they were all assembled in the dining-hall.

Q. While you were there how many prisoners were they who could not understand the English language?

A. I couldn't tell you, sir; all I know about it is there were some Germans there.

A. A. ALLEN SWORN.

Examined by Senator Webber:

Q. Where do you reside?
A. In Jackson.
Q. What business are you now engaged in?
A. I am now engaged in selling music for S. D. Bullock.
Q. Have you been employed at or about the State prison?
A. Yes, sir.
Q. When, and how long?
A. I went there in the spring of 1871, about the first of April, I think; I don't recollect the day of the month; I remained at the prison until December 15, 1872.
Q. In what capacity were you employed?
A. I went there as a guard, and did duty about two months as such, and then, after that, I acted as a keeper.
Q. Were you assigned to any particular portion of the prison?
A. I had a regular shop that I kept, although I did duty at times in other places when keepers were sick.
Q. Were your duties such as to enable you to know of the punishments inflicted in the prison?
A. No, sir.
Q. Did you ever witness any punishments inflicted in the prison?
A. I helped take one man from the cross, that was all.
Q. Do you know how long he had been there?

A. Only from what the deputy told me ; it was in the evening ; I was standing for another guard while he went up into the city ; I stood until nine o'clock ; just before I came off the deputy came in and wanted me to go and help take a man off the cross.

Q. Describe the manner of taking him down from the cross.

A. The man was fastened with straps around his wrists, his arms stretched straight out ; we had simply to unbuckle the straps and loose the man.

Q. Was he fastened in any other way than by the straps about the wrists ?

A. No, sir, I don't think he was ; I think there was a way of putting straps about the ankles, but I don't think they were on his.

Q. State whether the man appeared to be in any way injured or affected by that punishment ?

A. Well, he seemed to be in a good deal of pain, but I presumed it would not result in any permanent injury ; his wrists were swollen some ; he staggered some, but went without our helping him ; he got down himself.

Q. How high was he placed above the level of the floor ?

A. I think he stood upon the floor.

Q. When you speak of his getting down, what do you mean ?

A. He was in the old solitary, and he had to come into the hall and then go down stairs to go to his own cell.

Q. Who was the deputy while you were there?

A. Mr. Martin.

Q. Did the deputy tell you how long this man had been on the cross ?

A. He told me he was put there in the forenoon. I think it was just before noon, and he remained there until just before the man relieved me. That was at nine o'clock in the evening.

Q. Do you know for what offense this convict was punished ?

A. Yes, sir; there was some trouble between him and another convict; as they went into the hall he struck the other convict, or struck at him. They fought there and created quite a melee and the officers stopped it. This man was put on there for that offense.

Q. What was the name of this convict?

A. The name he went by there, I think, was Dugan, although he had another name, but I don't remember it. At least I understood Dugan was not his right name.

Q. Is that the only punishment you ever witnessed ?

A. Yes, sir.

Q. Did you see Mr. Morris frequently in his intercourse with the convicts?

A. I saw him in the dining room on Sunday mornings when they used to assemble, and occasionally when he came through the shops with visitors.

Q. Did you ever see him use any violence in the treatment of convicts ?

A. No, sir; I never did.

Q. How old a man was Dugan ?

A. I should judge he was from 27 to 30 years, or thereabouts.

Q. When this man was on the cross, state whether his arms were so elevated as to make it difficult to stand with his whole weight on his feet.

A. I don't think they were. His hands were elevated, I should judge, just about even with the top of his head.

Q. So that by standing perfectly erect he could stand square on his feet?

A. Yes, sir.

Q. Did you ever know of any intercourse, in the way of conversation, between freemen and prisoners in the shops?
A. Yes, sir.
Q. State the practice in that regard.
A. Well, there were a great many times that there were things about the work that it would be necessary for a convict to know, and the keepers usually understood the work pretty well, and very often the convicts would ask the keeper if a certain kind of work should be done so and so.
Q. I spoke more particularly of their intercourse with freemen who are not officers, or those connected with the shops.
A. There were times that they talked with the foremen about matters that did not strictly pertain to their work.
Q. When such instances happened did punishment follow?
A. No, sir; I never knew of a man being punished for it.
Q State whether Mr. Morris in his intercourse with the convicts exhibited a uniform temper.
A. Why, no; I could not say it was uniform. I never saw Mr. Morris display any exceeding passion in presence of the convicts; it was not uniform; his tone was not always alike. All the intercourse I ever saw him have with the men was when he stood on the platform of the dining room and talked with them, or perhaps read to them.
Q. On these occasions was it his custom to read the prison rules to the prisoners?
A. I don't think I ever heard Mr. Morris read the prison rules. I heard him read a statute law to them, in regard to convicts at work outside the prison running away; and it being the same as breaking prison. I might have heard him read the prison rules, but I don't recollect it. Every convict had them in his cell, or was supposed to.
Q. What proportion of the convicts could read while you were there?
A. I could not answer the question. I don't know.
Q. What was the usage if a convict desired to enter a complaint of ill-treatment from a keeper? How did he make his complaint to the keeper?
A. If he wanted to see the agent or inspectors he usually made his application to his keeper. That was the general rule.
Q. Was it understood that he was at liberty to appeal to any officer except his keeper?
A. I think he could appeal to any officer.
Q. Do you know what the practice was as to examining into the truth or falsity of a complaint made?
A. No, sir; I was never present at an examination.
Q. Do you know what punishments were inflicted during the time you were there?
A. With the lash, the shower bath, the cross, with the shackle or weight on the leg. They were the only punishments I knew of; yes, they locked them in the bare cell also.
Q. What was the difference between this bare cell and the ordinary cell?
A. There was no difference except the bunk was taken out.
Q How long did you ever know a convict to be kept in a bare cell without food?
A. I don't know; I never heard of convicts being put in a bare cell and kept any great length of time without food. They had rations served to them. All

STATE PRISON INVESTIGATION. 101

I know about it is what I got from the officers. I think they were fed on bread and water, but how much I don't know.

Questioned by Senator Mellen:

Q. Did you ever know a convict to be punished in order to make him reveal information which he was supposed to be in possession of?

A. No, sir; I never saw a man showered or whipped; this man Smith was in my shop.

Q. Did you know this man Dugan's general reputation?

A. It was not very good; I don't know of any trouble he had only once; I knew he had some trouble with another convict; they got to fighting out in the iron shed; they had a pretty hard fight, for they were bruisers.

Q. Was he considered as one of the hard cases?

A I think not to manage.

By Mr. Livingstone:

Q. When speaking of the lash, do you mean a strap or braided whip?

A. Braided whip.

Q. You say you have seen prisoners when they were punished?

A. This man Smith was one of my men.

Q. Was he a colored man?

A. Yes, sir.

Q. Did you ever see a man who could not work from the effect of punishments?

A. Smith could not work; I sent for the deputy to take him away.

Q. How long before he went to work again?

A. I could not tell you just how long—whether he went to work in less than three days or not.

Q. Was that the man who was tied up by the wrists?

A. No, sir; he was the one who was whipped.

Q. Did the lash cut him much?

A. He was cut pretty bad; I gave him some oil to put on his wounds.

Q. How long ago was that?

A. I think it was in the summer of 1871; I cannot tell the month, the books would show that; I think in August or September.

Q. Who did the whipping?

A. Mr. Martin, I suppose; he said he did.

Q. Was that before or after Mr. Morris took charge of the prison?

A. It was after Mr. Morris took charge.

Q How long did they retain that whip?

A. All the time I was there.

Q. How long were you there?

A. I was there from April 1, 1871, to December 15, 1872.

Q. During the time you were there did you know of any one else being whipped as severely as this man?

A. There was a man punished by the name of Collins (I only know this from the officers) who received more lashes than Smith did.

Q. On what part of Smith's person were these wounds?

A. Around his body, on his sides, and in front; when he raised his arms to strike these wounds were very painful, so much so he could not work; he showed a disposition to work but he could not.

Q. Some of them were across his breast in front?

102   STATE PRISON INVESTIGATION.

A. I am not so positive whether they came clear across his breast ; he opened his shirt, and I thought him in a condition that he could not work.

Q. Do you know whether he received the most of the whipping on his back or side?

A. I could not tell ; the lash would wind around the body when the blow was struck.

Q. Did this man deserve the punishment?

A. I think he deserved a very severe punishment.

Q. Was that the general impression of the keepers ?

A. Yes, sir. I did not hear any keeper say but what the man ought to be punished, because it was one of those offenses if you let it go you could not maintain discipline at all.

Q. Were cases frequent where men were whipped ?

A. Quite a number.

Q. Do you know from your own personal knowledge how many blows this man received?

A. I do not. The deputy told me that he gave him 36. One of the other officers said 35.

Q. You say there was no change in this whip while you remained there during the 20 months ?

A. No, sir, I think it was the same whip. If it was not it was one so near like it that you could not tell the difference.

Q. Did you ever know of any one being punished who you thought did not deserve it?

A. Well, there was one case I was in doubt about. There was a couple of men under another keeper who got into a fight—a negro and a white man. The negro got the white man down and was giving it to him with a bar of iron, when the keeper came up and pulled him off. He cut his head pretty bad. Both of the men were punished. The negro had always been a good man in the shop. I don't know whether the white man irritated him so that he pitched on to him or not. The white man claimed he ought not to have been punished. I don't know how it was, but as long as the white man claimed that he ought not to have been punished I should have investigated the matter.

Q. Did you ever know of any punishments in the prison which betrayed any animus on the part of Mr. Morris toward a prisoner?

A. I don't understand you.

Q. Did you ever know of any convict being punished for any other purpose than to preserve discipline?

A. I never saw any man undergoing punishment except Dugan.

Q. Do you know of your own personal knowledge of any of the convicts being treated unfairly or punished unnecessarily ?

A. As regards these two men, the negro and white man, if the matter had been mine I should have investigated to know whether the white man needed flogging or not. Perhaps the punishment was just, but I had my ideas about it.

Questioned by Mr. Morse :

Q. Was there any investigation of this matter made ?

A. Not much, I guess, because the men were punished within half an hour after the fight occurred. The men came right back through the hall.

[Mr. Webber read from the prison record book as follows :

July 17, 1872. David Smith was treated yesterday. At 9 o'clock in the evening he called a guard to give him water, and when the guard came he said he had water and did not want any. In a few minutes he called again for water, and the guard (Lewis) asked him why he did not take the water when he was passing. Said he had water then, and did not want any. The guard said if he had a supply of water a few minutes before he did not need any now. Thereupon he became very angry, and began to call the guard all manner of filthy names, and made violent threats. Finally he seized his bucket and dashed the contents through the cell door into the face of guard Lewis. Was on the cross 12 hours, and closed up with 30 lashes. The first refreshment of the kind this season.]

Examination resumed by Mr. Webber:

Q. Did you know of David Smith's being on the cross?
A. I know David Smith was on the cross; but whether for that offense I cannot tell.
Q. Do you know whether his being on the cross 12 hours had anything to do with his inability to work?
A. It might have had.
Q. You cannot say as to that?
A. No, I can not.
Q. While you were at the prison did you understand that, in all cases, punishment was suspended as soon as the prisoner gave up, and begged, and promised to do better?
A. No, sir, I did not understand it was.

S. H. HENDEE SWORN.

Examined by Mr. Webber:

Q. Are you employed at the prison?
A. No, sir.
Q. Have you ever been?
A. Yes, sir.
Q. In what capacity?
A. As guard.
Q. When did your employment commence?
A. About April, in the spring of 1871.
Q, When did it end?
A. I continued until the last of October, I think, of the same year.
Q. By whom were you employed?
A. By Mr. Morris.
Q. What department of the prison were you assigned to?
A. My duty was to take visitors through in the afternoon, and from 6 to 12 o'clock I stood in the hall in the east wing.
Q. State whether you ever witnessed any punishments in the prison?
A. I did.
Q. What kind of punishments?
A. I saw three or four men while on the cross. Those are all the punishments I ever witnessed. Yes, I saw a man locked in the dark cell, as we called it, and and I saw one man with an iron on his ankle. I never saw a man whipped.
Q. Do you know of any man being whipped while you were there?
A. I did.
Q. State whether you saw any of these men when taken down from the cross?
A. I did, two of them.
Q. What was their physical condition?

A. Mr. Smith, whom you talked about, was so he could walk.

Q. Did you notice any swelling of the wrists?

A. I don't know as I noticed his wrists. I know I helped unbuckle him from the cross.

Q How did he walk when he left the cross?

A He could walk without assistance.

Q. Who was the other one you saw taken down?

A. I don't know who he was. The other one was a white man,—one of the convicts in the yard, and I did not know what shop he was employed in.

Q. Do you know how long he had been there?

A I know he was on the cross at noon, and I helped take him down in the evening, about 9 or 10; I cannot state the exact hour.

Q. What was his physical condition when taken down?

A. We carried him down stairs, that is, Mr. Martin and I. Can't say whether Mr. Morris was there or not.

Q Why did you carry him down stairs?

A. He was in a condition that he could not walk. That is, he did not try to walk, and we had to carry him.*

Q. Did you discover any swelling of his wrists?

A. I did not notice.

Q. What did you do with him when you carried him down stairs?

A. He was put into his cell.

Q. Do you know how soon after he was able to work?

A. I do not.

Q. Do you know for what offense he was put upon the cross?

A. I do not.

Q. Can you tell when that was?

A. No, sir; it might have been in the latter part of the summer of 1871.

Questioned by Mr. Bartow:

Q You don't know what offense he was there for?

A. I do not.

Questioned by Mr. Webber:

Q What cases of whipping with the lash did you know of while there?

A. I knew the case of Mr. Smith, and there was a convict on my side that was punished, but for what offense I don't know. I believe it was for insolence.

Q. In any instance were they injured by punishment so as to interfere with their capacity for labor?

A. Not to my knowledge.

Q. What time did you say you went there?

A. In the spring of 1871; in April, I think.

Q. Are you sure as to the year?

A. Yes, sir; I came away in the fall of the same year. I think the last of October, If I remember correctly.

Q. You spoke of David Smith being on the cross and being whipped.

A. As regards the whipping I don't know any thing about that. I did not say he was whipped; I know he was on the cross.

Q. Are you not mistaken in regard to the time of punishment?

A. I am not.

Q The record says 1872.

A. I was there in 1872 also.

Q. What time did you go there after you left in the fall of 1871?

A. About the middle of May the next spring.
Q. How long did you remain then?
A. I continued until not far from the first of August.
Q. Did you witness any punishments while there in 1872?
A. I did one that I know of.
R. What one?
A. This man was on the cross.
Q. Do you know his name?
A. He went by the name of Yankee Robinson.
Q. Do you know what he was put there for?
A. No, sir.
Q. Did you see him when he came down from the cross?
A. No, sir.
Q. Do you know what his physical condition was when he was taken down from the cross?
A. I think he was able to walk. I don't think he was on the cross long.
Q. When prisoners were punished by being placed upon the cross, state whether they were left alone, or whether any one was left with them.
A. They were left alone. When they were placed in the old solitary, I stood in the hall, and it was my duty to look in occasionally upon them, to see that they did not break out.
Q. Did you ever know of any convict being punished after he had yielded and promised to do better?
A. Not to my knowledge.
Q. When you went to see these men on the cross, did any conversation pass between you at the time of your visits?
A. No, sir.
Q. Did they speak to you?
A. No, sir; the door was so I could look through and see them without their seeing me.
Q. They would not know you were there then?
A. No, sir.
Q. Could they not hear your step?
A. No, sir; I wore cloth slippers.
Q. Did you ever discover any unevenness of temper, on the part of Mr. Morris, in his treatment of convicts?
A. No, sir.
Q. Have you been employed at the prison since 1872?
A. No, sir.
Q. Did you have anything to do with copying the record?
A. No, sir.
Q. Do you know whether a record was made of every punishment?
A. I suppose there was, yet I do not know.
Q. Was there any abuse of discretion on the part of the Agent that came to your knowledge while you were there?
A. No, sir, not aside from this man that I went to help bring from the cross. I thought at the time it was rather severe, yet I did not know what the offense was, or how much punishment he deserved.
Q. Was it understood that the keepers and guards were at liberty to criticise the punishments inflicted?
A. No, sir; I did not understand that they were at liberty to criticise.

STATE PRISON INVESTIGATION.

E. S. PERRY SWORN.

Examined by Senator Webber:

Q. Where do you reside?
A. In Ann Arbor.
Q. How long have you lived there?
A. About 18 years.
Q. Have you been employed at the prison at any time since Mr. Morris has been agent?
A. Yes, sir.
Q. What time did your employment first commence?
A. I first went there in the spring of 1870.
Q. Was he agent then?
A. No, sir.
Q. How long did you remain there?
A. Until sometime in 1873. I left there in May, I think.
Q. Have you been employed there since?
A. No, sir.
Q. In what capacity were you employed?
A. First as a guard.
Q. In what department of the prison?
A. Well, nights I was inside in the wings, and in the day time I was on the walls.
Q. Did you ever witness any punishment of convicts?
A. Never but one.
Q. What one was that?
A. A man by the name of Thurston.
Q. Was that after Mr. Morris became agent?
A. Yes, sir.
Q. Did you see him punished more than once?
A. No, sir.
Q. What was the character of the punishment?
A. I heard he threatened the Agent's life, and he was flogged with a whip.
Q. Were you present during the flogging?
A. Yes, sir.
Q. Did you count the lashes?
A. No, sir.
Q. Who inflicted the punishment?
A. Mr. Morris.
Q. State whether the punishment was severe or otherwise?
A. I don't think it was.
Q. Describe the punishment?
A. Well, he was whipped with the whip that has been spoken of. His clothes were taken off from him, all but his pants.
Q. Did you see him after the whipping?
A. I did not see him after he was taken away.
Q. Did you examine his person to see the effect of this whipping?
A. No, sir.
Q. Do you know whether the skin was broken by that whipping?
A. I could not say as it was.
Q. Can you judge as to the number of lashes?

A. Well, I should think in the neighborhood of 100. It might not have been so many. Could not say positive, between 50 and 100.
Q. On what part of the person were the blows given?
A. Partly over the shoulder.
Q. Would the blow fall on the front, or back part of a person?
A. They fell mostly on his side, and over his shoulder.
Q. Over which shoulder?
A. I think it was over the left shoulder.
Q. Did he stand with his face or his back to Mr. Morris?
A. With his back, or rather sidewise, with his left side towards Mr. Morris.
Q. Was he made fast to receive the punishment?
A. His hands were tied over his head to a post.
Q. Is that the only punishment you ever witnessed?
A. That is the only one.
Q. Did you ever know of any other punishments being inflicted by Mr. Morris while you were there?
A. Only by hearsay.
Q. Do you know what modes of punishment were resorted to while you were there?
A. Yes, sir; there was the lash, the cross, the clogs or irons which were fastened around the ankles, and the dark cell.
Q. Any riding of a wooden horse?
A. No, sir.
Q. Any wire caps worn?
A. No, sir.
Q. Was it any part of your duty to communicate rules to the prisoners?
A. No, sir.
Q. Do you know what opportunity they had of knowing the rules?
A. Yes, sir.
Q. What was it?
A. They had them right in their cells.
Q Do you know how many there were who could not read?
A. No, sir; I do not.
Q. Were there any?
A. Some; but I don't know how many.
Q. While there, did you discover any unevenness of temper on the part of Mr. Morris with his intercourse with the convicts?
A. No, sir, I did not.
Q. What opportunities had you to observe the manner he treated the convicts?
A. Not much to speak of. In the day time I was on the wall, and in the evening I went on at 12 o'clock, and staid until 6 o'clock the next morning. Then I went home and staid until 12 o'clock the next noon.
Q. Did you have occasion to report any convicts while you were there?
A. Once in a while.
Q. To whom did you report?
A. To the deputy.
Q. Who was deputy at that time?
A. Mr. Martin was when I first went there, but afterwards Mr. Winans was.
Q. Did Mr. Martin remain as deputy after Mr. Morris became Agent?
A. For a while.

Questioned by Mr. Barlow:
Q. Do you know whether Mr. Thurston was whipped before or after this time you describe?
A. I think b fore.
Q. Do you know his offense?
A. I don't know, only from hearsay.

A. E. HAWLEY SWORN.

Examined by Mr. Webber:
Q. State your age, residence, and occupation.
A. I am 48 years old, live in the city of Jackson, am a fork-maker by trade.
Q. Have you ever been employed at or about the State prison?
A. I have, sir.
Q. What time did your employment commence?
A. April, 1871.
Q. How long did you continue?
A. Until July, 1873.
Q. You have not been employed there since?
A. No, sir.
Q. In what capacity were you employed?
A. As foreman of the trip-hammer shop.
Q. How many convicts were employed in that shop?
A. We had from 35 to 40 odd.
Q. What opportunity did you have while there to observe the discipline of the prison?
A. I had very little, only so far as my shop was concerned.
Q. Did you know of any convicts being punished while you were there?
A. Some in my shop.
Q. What was the character of the punishment inflicted?
A. I think but one of my men was whipped while I was there; two were in the dark cell, I think, and two, I think, were on the cross.
Q. What opportunity did you have to observe Mr. Morris in his personal intercourse with the convicts?
A. Nothing of any account, only as he passed through the shops.
Q. Did any instance of severe punishment come under your observation?
A. Not but one as I recollect.
Q. Do you remember the name of that convict?
A. I think his name was Williams; I may not recollect exactly.
Q. How was he punished?
A. He was whipped.
Q. Can you state when this was?
A. I think in the fall of 1872.
Q. Did you know what his offense was?
A. For trying to scale the wall.
Q. Describe the punishment which he received.
A. I did not see him punished; I only saw him after he came back to the shop.
Q. Describe his condition?
A. While he was changing his clothes I saw there were gashes cut in his side, under the arms.
Q. How many?
A. Two or three; I think three.

Q. Describe their length?
A. I think they were more than two inches long in the right side. His work was such that he had to use his arms, and he complained that he could not work. The keeper kept him at work. He also at the same time had a clog upon his leg.
Q. How heavy was this iron attached to his feet?
A. That I could not tell you more than by guess work. I should think it would weigh somewhere from 8 to 9 pounds.
Q. Were these wounds fresh when you saw them?
A. They were fresh as if the punishment had been administered recently; there was blood on them when I saw them.
Q. What were the opportunities for conversation between the freemen employed in the shop and the convicts?
A. I never had any printed rules, but it was understood that the convicts could talk with the free men about their work; nothing more.
Q. As a matter of fact, did other conversation take place between them?
A. Oh yes, sir; frequently.
Q. When such other conversation did take place between them was it reported as a breach of discipline?
A. Not that I know of.
Q. Did you ever see Mr. Morris show anger in his treatment of convicts?
A. I don't know that I did.
Q. State what you observed in that direction?
A. All the knowledge I had, and it may be merely a matter of opinion, he would punish some men for light offenses, when others for large offenses would get nothing done to them.

AFTERNOON SESSION.

EXPLANATION BY MR. WILCOX.

I would like the attention of this Investigating Committee for a moment, and suggest that it would be very difficult for the prison authorities, or for the Inspectors, to comply with this resolution of Senator Webber. The books are very numerous, and some of them are needed there every day. We have no deputy clerk now who understands the clerical work of the prison, and the clerk is required there every hour in the day.

The physician has to be there every day and is liable to be called any hour,— any accident in the prison; and I would suggest that after taking all the testimony that you please to here, that you adjourn to the prison, where you will have access to the books, and to other evidence that you have not here, and it will give you a better opportunity.

Next Wednesday is the monthly meeting of the board, and at that meeting we determine the good time of convicts who, if they have lost no good time, will go out this month, and we have to have the record of their punishment, and other records to determine that.

We have no right to detain them, if we have no charges against them. If there are convicts there who have no charges against them, of course they go out; but if they are on the records, we examine them, and from our best judgment determine their good time.

I think that would be less demoralizing upon the prison, than it would to bring all of the officers here.

When I went to the prison six years ago, I found it in revolt,—every man locked in a cell. I know some of the perils connected with a revolt in a prison. It was a long time before we got the prison into working order, and I am very solicitous that there should be no demoralizing of the convicts, if there is of the Inspectors.

E. A. HAWLEY, RECALLED.

Examined by Mr. Webber:

Q. Do you know of any infraction of the rules, or flagrant misdemeanors, while you were in the prison, which were reported to Mr. Morris, of which no notice was taken; if so, state them.

A. Well, I know of one or two instances that I suppose was in that shape.

Q. Please give the particulars.

A. One man made very violent threats, and said he would not do his work, nor Mr. Morris could not make him do his work. There was nothing done with him then.

Q. Do you recollect the name of the convict?

A. Talbert.

Q. Do you know whether those threats were reported to Mr. Morris?

A. I talked with Mr. Morris about it one night as I came out of the yard, and he made me this reply, he said: Talbert was a bad man. That was about all the reply he made to me. The convict did not threaten me, he threatened the contractor. He said he could do his work, and get it done at four o'clock, but he would not, nor Mr. Morris could not make him; and he said, if the contractor came into his corner there, and asked him to do it, he would take his heart's blood. That is the way he spoke.

Q. And you reported this conversation, as you have now given it?

A. I reported it to the keeper; and when I came out, I was talking with Mr. Morris about it at night, what they were going to do with him, and he made me that reply: that he was a bad man.

Q What time was this?

A. I think that was in the fall of 1872, or some time in the winter,—somewhere along there.

Q. Any other case of like character within your knowledge?

A. Well, there was one other that I have in my mind. Mr. Martin came in, there was a couple of them got to quarreling one day over their work, and spoiled some considerable work, and I shut their fire down, and stopped their working. And I sent for Mr. Martin, and he came and talked with one of them; and he told him, says he, "If there is any more of this, I will" do so and so to you,—" whip you." The convict says: "I should think more of it if some other man would say so; I don't think much of it now." They had been quarreling all the forenoon, a couple of them, working together. Well, Martin took him right in, and in fifteen or twenty minutes he came back laughing, and said there was nothing the matter. He said Mr. Morris said he must not talk. That is what he told the other convict. I overheard the conversation.

Q Do you recollect the name of this last convict that you speak of?

A. I don't recollect his name now.

Q. That was in the summer of 1872, along in July or August?

A. I think it was.
Q. Any other instances of like character?
A. No, I don't recollect of any other.
Q. Do you recollect ever hearing that Mr. Cooley's life was threatened?
A. Well, that black fellow threatened it there, at that time I was talking with him. I told him what his work was, and he said he would not do it. I made him the reply that the easiest way was the best way, and when I went in he was talking in that way. I did not have any more words with him.

CROSS-EXAMINATION.

By Mr. Conelly:
Q. By the black fellow, do you mean Talbert?
A. Yes, sir.
Q. That was in the fall of 1872?
A. Yes, sir.
Q. He did not make any threat directly to Mr. Cooley?
A. No; I had not seen Mr. Cooley in that corner for some little time.
Q. But he stated if Mr. Cooley were to ask him to do the work that he would take his heart's blood?
A. Yes, sir; he told me so right to my face.
Q. To whom did you report it?
A. I talked with the keeper about it.
Q. Who was the keeper?
A. I don't recollect now. We changed keepers there; I don't know who it was.
Q. Did you report that to Mr. Martin?
A. No, sir.
Q. Did you make a report of that to Mr. Morris?
A. No; I was speaking to Mr. Morris about it when I came out, that was all. My report was all made to the keeper.
Q. Now, what did you tell Mr. Morris, when you spoke about it?
A. Why, I think I asked him the question whether he was going to be made to do his work or not, something of that kind.
Q. What did you say to him about the man having threatened Mr. Cooley,— did you ever mention that to him, at any time?
A. I mentioned the conversation I had with him at the time.
Q. Well, now, why not answer my question: did you ever tell Mr. Morris that he had threatened Mr. Cooley?
A. Well, I think I did. I could not say for certain the conversation that I had with Mr. Morris there, at the time I was going out.
Q. You can't say then, you told Mr. Morris?
A. I can't say whether I told him that, or whether I asked him if he was going to make him do his work.
Q. Now, as to the other man,—I think you said you did not remember the other man's name?
A. No, sir; I don't now.
Q. What you have related occurred in the presence of Mr. Martin?
A. Yes, sir; Mr. Martin was talking with him; I stood right beside him, and we made him that reply, taking him in.
Q. By taking him in, you mean taking him from the shop into the building where the cells are?

A. Yes, sir.
Q And you saw the convict when he returned?
A. Yes, sir.
Q. Was Mr. Martin with him when he returned?
A. No, sir.
Q. Was Mr. Morris?
A. No, sir; he was sent back.
Q. And you had a conversation with him?
A. I wanted to see whether he was going to work or not.
Q. Did you speak with him?
A. He said he was going to work. He made the remark to a convict. He asked him what he got. He said Mr. Morris told him not to use such language, or not to talk so, or something of that kind.
Q. My question is, did you speak with him?
A. I asked him if he was going to work?
Q Did you say anything else to him?
A. Not in regard to his punishment.
Q. He told that to another convict.
A. Yes, sir.
Q Not in the presence of Mr. Martin?
A. No, sir.
Q. Then you have no personal knowledge, yourself, whether Mr. Morris disciplined him at that time or not?
A. No, sir.
Q. You never heard him say?
A. All I judged by was the time he was gone.
Q How long was he gone?
A. Probably from ten to fifteen minutes.
Q. You heard him say to the other convict, what,—repeat that?
A. That Mr. Morrison told him that he must not use such language, or something of that kind ; must not talk so.
Q. Well, did he say anything about having been disciplined in any way?
A. He said he had not been.
Q. How did he behave himself after that?
A. Oh, they went to work after that a little better.

GEORGE BANISTER SWORN.

Examined by Mr. Webber :

Q. State your age, residence, and occupation.
A. I am forty-two years of age, reside at Jackson, and am employed as foreman for Withington, Cooley & Co., contractors in the trip-hammer shop.
Q. Are you employed there now.
A. I am, sir.
Q How long have you been employed there?
A. I came there in July, 1873.
Q And have been ever since?
A. I have.
Q How many convicts are employed in your department?
A. I have thirty-six now. It has averaged from thirty-five to thirty-nine.
Q How many freemen besides these, are employed in that shop?
A. I have one now. Most of the time there is none but myself.

STATE PRISON INVESTIGATION. 113

Q Have you ever witnessed any punishment in the prison?
A. Not but once, and that very slight.
Q What was the character of the punishment in that instance?
A. A man was being showered on his feet; had his pants rolled up about to his knees, and being showered on his feet.
Q. Was he one of your men?
A. No, sir; he was not.
Q. Have you known of any punishment being inflicted?
A. Only by hearsay, with that one exception.
Q. Have any men in your department been guilty of any breaches of discipline while you have been there?
A. Yes, sir; quite often.
Q In such cases what do you do?
A. Well, my remedy is to report them to the keeper.
Q And then what is done with the men?
A. They are reported to the deputy, so called, and if he deems the offense sufficient, they are punished, I suppose.
Q Well, state whether, of your own knowledge, any have been taken from the shop ostensibly for that purpose.
A. There has; I could not say just how many; I should say four or five in the time that I have been there; since I have been there.
Q. While you were there were any in your shop punished so as to unfit them for labor.
A. No, sir.
Q State whether any of the men under your charge have been punished by flogging.
A. There has one, so I hear.
Q. Well, did you see him after he was flogged?
A. Yes, sir; I saw him at work. He came back and was at work again; I did not see his person.
Q You never examined to see the effect of the flogging?
A No, sir.
Q. What opportunity had you for observing Mr. Morris' intercourse with the convicts?
A. Oh, very little.
Q. Did you ever see any thing there to indicate that any discrimination was made between convicts in their treatment for breaches of discipline?
A. Well, that would be a matter of opinion on my part, so far as that is concerned. I don't know as I could really testify to any now, sir.
Q. Have you known any cases where you reported to the keeper the breaches of discipline where punishment did not follow?
A. No, sir; I have done but very little reporting since I have been there. There has been no case where I have reported a man,—really reported a man,—and with a request that the keeper should give him punishment, where it has not been done.
Q What investigation is made as to the truth of the charges which are made when reports are made in that way?
A. Really, sir, I could not tell you; I never have been questioned but once or twice in regard to men that I have reported.
Q Have you, in any instance, been called upon by the Agent, before him, in the presence of the convict against whom the complaint was made?

A. I have, in one instance.
Q. For an examination?
A. Yes, sir.
Q. What was the offense with which the convict was then charged?
A. Charged with refusing to do his task.

Q, Relate what took place at the interview when you were called before the Agent?

A. It is some time ago, and I have not called the matter to mind since; I had a "life man," that done a considerable grumbling in regard to his fire; he did not do his day's work; I did not think his fault was consistent, and I reported him; he was taken to the hall, and after a time, I think Mr. Morris sent for me,—I could not swear whether he did or not,—and questioned me in regard to it; and I stated to him the facts as I understood them, and in the presence of this convict; he denied some things, that is, I think he denied he had done what was called a task; I told Mr. Morris that I could show it to him on my books, that he had done it right along; I guess that was about all that was said in regard to him; I might have complained to Mr. Morris something in regard to his complaints about his fire—something of that kind; I don't remember now.

Q. Do you know whether the man was punished?
A. I could not swear that he was; I understood that he was "showered" a little at the time.

Q. State whether you ever observed anything in the intercourse of Mr. Morris with the convicts which indicated a want of uniformity in temper or disposition.

A. I have not seen but very little: that is, I have not seen Mr. Morris have but very little intercourse with the convicts; I might have an opinion of my own, still I would not give anything of the kind as evidence; I think he treats them all well.

Q. How many hours a day are they required to labor?
A. The average, I think, is a trifle less than ten hours; in the winter time, short days, it amounts to about eight; long days, in the summer, the longest time is a little over eleven hours.

Q. How does the work performed by convicts compare with the labor of freemen for the same length of time?

A. Well, the most of them that have tasks do more work than freemen will do in the same, that is, they accomplish the task in less time than freemen will do it, as a rule.

Q. When they work without tasks how does the quantity of labor performed by them compare with the quantity which would be performed by freemen in the same length of time?

A. I think it is probably less.
Q. Well, in what does it differ?
A. Well, it depends some upon circumstances; how much they are watched, perhaps I might say *forced* to; it depends a good deal upon the foreman in regard to that matter.

Q. What is the practice in your department as to conversing with the convicts while at work?

A Well, it is the practice—at least I have practiced it—to talk with them as I would with freemen, that is, when it was necessary.

STATE PRISON INVESTIGATION. 115

Q. Do you converse on any other subjects with them, except the matter immediately connected with the work?
A. Well, perhaps, sometimes, yes.
Q. Such conversation you don't understand to be a breach of discipline?
A. Well, strictly, I suppose it is.
Q. Well, is it one that is passed over without notice, ordinarily?
A. It is, sir ; in fact, I don't know that the prison authorities can have cognizance, or know whether a foreman is talking strictly about the business, or whether he is talking about something else.
Q How many keepers are employed in the shop over which you are foreman?
A. I don't know.
Q. Are there any guards in addition to the keeper in that shop?
A. There are not.
Q. Has any instance of harsh or severe treatment of any of the convicts, by any of the keepers or guards, ever came to your notice since you have been there?
A. There has not.

JESSE PARMENTER SWORN.

Examined by Mr. Webber:
Q. State your age, residence and occupation.
A. I am 34 years old; live in Jackson; am selling pianos and organs for Mr. Bullock.
Q. Have you ever had any thing to do with the management of the prison?
A. I worked there for some four years and a little over.
Q In what capacity?
A. As keeper.
Q. What time did your employment commence?
A. It commenced,—I cannot just remember the date,—well, I left there the 19th of January, 1873, and I had been there four years, something over.
Q. You have not been there since?
A. No, sir.
Q. Were you there before Mr. Morris took charge of the prison?
A. Yes, sir; I was there under Mr. Bingham and continued right along under Mr. Morris until—
Q. You quit.
A. Yes, sir; until I quit by invitation.
Q What department of the prison were you stationed in as keeper?
A. Well, I worked in almost every shop and in the yard at different times. I worked principally on the wagon contract; I had charge of the paint shop for something over two years; I had charge of the hospital for six months as hospital keeper,—about six months, I think. I worked in the wood shop on the wagon contract about six or eight months.
Q. While you were there after Mr. Morris became Agent did you witness any punishments of the convicts?
A. Well, yes; I did in two or three instances.
Q. Any instance of unusual severity?
A. No, sir.
Q. What character of punishment was inflicted upon convicts?
A. Well, the custom was sometimes to lock them up in a cell without a bed, and after Mr. Morris came there they introduced showering, and there was a

cross arrangement put in the old "solitary" that they tied men to for a time; and as a last resort we had—

Q. How many instances do you recollect where the whip was resorted to?

A. I never saw the whip resorted to under Mr. Morris; I knew of men being punished with the whip, but I never saw it.

Q. Did you ever see any men that were punished by the whip after they were punished, to examine their person?

A. I had one man punished in my shop; I took care of his little afflictions afterwards myself.

Q. Describe how the prisoner appeared when you examined him.

A. He had received, I guess, about fifteen lashes; there was some pretty severe ridges on his back; I took and greased them for him with sweet oil, and put an old cloth onto it, so they would not scar, and it was as good a dose of medicine as the man ever had in his life, probably.

Q. Do you recollect the name of that convict?

A. Yes, sir.

Q. What was it?

A. Now, I do not know whether I do or not; his name was Johnny Layton; he was the only one ever whipped that was under me while Mr. Morris was Agent; but I did not see that chastisement, you understand; I saw him after he was punished, but I did not see the punishment inflicted.

Q. What was the offense with which he was charged?

A. Well, he had refused to work and had been acting badly for a long time. There was something singular about him; I did not know why he should act so, and after that he returned and took hold and did his work as long as I had him under my charge. He had refused positively to do any more work under any circumstances when he was punished.

Q. What was the custom in regard to inquiring into the truth of the charges which were made against convicts when they were reported?

A. Well, my impression is that there were instances there, under Mr. Morris, when there were reports made that were not investigated.

Q. Any such instance now in your mind?

A. No, sir, there never was an instance of that kind as far as I was concerned as a subordinate. Whenever I made a report it was always attended to promptly. I never made but a few reports, but it was a common complaint among some of the subordinate officers—I heard of it—that they were not sustained.

Q. That the officers were not sustained in making their reports?

A. Yes, sir; but I could not recall any instance.

Q. Do you know what the practice of the Agent or deputy was, as to the means of determining the truth or falsity of those reports, when they were made?

A. I know what the rule is, and the practice; yes, sir.

Q. Well, state it.

A. The rule is, if a keeper—when a man gets out from under his control, so he cannot any longer control him under his influence, to report him to the deputy keeper; the deputy talks with the man in the shop, and if he considers the matter of any moment, takes him to the hall, and reports him to the Agent or locks him up, at his discretion.

Q. Is the report made always in the presence of the convict?

A. Well, it always was with me. I never reported a man without calling him up, and having him hear just what I had to say, and I guess that was the cus-

STATE PRISON INVESTIGATION.   117

tom; it was the practice with most officers, but occasionally report a man in the hall at night, after bell, when the man would not be present. Usually if they had a man to report in the shop, they would send and get the deputy keeper, and then call the man up and make the statement in the presence of the man.

Q. Were these reports made in the presence of the other convicts?
A. No, sir.
Q. Did you ever know, while you were acting in the hospital department, of any punishment being inflicted upon convicts who were in the hospital?
A. Yes, sir.
Q. What was the character of the punishment inflicted there?
A. We had a hospital steward there by the name of Leonard—
Q. I mean under Mr. Morris?
A. Yes, sir; under Mr. Morris. I was in the hospital under Mr. Morris. Leonard got the disease we used to call the big-head, you know, and Mr. Morris had allowed him, without discretion, I thought, to fix up his clothes very nicely. He was very much of an affected gentleman, and after I went into the hospital, he and I could not agree, and finally Mr. Morris and him got into a difficulty. I did not report him, because I thought he had more authority there than I did at the time; but Mr. Morris took and put the very worst suit of clothes on him he could find in the prison, and made him empty buckets for three or four days. That was the only man I ever knew punished in the hospital.
Q. This man you speak of being punished in this way was not one of the patients in the hospital?
A. No, sir; he was hospital steward. One of the attendants, you know. He was a healthy man.
Q. But a convict?
A. Yes, sir, and that acted directly upon his conscience, I think, the same as calomel does on the liver. I know it had a very wholesome effect on him.
Q. I intended to direct my inquiry to those who were in the hospital as patients?
A. Oh, well, I never knew of a patient being punished. Let me see; not that I remember.
Q. Did you observe anything there that indicated a discrimination in favor of any particular convicts?
A. Yes, sir.
Q. State what you saw?
A. Well, there was a certain class of convicts in the prison that I thought Mr. Morris was too familiar with the first year he was there, in fact more or less all the time that I was there. There was a certain class of convicts that Mr. Morris used to treat fully as well as he did the officers.
Q. What was that class?
A. The most intelligent, intellectual men that were sent there. One man that I have in mind was sent from Detroit. He was a detective. This Leonard was another one. A man that was sent from Adrian by the name of Rice; he had more privileges there than ever I had there under Mr. Morris.
Q. Well, were those privileged men required to perform labor?
A. Oh, usually, yes, sir.
Q. The same as other convicts?
A. Well, they used to get favors, you know. Kissing goes by favors. There is always convicts combined together in the prison to carry the thing in favor of

their interest in everything, and these men that were in cahouts with the Agent there, they had a certain influence that was, I thought, detrimental to the discipline of the prison. I thought it had a bad effect. There would be some punishing done, and then this undue familiarity, I called it, which tended to neutralize the influence that he could otherwise have had as a disciplinarian. There was another instance of punishment Mr. Morris and I participated in together. One of my men, his day's work had been raised, and he refused and got an iron that looked like a meat cleaver and ground it up sharp—he was a colored man —and in the morning he did not come out of his cell. We went there and he would not come out; he had that cleaver and said he would brain any man that would come in there. Well, it had been practiced there, that thing was not an isolated case, the convicts frequently did that thing, and they had let them stay there sometimes a day or so or three, until they got hungry enough and thirsty enough to come out and give up their weapons, whatever they had, but in this instance Mr. Morris thought, perhaps, that was not the best way; so he gets an iron heated, about ten feet long, and under his instructions I went to work and punched the fellow with that hot iron until he agreed to hand out the cleaver. He did so, and then they took him to the lower end of the hall and whipped him, but I did not see the whipping. I did not go down there.

Q. State whether this iron was applied in such a way as to inflict any burn upon his person?

A. Oh, burning a little on the hands. The intention was not so much to burn him as it was to scare him out. I approved of that; I thought it was right; I think so now.

Q. I am not asking about your opinion of things, I am getting at the facts.

A. Well, that is the facts in the case. It burned him a little across his arm, and I think it burned him a little here [indicating], just touched; not enough to injure him at all.

Q. At what time did that occur?

A. Well, sir, I could not answer that question.

Q. Can you give me the name of that convict?

A. No; that was a colored man,—nigger Albert. That is the only name that I ever knew for him.

Q. Did you ever know of any thing that in your judgment was injurious or detrimental to the discipline of the prison, in which women were concerned, in or about the prison?

A. That was injurious or detrimental to the discipline of the prison?

Q. Yes, sir.

A. No, sir.

Q. Did you every know of any thing in which any of the officers,—any thing in which any of the officers indulged in any improper familiarities with women, any that were connected with the prison,—connected with the officers of the prison?

A. I do not understand the question.

Q. Did you ever know of any instance in which the Agent or any of the officers of the prison, while they were there, endeavored in any way to use their official position to give them familiarity with females or any female?

A. I never knew of any such instance; no sir; never knew of it.

Q. What information have you on the subject?

A. Well [witness hesitates].

Mr. Conely—I would like to say a word to the committee, as to the latitude

STATE PRISON INVESTIGATION.   119

that this inquiry takes; whether it is right, proper, and expedient, under the guise of a legislative investigation, that professes to be, and is probably intended to be, for the benefit of the State, to go into an examination of a thing of this kind, to have spread here upon the record; the witness has stated that he does not know of anything of that kind.

Witness—No; I have not stated that.

Mr. Conely—Well, the next question is, what information have you upon the subject. I think that is the present question. Now, it seems to me that this is not what is wanted in this investigation; what delinquencies these various officers may have been guilty of, with reference to persons not connected with the prison, they have a remedy in the law courts; and an appropriate remedy. A man is not permitted to be dragged before even a justice of the peace, except upon a sworn complaint. Under the laws of this State he is not to be put upon his defense upon an accusation of that sort, except upon a sworn complaint, and then he is so far protected that there is not allowed to be produced against him anything but positive testimony,—things that people know; but this question goes beyond that. This question goes to the extent that this witness shall be asked what information he may have had from other people, of this character. Spread here before this people, its tendency must necessarily be,—if he has any information upon this subject,—it must necessarily be to blacken the character of those against whom he may have received such information. Without the opportunity to defend themselves from such accusations, and that which our laws give every man, in the court, that there ought to be first proffered against him a sworn complaint, specifying the time and the place. Now, I submit, in an investigation of this character, unless it is clearly for the public good, it ought to be confined to the official acts of those persons and to their conduct within the prison, and when it reaches a thing of this kind it ought to be so far agreed that no witness shall be allowed to tell except what he may know himself; and that circumstances that tend to blacken the character of a person, that must tend to it, they shall not be permitted to tell unless they have some positive knowledge of the facts themselves. In fact, I do not see what good it can possibly have, so far is this investigation is concerned, to bring to light here, and have brought before the public and through the press of this State, things of this kind. It does not seem to me it is necessary for the welfare of the prison, and I would ask that the committee consider well before they say that they will go into an inquiry based entirely upon hearsay,—what information an individual may have had from some person. If anything has been done within the prison that interferes with its discipline, whether by the Agent himself, or by any subordinate, or by any Inspector, of so serious a character as that, it seems to me that the witness should be confined to what he knows. I think this investigation that you have began, is too indefinite, any way; but when they pursue so wide a range as to permit Tom, Dick, and Harry to come in here and say what they have heard from other people, it seems to me we ought to consider whether the public good demands it. I think this question, gentleman, ought not to be permitted here.

Mr. Webber—I would say to the committee that I have not conversed with the witness, and am not aware what testimony may be given in response to the inquiry which I make; but I have been informed that certain officers connected with the administration of the prison have, in some instances, made use of their official position with female relatives of the convicts, to solicit improper favors. And in my judgment, as a member of the committee, if such facts exist,—and I presume all members of the committee know of such rumors existing,—if such facts exist, the public interest would be promoted by knowing against whom such facts exist. I do not intend to allow the witness to go outside of information received from persons who were officers of the prison. But I intend to confine the question to information received from officers of the prison. The question being objected to, it is proper for the committee to decide whether it is proper to be answered.

Mr. Conely—Perhaps I may add one word; I will not say anything beyond that. Now, I never heard anything of this sort until this morning, after coming here, I was informed that the inquiry was to partake of that character, and it struck me as being entirely beyond the scope and what was authorized by the resolution. Whatever may have occurred within the prison, of course, we concede is within the spirit of the inquiry, but, suppose it be true that some person connected with the prison has taken advantage of the fact that he was the Agent, or deputy, keeper, or some other official of the prison, to solicit some favor from some woman, a relative of a convict, is that to be the subject of inquiry here? Is it a proper subject of inquiry here? Does the public interest demand that that should be inquired into here? Shall not a person who may be charged with an offense have the ordinary rights that may be conceded criminals, that there shall be some specific time and place? All these people have notice of now is that this inquiry is for the public good; for the purpose of ascertaining what remedy, if any, as to the abuses that exist within the prison; what reforms are needed within the prison, if you please, but the personal conduct of any officer outside of it is just as much beyond the scope of this inquiry, in my mind, just as much beyond the powers of this Legislature as anything can be. It seems to me that this legislative committee have no more power to inquire into the private conduct outside of the walls of this prison of Mr. Morris, or any of his deputies, than they have any one of yourselves, or of myself. Suppose it be said it interferes with his influence, if you please. Let that be so. Does this committee sit for that purpose—to inquire whether these people outside may smoke, drink, or swear, or commit larceny, if you please, or commit adultery? Are not our courts open for that? Why, they would not let a member of the bar be tried for such a thing as that, to see whether he is entitled to the position of attorney at law. The Supreme Court has stated in one case that a man cannot be removed from the bar without his trial in the common law courts, upon an indictment filed against him in the ordinary way. And here we say, if any of these men have been guilty of these things, the proper complaints can be made against him in the ordinary courts, and that would be a matter why these men should be removed. But this is not a matter that can be inquired into in this investigation, whether it is true or whether it is false. It cannot suggest to this committee any reforms that are needed in the prison management. Not at all. It might suggest this, that the incumbent of that position was not the person for it, but what power would this committee have over that? What power would the Legislature have over that? What power has the Legislature over Mr. Morris, whether he shall go or whether he shall stay? Not a particle. The whole power of the Legislature is simply to cure abuses that may exist there. Their power is to cure what abuses may exist there in the management, should any exist, relative to the convicts or relative to offenses, but the private character of individuals, it seems to me, is beyond their inquiry, and it seems to me it would be an exceedingly unfit thing, to go now and ascertain what had been done by those persons outside, under the guise or because there was a convict in the prison, and a person was an officer of the prison, therefore he went to a female relative of a convict and procured from her some improper favors. I think, gentlemen, such testimony as that should be excluded. You see a very wide door may be opened, and very great injustice may be done, because a person has not the same opportunity of defense before an investigating committee that he would have in the courts. And these officers who may be implicated are not here; there is only one of them here, and that is Mr. Morris, the rest of them are not here to defend themselves.

Mr. Barlow.—I think this matter is something like this: Our friend from Jackson says we should not go outside of the prison in our investigation. That is my opinion, too; but while that is true, if a person holds an official position in the prison, and by virtue of that position he should take advantage of females who should visit their relatives in the prison, it would tend to demoralize the management and discipline of the prison; that while we have not the power, or really the right, to go outside of the prison and inquire what a man does,— he may play billiards, he may smoke or chew, he may take improper liberties with females outside of the prison,—yet if their conduct and demeanor within the prison is such that would be proper, although we have no business to inquire what he would do outside. But if, on account of his position, he has taken advantage of visitors who have been there, or he has taken advantage of his position in any way inside of the prison to introduce immoral conduct there in the presence of the officers or inmates of the prison, it would be a proper subject of inquiry.

Now, our friend from Jackson says it is the object of this inquiry to inquire into the management of the prison; it seems to me the conduct of an officer inside the prison, and in the presence of prison officials, is a part of the management of that prison.

Mr. Conely—That we make no objection to.

Mr. Jones—I was out at the time the question under discussion was asked; I would like to know what the question was.

Mr. Barlow—The substance of it was this: to make inquiries as to whether any official of the prison had taken advantage of his official position to take improper liberties with females, relatives of the convicts there.

Mr. Nelson—As a member of this committee I should object to anything of that kind,—of any questions of that kind being asked or introduced before the committee.

Mr. Mellen—It seems to me to be a proper subject of inquiry if it was connected with the prison. If it was done outside of the prison, with a person not connected with it, I do not think it is any business of this committee.

Mr. Nelson—I cannot see as a question of that kind has anything to do with the discipline of the prison. I think it is outside, entirely, of our jurisdiction.

Mr. Barlow—Suppose a person was a convict, a father, or a brother or son of the female, and that female should come to the prison and the official of the prison should say to the female who was there to visit the friend or relative, that "If you will submit to such and such things here in the prison, or with me, that you shall be permitted to do so and so, that is, you shall be permitted to see your relative when you wish and to stay as long as you wish, and you shall be granted certain favors if you will comply with such solicitations." Would you think that would be a proper subject of inquiry?

Mr. Nelson—That is dealing wholly with outside parties, not with the convict. It has relation to parties wholly outside of the prison, except as to the person making the advances. I do not see as it has anything to do with the convict, or with the prison management whatever.

Mr. Morse—It seems to me if any officer of the prison is guilty of anything of that kind he is liable to a criminal prosecution.

Mr. Webber—It strikes me, Mr. Chairman, that these officers concerning whom these inquiries are made, are not on trial. This committee cannot, neither can the Legislature, impose any punishment upon them in consequence of any inquiries they may make here, so that it does not occur to me that it is a case like the one alluded to by Mr. Conely, where parties are allowed certain rights in court, because there, the conclusion might be to inflict a penalty or a punishment upon the individual; but I am not aware of anything that in my judgment would be more demoralizing to the discipline of the prison than to have it understood that relatives of the convicts, female relatives of convicts, were subject to any improper solicitations from the officials connected with the administration of the prison as a price for procuring for their friends favors in the prison or as a price for procuring admission to visit their friends in prison. I do not know that any question which I may ask will lead to any such information, but from the rumors which have reached me it seems to me a proper question to ask.

Mr. Bartow—Well, I would say, such things if they should be done in the prison, so that the officers knew that they were going on, would tend to the demoralization of the prison rule. I might have my doubts about it being a proper subject of inquiry under our resolutions or any resolution that the Legislature might make.

Mr. Nelson—That is my objection. It is outside of our jurisdiction, entirely, to inquire into anything of that kind.

Mr. Bartow—Well, gentlemen, you heard the proposition here. I would like a vote upon it; it would be arbitrary for one man to assume to reject testimony. I would like to have an expression of the committee upon it; I do not want to dictate in a matter of that kind whether a question shall be put or not, or whether the investigation shall be gone into or not. If it was in regard to a particular question, I would decide the admissibility or inadmissibility of the question. In regard to the subject matter, I would like to have each member of the committee express themselves, whether they consider it a proper subject of inquiry.

Mr. Seager—Mr. Chairman: I did not intend to say a word upon this question, but if I understand the difference between the members of the committee, it is upon this point: if there was any claim here that there was a practice of this kind prevalent in the prison, or that it was customary, that it was usual to subject relatives of the prisoners visiting the prison to any solicitations of this character, there would then be, I think, propriety in the Legislature, under certain restrictions, going into the inquiry; but I do not understand that there is even a rumor of that kind afloat. The most that is attempted to be urged here is one isolated case possibly, and that isolated case relates simply to the person soliciting and the person to whom the solicitation was made. Whether that report is true or false, I know nothing about it whatever. While it is true, as stated by Mr. Webber, that it is not in the power of this committee, it is not in the power of the Legislature to inflict any punishment, it is equally true that this investigation has back of it a character that is not given to an ordinary trial for what you do here to-day, to-morrow is read in every family, almost, throughout the entire State, through the medium of the daily press. You bring up a man, he may not be here, he has no opportunity to meet this accusation, and you will admit here merely hearsay testimony to which, if the committee sees fit to go into this thing, let them subpœna before them the witnesses who do know the facts, and not take testimony which should not be taken in the ordinary police courts.

Mr. Bartow—well, I should think it would be proper to ask the witness the question as to what he knew and what transpired in the presence and within the knowledge of the prison officials tending to demoralize the morality and management of the prison. I should think it would be improper to go into a general examination of the matter without confining it to what was done inside of the prison and in the presence and within the knowledge of the prison officials. Suppose a person visit the prison, and it was done in such a way that it did not tend to demoralize the prison by being done openly or within the knowledge of the prison officials, then it is a question whether it is really proper to investigate it.

Mr. Mellen—It seems to me proper.

Mr. Conely—I might suggest that this witness has stated that he has no knowledge on the subject, and at this time it is not, perhaps, practicable to make any determination, if this witness knows nothing of it, the further consideration of it can be postponed until the question comes up again.

By *Mr. Bartow* :

Q. Do you know anything personally ?

A. No, sir.

Mr. Webber—I am not satisfied fully with that answer. The manner in which it is given leads me to believe that the witness has more knowledge on the subject, and I desire to ask him this question :

Q. Have you ever had any conversation with Mr. Morris, while he was Agent, on the subject ?

A. No, sir.

Q. Have you ever heard him, in speaking of that subject to you, or to any one else, make any statements which, in your judgment, had any meaning in that direction ?

A. You confine that to persons that are connected with the prison, or have friends that are connected with the prison ?

Q. Yes, sir.

A. No, sir.

Q. I then ask it with reference to any female visiting the prison ?

Mr. Conely—Well, that we object to. The grounds of our objection are already stated. It is not necessary to repeat what we have stated before.

Mr. Bartow—I guess we had better withhold it until we have a consultation of the committee alone.

Mr. Webber—I desire to ask the witness this question. [Reads question, as follows :] While you were at the prison, and Mr. Morris was Agent, have you any knowledge of your own, or from information derived from Mr. Morris, that any female visiting the prison was treated by any official of the prison in any improper manner or that any improper language was addressed to her by any such officer ? If so, state the circumstances thereof.

Mr. Morris—So far as I am personally concerned, I do not object to the question at all.

Mr. Conely—Now, this question, with certain limitations, we shall not object to. I do not know but what Mr. Webber may be willing to embody these limitations in the question when they are suggested: "While you were at the prison, and Mr. Morris was Agent, have you any knowledge of your own, or from information derived from Mr. Morris," with the understanding that means information obtained directly from Mr. Morris, and not from other sources, "that any female visiting the prison was treated by any official of the prison in any improper manner," now, if that is confined to treatment that she received while at the prison, I see no objection to it, "or that any improper language was addressed to her by any such official." If that is confined to language addressed to her while in the prison, I see no objection to the question; so that, if this question is either modified by writing it, or by explaining it to the witness, that he is to confine his answers to what occurred in the prison, we have no objection to it.

Mr. *Webber*—Shall the question be asked?

Mr. *Bartow*—I do not see any objection to it.

Mr. *Webber*—I do not wish to ask the question with any verbal explanation in connection with it. I desire to ask the question and let the witness answer the identical question which I ask, without having any verbal explanation connected with it, to tell him what it means. If the question is not specific enough so he can understand what it means, then the question is not specific enough to be asked.

Mr. *Conely*—I would ask Mr. Webber if there is any objection to having written there, the words "while at the prison," in the two places that I suggested?

Mr. *Livingstone*—I think the question better be answered just as Mr. Webber puts it.

[Question read by the stenographer]
A. I have no such knowledge whatever.

By Mr. Webber:

Q. Were you present at any time when Mr. Morris was reading to the convicts assembled, or any considerable part of them?

A. Yes, sir; quite frequently.

Q. State whether on any occasion, Mr. Morris' manner or his language, when reading and speaking to the convicts, was of such a character as to affect injuriously the discipline of the prison?

A. In my opinion, that would be?

Q. Yes, sir, of course it would be only that.

A. State the question again, please.

[Question read by the stenographer.]

A. Well, in my opinion, it was at times.

Q. Describe wherein?

A. There were some instances,—some matter that Mr. Morris read that I regarded as very improper to be read before those convicts; simply a matter of opinion of course.

Q. State it, and describe the language?

A. I may not be able to recall but a portion of them. There were a great many. At one time Mr. Morris was reading an article to the boys, and it seemed that where the article—he interlined on a paper something that was original with himself; he read a portion of it from a book, and a portion of it from his manuscript, and I remember distinctly one remark that was from this manuscript as he read it, describing a flock of sheep; when a stranger approached them in the field, that they would all start and run, and then would turn their heads around and look back. And Mr. Morris said the reason why they turned their heads around was because they had no eyes in the other extremity. That I regarded as improper; perhaps others might not.

Q Any other instance of that kind, that occurs to you?

A. Well, there was another matter in very much the same line that I remember. I recollect Mr. Morris was reading an article,—I am not positive, but I think it was his own production, something that was original with himself,—he was describing the influence of frienship. I cannot remember much of the article, only the point that I want to make is this: he said to them, speaking of their wives and sisters, "if they hadn't any sisters they could love someb dy else's sisters." I thought to these convicts that expression tended to degrade him with them; that is how I looked at it.

Q. Any other cases of that kind?

A. Not that I recollect at present; there were a great many cases, but I do not recollect.

Q. State whether his manner with the convicts was uniformly dignified and reserved, or whether it was sometimes in that manner, and sometimes familiar?

A. Well, in Mr. Morris, the fore part of his administration, as I said before, there was a good deal of undue familiarity, that is, in the beginning. He overcome that, to some extent, before I left there. I was there nearly two years with Mr. Morris, and the first season that he was there—the first year that he was there, there certainly was an undue familiarity, and it tended to demoralize the prison; it had that tendency; it affected the discipline of the prison, and every subordinate officer that was there, that had had more experience than Mr. Morris, felt it. They attributed it to inexperience on the part of the Agent, and I thought it was in a great degree so. You understand me; a general feeling of insecurity on the part of the officers. Now, Mr. Morris is charged here with undue cruelty, which I never saw anything of. I think I stated that; but there was an undue familiarity there—an undue sympathy that was not tempered with good judgment.

Q. While you were there did you ever know of any of the convicts being punished by being tied up by the wrists and left in that position, with their wrists above their heads?

A. There was one man—oh, tied up in this shape? [Witness holding hands above his head.]

Q Yes, sir?

A. No, sir, I never did.

Q. Do you recollect of a convict there by the name of Spencer?

A. Yes.

Q Do you recollect of the occasion of the visit of his wife to the prison?

A. I never knew her or saw her in the world.

Q You have no knowledge on that subject?

A. No, sir, no personal knowledge.

By Mr. Livingstone:

Q. Were you there during Mr. Bingham's administration?

A. Yes, sir, for about two and a half years, I think.

Q What was the state of discipline during Mr. Bingham's administration, the time that you were there, previous to Mr. Morris taking hold, as compared with Mr. Morris' regime?

A. Well, Mr. Bingham—he was rather vindictive. Bingham was a very thorough business man.

Q. Do I understand you that Mr. Bingham was very vindictive?

A. I think so. He was sometimes very vindictive; but he never had any pets in the prison. He said to me, one day after he resigned, "I think I have never had any pets in the prison." I think he never had: I never knew him to have any. His style was if a convict or free man got in the way, their toes got hurt every time; on the whole, I think he was a good man; but there was some things that I thought, in his discipline, was very severe. He had a fine state of discipline, and his finances show that.

Q The point I want to get at is this : were the punishments that were inflicted during Mr. Bingham's administration more severe than those that were inflicted during Mr. Morris' administration?

A. I think they were.

Mr. Bartow—Well, I do not know why we should be going into Mr. Bingham's administration, because there is no resolution directing any inquiry there, and Mr. Bingham is not there. And we could not do any good in that respect even if it were directed to him. It is certainly outside of any resolution of inquiry ; and it would be extending it much more than we ought to do ; I think it will take up time, and space, and expense that we have no right to go into.

Mr. Livingstone—I did not ask the question with the intention of going into Mr. Bingham's administration. I asked it for another purpose ; but, however, I am perfectly willing to withdraw it if the committee object.

Mr. Bartow—It seems to me that it would be unnecessarily extending it.

Mr. Livingstone—Well, I am not sure but there has been other questions asked here that might have been objected to on that same ground.

Mr. Bartow—That may be. As a comparison between the two, Mr. Morris might be an improvement.

Mr. Morse :

Q. How long were you in the prison?

A. About four years and three months I think I was there.

Q. You resigned your position there?

A. No, sir ; I was discharged.

Q. Who by?

A. By Mr. Morris.

Q. What were you discharged for?

A. For opposing his re-appointment, two years ago.

Q. How do you know that was the reason?

A. There was no other reason stated. He wrote me a letter relieving me from duty.

Mr. Conely—Have you got that letter?

A. Yes, sir, I have the letter, but not with me.

Mr. Conely—Well, the letter better be produced if it is desired to be used.

Mr. Livingstone—Not being a lawyer, I do not know whether it would be a proper question or not, but I would like to ask the witness whether there is any animus existing between Mr. Morris and himself,—whether he feels perfectly friendly towards Mr. Morris or not?

A. Now, in answering that question, I might explain my relations with Mr. Morris.

Mr. Conely—Oh, just answer the question.

Mr. Webber—The witness has a right to answer it in a qualified way.

The Witness—It won't take me very long.

Mr. Conely—I withdraw any objection so far as I am concerned.

STATE PRISON INVESTIGATION. 127

Witness—I did not like Mr. Morris' administration as an agent. He never did me any harm in the world. He never interfered with me as an officer in any way. There was another man applied for the place, and when the man came up as between the two men, I said I should support Mr. Lane, and the matter finally came up between Mr. Morris and myself, and in regard to the matter—he opened a letter of mine that was directed by a convict, and retained it and presented it to the board of inspectors. I went in and asked him for the letter. At that time I told him, says I, " personally I have no feeling in the matter—I don't believe in you as an Agent. If I have any influence, I am going to help the other man." And he did just exactly as I would have done, when he relieved us fellows that opposed him. I never blamed him a particle, nor never had any feelings, not a particle. Afterwards Mr. Morris approached me in the street and he said there was some reason at present in regard to my conduct there that was dark and bad, and he forbid me coming in there to see a convict that I was endeavoring to get pardoned. I do not think he told the truth, because I asked Mr. Wilcox—he was to investigate the matter. From that time I felt as though he did me injustice, because I always endeavored to do my duty there as an officer, and so far as the discharge was concerned, there never was no feeling, he done just as any man would have done. We opposed him, and he beat us, and we took a back seat. That was all square work. That is my explanation of the whole circumstance.

Mr. Eggleston:
Q. Did you ever hear of any case of whipping in the prison besides the case of John Layton?
A. That was the only case that grew out of a report of mine. I stated this nigger Albert that was whipped in my shop; he was one of my men, but it did not grow out of my report. His day's work had been raised and he had this iron and he shut himself up and he said he never would come out until his day's work was taken down, and Mr. Morris took measures to get him out.

Mr. Livingstone—Mr. Eggleston asked you if you ever knew of any other case?
A. I have heard spoken of them.
Q. Was he whipped severely?
A. I do not think the whip was ever used severely after Mr. Morris came there. I never knew of an instance.

Mr. Mellen—Did you know of Thurston being whipped while you were there?
A. I knew a man by the name of Thurston—an old man, but I did not ever know of his being whipped.

Mr. Webber:
Q. What do you call a severe whipping?
A. Well, when I was an officer of the prison my mode of arranging matters was to be just as kind to them as they would allow me to; I never gave a man an order when a request would accomplish the object. In my shop, instead of sitting up in the seat all day, I would go around among the men and encourage them, talk to them and do the best I could to make them friends to me. And my theory of prison discipline is, when a man got up and positively opposed the authorities, the quicker you got him off from that pony the better it was for the prison.
Q. You have not answered my question. What would you consider a severe whipping?
A. Well, to whip a man until he says "enough," I would not consider severe. A man knows his own business. If a man gets up there, if he has been care-

fully managed by the officer, and he has forced the officer to report him, if he forced himself in that position, then I say punish him until he gets off his horse; or, in other words, until he will get down and say "enough," and be a man. Now, there was the dark cell; that used to have no immediate eff ct. Of course in a short time,—in 24 hours,—it would injure a man's health more than half a dozen whippings. You never injure a man by whipping; you never hurt anything but his will. I always regarded the whipping as the more humane.

Q. You do not answer my question yet. What would you consider a severe punishment? How many blows?

A. Well, sir, I cannot answer that question; I don't know how to do it.

Q. Would you consider a hundred lashes a severe punishment?

A. Yes, sir; I should consider it outrageous.

Q. Would you consider fifty a severe whipping?

A. Well, I know one man that I think got fifty; I think he deserved it. I do not think it was severe.

Q. I am trying to get at your idea of a severe whipping.

A. Well, I think a hundred lashes would be severe under any circumstances.

Q. Well, would you consider fifty severe?

A. Ordinarily I should think it would be. There are cases, I say, when fifty lashes was not any too severe.

Q. Well, would it not be severe anyhow?

A. It would be severe, of course; fifteen lashes would be severe.

Q. Now, in your judgment, would fifty lashes be severe punishment?

A. Yes, sir; it would be a severe punishment, and yet there are instances where an Agent would be perfectly justified; there is no question about that.

Mr. Bartow—What kind of a whip did they use for whipping when you were there?

A. Always when I was there they used a common raw-hide.

Mr. Livingstone—Did you ever know a whip to be used with wires braided in the lash?

A. No, sir.

Mr. Bartow—Were you there when the strap was substituted for the lash?

A. No, the whip hung in the hall, I think, when I left.

Mr. Livingstone—Which, in your judgment, would be the most severe, being whipped with the lash or being whipped with the strap?

A. I never had either one, consequently I cannot answer it. They used to use the paddle when I first went there. That was a mode of punishment that Mr. Morris never used.

Mr. Eggleston—Was the Agent, Mr. Morris, partial to any class of convicts, in your judgment?

A. Yes, sir; he was.

Q. State the class.

A. The class of men that had my sympathy the least used to get his the most. We all, of course, that were there had a theory of prison discipline. I had a theory of my own, and the class of men that came to the prison that had never had any friends, that had drifted right into crime naturally, and had fallen simply into State prison, and were ignoramuses, was the class of men that I could put up with more than any other class of men in the prison, because I sympathised with them. One boy by the name of Guile, he never had any friends, never had any parents to take care of him; he had slept in dry goods boxes, around blacking boots, and the first thing he knew, when he got old enough, they sent him to prison. But there was a class of convicts in the prison that were educated men; they were men, when they were outside, of refinement; men that had held positions of profit and trust, and had betrayed that trust and got into prison; and that was the class that received his favors, and I disapproved of it. It was invariably the case.

Mr. Morse—Did Mr. Morris have the reputation for cruelty among his subordinates in his punishment?

A. Never that I heard any thing of the kind.

Cross-examined by Mr. Conely:

Q. The reputation during the early part of Mr. Morris' administration was right the other way, was it not? He was too lax; too lenient?

A. Yes, sir.

Q. He came there with some theories in regard to humanity in prison management that differed from the formerly accepted theories of state prison management, did he not, that he undertook to put in practice?

A. Now, I never accepted Mr. Bingham's theory of prison management any more fully than I did Mr. Morri's.

Q. Well, I speak of those that had been put in practice. He came there with theories different from those that had been put in practice in prison?

A. Yes, sir.

Q. That would be regarded, at any rate, as more humane?

A. Yes, sir. He tried a long while to get along without using the whip, as I said before : The time was, I say, before the whip was bought and introduced, that there was no discipline in the prison, and no officer was safe to take issue with a convict.

Q. The system, then, under which he first started there, in your judgment, proved a failure?

A. Yes, sir, it did.

Q. Now how was this sympathy for the educated class, as you style them, manifested?

A. Well, I had one in my shop, his name was Talliday, he was a major in the army. Mr. Morris came in the shop frequently and conversed with him from half an hour to an hour or an hour and a half, sitting in the shop and conversing with him.

Q. Do you know of any other instance?

A. Yes, sir.

Q. What was that?

A. I do not know that I can recall the name,—that hospital steward—Leonard.

Q. He is the fellow that got cured of that sickness?

A. Yes, sir, he insulted Mr Morris; he got the big-head, you know.

Q. What did he do to indicate that he had special sympathy for him?

A. He used to visit with him ; Mr. Rice of Adrian, a man that came there for two years, Mr. Morris made a good deal of him—really associated with him, as he did not with other convicts.

Q. Did you know this Rice?

A. I knew him, certainly, before he came there.

Q. You know that he came there on a plea of guilty of forgery?

A. I think he told me that he did ; yes, sir.

Q. Do you not remember that the circumstances under which he committed the forgery were circumstances of great temptation?

A. Well, different men might differ on that subject.
Q. Well, did not you hear that to be the fact?
A. Yes, sir; I heard him state it.
Q. Was not the sympathy of the whole southeastern portion of the State, at the time of his conviction, aroused in favor of this man Rice?
A. I do not think it was, from my knowledge that I have had since I left the prison; I have had business with him down there, and that was not the case, sir, among people that knew him; he got up sympathy in the prison.
Q. Did not he have the sympathy of everybody that was acquainted with him at the time of his conviction?
A. I do not know whether he did or not; I know that he has not the sympathy of people that I always was led to believe he did until I had some business with him.
Q. Now, I understand you to say that this sympathy of Mr. Morris manifested itself in the giving of books and magazines?
A. There has not been any question asked in regard to that; that I regarded as a very wise and judicious measure in prison discipline; always did.
Q. He introduced that, did he?
A. Yes, sir; the magazine matter he introduced in lieu of tobacco, which, certainly, must be a good thing.
Q. Do you remember of any other person in whose favor discrimination was made than those you have named?
A Yes, sir.
Q. To whom?
A. That Spencer was one that was spoken of.
Q. Well, to what did it extend in his case?
A. He was allowed to go outside, and run all over the prison, and be as saucy as he pleased to any one.
Q. To whom was he saucy?
A. To any officer that crossed his path.
Q. What particular officer do you mean?
A. Well, there was a general disposition of impertinence on his part while he run loose in the hall.
Q. Was he ever saucy to you?
A. Yes, sir.
Q. Did you report it?
A. No, sir.
Q. Was he ever saucy to any other officer to your knowledge?
A. Not to my personal knowledge, that I recollect.
Q. You say he went outside; to what extent did he go outside?
A. I do not know; I have seen him outside several times.
Q. Do you know how long before his time expired?
A. No, I do not; four or five months, three or four months, it might not have been more than two.
Q. Every man is allowed to go outside whose time is pretty much through, ain't he?
A. Certainly; the difference was here: he was gate-runner, this Charley Spencer, and they allowed him to run all over the yard; they sent him all over the yard by virtue of the position he held; and in consequence of something, I do not know what, he was different from any other gate-runner we ever had; he

ranked himself, in his own feelings at least, in his department as high as any other man in the prison, and we used to attribute it to that thing.

Q. Now, this influence that you speak of as favoritism occurred during the time that Mr. Morris was trying to have established there his theory of humanity, did not they?

A. Well, not wholly; I think the whip was introduced within two or three months after Mr. Morris came there; I do not remember, however, I am not clear; I think Mr. Morris withheld the whip as long as he could, and when he finally used it, I think he whipped two men the first day, and then from that time the whip was used occasionally.

Q. Did Mr. Morris always maintain a disposition of humanity in the prison as a whole?

A. Oh, we had nothing to do with his favoritism; that was an outside issue.

By Mr. Jones:

Q. From your experience there in prison, did you consider yourself an expert in the management and discipline of a prison?

A. Oh, not more so than others; I gave that my attention when I was there; I gave it my whole attention; when I left it I let it alone, and since that I have had something else to do.

EDMUND LEAVENWORTH, SWORN.

Examined by Mr. Bartow:

Q. Where do you reside?
A. Leslie, in this county.
Q. Have you ever been engaged at the prison?
A. I was there; yes, sir.
Q. From what time to what time?
A. Well, about the last of October or first of September, 1871, I commenced there. I was there until May, 1873.
Q. In what capacity were you engaged at the prison.
A. I commenced as a guard. I was afterwards a keeper, and was gate keeper at the front gate.
Q. At what time did you say your time determined there?
A. I think the last of Oct., 1871; it might have been in Sept.
Q. No, no; what time did you quit?
A. The last of April, or the first of May, 1873.
Q. What part of the prison were you in during the time you were guard there?
A. I was in the trip-hammer shop a short time, then went into the blacksmith shop, and was there, I think, nearly a year.
Q. What were your duties as guard?
A. Well, the same as any other guard. I was on duty six hours.
Q. Well, I mean simply what was your business. What part of the business did you perform as guard?
A. Well, while I was guard proper, I was an all night guard in the east wing. I went there in the first place to do substitute business, that is, if the keeper was sick a day or two, I would take his place; if a guard was sick, I took his place.
Q. While acting as an officer, were you a good deal of the time in the company of Mr. Morris?
A. No, sir.

Q. Did you witness punishment for offenses while you were there?
A. Never but one, while I was a keeper in the shop.
Q. Well, while you were engaged at the prison, I mean?
A. I saw some cases of showering after I went around to the front gate.
Q. Well, describe the mode of this showering.
A. Well, the convict is stripped of his clothes, or left on, as the case may be, sometimes one, and sometimes the other, his hands are tied behind him, to an iron gate generally, and the hose is handled—they use the Holly water—a small stream of water, and it is thrown on to the convict all over.
Q. Who inflicted the punishment that you witnessed?
A. I think as a general thing when I saw it, Mr. Morris did it; sometimes a deputy.
Q. Now, where was this stream of water directed against the person that was punished?
A. It was a punishment.
Q. I say, where was it directed against them,—what part of their body?
A. Oh, all over generally,—sometimes only the feet were showered.
Q. Did it seem to be directed to any particular part of the body?
A. I never saw one punished when it seemed to be directed entirely to one place.
Q. How long did you see any person punished with the shower bath?
A. Well, I can't hardly say; perhaps sometimes twenty minutes in all, with intervals.
Q. How long was the longest that you ever saw any one?
A. I say perhaps twenty minutes, but showered at intervals, not twenty minutes constant showering.
Q. Well, during how long a time would it be that he was showered. This twenty minutes, you mean that the stream was directed upon him twenty minutes?
A. Most of the time; generally shower him a little while, and then stop and ask him if he had anything to say, any promises to make, anything of that kind. If he did not, the water was applied again, or if his reply was saucy or defiant, as it sometimes was.
Q. Can you recall any particular case now, where a convict was showered as punishment?
A. I don't call to mind now any particular man. I was at the front gate. Sometimes, nothing else to do, I would step inside and see the convict showered,—not a great many times.
Q. Have you ever seen any other means of punishment inflicted there than the shower bath?
A. I saw one colored man whipped.
Q. Do you remember his name?
A. Well, I think his name was Albert; I don't know any other name. I don't know but he was in Mr. Parmenter's shop; I don't recollect exactly whether he was, or Mr. Adams'.
Q. Do you know what he was punished for?
A. I don't; I never inquired.
Q. Do you know for what offense any of the men were showered?
A. No.
Q. Who reported these men for offenses?

A. Well, the keeper generally reported the men to the deputy, and he either took the man in, or went in and reported the case, as I understood it.

Q. Well, when those cases were reported for any infraction of the rules, what mode was instituted for investigating the truth of the charge?

A. Well, I don't know,—not after he left the shop.

Q. You were not present during the investigation of any of the charges?

A. The deputy when he would come out of the shop, if he was sent for, would generally inquire into the case, of the keeper, get what information he could from him, talk the matter over a little (he did with me), to find out what there was of the case.

Q. You say you saw this one man whipped?

A. Yes, sir.

Q. How many lashes were applied?

A. I could not say.

Q. How was the man prepared for being whipped?

A. I don't remember whether his shirt was taken off or not, now. His wrists were tied together and drawn up.

Q. You don't know whether he was entirely naked, or not?

A. No; I know he had his pants on. I think he had his pantaloons on. I am not positive whether his shirt was on or not.

Q. Well, do you know whether there was any marks left after the whipping, from the whipping?

A. No; I did not examine him at all.

Q. Have you stated now all that you know about the punishment of convicts while you were there?

A. I think I have stated all I know about it.

A. A. ALLEN RECALLED.

Examined by Mr. Bartow:

Q. During the time that you were there as keeper, did you witness partiality shown to the prisoners by Mr. Morris?

A. Well, I saw what looked to me to be a difference in treatment of convicts sometimes; things that was not in accordance with my ideas.

Q. Well, did you notice any difference in times, whether a convict would be punished for an offense at one time, and at other times would seemingly escape for the same offense?

A. No, sir; I never reported a man but once but what he was punished, and then I reported him as a protection to myself. Mr. Webster was a little rigorous. I was told when I went on to that track, that he would, in a measure, run me, or he would run me out. Well, this man Smith, that we had this discussion about; this foreman was a high tempered man, and a very bad man to manage; and he had been punished for this offense of throwing the contents of this bucket. Well, there was several things come out; I had done the best I could with him to keep him from punishment; to make him behave himself. They put him on to boxing wheels, the man that worked with him had the management of it, and a man wants to be skillful and experienced to do that kind of work. He was taken sick; I thought he was playing off, and reported him, this man Raymer. I always made my reports to Mr. Martin, only in just this one instance, I told Mr. Morris what I thought about Raymer. I thought he was playing off, but he could tell a smooth story. And that throwed the work onto Smith, and he could not understand it, and made a mistake in boxing eighty wheels, and the wheels did not tram,—what they call tram; and Webster came there and was very wroth from it, and he said the man had got to be reported. He said I should report him. I told him I would not; I did not think the man was vicious, I thought it was a mistake, I thought he did the best he could. He said so much about it that I did not report him in the ordinary way. After the men were locked that night I went in, and Mr. Morris and Mr. Martin were sitting in the window, and I stated to them what Smith had done with the boxes; that he had boxed eighty wheels so the work had all got to be did over again. Mr. Martin thought he had better be punished, and I thought not. Mr. Martin said it was none of my busines, and Mr. Morris intimated that they would decide on that question; I told them of course they would, but I should plead for the man, because I knew his temper. I did not want him punished; if they would hold that over him, and let me manage him, I would manage him a good while then without any reports. They did not say whether they would do it or not; but I talked awhile, and in the morning he came out, and he was not punished. This man Raymer, I thought that he ought to have been punished and sent back and made to work. But he was one of that class of men that if there was anybody there that would get favors, he would get it, because he was a smooth talker.

Q. Now, did there seem to be a class of men that would get favors in preference to any other class?

A. Well, I think there was.

Q. What was the class that seemed to receive his favors?

A. They were the most intelligent, refined, and gentlemanly appearing men; men that knew how to be gentlemen. Because there is lots of those fellows there that do know how to be gentlemen. If there was a good place they would pull for it, and they were likely to get it. That Spencer that was spoken of; they came into my shop once; I had a seat built up so I could overlook the shop, and he took his place very dignifiedly in my seat, and I pushed him out of it. I did not report him; I don't know whether he did me or not. I did not hear anything of it.

Q. Did you notice anything while you were there, in regard to Mr. Morris' moral conduct, in the presence of the keepers, or any of the officials there, or convicts?

A. Well, that was objectionable?

Q. Yes.

A. No, sir; I don't think I did.

Cross-examination by Conely:

Q. Were you discharged at the same time Mr. Parmenter was?

A. I was not discharged at all.

Q. You resigned, did you?

A. I did.

Q. You were one of those who sustained Mr. Lane very strongly two years ago?

A. Well, I sustained Mr. Lane strongly after I left the prison; I did not before. I sustained him in my mind all the time; but I made no effort, no work for him until after I left the prison.

The further examination of witnesses was here adjourned until to-morrow morning at nine o'clock.

STATE PRISON INVESTIGATION.

SATURDAY MORNING, APRIL 10, 1875.

JOHN BEDFORD, SWORN.

Examined by Mr. Webber:

Mr. *Webber*—Mr. Chairman, before proceeding to the examination of witnesses this morning, to correct any impression that might be injurious to Mr. Morris, from the objection to the question asked the witness, Parmenter, yesterday, while on the stand, concerning improper language or treatment of females, by prison officials, I wish to say that I was led to ask the question by information which I had received, and which by subsequent conversation with the witness, I found was unfounded. Had I known before what I learned from the witness after he left the stand, I should not have asked the question.

Q. Mr. Bedford, state your age, residence, and occupation?
A. My residence is Jackson, Michigan; my age is forty-nine, sir.
Q. Occupation?
A. Restaurant.
Q. How long have you resided at Jackson?
A. Six years this month. Six years about the first of May.
Q. Have you ever been employed at the prison?
A. I have, sir.
Q. In what capacity and when?
A. I went to the prison six years ago, somewhere about the first of May; and have been employed there until last April, as a keeper.
Q. Until April 1874?
A. Yes, sir; one year ago about, I was there nearly five years, lacking a few days of it.
Q. Do you remember at what time Mr. Morris took charge of the prison, as Agent?
A. I do, sir.
Q. Confine your testimony to matters that took place after Mr. Morris took charge as Agent; will you state what punishment was inflicted in the prison while you were there,—the kinds of punishment, I mean?
A. When Mr. Morris came there the whip was used, confinement in the cell, and clogged,—what we call clogged; I believe it was termed in that way; that was an iron band around the ankle.
Q. After Mr. Morris came there I speak of,—what were the punishments?
A. After Mr. Morris came there?
Q. Yes.
A. I understood you to say at the time Mr. Morris came there.
Q. No, confine your testimony, I say, to the time after he took charge of the prison; what were the punishments resorted to?
A. Showering, some with the lash, the wire cap, confining in cells, I believe were the punishments that he used. I heard that there was a cross, but I never saw it; that I don't know nothing about; I never saw it in my life.
Q. What opportunities had you to observe the punishments inflicted on convicts?
A. Not a great deal; my business was in the shop, and convicts were not punished there. Occasionally, in going to and fro, I might have seen something

STATE PRISON INVESTIGATION.

of the kind. My opportunities for seeing were not very frequent. I was confined to the shop strictly.

Q. Did you have opportunities to observe the manner in which Mr. Morris treated convicts, as to whether there was a uniform equanimity of temper or otherwise?

A. I don't know that I ever saw Mr. Morris show any temper to a convict but once.

Q. When was that?

A. At the time Thurston had the knife.

Q. And Thurston was the convict you mean?

A. Yes, sir; Thurston was the convict; that was at the time Mr. Morris took the knife from him.

Q. Did you witness Thurston's punishment?

A. I did part of it, sir.

Q. Which, the first or second?

A. The second; the first one I think I did not; I heard of it and I saw Thurston in the bare cell. It was my duty to lock that tier of cells, and when I got to that cell Thurston was in it and was very boisterous; made some heavy threats; I believe one threat he made was that he would cut Mr. Morris' guts out, to use the expression that he used. I reported the fact to the deputy, and also advised Thurston to keep quiet, that that would only get him into trouble, making any such threats as those. This was previous to his first punishment that he made those threats.

Q. What evidence of anger did Mr. Morris exhibit at that time?

A. Well, he ordered Thurston to give him that knife; he was a little red in the face, and I probably should have been the same when I knew that the man had prepared a knife to kill me with it, if he could.

Q. Did you observe any other evidence of anger?

A. No, sir; not particularly; he did not show nothing. He was quite red in the face; there were several keepers present, quite a number of them, and I guess they all probably were a little red in the face.

Q. Well, just confine yourself to the question. Do you know of a convict named Budlong in the prison?

A. I can't remember him by name?

Q. Did you ever witness any showering in the prison?

A. Yes, sir, I did.

Q. Describe the manner in which that punishment was inflicted?

A. Sometimes it was a man's pants rolled up above his knees, and his feet showered; sometimes I have seen the man naked and showered.

Q. On what part of the person was the stream applied when stripped naked?

A. Oh, all over the body alike; a moment here and a moment there.

Q. Was the showering applied on the front or rear of the person?

A. The front, sir, whenever I saw it.

Q. State whether you ever witnessed any instance of severe showering?

A. I did once, sir; a man was showered in the wash-house; I saw the showering by Capt. Winans in the wash-house. I can't speak the name of the convict, but he was a red-headed fellow that worked in the cabinet shop. Names I can't remember very well. I think Mr. Winans showered him unjustly; or not unjustly, but with too much severity.

Q. With undue severity?

A. With undue severity; yes, sir; showered too long.

STATE PRISON INVESTIGATION. 137

Q. What effect followed the showering?
A. The man was sent to the shop, I believe.
Q. What indication did you discover that led you to suppose that it was unduly severe?
A. Because I was close by at the time; I was in the shoe shop; I was close by, and I knew about when he commenced and I knew about when he quit.
Q. How long did it continue?
A. I could not tell you, sir; I paid no attention to it; it was rather unusual. Mr. Morris wasn't there, but whether he was about the premises anywhere I don't know; but he was not there at that time.
Q. Describe the physical condition of this convict after having received the showering, as to whether he was apparently or really injured by the showering?
A. I could not say that the man was injured, because I was not near enough to him, nor did not see enough of him afterwards for a few days. I believe the next time I saw him he was at the meal table in the dining-room; I was not close enough to see that the man was injured. The man hollered out a little, considerable. I know he got a pretty good showering.
Q. Did you ever witness any other instance of showering that you thought was severe?
A. I witnessed the showering of two men that hid out one night in the yard; crept under what was termed the "old tannery building." I saw those two showered. Well, I should think they were showered probably from three to five minutes; nothing severe about it at all; that is, no injury could arise.
Q. Any other instance of punishment that you witnessed?
A. I saw a man wear a wire cap for a long time.
Q. For how long a time would that wire cap be worn?
A. Well, my impression is that it would go from ten to thirty days, according to the charges preferred against the man. I think there was a case where a man wore a wire cap thirty days; but I guess they had made their escape over the wall. Sometimes for minor offenses the cap was probably put on for ten or twelve days, something of that kind; it is a matter I never paid any particular attention to.
Q. Describe this wire cap.
A. Well, sir, it is a small collar on the neck, and two pieces of wire going this way, and two pieces this way. This little collar was fastened with a lock and collar, about—well, a half inch or five-eighths, light material, just sufficient to hold this wire. Those little wires are probably about the thickness of that [indicating].
Q. Describe the cap.
A. Well, I could not give you the size of the wire.
Q. One-eighth of an inch?
A. It would be about the size of a common bale of a patent pail.
Mr. Bartow—Were these two wires all, or were they all braided in meshes?
A. No, sir; there was only the four wires; one coming up this way, and one this way; that would make two wires doubled up across the center of the head large enough so a man could put his every-day-cap right on under that wire and wear it as usual.
Q. State whether convicts wearing that wire cap were sent to work as usual.
A. Yes, sir; it did not hinder them.
Q. Were the caps removed at meal-time?
A. No, sir.

Q. Were they removed at night?

A. I think not, sir; the men came in with them on in the morning.

Q. What would you consider the milder punishment?

A. The showering of the feet, and putting this cap on them, was considered very mild puishment. Locking them in the bare cell was considered mild punishment. A man put in at evening when they were marched in after the day's work, put into the cell, and along, I think, as a usual rule, between eight and nine o'clock, for little, minor offenses, they were unlocked and sent to their cells. If the offense had been rather great, he would be kept in until morning.

Q. How long did you ever know a convict to be kept in a bare cell the longest?

A. Well, I don't know but what I have known a convict to be kept in the second night. I think Thurston was in, if I recollect right. He was in the second morning when I unlocked my tier. I rather think that is the longest that ever I knew of it. That is the longest that I can remember of, at least.

Q. While in the bare cell, state whether any provisions was taken them, and, if so, what?

A. That, I could not say; after we went to the shops in the morning, after breakfast, my opportunities to see anything of the kind were very limited indeed.

Q. State whether you ever witnessed any boxing of ears, or slapping in the the face, or kicking, by Mr. Morris, of convicts.

A. I never saw any, sir, not to my knowledge. I don't think I ever saw Mr. Morris box a convict's ears. I heard of it, but I did not see it.

Q. What opportunities had the convicts to converse with free men who were workmen in the shops?

A. They were allowed to converse with them on anything relative to their work. But they were not, but they did, and quite a number of times,—twice I am certain of,—I reported the foreman for that offense.

Q. For talking concerning other matters than their work?

A. Yes, sir. But the usual rule was, if you saw a foreman talking to a convict, and you thought he was talking a little too long, to go to see what it was about, and, perhaps, make the observation that he was doing a little unnecessary talking. Well, it was about this piece of work, or it was about that piece of work, so a keeper could not say anything; but it was against the rules if they did.

Q. State whether you ever knew a foreman discharged for a breach of the regulations; for talking to convicts concerning other matters than the work?

A. I have known them to be shut out of the yard for their intercourse with the convicts; I don't know that I ever knew of a case where he was shut out exactly for talking to him; I don't think of any at present; for their intercourse with the convicts they have been shut out of the yard.

Q. What do you mean by intercourse?

A. Well, trafficking with them; perhaps bringing them in something that was against the rules to bring in.

Q. State whether while you were there you observed any improper treatment of convicts by the keepers other than you have stated?

A. Well, sir, my opportunities to see that were very small, except right in my own shop; the keepers are confined strictly to their own shops—they have no business anywhere else; that is their duty, right there.

Q. Was any discretion allowed the keepers as to what offenses they would report and what they would not?

STATE PRISON INVESTIGATION. 139

A. The rules was that every offense should be reported, let it be small or great; it was not alwas complied with, sir; sometimes like a man's talking— something of that kind, perhaps by talking to a man. or perhaps some graver offense, the keeper did not think it was sufficient, and a man promising to desist or would do better, he might not report him; I know that was my way of doing business, but as for the rest I can't answer; but I neglected to do that a number of times, when I did not think it was really necessary to do it.

Q. Were the reports made to the deputy in writing, or orally?

A. The keepers made them orally, sir; I think I never was called on but once to make a written report; that was under Mr. Bingham, not under Mr. Morris.

Q. When offenses were reported against convicts, what was the custom of the deputy as to inquiring into the truth of those reports?

A. As a general rule, if a man done anything wrong, why I sent for the deputy; the deputy came, and if he did not think it was hardly necessary to take the man in for the offense, perhaps he would reprimand him right there in the shop, and tell him what he might depend on if he done it again,—something of that kind; perhaps he would say, to-night you report him when you come in; but the agent in some grave offenses would perhaps send for the foreman, and perhaps send for the keeper, to inquire into this case, to find out what there was about it; I believe Mr. Morris has sent for me; I know he has, to inquire into the case to see what there was of it.

Q. Do you remember how many times you have been called before Mr. Morris to be examined concerning cases that you have reported?

A. Well, I have quite a number of times, but I could not tell you anything about the number.

Q. What proportion of the cases reported would you be called on to be examined concerning them?

A. I could not tell you that.

Q. Well, half the cases?

A. Well, I might, perhaps, one in every ten; nothing unless it was a case rather unusual—something of that kind.

Q. When you reported to the deputy, was it his custom to take down your report in writing at once in your presence?

A. I have seen it done right as I gave it; take out his book and write it right down as I gave it; other times I have not.

Q. What was the general custom in that regard?

A. Well, the general custom was not to do it, but then I have seen it done.

Q. Do you know at what time, when he did not do it in your presence, it was done?

A. No, sir, I could not tell you.

Q. Did you have any opportunity to examine the record to see whether all the reports which you made were upon the books?

A. No, sir; not under Mr. Morris' term.

Q. Did you discover any evidences while you were there of any discrimination in the treatment of the convicts, treating some more lenient than others; punishing some for offenses, when others, for like offenses, would be permitted to go unpunished?

A. I can't say that I did, not for two men with the same offense; I could not say that I ever knew of one getting punished unless the other did.

Mr. Bartow:

Q. Did you ever witness the punishment of riding the wooden cross?

A. Never but once, sir.

Q. Did you ever know of their being immersed in a cold bath?

A. In water?

Q. Yes.

A. No, sir; all the immersing ever I knew of was when a man first came there he was taken to the wash-house in a large tub and washed.

Q. Did you ever know of their being tied up by their hands?

A. Yes, sir.

Q. Describe how that was done.

A. Rope around the wrists in that way [indicating].

Q. Well, were they suspended?

A. Do I understand you from the floor?

Q. Yes.

A. No, sir.

Q. Would they be punished with the different modes of punishment for the different offenses, or would it be sometimes one mode of punishment and sometimes another for the same offense? The question is, whether for the same kind of an offense they would be whipped, or showered, or ride the wooden horse, or be clogged for the same class of offenses, in the discretion of the Agent. The question is, would the Agent use his discretion as to the mode of punishment for the same class of offenses, or whether a rule prescribing that they should be punished with one or the other of the modes for a certain class of offenses?

A. There is no rule that I ever knew of for any class of offenses.

Q. You think that the mode of punishment was entirely with the Agent, the mode of punishment, and according to the offense committed? I guess perhaps you don't understand me really now. I don't know as I properly express myself. The question is, supposing for the same class of offenses, could the Agent select his mode of punishment,—use his own discretion?

A. I think he could, sir.

Q. You think there was no rule prescribing any sort of punishment for any offense?

A. I think not, sir; I never saw any.

Q. Well, now, have you witnessed different punishments for the same class of offenses?

A. Yes, sir.

Q. Well, were some of them much more severe than others for the same class of offenses?

A. Twice that I know of personally, they both were about the same thing, as near as I could tell.

Q. Punished about alike?

A. Punished about alike.

Q. For the same offense?

A. For the same offense; that is all that came under my observation.

Q. The question was, whether you witnessed cases of punishment where some of them was much more severe than others for the same class of offenses?

A. I understand your question to be, whether a man for the same offense, would receive the same punishment.

Q. For the same class of offenses, whether he would sometimes be punished much more severely than others?

A. I think not; I stated to you that I knew of two cases, and they were both punished alike.

Q. You stated also that they were punished with different modes of punishment for the same class of offenses?
A. Yes, sir; two cases that I have in my mind that I knew.
Mr. Mellen:
Q. In that severe case of showering that you saw, did the showering continue after the convict hallooed?
A. Yes, sir.
Q. About how long should you think?
A. I could not tell you, sir, I had fifty men under my charge at that time, and my business was looking after them; I could not give you any idea of the time.
Q. Why was it that you got the impression that it was too severe?
A. It run too long; the man hallooed too much.
Q. Did his cries grow weaker as the showering continued?
A. I think not; he was a very heavy, large man, as heavy as myself, I think, or very near.
Mr. Nelson:
Q. What did he do when he was hallooing?
A. Oh, he said he would not do it again.
Q. Did he say that he submitted, or would submit to the rules of the prison?
A. He said, "I will not do it again if you will quit, I will never do it again if you will let me go this time, I will never do it again."
Mr. Mellen:
Q. You have no recollection how long the showering continued after he said that?
A. No, sir, I could not tell you.
Mr. Jones:
Q. Did it continue any length of time after he said that?
A. Well, some little time; perhaps two or three minutes, perhaps five, perhaps more; I could not confine myself to time.
Mr. Morse:
Q. What was this man's history in the prison that you speak of?
A. My impression is that the man was not very good in the upper story; I considered him a fool.
Q. Was he a troublesome man?
A. He would get troublesome occasionally, and occasionally he would be very good.
Q. Had he ever been punished before?
A. I think he had been punished before; not to my knowledge; that is I never saw it done.
Mr. Jones:
Q. Do you wish to be understood that he was a man not of sound mind?
A. I do, sir.
Mr. Mellen:
Q. What was his name?
A. I can't tell you his name, although I had him some under my charge.
Mr. Morris:
Q. Was it Bedlong that you refer to?
A. A red headed man at the upper cabinet shop; Bedlong, that is the name.
Mr. Jones:
Q. Was it because you thought he was of an unsound mind that you thought the punishment was too severe?

A. Well, sir, in order to answer that question, I have got to answer it twice. I thought it was too severe on such a man as he was.

Q. Do you know what his offense was?

A. I don't know, but I understood it was something about tearing his blankets in his cell; something about that, but I could not tell you what it was now.

Cross-examination by Mr. Seager:

Q. In addition to the other punishments that you mentioned being in use when Mr. Morris took the agency there, was the paddle used under the former administration, I mean?

A. It was, sir.

Q. What punishments were abolished by Mr. Morris when he came there?

A. I think the clog went out of use very quick after he came there; I think he ordered them off unanimously; I could not tell you the time, but I know they were taken off.

Q. What other punishments did he abolish; did he abolish the lash?

A. He abolished the lash for a considerable time.

Q. Did he the paddle?

A. I never heard a case of the paddle being used while Mr. Morris was there.

Q. Were those the most severe punishments in use in the prison,—the lash, the paddle, and the clog, at the time Mr. Morris went there?

A. I think they were, sir.

Q. What other measures, if any, that you regard as more humane, did he introduce into the management?

A. The men were allowed a half a sheet of paper once in three months when he went there; if my memory serves me right, he had been there but a very short time, when he told them if they would not abuse the privilege, that he would give them a sheet of paper, and they should write once a month. He held that out as an inducement for good behavior.

Q. Did he make the time from three months to one month, or reduce it gradually?

A. I believe he reduced it to two months first, and in a very short time reduced it to one month.

Q. What was the effect of that, so far as you observed it?

A. I think the effect was very good, sir.

Q. What reforms, if any, or changes, if any, in regard to books and magazines, reading matter generally, did he introduce?

A. He began to talk about introducing magazines, and finally made a statement to the convicts in the dining-room,—I am not giving this word for word as it was, it is a good while ago; I will give you the thing in substance,—that any man that had got to stay a year in the prison, that he would give him the privilege, or would furnish him with a magazine for that year, providin would give up his tobacco.

Q. They had a ration of tobacco given to them at that time, did they?

A. Yes, sir, they had.

Q. The proposition was if they would give up the tobacco, in the place of that he would give the man that gave it up, a magazine?

A. Yes, sir.

Q. Did he name the magazine that would be given to them—did he name them and let them pick from them?

A. I think he did name the magazines.

Q. Men allowed to select from them which one they would take?

STATE PRISON INVESTIGATION.   143

A. Yes, sir; he gave a list of such and such magazines, as I understood it.
Q. What was the effect of that proposition?
A. Very good, sir.
Q. Many of the men avail themselves of it?
A. Quite a large number, sir.
Q. Gave up the tobacco and took, instead, the magazine?
A. Yes, sir.
Q. Is that arrangement still continuing at the prison at the present time, or was at the time you left, I mean?
A. At the time I left those magazines were passing from cell to cell.
Q. How about newspapers?
A. Well, Mr. Morris had several talks with the men in the dining-room; that is, he talked several times to them in the dining-room relative to papers; told them how he had labored with the board, and, I think, also with the Governor, about introducing papers, and if they would not abuse it that he thought in time he would get the papers for them.
Q. You may state the circumstances under which and the reasons for which the whip was again introduced into the prison, after being abolished, and the clog.
A. The whip was introduced for a man in his cell throwing the contents of his bucket into the night-guard's face, as I understood the thing; I saw the guard and the guard told me; I did not see it; the guard told me that the man threw the contents of his cell onto him.
Q. What was the condition of the discipline, if there had been any change in it, in the prison, at the time the whip was again introduced? Had it become necessary to resort to some more violent punishment or not?
A. It had, sir.
Q. For what reason do you think so?
A. Well, sir, I can tell you some instances. The foreman, for instance, would say to a man, You do a piece of work, and he would refuse to do it, and he would tell you he would not do it, perhaps, and would use some bad language to him; perhaps be very saucy; something of that kind; and one case that come under my observation very closely: a man pulled up his sleeves and called me an old son-of-a-bitch, said he could lick me, and squared away ready for a fight; that was the only man that ever attempted to strike me while I was in the prison; that man done it and he was not punished.
Q. Was that before the whip was introduced, or after?
A. It was before that, sir. How much he might have been reprimanded, or anything of that kind, I don't know, but he was not punished; it became a little bit tickleish to stay there.
Q. Do you remember who that man was?
A. His name was Armstrong, sir.
Mr. Morris—Charley Armstrong?
A. Yes, sir, Charley Armstrong; he was under Deputy Martin's administration.
Q. Do you know whether it was reported to the Agent or not?
A. I think it was.
Q. How long a time was it after Mr. Morris went there?
A. Well, that I could not tell you.
Q. Well, about how long? Was it before the whip was introduced, after Mr. Morris went there?

A. I could not tell you; I could not give you any dates; I never charged my mind with any thing of that kind.

Q. This punishment with the wire cap you speak of; does that inflict punishment, or is it a disgrace?

A. It is rather more of a disgrace.

Q. Is it painful?

A. I think not, sir.

Q. Can a man eat in it?

A. Oh, yes, sir.

Q. Loose on the head is it?

A. Loose.

Q. How is it about sleeping?

A. I don't know what the effect would be with a man's lying down on it; I could not tell.

Q. I think you stated, but I would like it a little more fully, what was the rule and practice in regard to conversing with freemen? What were your instructions in regard to it?

A. The general rule was that freemen should not converse with convicts, and were shut out of the yard for so doing, and trafficking with them. Let me see, I believe there was one man shut out of the cabinet shop, if I recollect right.

Q. For what?

A. I think Mr. Winans caught the man at it, and reprimanded him, and I think afterwards shut him out of the yard for talking to a convict.

Q. What do you mean by shutting out of the yard?

.A I mean when he comes to the gate he can't get in; the gate is shut against him.

Q. That is, men that are employed by contractors as foremen?

A. Yes, sir.

Q. The Agent shuts the door in their faces? Don't let them come in the prison again?

A. Don't allow them to come in without giving satisfaction; some of them showing by investigation, the Agent will perhaps let them back again.

Q. Some reports, you say, were written by the deputy at the time given, and others were not. What was the character of those that he took down at once, as compared with the others that he did not write?

A. Oh, in a case that was considered a bad case I have seen him take it down just as you would give it to him.

Q. But the minor offenses he did not usually do it?

A. He did not usually do it, not many; any that required looking into a considerable I have seen him haul out his pocket-book and take it down.

Q. You stated that you did not know whether the reports that you made were put upon the books. Did you ever examine the books at all?

A. I never saw the books.

Q. It is for that reason that you don't know?

A. Now, just wait one moment. You asked me if I knew whether all those reports were reported to the Agent?

Q. Yes, sir.

A. I know of one report that I made to the deputy that was not reported to the Agent; or at least I found out afterwards so.

Q. What was the character of the offense?

A. Well, it was a man running a slung-shot out of a piece of lead about the size of an egg,—or babbit, I guess it was, instead of lead.

STATE PRISON INVESTIGATION.   145

Mr. Webber:
Q. Was the man punished in that case?
A. He was not at the time the report was made. I afterwards reported the case to the Agent myself.
Q. Do you know the reason the man was not punished at the time?
A. I think, sir, the deputy did not report the thing to the Agent.
Q. Do you know anything about this man's claim in regard to this slung-shot?
A. He claimed that it was for me, or another keeper, I learned afterwards; I did not just at that time.
Q. I mean on the investigation of the thing,—what did the man claim this piece of babbit metal he had was for; what did he declare it was for?
A. On his examination? I don't know; but he told another man in the shop that it was for me or for Mr. Woodruff.
Q. Who was this man?
A. The name was Thurston.
Q. Well, what was the general character of this man Thurston?
Mr. Morris:
Q. Let me ask Mr. Bedford one question. You did not get the idea what perhaps he meant that for; what did he claim this slung-shot was, or what piece of mechanism?
A. Oh, he said he was running it for one of the masons,—plumb-bob for one of the masons.
Q. How was it shaped?
A. It was very near round.
Q Like the bob that the masons used there in their work sometimes?
A. Somewhat round I believe; they are a little octagon shape, but this was rather round.
Q. But that is what he claimed that it was?
A. Yes, sir.
Q. You may state very briefly what you know of this man Thurston?
A. I think that I had the control of Thurston for some two years and a half, and he made me a good deal of trouble; perhaps more trouble than all the rest of the men I had in my shop at that time; I considered him a very bad, vicious man, and was always on the alert for him.
Q. Was you afraid of him?
A. I was not, because I thought I could handle him if it came to that; if a keeper shows fear there I think he may as well walk out.
Q. Was he a dangerous man?
A. Yes, sir; he was; he was a very bad man before he came into the prison; I knew him by report before he came there.
Q What means were used before he was whipped, if any; what other punishments tried?
A. He was in the engine-room, and was removed from the engine-room and put into the shop, and then he began to feign sickness, and he was running around considerable, but whether he was punished or not I never knew; but he was frequently reported; he was shut in the bare cell, that I know.
Q. What was the offense for which he was whipped the last time; at the time you saw him whipped?
A. That was at the time that he prepared this knife; and I presume threats that he made.

Q. Were you there when the knife was taken away from him?

A. I was, sir; but the knife was not took away from him; the spit-box stood close to him, and he slipped the knife into the saw-dust in the spitoon; he had been seated on a bench after he took this knife, and slipped it into this spittoon to get it out of sight; the first I knew of the knife was after we had done locking up; Mr. Morris says: "Bring me that knife," and he got it out of the spitoon and brought it to him.

Q. What did he say about the knife,—what it was for?

A. I could not tell you the reply he made to that question.

Q. Well, the substance of it; what threats, if any, were made?

A. Well, he did not make any threats then, but when he was in his bare cell he did make threats; he said he would rip Morris' guts out of him.

Q. What was his behavior when he was being whipped?

A. Do you mean at the time I saw him with it?

Q. Yes, at the time you saw him with it.

A. Well, sir, he danced around a considerable.

Q. What did he say?

A. After he took the knife, Mr. Morris told him, he says, I believe, something like this: says he, I told you that if I ever caught any man this way with a knife I would punish them. And Thurston made some reply, I don't know what. But Mr. Morris whipped him.

Q. Were you there while he was being whipped?

A. I was.

Q. What have you to say in regard to that whipping,—was it, or was it not, unduly severe?

A. Well, sir, I should say he did not get enough of it; I think if I had been placed in his position he would have got more.

Mr. Webber—What was that last answer?

A. I say, I think if I had been in Mr. Morris' place he would have got more.

Q. Was he disabled at all by that whipping?

A. No, sir.

Q. Show any signs of exhaustion?

A. No, sir; he put his clothes on and went right back to the hall; that is, he was sent right back to the cell, I think; the keeper was called that locked his gallery and took him right to his cell.

Q. What was his behavior subsequent to that whipping?

A. Bad.

Q. I mean after that; not that day, but his subsequent behavior in the shops and the places where he worked, was he, or was he not, improved in conduct by the whipping?

A. Afterwards?

Q. Yes.

A. Yes, sir.

Q. Well, which do you mean, that he was, or was not?

A. I mean I think that it done him good; I think it improved his conduct in the prison.

Q. In this punishment of tying by the hands that you have spoken of, was the prisoner ever, at any time that you saw, elevated from his feet at all?

A. No, sir; I never saw any. He stood square on his feet.

Q. This punishment, then, was simply the fatigue of holding his hands over his head for the length of time that they were there?

A. Yes, sir.

Q. Could they take hold of the rope so as to rest their arms when they were up there?

A. Yes, sir; by twisting their hands they could catch hold of the rope. I never saw but one case of that to my recollection.

Q. Was, or was not whipping a frequent punishment?

A. Do you mean after Mr. Morris came there?

Q. Yes.

A. Not very frequent.

Q. How many cases do you know of, probably, while you were there?

A. Oh, I could not tell you; I never saw, I believe, but this once; I heard of it, but that I did not see. But it was only in rather extreme cases, I believe, that the whip was applied; where other means had been used and would not answer.

Q. What about the exercises of the prison Sundays, while you were there,— what were they?

A. Shall I give them in detail?

Q No; what were their general character,—were they interesting and pleasant for the men?

A. Yes, sir; I considered them so as a general thing; Mr. Morris generally read a piece after the commencement of church hour. Well, after breakfast the men went to their cells, and when they came out to church, Mr. Morris generally read a piece when he was present, and the chaplain had his services, Sabbath-school, writing; the Sabbath-school and writing was before church.

Q. Did you ever know Mr. Morris to be absent from those exercises?

A. Never when he was at home, I don't think sir, unless it might have been once or twice that he was sick; but it was very seldom that he was ever absent at church, and very frequently, at Sabbath school; he took a class in the Sabath school, just before I left, himself, learning the men to read.

Q. How was the management in point of severity; the general management of the prison, under Mr. Morris, compared with that under Mr. Bingham, Mr. Morris' predecessor?

A. Quite an improvement, sir; the whip never was used as severe, to my knowledge, nor begin to be, as it was under Mr. Bingham.

Mr. Webber:

Q Was locking in bare cells a mode of punishment resorted to by Mr. Bingham?

A. Yes, sir; but in a different manner to what Mr. Morris done it.

Q. You say that you reported a man—Charley Armstrong, for having used threatening language to you?

A. Yes, sir.

Q. And that he was not punished?

A. Yes, sir.

Q. Now, why was he not punished?

A. I think sir, at that time, the deputy did not report that case at the time of it; and I afterwards reported it to Mr. Morris; whether Mr. Morris done anything with the man after that, or not, I don't know; I could not say that he did or did not.

Q. Did you hear of anything being done to the man?

A. No, sir; I was in another shop at that time; my opportunity was not very good to find out.

Q. What means did you resort to to quiet this man when he made these threats to you?

A. I stood and looked him in the face for a few seconds, I finally told him, says I: "You go right to your place of work, sir," turned to my man and sent for the deputy.

Q. Did he go to his work?

A. When he saw me send for the deputy he went back to his place of work.

Q. Did the deputy come?

A. Yes, sir, he did.

Q. When you made your report, usually, did you make them in the presence of the convict?

A. As a general rule I would call the convict right to me, and the deputy came and I made my report right in his presence, whatever I had got to say, as a general thing; sometimes I have reported a man and then called the convict up afterwards—after I told the deputy, and made my report right over again in the presence of the convict.

Q. Was it the custom always to do either one or the other, so that the convict knew that the report was made, and knew what it was: was it a uniform custom?

A. It was a uniform custom. If a convict was reported, he knew what he was reported for; it was always in my shop; I can't answer for other keepers; that was my mode in making my reports before the convicts.

Q. Was it the uniform that the convict, the keeper, and the deputy would be together at the time this report was made, or that they would be together afterwards, when the report would be repeated?

A. As I stated, it was my general custom; but what other keepers done I could not say.

Q. I don't say generally, I say uniform?

A. I said it was with me.

Q. I understood you to say you never saw a man go to bed with one of those wire caps on?

A. I never saw him get into his bed with one on, sir, in the world.

Q. With one on could he sleep comfortably?

A. It would not be a very comfortable thing to sleep in. I don't know as it would cause him any particular pain.

Q. Do you know whether it was their practice to set up and sleep while they wore those?

A. I never heard of a case of it; I never saw one.

Q. Well, you never saw one lie down either?

A. I never saw one lie down because I left the prison always immediately on locking up, and they would not go to bed until they got ready.

Q. I understood you to say that it was only the minor offenses that the deputy neglected to take down in writing, when you reported them to him?

A. I said in some grave cases I have seen him take the book out and write; but that was not a general practice.

Q. Well, did he always do it when the offense was a grave one?

A. I can't say that he did, sir.

Q. What class of offenses were regarded as minor offenses?

A. Oh, perhaps talking in the dining-room, perhaps talking in the ranks, perhaps some little thing in the shop that was not worth while to notice them; many little things that occur there in the shops that are not worth mentioning, yet at the same time you have got to look after them in order to keep up your discipline. If you allow them to go one foot they will take two.

Q. I understood you to say, you thought Thurston was not whipped enough at this second whipping?
A. I did.
Q Did you examine him after the whipping to see how his person was marked?
A. No, sir, I did not examine him, I saw it done.
Q. Do you know on what part of the body the blows were inflicted?
A. Well, I should think mostly up around his shoulders; the heft of the blows I should think was up about his shoulders.
Q Were there any blows inflicted on the front part of his person?
A. I think there was some around his chest here.
Q. And around his abdomen?
A. I could not say that there was any on his abdomen.
Q. Did you examine to see?
A. No, sir, I did not.
Q. Did Thurston, while that whipping was in progress, make any offers to do better?
A. Yes, sir, he told Mr. Morris that he never would have another knife in his possession as long as he staid there.
Q. Well, state whether he begged him to desist from the whipping?
A. Why, he told him if he would not whip him any more that he would promise to do better, and he would do anything that was asked him to do that he could do.
Q. State whether the whipping was continued after he made such promises?
A. Well, I rather think not, if any but light afterwards. I think when he promised Mr. Morris that he would do anything in the future that was asked, I think Mr. Morris quit.
Q. Do you know how many lashes Mr. Morris gave him at that time?
A. I could not tell you.
Q. Were they all given continuously from the beginning until the end?
A. No, sir.
Q. How many were given continuously at first?
A. I could not tell you.
Q. Well, what proportion of them?
A. There might have been twenty.
Q. Then how long an intermission?
A. Well, for a few moments. Mr. Morris asked him some questions and he would not give satisfactory answers, but what those question was, or what the answers was, I could not tell you now, but I know there was conversation between them.
Q. Did Mr. Morris appear to be angry while administering that punishment?
A. While he was whipping him?
Q. Yes?
A. No, sir, he did not show but very little anger, I did not think, at all, only the time he took the knife away from him.
Q Well, confine yourself to the question. We won't spread over so much ground. After the first intermission how many blows were given before another intermission?
A. I could not tell you; I did not count them.

Q. How many intermissions were there?
A. Oh, there was probably two or three; I could not say.
Q. Did Thurston at any of those intermissions make any promises of better behavior?
A. He asked Mr. Morris to not whip him any more; he would not answer the questions as I understand it.
Q. Well, you had a chance to hear, didn't you?
A. Yes sir, but it is a long while ago, sir, to remember very minutely that.
Q. Were you any ways shocked at that punishment?
A. No sir, I was not.
Q. Why do you think he ought to have more punishment?
A. I thought, in the manner in which Mr. Morris used the whip, that he might have been punished a good deal severer; I have seen it used a great deal severer. If you will allow me, I can show you just exactly how Mr. Morris handled it. [Laughter.]
Q. Will you answer my question?
A. Well, there is a great deal of difference in using a whip.
Q. I think I am aware of that fact. I desire now, to repeat my question, and hope you will answer it. Why did you think the whipping was not sufficiently severe?
A. In the manner in which Mr. Morris used the whip, and very little effect it had upon the body.
Q. What result would you have expected to attain from a more severe punishment?
A. Because I did not think the man was subdued; I thought it necessary to do it.
Q. What did you discover in the man's appearance that would lead you to believe that he was not subdued?
A. Because I knew the man well.
Q. Had you any spite against him?
A. I had none.
Q. You judged that the punishment was not sufficiently severe from your knowledge of the man's character rather than from the particular facts at that time before you, as I understand you?
A. I have stated for the reason that I did not think the man subdued.
Q. I ask you then what indication you discovered of the want of subjection?
A. The man's general appearance.
Q. Did he use any language which indicated that he was not subdued?
A. No sir.
Q. What particular appearance indicated to you the want of subjection?
A. By the look of his eye and his appearance.
Q. Did you stand where you could see his eyes?
A. I did and looked at him.
Q. What position did you stand in, in relation to where Mr. Morris stood, at the time the punishment was inflicted?
A. I stood in several different positions; I could not tell you, sir.
Q. Were you walking about while the punishment was being inflicted?
A. I would walk about some, sir.
Q. Was there any consultation between you and Mr. Morris at any of the intermissions?

A. No, sir; he never spoke to me, nor a man in the house, I don't think. I spoke to some of the other keepers.

Q. I understood you that Mr. Thurston not only begged Mr. Morris to quit, but also promised that he would do as he was told, and submit to the rules?

A. Yes, sir; he promised Mr. Morris that he would not carry a knife. He would do anything that was required of him, if he would let him off, I believe was the words he used: "If you will let me off this time."

Q. Now, as to the conduct of this man afterwards, I understood you to say it was better?

A. Yes, sir; I think he was.

Q Did he remain in your shop after this?

A. He was not in my shop at the time.

Q. What opportunity had you, then, to observe his conduct?

A. Some time afterwards I was put in the yard, and he was then put under my charge again.

Q. For how long?

A. Well, I could not tell you; I was doing some grading of the yard; I could not tell you how long I was in the yard.

Q. Have you any peculiar opinion of prison discipline of your own?

A. Yes, sir; I have.

Q. Is it your opinion that a severe course of treatment with convicts will ensure better discipline than a milder course?

A. No, sir; I do not think that a severe discipline would be the best, but I do think that it is necessary to have something that will make them afraid; in other words, I do not think that a prison can be run satisfactorily, without you have a penalty to it for offenses. I think, sir, that there would be a great deal of fighting, both among themselves,—and that it would be unsafe for keepers to be there, or any body else, if there was not a severe discipline kept up by some mode or another.

Q. Is it your judgment, that whipping is to be preferred, rather than solitary confinement, as a punishment?

A That I cannot say; it would be altogether owing to what your solitary confinement would be, sir. I think the locking of the cell, as Mr. Morris has, is not very good, unless the prisoner was confined in it quite a number of days.

Q. Suppose he was confined long enough so as to make it a punishment. Let me ask you if you have known of a case where a prisoner was confined in solitary confinement for ten or twenty days together?

A. Not in this State. I have known of prisoners being locked in cells for quite a number of days; understand that was in one cell, but not what you call in this prison the bare cell. The bare cell here is just the same, except the bedding is taken out and everything. The cell is bare.

Q. Is there light enough in the cell to read by?

A. Yes, sir; just the same as any other cell.

Q. What is the effect of solitary confinement in a bare cell upon hardened convicts for a period of say ten days?

A. I never knew of one locked in a bare cell for ten days.

Q. Do you know of any reason why that mode of punishment has not been resorted to?

A. In this prison?

Q. Yes.

A. I do not, sir.

Q. In your judgment would it be more humane or less humane to lie in the bare cell until the prisoner was subjected than whipping with the lash?

A. On some men the effect would be very good, locking in the bare cell. Some men twenty-four hours in the bare cell would be a very, very severe punishment; in other cases, I think that two or three months would not be as much to them as the twenty-four hours would be to other men; men are different; some men would rather stay locked up than to work.

Mr. Bartow:

Q. Did you ever know of convicts punished there on the Sabbath day?

A. By putting in the bare cell I have.

Q. Is that all the mode of punishment you have known inflicted on Sunday?

A. I think I never saw a man punished there on Sunday except by being put in this bare cell.

Q. Did you use to tend services there on Sunday?

A. Did I?

Q. Yes.

A. Yes, sir, every Sunday.

Q. Did you ever see any man slapped in the face on Sunday during service?

A. I did not see it; I heard of it.

Q. Who did that?

A. I was told that Mr. Morris did it, but I did not see it; I was at the back end of the dining-room.

Q. You state now that you think Mr. Thurston was not whipped unduly severe. How many lashes did he receive that whipping that you witnessed?

A. I could not tell you; I have not but very little idea; it might have been 40, 50, or 60, but I would not state any number, because I do not know.

Q. Did punishment immediately follow the report of infraction of the rules?

A. Do you mean generally in the prison?

Q. Yes.

A. It did generally follow the report of the infraction; in some cases I knew it to follow immediately; others I knew it to go a day or so; perhaps an investigation was necessary; in such cases, why it was postponed.

Q. Did Mr. Morris usually investigate a report of infraction, to know whether it was true or false?

A. No, not as a general rule.

Q. He did not?

A. I think not; the keeper's report was supposed to be truthful; but in what we call rather gross offenses I believe he generally used to inquire into them; I have seen half a dozen men called to the hall to investigate.

Cross-examination by Mr. Seager:

Q. Did not the convicts usually admit the truth of the keeper's report, or did they deny them as a general rule?

A. They always admitted that the keepers made the proper report.

Q. In what cases then, was the investigation had?

A. Well, I cannot refer to them.

Q. I do not mean by reference here; you say as a rule they generally admitted the truth of the report?

A. Yes, sir.

Q. Did the agent investigate when it was denied, as far as you know, when the convict denied that he had committed the offense?

A. I know of two cases that came directly under my observation, where men refused to do the quantity of work, and the investigation would last some length of time, to satisfy Mr. Morris that this was just and right. Those reports would come from the foreman to the keepers, and from the keepers to the deputy, and from the deputy to the Agent, as a general rule. There was one case in my shop. I was in the shoe-shop. The foreman required so much work of the man; the man said he could not do it. I reported the case, and it ran along two or three days. I saw Mr. Morris talk with the man about it; he told me to investigate the case and see what I thought about. I was about three weeks investigating the case, whether the man could do that work or not. I timed the man by the watch at certain portions of the work. I had several conversations with Mr. Morris at this time, and I finally told Mr. Morris that the man could do the work,—and he punished him. The next day his work was all done by two o'clock, and I never knew the man to be after three o'clock doing his day's work afterwards.

Q. Do you know what became of Thurston the day he left the prison?
A. I do, by report.
Q. Well, what was it?
A. Well, the report was that he got into a row and had to jump the town that night. That I do not know of my own knowledge.
Q. Suppose a convict should swear that he would not do a stroke of labor to-day, what punishment would be used for him?
Mr. Morris—In the presence of forty other men, perhaps, what would you do with him?
Mr. Webber—It is hardly worth while to go into that, is it?

JAMES L. PERKINS SWORN.

Examined by Mr. Webber:

Q. State your age, occupation and residence.
A. I am 50 years old, I reside in Jackson, profession of attorney at law.
Q. Have you ever had anything to do with the management of the prison?
A. No, sir, nothing further than I have been a prisoner there.
Q. You have been a prisoner?
A. Yes, sir.
Q. At what time were you there?
A. I was there up to the 10th day of last month, thirty months.
Q. In what shop were you engaged while you were there, or in what part of the prison?
A. In the shoe shop during the first year, and nearly a year afterwards I was at work in the yard, and from there I was put in the asylum. I worked there for some about eight months, and after that time I was at work in the yard outside, and in various places, wherever they saw fit to call on me to do work.
Q. Did you ever witness any instances of punishment while you were there?
A. I have, sir.
Q. Describe the punishment you have known to be inflicted while you were there.
A. I have known men to be punished by wearing the clogg, and by being locked in the bare cell, and showered with the hose that they used there for that purpose, wearing the wire cap and riding the wooden horse.
Q Did you ever see any flogging?
A. I never saw any flogging, but I have heard it; heard the effects of it and seen the effects of it. I heard men that were undergoing the operation, and seen them soon after they were.

Q. What instances ever came under your observation where you have seen the prisoners after the flogging was inflicted?

A. The first instance I saw was a man by the name of Wilson,—not the Wilson that has been spoken of here in the testimony,—but another man that worked in the shoe shop. I guess they were both at work in the shoe shop for a while; but this was James Wilson. He worked right by the side of where I was at work. He was reported by Mr. Bedford for what they call "playing off;" he did not work enough; he claimed to be sick; to be unwell; that he could not do his day's work. They required a pretty hard day's work of him, and it was for several days that he did not do it, and said he could not do it, and looked sick; but Mr. Bedford,—I heard him tell him he thought he was playing off — and he reported him. He was taken in and flogged inside. I did not see him flogged, but when he came out he came back to his work, he told me he had been whipped.

Q. What evidence did he exhibit to you that he had been whipped?

A. He opened his shirt here, let me see where the lash had come around under his arm and across his breast. I did not examine his breast at that time, but I saw his breast, his whole breast.

Q. How was he affected by the punishment?

A. He was all cut up; badly cut and bloody.

Q. Did you notice how many marks of the lash there was upon him?

A. I did not count them, but there was a number of them.

Q. How low down on his breast did you discover those marks?

A. As far as he could open his shirt. He opened his shirt here and let me see. He had his coat and vest off when he went to work. He turned around and showed me his breast.

Q. Any other cases come under your observation,—or let me ask you about what time this was?

A. Well, sir, I cannot tell the time exactly. It was during the latter part of the first year that I was there, while the shoe shop was running.

Q. Any other cases of punishment by the whip that came under your observation while you were there?

A. Yes, sir; the shoe shop, where I was at work, and a number of others, looked right out of the window upon the men that were at work there digging a cellar to the kitchen—the new kitchen and dining room—and there was a transaction that took place there; there was a keeper there by the name of Warner, and he got into a difficulty with a man by the name of St. Clair, a prisoner, and he punched him with his cane.

Q. The keeper did?

A. The keeper punched him with his cane, and St. Clair struck him with his shovel, and the keeper ran and hallooed "murder," and St. Clair was reported and taken in and whipped. That is, it was said he was whipped, and I saw him —he was not showing the whipping to me, but to another man—I came down, and he was right at the corner of the shop, and he had his shirt open here, and showing another man that stood around the corner, and I saw his breast. I did not see his back at that time, but I saw his breast here, where he was whipped, as far as he could open his shirt; it looked like the other man's; badly cut up.

Q. How long after the punishment was this, that you saw it?

A. He had just come out.

Q. So it was fresh?

A. Yes, sir.
Q. Any blood from the wounds?
A. Yes, sir.
Q. How many marks did you observe?
A. Well, I did not count them; there was a good many.
Q. Any other cases that came under your knowledge, of whipping with the lash?
A. Well, I could not tell whether it was with a lash. I had occasion to go into the hall one day, and I saw, in the north hall of the west wing, about half way down, I saw Mr. Morris and two or three going in at the lower door; they was taking a prisoner in with them; it was but a few minutes after that I heard him scream and heard the instrument, whatever it was, a lash, or strap some said it was, being applied to him, and I heard his screams, but I did not see him.
Q. You did not see him afterwards?
A. No, sir.
Q. You do not know what the offense was?
A. I do not know what the offense was. I passed down from the hall after they took him out, and went out at the lower door of the hall, and the men that had charge of the hall, and some others that were working in the hall, were cleaning up where the excrement run from him during the whipping, so they told me. I saw that, and they told me what took place.
Q. Did you ever witness the punishment by showering?
A. Yes, sir.
Q. State any instance of severe punishment by showering of a prisoner under your observation.
A. Well, sir, I used to be very frequently, sometimes every day in the week while I was at the asylum, between eight and nine months, back and forth and about the hall and different shops on different business, more particularly into the hall and cellar where they kept the provisions — my business was cooking there — and I was there very frequently when I went over there into the hall into this cellar. The cellar was on one side of the stairs as I went out of the prison entrance; the showering was done on the other side, and men were fastened up to the door that went from there out into the east wing; it was swung back and they were drawn up there by the arms and fastened, and undergoing the operation. I frequently saw them when I was going in there and out, and I frequently stopped there and witnessed the operation, a great many times.
Q. How long have you ever known that punishment to be continued?
A. Well, sir, I could not tell, but it looked like a good while; I could not tell the time.
Q. Did you ever notice whether the stream from the hose was directed to any particular part of the person?
A. Well, I have seen it directed to all parts.
Q. Well, if you have noticed it being directed to one particular part more than another?
A. Oh, at times during the operation, they would direct it to one particular part more than another. I have seen Mr. Morris, when men were screaming and making a great outcry, tell them to shut up, and direct it right into their mouth, and hold it there until they would be almost completely drowned down, so that they could not make a noise, and then direct it to some other part. They were fastened with their arms stretched out to the door and a strap under the chin, fast.

Q. Could they do anything more than to turn their head?
A. No, sir.
Q. Can you name any of the convicts that you have seen punished in that way?
A. No, sir; I do not know that I can. There was a man that had formerly worked in the shoe shop that I know his name, but I cannot think of it now, and at one time that I was there another man, and other men that were strangers to me, that worked in other shops.
Q. How common an occurrence was it to see this punishment by showering inflicted?
A. I used to see it very frequently. I cannot tell; sometimes during the week I would see it several times, and some weeks not so many times. Sometimes I would see it every day when I would have occasion to go there.
Q. Did you ever witness the infliction of punishment by riding the wooden horse?
A. Yes, sir.
Q Describe this wooden horse.
A. Well, sir, the horse, I should judge—I never went to it to examine it particularly, but I should judge it was made of scantling—square scantling; men sat straddle of it.
Q. 4x4 scantling?
A. I do not know the size of it, I never measured it; quite a good sized scantling.
Q. State whether the man had his clothes on when punished in that way?
A. I think he had; yes, sir, I am certain he had when I saw it.
Q. Do you know how long they were detained there?
A. I do not, because I did not stay to see how long they were kept there. I have heard, in one instance, they were kept there five hours. I do not know anything about it, only what I have heard.
Q. How many instances have you observed of punishing in that manner?
A. I never saw but one.
Q. Punishing by the wire cap; was that a frequent occurrence?
A. Yes, sir; whenever a man made any attempt to escape, I understood that was the offense that that penalty was made use of for, and such attempts were very frequent.
Q. Can you tell how many you have known to be undergoing that punishment at one time?
A. The wire cap.
Q. Yes, sir?
A. Oh, I have seen—I never saw over two or three at the same time wearing it.
Q. What would be the effect of wearing that cap, in your judgment, upon lying down to sleep?
A. Well, you can tell that as well as I. It was a little iron collar around the neck here, with wires, a wire, perhaps three-eighths wire, I should judge, nearly, quite a large-sized wire went over here; there was two wires that crossed over the head, and it was afterwards re-modeled so that I think there was three. I saw a tinner fixing the thing up at the old blacksmith shop; he was putting in his repairs, another wire over it, so that there was three crossed over the head. I think he told me that was what he was doing with it. He was at work with it. It came up over the head so that a man could put his cap on under it, that

is, a cap such as a good many men wear there—those skull caps, made of streaked cloth.

Q. How common an occurrence was it for the punishment by the clog to be resorted to?

A. I do not recollect now, particularly, of but one instance. There was one man wearing it not a great while before I left there, a man that undertook to get out. I think it was Thanksgiving, or some day that they had some doings there, and he made an attempt to escape; La Mountain I think his name was. He had a large iron collar around his clog, I guess an iron clog around his leg that he was wearing?

Q. What means had the prisoners of knowing what particular punishment would follow any particular offense?

A. They had no means at all, sir.

Q. While you were there, state what means you had of knowing what the prison rules and regulations were?

A. I saw the printed rules; I saw them hung up in the cell; I had been there a year and over before I ever saw them. When I first went there,—I had known there was something said afterwards, I think the rules were printed and hung up in the cells afterwards.

Q You say for a year after you went there there were none?

A. It was, I think, a year. It might have been a little more or a little less before I ever saw the printed rules.

Q. Were there any instructions given the prisoners at the meetings that were held, when they were assembled together at any time to your knowledge, as to any particular punishment following any particular offense?

A. No, sir.

Q. Was there anything as to a certain class of punishment for a certain class of offenses?

A. No, sir.

Q. State generally what the understanding was among the convicts, so far as you could learn, as to the offenses for which punishment would be inflicted, and the character of punishment that would follow any particular offense?

A. I never knew that they had; no information or idea in regard to the punishment that would follow offenses, anything more than it was entirely arbitrary with the Agent with the punishment he should inflict. They might get showered; they might get whipped; they might get something else, as far as I ever heard them talk, or had any knowledge.

Q. Did you ever discover any indications of discrimination in the treatment of prisoners there, favoring some more than others?

A. Well, I have. I have seen quite a number stepping around, pretty well dressed up, with their starched bosoms and collars on, with their calf boots or slippers; they did not seem to have any thing to do.

Q Was there a rule in regard to that, or was it a matter entirely in the will of the Agent?

A. It was entirely with the authorities there, as to the treatment a man got in that respect or any other.

Q. Was there any understanding to your knowledge among the prisoners, that for any particular observance of the rules, any particular recompense or rewards would follow, and if so, what?

A. I do not understand your question.

[Question read by the stenographer.]

A. Why, there was an understanding that if they obeyed the rules that there would be a certain amount of time deducted from their sentence.

Q. Anything further than that, to your knowledge?

A. No, sir.

Q. Was there any instructions given when the prisoners were assembled, by the Agent, as to any means generally by which the convicts could be allowed the same privileges that were allowed to those you speak of, with starched bosoms and calf boots?

A. No, sir.

Q. Was there any explanation given by the agent at any time to the convicts of the reason why some were allowed greater liberties than others?

A. Not that I ever heard.

Q. How long a time have you known of the punishment of the locking in the bare cells to be inflicted at one time, if any such instances have come within your notice?

A. Well, I do not know; I have seen men put in at night and locked up and kept there all night. I have seen men put in at night after the bell rang and the men were marched in, and kept there until twelve o'clock at night and let out. I have seen them put in at night, and were there when I went out in the morning, and were there when I went in at night again; how long they were kept, I cannot say. They were put in the bare cell and there was a sign hung upon the door "nothing to eat or drink," and kept there different lengths of time. These cells where they were locked up for the last four or five months that I stayed there, was on the side of the hall where I slept. A great many men were out in the bunks in the hall, so that I passed right by them in going in or out.

Q. Did you notice any discrimination among the convicts, as to the punishment being inflicted on some for offenses, when others with the same offenses would not be punished?

A. Yes, sir; I have seen men punished, or known of their being punished, for having tobacco; for using tobacco; being reported for it and caught with it. I have seen others carry it with perfect impunity, and use it before the officers and keepers. I have seen them pass it to the keepers, and the keepers to them.

Q. And no complaint of it?

A. No, sir; others that were caught with it were severely punished.

Q. Can you recollect any instance—the name of any one that you saw using tobacco and passing it to a keeper, or a keeper to him?

A. Yes, sir; I can mention a number of them.

Q. Name such as you can remember.

A. One man's name was Perkins; another was a barber.

Q. Perkins, that's yourself?

A. Yes, sir; and the hospital steward; his name is—I can't think of his name now; and there was a great many others. A man that had charge of the halls, the wing boss as they call themselves.

Q. Were those wing bosses prisoners?

A. Yes, sir.

Q. Was there any discrimination made between them, as to the amount of labor required of convicts; some being favored in that respect over others?

A. Well, I don't know; I always noticed that there were a number that were around the yard, around the State shops, and around the hospital, around the

STATE PRISON INVESTIGATION. 159

wings, that did not seem to be doing much, nor having much to do; others that were around the shops were worked very hard.

Q. Any reason known to you why some should be permitted to go without severe labor, and others have it imposed on them?

A. No, sir; I know of no reason. There is some two, or three or four most of the time in the blacksmith shop—State shop they call it; the carpenter shop, that did not, as a general thing, do an hour's work in a day; I should judge not, on an average, and others on the outside that did not do much work.

Q. Did you ever witness the punishment of being strung up with the hands over their head?

A. No, sir; I never saw a man in that predicament; I frequently heard of it; heard men relate it that had undergone the pain.

Mr. Bartow—

Q. Did you use to attend religious services on Sunday?

A. Yes, sir.

Q. During those religious services have you seen men punished there?

A. I saw a colored man get pretty severely slapped one day during prayer.

Q. Who did that?

A. Mr. Morris.

Q. What was the offense?

B. He claimed that he laughed.

Q. Did he punish him there in the presence of the rest of the prisoners?

A. Yes, sir; right before the whole of them.

Q. What was Mr. Morris' temper so far as your observation extended—even or uneven?

A. Mr. Morris was always at times very good natured; at other times he was very much the other way, as far as I have seen him.

Q. Did you attend some time in the hospital?

A. Yes, sir.

Q. Did you see a man in the hospital there that was called a crazy man? Did you see water poured on him to test his sanity?

A. No, sir; I did not see that.

Q. Did you hear of it?

A. I heard of it, yes, sir.

Q. What kind of a man was he? Was he troublesome; describe to the committee what kind of a man he was.

A. Well, I never knew any particular trouble with him, anything farther than he seemed to be out of his head; that is, either feigning it or was actually so. I believe a good many of them thought he was playing off, as they call it,— playing crazy,—and others thought he was actually insane. He was sent to the asylum and kept there for some length of time.

Q. Did you ever see men taken out of the ranks during their marching to or from the dining-room and punished or slapped.

A. No, sir; I have seen them taken out of the ranks, and after being marched in, put into the dark cell.

Q. But not immediately punished?

A. No.

Q. Well, did punishment usually immediately follow the report of an infraction, or would some time elapse before they were punished?

A. Well, men were reported and put in a dark cell at night and kept until the next day and punished.

Q. Have you known of punishment to immediately follow the report?
A. Yes, sir; I have seen them taken right in and punished.
Q. During the application of the punishment, what was Mr. Morris' appearance in regard to temper?
A. Well, sir, I have seen him sometimes when he appeared to be very much out of humor quite a number of times.
Q. Did he appear to apply the punishment vindictively, or coolly?
A. Most of the punishment that I have seen of the showering was where men were undergoing punishment for some offense; the most of the punishments that I have seen was always in relation to tobacco that men had taken from the cigar shop, or had been found with it in their possession, and I have seen Mr. Morris showering men and demanding of them that they tell where they got it. Sometimes they would tell and he would not be satisfied with their story that they told, and I have seen them punished a long time in order to get from them a statement of some kind as to who gave them the tobacco, or how they came by it,—something of that nature.
Q. Would they, from what you afterwards learned. sometimes tell an untruth as to what they had done, for the purpose of escaping from the punishment?
A. I have heard them say,—I don't know anything further than what they said,—that they told the truth in the first place and changed it to get out of the fire.
Q. You only have it from what they said?
A. Only from what they said; not that I have any knowledge of it.
Mr. Mellen:
Q. I did not fully understand your answer before as to the manner they were placed when they were showered,
A. They were drawn up to the grate door; it was turned back against the wall. They were drawn up and tied up there by their arms, and there was a strap hung there. I have seen men undergoing the operation without this under their chin, and I have seen them with it. That fastened their head up there so they stood fronting the fire from the hose,—or water, rather.

The committee here adjourned until 2 o'clock P. M.

AFTERNOON SESSION.

JAMES L. PERKINS RECALLED.

Cross-examined by Mr. Seager:
Q. Mr. Perkins, what duty were you put at when you first went to the prison?
A. Book-keeper for Mr. Hatch, shoe contractor in the shoe shop.
Q. How long were you there?
A. I was in that shop, I think, nearly a year; I can't recollect the precise time; it is about a year.
Q. From there where did you go?
A. From there, when the shoe contract broke up, I went to work in the yard, at one thing or another.
Q. How long were you there?
A. Well, I was there not more than three or four or five days, thereabouts.

At that time Mr. Morris came to me and sent me over to the asylum to work; that is where they keep the insane convicts.

Q. Where is the asylum?

A. It is outside of the wall.

Q. How long were you there?

A. I was there between eight and nine months.

Q. What were your duties at the asylum?

A. Cooking.

Q. How many other men were there employed about the asylum?

A. There was one other at the time I was there,—that is prisoners.

Q. What restraint were you under there at the asylum? You say it is outside of the prison walls entirely.

A. I was under no restraint, that is, no further than I attended to my business.

Q. Nothing to prevent your escaping, was there, that is, so far as guard was concerned?

A. No, sir.

Q. How long did you say you were there?

A. I was between eight and nine months; pretty well towards nine months, I think.

Q. You spoke this morning of the difference in the duties that were assigned the different prisoners in the different shops and about the yard. As a matter of fact, it is true, is it not, that some of the duties about the prison are a great deal easier than others?

A. Yes, sir.

Q. To what class of convicts, as a rule, was this lighter kind of work given? I mean of good behaviour or of vicious men?

A. Well, sir, I don't know.

Q. Well, as far as your observation went?

A. I don't know whether the different positions were assigned on account of conduct or not.

Q. Take your own case, for instance; you had no restraint over you at the asylum, you say, at all. It would not be possible, would it, to assign a place of that kind to a man of dangerous character?

A. A man was so circumstanced that it was pretty certain that he would not leave. I presume there would be no hesitancy in putting most any man there, that is, that could do the business.

Q. Were there men there to any considerable number that were not able to do full work, what were called infirm, feeble men?

A. Yes, sir; I know of several such men.

Q. How many?

A. Some very old men and some that were cripples; some men that were sick most of the time.

Q. Was not the labor that each man was assigned to fixed with reference to the ability of the man to perform it?

A. I think it was not in some instances.

Q. What instances?

A. Well, the men that worked in these shops that I spoke of,—the blacksmith shop, the State carpenter shop, and the cooper shop, and such places. I used to have opportunities of seeing and knowing about how much they were doing, and it was very little at that time.

21

Q. What opportunities did you have of knowing while you were book-keeper, for instance?
A. I did not have so favorable opportunities as I had afterwards.
Q What opportunity did you have while you were in the asylum?
A. I had the opportunity of being through the yards and through the shops; sent there to the shops on errands for the keeper, and frequently stopped there when I was going back and forth to the prison to get provisions, groceries, etc.
Q. Did those men do all that was required of them to do?
A. I suppose they did; I knew of there being any one with them.
Q. Were not the duties that they were assigned, duties that must be performed by somebody?
A. Sometimes they had some work to do, and a great many times they hadn't anything to do.
Q. That was so in your own case, wasn't it, over to the asylum?
A. No, sir; it was not. I had all that I could do all the time, every day.
Q. Why did you leave the asylum?
A. I left it because I was ordered to do so and put at other work.
Q. What were you ordered away for?
A. I don't know, sir, anything about it.
Q. While you were at the asylum were you allowed to see your family?
A. Yes, sir.
Q. How often?
A. Sometimes once in two weeks, sometimes once a week, and sometimes in four weeks; no oftener than I had been when I was in the yard.
Q. Did the Agent always know when they came to see you when you were over to the asylum, outside of the walls? What means did the Agent have of knowing how often your family came to see you, unless you reported yourself?
A. The keeper was there; he had the means of knowing all about it.
Q. Any body but yourself and the keeper at the asylum?
A. The man that was at work there.
Q There was a keeper, yourself, and another man there at the asylum?
A. Yes, sir?
Q. Keeper there constantly?
A. Yes, sir.
Q. Never left yourself alone there?
A. Oh, I have been there alone when he would run over into the yard; been there alone with the other man, when he would go down town a short time,— down to the grocery.
Q. As far as you and the other man were concerned, whether there was any attempted oversight ovrr you and him on the part of the keeper?
A. No, sir, only when he went off down in the town in the evening, then we were in the hall and locked up there, that is, just a common wooden door.
Q. During the day did you leave the asylum when you were a mind to, if you had no duty to perform there at the time—were you obliged to remain there?
A. I never asked; I never knew whether I was obliged to or not; I never did leave any farther than around the premises through into the yard and back again.
Q. Were you there at the asylum, subjected to the same rules that the other convicts were?
A. Do you mean the rules.

Q. Yes, sir; the general rules that applied to the other convicts. Were you subjected to them over there?

A. Why, there are rules that convicts are not allowed to talk; we were allowed to talk there all we pleased, and to talk with any one that happened to come along, or any one that was there; at least we always done so, and I never heard any complaints about it.

Q Was there any rule in your case in regard to correspondence? Could you write letters whenever you wanted to?

A. I could have written letters whenever I wanted to; I never did write any letters only one. Mr. Dyer gave me the privilege.

Q Do you use tobacco yourself?

A. Yes, sir.

Q. Who furnished it when you were there?

A. I furnished it myself.

Q. How did you furnish it—where did you get it from?

A. I used to send down town and buy it.

Q. Who did you send by?

A. I have sent a great many times by Mr. Dyer, the keeper.

Q. Do you know that there were a class of men in the prison that were allowed to use tobacco?

A. Yes, sir; I knew there was.

Q. About how many were there of them?

A. Well, sir, I don't know how many there was.

Q. Why were they allowed to use it?

A. I don't know.

Q. You spoke of there being a difference in the treatment of prisoners in regard to this tobacco question. Do you not know that it was a matter of fact that there were some sixty or seventy convicts there that were allowed to use tobacco. The long time men, that did not give up their tobacco?

A. Yes, sir, I have heard him say that there was old men there, he did not choose to deprive them of their tobacco.

Q. Mostly life convicts, were they not, or very long time men?

A. Well, about that I don't know the length of time; I know he spoke particularly about some old men that were there; he did not see fit to deprive them of the use of tobacco.

Q. Do you know of any instance of convicts admitted there within the last year that were allowed tobacco with the Agent's knowledge and consent?

A. No, sir; I don't.

Q. These cases that you speak of men using tobacco, were the cases that used under the old rule where the men did not give up their tobacco?

A. No, sir; not that I know of. They were not old men, these men that I speak of.

Q. I don't mean old men ; I mean men who had been there some time—old in the prison ; there before the rule was made, and who did not come under the rule?

A. Well, sir, there was some that must have come under the rule, because they had been there a less time than I had.

Q. What men were they,—name them,—that were allowed to use tobacco?

A. I don't know whether they were allowed to do it ; I don't know whether they had Mr. Morris' consent, or anybody else's ; I always saw them have it ;

frequently used it; and I have frequently known them, and heard the keepers ask them for a chew of tobacco, and take out a bundle.

Q Well, give me the names of some of the men.

A. Well, there was one man, Leonard I think his name is; he always carried his tobacco,—plenty of it.

Q. When did Leonard come there; was he there when you went there?

A. Yes, sir.

Q. Well, that is not the case we want then.

A. One man that worked in the barber-shop,—some two or three that worked there.

Q. Please give me their names?

A. I can't give you their names; I don't recollect their names.

Q. These men that you speak of,—in the barber-shop,—men that came after you did?

A. Yes, sir.

Q. You don't know their names?

A. I don't recollect their names.

Q. How many men are there in the barber-shop, Mr. Morris?

Mr. Morris:

A. Four men in the barber-shop.

Q. Can you give the names of any of the men that was in the barber-shop?

A. No, sir; I can't recollect the men's names; I used to see them—

Q. But there were two or three men in the barber-shop that came there after you did, who were allowed to use tobacco?

A. That did use it.

Q Openly?

A. Yes, sir.

Q Before the keepers?

A. Yes, sir.

Q. Was there any keeper in the barber-shop?

A. No, sir; not that I know of.

Q. Well, what other instance of the use of tobacco?

A. Well, sir, those men that work at the shops.

Q. Well, what men; in what shop?

A. There was a man that works in the blacksmith shop.

Q. What is his name?

A. I presume that he had the right that you speak of.

Q. Very well; we don't want his case then; what I want is instances, if you know of them, of partiality in the matter of this use of tobacco; where some men were allowed to use it, and where, under the same rule, other men were not allowed to use it?

A. Well, sir, these men that worked in the wings, they always had plenty of tobacco.

Q. What name?

A. Well, there is one by the name—Mr. Morris knows his name; I can't think of it now. He has charge of the west wing. My recollection of names is very poor. I can't possibly recollect the man's name. I know him as well as I know you.

Mr. Morris—John Clark?

A. No, sir; when he was there, he always carried his tobacco, and used it openly.

Q. How long had he been there?

A. He had been there some time, but he was not an old man; he was a young man.

Q That is not what we are speaking of. What I am speaking of, is, men who came there since the adoption of the rule. There are conceded to be about forty or sixty men in the prison, who are allowed to use tobacco, openly, to-day.

A. This man's name who had charge of the wing was Douglass.

Q. When did he come there?

A That I don't know.

Q. Was he there when you came there?

A. Yes, sir; I think so.

Q. I want to get the name of some man who came within the last year and two years who was allowed to use tobacco?

A. Well, sir, I told you I did not know anything about the allowance; I know the fact.

Q. Who does use it, not a question of allowance, but who does use it?

A. Well, sir, there is one man that is in the barber shop; I think his name is Fiddler; I have heard him called by that name.

Q. Now you have spoken of two men in the barber shop?

A. Well, I think that is his name.

Q. Do you know when he came there?

A. He came there some time since I came there.

Q. Well, that is one man. How do you know that he is allowed to use tobacco?

A. Because I have seen him use it.

Q. There is no keeper in the barber shop,—did you ever see him use it in the presence of any keeper?

A. Yes, sir.

Q. What keeper?

A. Mr. Wood.

Q. Before any other keeper?

A. I don't know that I have; I don't now recollect.

Q. How many times did you ever see him use it before Mr. Wood?

A. I don't recollect ever seeing him use it but once before Mr. Wood?

Q. What kind of tobacco was it?

A. Fine cut.

Q. Where did he get it?

A. I don't know.

Q You know Mr. Wood saw him use it?

A. I am sure he did.

Q. How long ago was that?

A. It is over six months ago.

Q. Well, what other men did you ever see use tobacco—not of the old stayers, I don't mean—not of the long time men—the men that were there before you went there, but the men that came there subsequent to the time the rules were adopted,—about the time you came there?

A. I know that the rules, as I understood it, in relation to the men's using tobacco, applied to those only that tobacco was issued to. None others had any right to use it; that is, that was the rule; and I know that I have seen a great many that tobacco was not issued to,—that was not using tobacco that was issued there,—using their tobacco freely and openly.

Q. Well, give me their names. If there were a great many, you must remember some of them?
A. Well, sir, I have told you all the names I can recollect now.
Q. The only man you recollect, then, is this man Fiddler?
A. That is the only man I recollect, and know of his coming there since I did.
Q. Where did you go to from the Asylum?
A. I went into the yard for a few days, and then outside onto the State lot. They were building a hog-pen, and their work there in the lot, ditching.
Q. Where did you go from there?
A. Well, sir, I worked there when they had work for me to do, and was inside the yard when they had work for me to do. Was out there sometimes a day, and other times a day or two inside.
Q. You spoke this morning of the punishment of James Wilson; you remember the case do you?
A. Yes, sir.
Q. Do you remember whether there were found under Mr. Wilson's bench, while he was at work there, or near him, pants that he was dying for the purpose of making his escape?
A. I know that he was punished for that before this time that I speak of. I don't know what punishment he underwent at that time; whether he was whipped or showered.
Q. He was punished before the time you speak of once, for having some clothes in his possession he was dying black, for the purpose of making his escape?
A. Yes, sir.
Q. Was he in the same shop with you when he was punished then?
A. Yes, sir.
Q. Was he severely punished at the time he was dying his pants to escape?
A. I don't know what punishment he underwent at that time.
Q. But he was in the same shop with you?
A. Yes, sir. I heard at the time, but I don't recollect now.
Q. Where did Wilson come from?
A. I think he came from Detroit. He was sent from Detroit.
Q. What was Wilson's reputation in the shop,—what kind of a man was he?
A. I don't know that he had any particular reputation at the time that he was punished for dying the clothes. He had been there only a few days.
Q. At the time he was punished the second time?
A. At the time he was punished the second time, I never heard anything particular; never saw anything in relation to the man.
Q. Ever heard any complaints about him?
A. No, sir; complaints occasionally for talking, as most men were. I heard the keeper rake him down for talking.
Q. How long a time after this attempt to escape before he was punished at the time you speak of? I simply want to get at it approximately, so as to locate it to look up the record.
A. Well, sir, I should think it was,—it might have been four, it might have been six months; it was some little time.
Q. When was it that you saw this showering?
A. It was while I was at the asylum that I saw most of it; when I was back and forth from there to the cellar. The cellar was on one side of the stairway, where we went up to the prison entrance, and the place of showering was right

on the other side. When I went in there, if there was men being showered by the door I could not help but see it.

Q. Was it during that time that you saw this showering you referred to this morning?
A. Yes, sir.
Q. While you were at the asylum?
A. Yes, sir.
Q. How long ago was it?
A. Well, it was a year.
Q. Who was the convict that was being punished and screaming when Mr. Morris turned the nozzle and threw the water into his mouth?
A. I don't know his name.
Q. Black man or white man?
A. White man.
Q. Do you know what his name was?
A. No, sir.
Q. Who else was there besides Mr. Morris?
A. There was some one of the keepers that was there. One of the officers that belonged there was there, sir.
Q. Which one?
A. Now I can't recollect. Mr. Cook was there,—Mr. Cook was then up at his desk, right at the stairs.
Q. Mr. Cook was there at that showering?
A. Yes, sir.
Q. You don't know what the man's name was?
A. No, sir, I don't.
Q. Was you there all the time he was being showered?
A. No, sir, they were showering him when I went in there.
Q. How long were you there?
A. Well, I stopped some little time, until they got through.
Q. You stopped to see it?
A. I saw it; yes, sir.
Q. Where were you going to?
A. I was going to get what I was after, and go right back to the asylum.
Q. Do you remember what you were after?
A. Yes, sir.
Q. What was it?
A. I was after coffee, in a can.
Q. Where was the coffee-can?
A. Kept in the cellar.
Q. Did you go up there to go through the cellar?
A. Yes, sir; I went right into the door and right into the cellar.
Q. Was there a cellar there a year ago?
A. Yes, sir; it was while I was work in the asylum; the exact time I can't tell you; it was about a year before I went over there; about that time; and then I was there between eight and nine months, and it was during the time that I was there.
Q. Did you ever see that in any other instance,—that showering you speak of,—throwing the water into the man's face?
A. Yes, I have seen men showered in the face.
Q. Men showered so as to choke him down?

A. No, sir; I don't know that I did to the extent that they showered that man in the face.
Q. Do you know what that man's offense was?
A. No, sir.
Q. Did you inquire of any body about it?
A. I did not make any inquiry.
Q. When did you first mention this to any body?
A. Well, sir, that I don't know.
Q. Well, about when?
A. I could not tell you; I frequently talked with the men about it.
Q. Since you came out, or before?
A. Before and since.
Q. Were you at liberty to speak to the inspectors when they went there?
A. Yes, sir.
Q. Did you ever make any complaints to the inspectors?
A. I never did.
Q. Was every man at liberty to speak to them if he saw fit to?
A. I don't know whether they were at liberty to.
Q. The rules prohibited the men speaking to the inspectors when they were going through the shops and the yards, didn't they?
A. What rules?
Q. The prison rules.
A. Yes, sir; I think so.
Q. What do you mean, then, by saying you were at liberty to speak to them?
A. Because I frequently saw them outside, where I had opportunity to speak to them, if I had occasion to, and did talk with them.
Q. Did you ever make any complaint of the severity of the punishment there?
A. No, sir.
Q. Did you ever have any conversation on the subject of punishment at all?
A. No, sir.
Q. Were you ever punished yourself?
A. No, sir.
Q. Why did not you work on contract?
A. I did work on contract for a year.
Q. Why did not you continue?
A. Because I was ordered to work elsewhere.
Q. Do you know why you were ordered to work elsewhere?
A. No, sir.
Q. You spoke of this colored man that was slapped at prayer times. When was it,—well, about the time,—of course I don't expect you to give the exact date?
A. Well, sir, I could not tell you; it was some little time ago. It might have been four months; it might have been not so long; it might have been a little longer.
Q. Was it during prayer?
A. Yes, sir.
Q. You are positive as to that?
A. I am not certain about it; I think so.
Q. Did you see him when he was slapped?
A. He stood with his back towards me; I did not see his face.
Q. Where was Mr. Morris?

A. Mr. Morris was there in the dining room.
A. How far were you from the colored man?
A. I was little past the middle of the room.
Q. This was done in the presence of all the prisoners, was it?
A. Well, there was most of them there?
Q Who was praying?
A. I don't know the man's name; it was not the chaplain.
Q Some stranger?
A. Yes, sir.
Q. Well, what did Mr. Morris do?
A. He slapped the man's face.
Q He was not sitting next to the man, was he?
A No, sir; I think he came down off from the stand.
Q. During the prayer?
A. That is my recollection of it.
Q. And went down and slapped the colored man's face?
A. Well, sir, I won't be certain that it was during the prayer, but I think it was.
Q. That is your recollection, that during prayer, he came down, and went to the colored man, and slapped his face in the presence of all the convicts there; Is that your recollection of it?
A. Why, it was during the service.
Q. Well, but this is your recollection of it, I say; is it, or is it not?
A. Well, sir, I don't recollect particularly all the items of it, and the particulars of the time; but I recollect distinctly the fact of the man getting his face slapped.
Q. Did you see Mr. Morris when he came down?
A. I don't know that I was looking at Mr. Morris when he came down. I could not say positively that he did come down. I don't recollect where he did start from.
Q. Did you see him slap the man?
A. I saw it as plain as you could see them, if a man was sitting with his face the other way.
Q. That is what I ask you,—you saw him slap the man?
A. Yes, sir.
Q. The colored man was sitting with his back towards you?
A, Yes, sir.
Q. Mr. Morris came towards you, and slapped the colored man, who was sitting ahead of you; is that it?
A. Yes, sir.
Q. Did he strike him more than once?
A. Well, sir, I could not be certain whether he struck him once or twice.
Q. Did he strike him a light, or heavy blow?
A. Well sir, I could not tell you whether it was a heavy blow, or a light one.
Q. You say he was as near to you as from here to the wall, yonder?
A. No, sir; I don't think he was.
Q How far from you?
A. Well, sir, I could not tell you the distance.
Q. Facing right towards you?
A. No, sir.
Q. Was not Mr. Morris facing toward you, when he struck the colored man?

A. Well, I think so.
Q. You can't tell whether the blow was a light, or heavy one?
A. I could not.
Q. You don't know whether he struck him once, or twice?
A. I don't recollect now.
Q. Did he say anything to the man?
A. Not that I heard.
Q. He simply came forward and struck him?
A. Yes, sir.
Q. How long a time were you in the prison,—thirty months, I think you said?
A. Yes, sir.
Q. Were you there before?
A. Yes, sir.
Q. Under the other management?
A. What other management?
Q. Before Mr. Morris came there, I mean?
A. Bingham?
Q. Yes.
A. No, sir.
Q. Was you ever in State prison before?
A. Yes, sir.
Q. Under whom?
A. Under Mr. Dox.
Q. How long a time were you there then?
A. I don't recollect. I was there a short time something over twenty years ago.

Mr. Bartow:
Q. Did you know Ben. Hill in the State prison?
A. No, sir; I don't recollect a man by that name.
Q. Did you know a man by the name of Henry Stimson?
A. Not by the name.
Q. Did you know Mike Harrigan?
A. No; I don't know them by that name.
Q. Did you know a man by the name of Waterman?
A. Yes, sir.
Q. Have you ever witnessed his punishment?
A. I think he is the man that escaped from there. I think he wore the wire cap when he got back. I won't be certain, but it is my impression that he did.
Q. Do you remember a man by the name of Smalley?
[No answer.]
Q. Do you remember a man called Jim Ballard?
A. Yes, sir.
Q. Where was he?
A. In the wash-room.
Q. Did you ever witness his punishment?
A. No, sir.
Q. Did you know a man by the name of O'Neil?
A. Yes, sir.
Q. Jim. Wilson—is that the one you have been describing here?
A. Yes, sir; his name is James Wilson.
Q. Do you know one called Bill Wilson?

A. There was another one by the name of Wilson; what his given name was I don't know.

Q. Did you know a man by the name of Rush?

A. There was a great many men that I was personally acquainted with for a long time that I did not know their names; my recollection of names is very poor.

Q. Did you know Costellow?

A. Not by the name.

Q. Willis?

A. Yes, sir.

Q. Do you remember Jim. Clark?

A. There was several men there by that name.

Q. I will describe him more particularly; do you remember the man that aided what they called Silver Jack to escape?

A. No, sir.

Q. Did you see Driscoll, the man that was shot after he escaped?

A. No, sir; not at the time he was in the hospital; I did not see him.

Q. Did you see him after he was shot?

A. Yes, sir; I saw him afterwards.

Q. Did you converse with him or Mr. Morris about the circumstance of the shooting?

A. No, sir; I never did.

Q. Did you ever hear Mr. Morris admit, in the presence of the prisoners, that he had punished men who had not deserved it, and he was willing to acknowledge it?

A. No, sir; I don't know that I ever did.

Mr. Webber:

Q. You knew Thurston?

A. Yes, sir.

Q. Drayton Thurston?

A. Yes, sir.

Q. Did you know him before he was in the prison?

A. No, sir.

Q. How familiarly acquainted with him were you in the prison?

A. Well, when I went to work in the yard I used to see him almost every day; frequenty talked with him.

Q. What was his mental condition, as to being uniform or otherwise?

A. Well, sir, I used to think that the man was considerably out of his face by spells; deranged, crazy; he acted so to me.

Q. Do you know of any facts which led him to that condition of mind?

A. Well, I frequently heard him talk about the difficulty with his wife that lived near by; about her getting a divorce from him and marrying another man that worked there in the yard; a foreman that had previously been a convict there; talked on about it; got quite wild about it; swore vengeance on all of them.

Q. Was that man that married his wife after her divorce from him at work there; around there where Thurston could see him?

A. Yes, sir.

Mr. Bartow:

Q. Mr. Perkins, did you come from Adrian?

A. Yes, sir; I came from there here; I have been there a week or so; my residence is in Jackson.

Mr. Webber:

Q. Was Thurston's manner when he talked on this subject of his troubles in regard to his wife, any different from what it was ordinarily, when that subject was not in his mind?

A. Yes, sir; very different; whenever he commenced to talk about it he used to continue until he got apparently beside himself; he went on like a crazy man; at other times he would seem to be rational, and quiet, and peaceable, attend to his own work, and mind his own business.

Re-cross-examination by Mr. Seager:

Q. Can you locate any more definitely this man. At the time that this man Wilson was punished that you speak of. I find here five instances on the pages that I have marked here, the dates of which he was punished. None of them seem to correspond with the one you speak of. I have got down to December, 1873; was it later than that?

A. The whipping, I think, was during the latter part of the year that I was in the shop; I think it was the latter part of that year. He had been there I know some little time; he was punished after he had been there but a short time for attempting to make his escape.

Q. Was it warm weather or cold weather. I see he was punished twice for trying to make an escape. Was it in warm weather or cold weather that this occurred?

A. Well, sir, I can't tell you.

Q. Did he ever escape that you know of?

A. No, sir. Mr. Bedford would recollect the time I presume; he could get at the time nearer than I can recollect it.

Q. Did he ever escape that you know of?

A. Yes, sir; I heard of his escaping I think afterwards, or making an attempt; I don't know whether he got away or not.

Q. How do you know anything about Thurston?

A. All I knew about him was from talking with him in the yard.

Q. Did you have any business to talk with him in the yard?

A. I did talk with him.

Q. Well, did you have any business to, I mean?

A. It was a common practice.

Q. Was it a violation of the rules?

A. No, sir, I don't think it was; the men used to talk; used to talk in the presence of the keeper.

Q. Was there a rule that you should or should not talk, or was there no rule on the subject?

A. Yes, sir; it was a rule that they should not talk in the shops, but they were allowed to talk in the yard freely, and done it in the presence of the keepers; the men all talked. They would get together up in the shops there, twenty or thirty, and be there a half a day at a time, and talk what they pleased, and when they pleased. That is, I mean the State shops, as they were called.

Q. Do you mean to say that men would leave their work, and go to the shop whenever they were a mind to and talk a half a day at a time?

A. I mean that were around the yards, that hadn't any work to do, as I know of.

Q. Did not they all have some work to do that were down there in the yard?

A. There was a number of days that there would be a large number of men that would not be employed at all; they used to gather around the yard and in the shops.
Q. Did not you have any person over you?
A. No, sir.
Q. Was there nobody whose business it was to look after you at such times?
A. Well, there was a good deal of the time that no one did look after them; whether any one had business to I don't know; the yard master would not be there, nor any one else.
Q. It was in the yard that you talked with Thurston?
A. Yes, sir.
Q. Was that before or after you came there from the hospital,—from the asylum, I should say?
A. It was after, I think.
Q. After you came from the asylum?
A. Yes, sir; it was not a great while before Thurston's time was out.
Q. Did you have any talk with Thurston while you were engaged on the bookkeeping over in the shoemakers' shop?
A. No, sir.
Q. He was not with you at all?
A. No, sir.
Q. Was not with you in the asylum?
A. No, sir.
Q. The talk you had with him then was about a year ago. You say you were a year in the shoeshop, eight months over in the asylum, which would make it twenty months, and you were there altogether about thirty months, and left about two months ago, so it was about a year ago when you had an opportunity to talk with Mr. Thurston?
A. Yes, sir; when Mr. Thurston was in the yard to work.
Q. It was within the last year?
A. I think so; some little time before his time expired.

Mr. Webber:

Q. You spoke of convicts having starched bosoms and calf boots. Can you give the names of those?
A. Well, they were men that were in the hospital, and in the kitchen, and around in different places.
Q. Can you name any of them?
A. Well, there was one in the kitchen,—Leonard was one.
Q. Any others?
A. Another man there,—a life man named Kidd, I think his name was; I don't recollect their names, all of them.
Q. You say that man was a man that was there for life?
A. Yes, sir.
Q. Were there any others that had any considerable length of time to serve that were permitted that kind of clothing?
A. Well, there is a number that are altogether better dressed than the generality of men there; several that are around the hall and the master's office, some two or three, and some around the kitchen and in the barber-shops that are dressed in those respects better than the other men altogether, and the others that worked in the halls, a good many of them.
Q. Do you know what their previous condition of life had been?

A. No, sir.
Q. Did you know one instance what the men were there for?
A. I did not.

Re-cross-examination by Mr. Seager:
Q. What kind of shirts did these men have?
A. Some of them had the shirts that are usually worn there,—that is the same, nearly, only made up in a different shape.
Q. How made up in different shape?
A. Made up with a bosom and collar; some had a different material,—this large checked stuff.
Q. Were these shirts that were made differently made in the prison?
A. I don' know where they were made.
Q. Did not they come in there on the convicts?
A. I don't think they did.
Q. Where do you think they come from?
A. They looked to me as though they were made of the same cloth that was worn there by the others, some of them.
Q. Who made them?
A. Made in the tailor-shop, I should conclude.
Q. Shirts made out of the same cloth as the others, but made with bosoms?
A. Some of them, and some of them made with different cloth; checked shirts?
Q. Any white shirts?
A. I don't recollect seeing any white shirts.
Q. How about the boots? you spoke about the men wearing calf-skin boots.
A. I have seen a good many men there wearing calf-skin boots nicely blacked up.
Q. Men were allowed to buy blacking and black their boots, were they not?
A. I don't know how that was; some men with their extra suit of clothes dressed up when they came to church, and others dirty and ragged.
Q. Where did they work?
A. Some of them worked in the shops, and some did not.
Q. Where they made their clothing dirty during the week?
A. No, sir; some that worked in the shoe shop, nothing that made it necessary for them to have an extra suit of clothes.
Q. Can you name them?
A. Only one I can name now,—Rabadow,—and Shoren. Well, quite a number.
Q. What is Shoren? Wasn't he the butcher?
A. He used to cut up the meat.
Q. Of course he had an extra suit of clothes. Who else? I don't know as I care to follow this up.
Mr. Morris—I will admit that there was a hundred men changed their clothes every Sunday.
Q. Those men you speak of being better dressed,—those doing their work,—how was it about the men that handled the food, waited on the table, and so on; were not they provided with clean clothes, to keep clean?
A. No, sir; some of them used to look pretty nasty, especially.
Q. Didn't they wear aprons or tunics?
A. They used to wear aprons when they were waiting on the table.

STATE PRISON INVESTIGATION.

JUNIUS AYERS SWORN.

Examined by Mr. Webber:

Q. Mr. Ayers, state your age, residence and occupation?
A. Age, 49; residence, Jackson; occupation, eating-house, or restaurant, as you choose to call it.
Q. How long have you resided at Jackson?
A. Nearly six years.
Q. Have you ever been employed at or about the prison?
A. Yes, sir. I came to the prison in the fore part of May, 1869.
Q. In what capacity?
A. First as a guard, and next as keeper.
Q. How long did you remain there after you went in there in May, 1869?
A. I left the last of September, 1873; I think the 25th or 26th of September.
Q. Who was Agent at the time you went there?
A. H. H Bingham.
Q. Do you recollect at what time Mr. Morris came there as Agent?
A. I think it was in the winter of 1871, or spring of 1871.
Q. What department were you employed in after Mr. Morris came there?
A. I was employed on the agricultural contract, shop No. 4.
Q. How many men were employed in that shop?
A. Well, some of the time during the time of my keeping the shop, I had as a steady thing from eighteen to thirty-nine. At times there were men brought in from different shops so that I had as high as fifty.
Q. What was the practice in regard to the convicts, who desired to speak to the agent or the inspectors. Were they at liberty to speak to them directly, as they came around through the shop?
A. They did do it.
Q. Without the intervention of the keeper?
A. Without the intervention of the keeper, so far as I was concerned.
Q. State whether that was a common occurrence for them to speak directly to the agent or inspectors without the intervention of the keeper?
A. So far as my shop. I can't speak for any other shop.
Q. I mean in your shop?
A. Yes, sir.
Q. It was a common occurrence?
A. Yes, sir. Very seldom that the inspectors passed through the shop without more or less of the convicts speaking to them.
Q. Were you familiar with the rules that were in force while you were there?
A. I was.
Q State whether that was in violation of the rules or not?
A. I think, under the forepart of the administration that I was under, I think it was rather in violation of the rules, but under Mr. Morris' administration I never knew of its being in violation of the rules for my superior officers to speak to the men passing through the prison.
Q. But for the men to speak to the officers?
A They used to speak to me first to know if they could have that permission, if they passed near their work. The men usually spoke to me about it before the inspectors passed through the shop.
Q. Were there any cases that came to your notice of any considerable number, where the convicts spoke directly to the superior officers, without asking your permission to do so?

A. I don't recollect at the present time of any, without speaking to me, before they came through the shop, unless it was an accidental visit of Mr. Morris through the shop, and of course I did not interfere.

Q. What was the custom when you were there about the convicts conversing with the freemen in the shop?

A. The rules in regard to the freemen connected with the institution was, that they should not converse with the convicts, only in regard to their work, either of the foremen or keepers.

Q. Was that rule observed?

A. Generally observed, so far as I know sir. The keeper cannot always tell whether the foreman is conversing strictly about the work or not, when he is a hundred, or a hundred and fifty feet away.

Q How large was this shop in which you were keeper?

A. I think the main shop was about two hundred feet long; then I had two side shops to look after.

Q You had three shops to look after?

A. Well, you can call it three shops,—there were two side shops.

Q. Under Mr. Morris' administration, did you observe any difference in his treatment of convicts; in other words whether he treated some with more kindness and consideration than he did others?

A So far as my shop was concerned,—I had but little opportunity to observe anything outside of the shop. My duties were confined wholly to the shop, from the time that I unlocked my men in the morning, until I locked them up again at night, then I left the prison as soon as possible.

Q. Well, so far as your shop was concerned, did you observe any discrimination?

A. I did not, sir.

Q. Did you ever witness any punishment inflicted in the prison, under Mr. Morris' administration?

A. I did.

Q. What punishments were inflicted?

A. I saw a man for a few moments once stretched upon that cross; it was only for a few minutes; perhaps I was in the room five minutes; I don't think to exceed that length of time. It was one of my men that was there. I tried to get him off the cross at work as soon as possible. He was put on the cross by a report that he made himself,—no report of mine. He reported me to Mr. Morris, and the report was so *absurd* that he punished him for making such a report.

Q. What was the report which this man had made of you?

A. Well, sir, I declare, Mr. Morris never explained the report to me. But he wished to get me out of the shop. I had previously reported the man; he was a man of bad conduct. I had reported him and he had been punished under Mr. Bingham.

Q. What was this convict's name.

A. Kincade. He is not at the prison now, sir.

Q. What was he there for?

A. I think,—taking his own statement, for it is all I know about it,—that it was called a bank swindle. He was a seven years man, sent from Detroit.

Q. He made a report to Mr. Morris concerning you?

A. Concerning me.

Q. Were you examined concerning the truth of that report?

A. I believe Mr. Morris said to me that he had inquired. This was in the early part of Mr. Morris' administration. He had inquired of the contractor and the different foremen, and of the contractor, Mr. Cooley, in regard to me as a keeper, and found that I was all right. That is what he said. Mr. Cooley says Mr. Ayers is all right as a keeper. That is all there is of it, as I recollect the conversation.

Q Then this man was ordered punished without bringing you and the convict together before the Agent?
A. Yes, sir.

Q. Do you know how long he had been on the cross when you went in to see him?
A. I do not.

Q Do you know how long he remained after you came away?
A. I don't recollect; I think not a great while. I think he was in the shop within an hour after I returned to the shop. Mr. Morris sent for me to come to the hall after he was placed on the cross, and after he had conversed with the foremen and contractor in regard to me being a good and reliable keeper, then he sent for me.

Q. How long after this convict had made a complaint to Mr. Morris concerning you was it before Mr. Morris punished him?
A. That I don't know, sir. He was in the hall and I was in the shop.

Q. Did you ever witness any other convict being punished.
A. One.

Q. What was the manner of that punishment?
A. He was flogged.

Q What was his name?
A. Thurston. I did not witness all of that punishment.

Q. Was Thurston in your shop?
A. He was not.

Q. Was he ever in your shop, under you as a keeper?
A. Not under my charge.

Q. Had you any opportunity to observe him closely or familiarly?
A. Well, he was used as an engineer on the cabinet contract, and a window opens where sometimes a portion of my men were called out of the shop on the platform to tie up the goods, a portion of them for shipment, and there was a window from the engine-room opening right out from this platform, and he would go out, or hang out of this window and talk with those men, and I reported him for it once.

Q. Do you know whether he was punished for that?
A. I think not; I don't know positively, but I think not, sir.

Q Well, what I want to get at is, whether you had opportunities enough to observe the conduct of the man closely, so as to be able to judge as to his mental condition?

A. Well, that was the only opportunity, as I could see him there. He afterwards came to the window and provoked one of my men in such a way with insulting language, that he threw a hammer at him and tried to kill him, and I wish he had. My boy was pretty severely punished, and he was not punished, through the intervention of some freeman there. Of course I don't know positively, but I think it was through the intervention of some freeman connected with the shop; I think it was the engineer. Mr. Martin was deputy at that

23

time, and he got off from being punished, and I wanted him punished; he deserved it, for he provoked the fuss.

Q. But your man was punished?

A. My man was punished.

Q. How was he punished?

A. All I know about it was what I saw and heard from the convict.

Q. Do you know how severely he was flogged?

A. Well, he did not receive a great number of lashes, but it was pretty severely laid on.

Q. Did you see his body after he came back?

A. I saw one pretty severe cut, if it had been twice as severe I would have been glad of it.

Q. Where was that cut that you saw?

A. That was I think, just under that rib here,—just below the rib, the worst one. I think he only received about ten lashes, according to his own statement; I did not count the number of scars.

Q. That cut that you saw just under the ribs and a little in front, was through the skin?

A. Yes, sir.

Q. How long a cut?

A. Well, sir, I don't recollect.

Q. What time was it that punishment was inflicted?

A. Well, sir, it would bother me to give you the date.

Q. Can you tell the year?

A. I think, I will not be positive, whether it was the first or second year of Mr. Morris' administration. It was along in the fore part of the season, when they were bundling up the horse rakes to ship; it was in the spring of the year; it must have been in the second year, because the whip was not brought into the yard. It was the second year of his admisistration, I think, and he was a very good boy after that.

Q. What was the name of that boy of yours?

A. He was under the name of Simpson.

Q. In the prison known as Simpson?

A. In the prison known as Simpson.

Q. Did you ever witness any other punishment?

A. I did not witness this punishment?

Q. Did you ever witness any other punishment?

A. None but Thurston, and only a portion of that. That was Thurston's last whipping, as I understand it.

Q. Do you know what other puishments were inflicted in the prison?

A. I have no means of knowing, only by reports.

Q. Had you any access to the prison records?

A. I don't know whether we were allowed—

Q. Did you ever look at them?

A. I never did. I don't know whether we were allowed that privilege or not. So far as I was concerned, my duties were arduous enough, without looking up prison records; I was glad to get out and home as soon as possible.

Q. What opportunities had the men that were in your shop of knowing what the prison rules required them to do?

A. The prison rules was read to the entire body of men, or the body of men that was in the prison, or dining-room at one time, by the chaplain. That is the only time I recollect of the prison rules being read to the men in general, any farther than they were explained to them by the keepers. But so far as I was concerned, I always made it a point, if a man came into my shop,—a new man, understand,—I talked with him and informed him, as far as possible, in regard to those rules, and what I should require of him, and, also, to give him to understand what the penalties would be, in case of a violation of those rules.

Q. Well, suppose that you informed him of this rule, for instance, the rule which prohibited conversation; what penalty did you tell him would follow if he should violate it?

A. I could not tell him what the punishment would be; it was not for me to know. A keeper don't know the punishment that a convict will receive for any conduct that he is reported for. As I understand this, it is left discretionary with the Agent and deputy, so far as I understand the prison rules.

Q. And that discretion is exercised after the report is made?

A. After the report is made, as I understand it.

Q. When you were informing new convicts that came in your shop, of the punishment that would follow an infraction of the rules, what information did you give them?

A. I told them that I did not know what the punishment would be, but they would find it severe enough. I wanted, in the first place, for them to understand that the punishment might be very severe, to deter them from committing these infractions of the rules, for the benefit of themselves.

Q. Did you ever report men for infraction of the rules who were not punished?

A. I have.

Q. How many such cases do you know of?

A. Well, I don't know how many, sir; I could not tell the number; I never kept any record of it.

Q. Were one-half of the cases that you reported punished?

A. I think not. There was a time during Mr. Morris' administration that the deputy neglected to report to Mr. Morris some very serious infractions of the rules. Deputy Martin I am speaking of.

Q. You say there was a time when Deputy Martin neglected to report?

A. I think he did, because he did not take the men in for some very serious, I considered, infraction of the rules, such as clinching each other, getting up rows; I had to pull them apart several times; reported them to Deputy Martin; considered them rather serious infractions of the rules.

Q. No punishment would follow?

A. No punishment; they were never taken out of the shop. I did not blame Mr. Morris for those instances, because I did not think he ever knew of it.

Q. Did you ever speak to Mr. Morris yourself about these?

A. Afterwards I did, when I found out the thing was going entirely too far.

Q. How long did it go on in this way before you reported direct to Mr. Morris?

A. Well, I think it is as much as four or five months; until I hadn't any discipline in the shop, nor could not enforce any; I was obliged to do it; the rules, understand, don't require the keeper to report to the Agent direct; there is no rule laid down where a keeper shall report a superior officer, that I have ever seen; my duty was to report to the deputy, and the deputy's duty to report to the Agent.

Q. When you found out the deputy was not doing his duty, you then reported him to Mr. Morris?

A. I went and had a talk with Mr. Morris, and he thought it was almost impossible that such things could be, but he soon found out that it was not impossible; it was very improbable that it could have been carried on for some time.

Q. How much longer did Mr. Martin remain as deputy?

A. I can't tell the exact time, but not a great while.

Q. Well, some months?

A. I should think perhaps two or three months; not more than that; I don't know as it was as long; but I should not think any more than two or three months.

Q. After you had had that talk with Mr. Morris, what instructions did Mr. Morris give you about reporting thereafter?

A. I don't recollect as he gave me any in particular.

Q. After that time did you report cases direct to Mr. Martin, as before

A. I don't recollect; I could say that I failed to report, because it was useless; I could control my men better without reporting them to Deputy Martin than I could to have a report and have no attention paid to it.

Q. Did you ever punish a man yourself in the prison?

A. I never did, sir.

Q. Were any of the keepers ever allowed to punish men in the prison?

A. Not to my knowledge.

Q. Well, after you had had this talk with Mr. Morris, were the reports which you made afterwards attended to promptly?

A. I don't recollect now, sir, that I ever made any other report to Mr. Martin; reports after there was a change of deputies was promptly attended to.

Q. When you had this talk with Mr. Morris, from that time until Martin left, did you have occasion to report anybody?

A. I think I did.

Q. Who did you report to then?

A. I did not report at all, as I said before.

Q. You did not make any report?

A. No, sir.

Q. Until after the deputy was changed?

A. Until after the deputy was changed; I could keep better discipline without than I could with it.

Q. What means did you resort to to preserve discipline, when you found things in such shape that reports did no good?

A. I used to treat my men kindly, and never report them unless actually necessary. My reports were not frequent.

Q. You found that treatment to be more effective?

A. I found that, in many instances, to be all that was necessary. In a few instances I found where nothing, I think, but brute force would control, but they were rare.

Q. I was going to ask you what proportion of the men that came under your notice, while you were there, that nothing but brute force would control?

A. I don't think it would exceed one to ten; not more than that; perhaps not as many as that; it would not more than that, at any rate.

Q. The nine-tenths you could get along with, without much trouble?

A. Without much trouble, sir. I never a very great deal of trouble myself, until after the report ceased to be of any effect.

Q. You took the men from the cells to the shop in the morning?

STATE PRISON INVESTIGATION. 181

A. Yes, sir.
A. And then back to their cells again when it came night?
A. I took them from the cells in the first place to the washing trough, from the wash trough to the dining-room, from the dining room to the shop, from the shop to the dining-room for dinner, from the dinner-table to the shop, and from there to their cells at night.
Q. Did they have their supper in their cells at night?
A. They had their supper in their cells ; it was issued to them in the halls, and they took it to their cells.
Q. In taking them from the shop to the dining-room, or to their cells, were they marched out in regular files?
A. Yes, sir ; close ranks.
Q. Was there ever any conversation among themselves in the ranks?
A. Sometimes men would speak, but in marching a company of forty men, which was usually the company that I took out, if my gallery was full, thirty-five, I think was the least, it was pretty difficult for a man to see the whole length of his ranks, in marching around the turns and corners of the wing, sometimes men would speak.
Q Was that an infraction of the rules?
A. It was.
Q. For such an infraction did you ever report anybody?
A. I reported for such infractions, but not often.
Q. Do you know what punishment was inflicted for such infractions?
A. I do not, sir.
Q. Did you ever have any trouble with your men on account of the use of tobacco?
A. I have had men find a great deal of fault on account of not receiving tobacco. I have had men under my charge which at one time we had the right to give tobacco, if we saw fit, and I bought tobacco and gave it to them ; that when they got out of their regular rations, that was issued weekly, that they were almost like a man that is in the habit of drinking a great deal, if they are cut off from their stimulant.
Q. Did you find that you could preserve better discipline by giving them tobacco than you could without it?
A I think it would be a great benefit to the institution if tobacco was issued; a reasonable amount to convicts.
Q. This is your opinion, from your experience in the prison?
A. From my observation in the prison, and from my own experience as a tobacco user. [Laughter.]
Q. How long time did you keep up this practice of buying tobacco yourself to supplement the short rations?
A. Until we were forbidden to do it.
Q. Well, I want to know about how long a time this was?
A. Until Mr. Morris cut the tobacco short on the new men that were coming into the prison.
Q. Yes, but that don't tell me how many months it was?
A. Well, sir, I can't tell you ; I think, if I recollect right, it was the fourth of July, 1873 ; I am not certain whether it was 1872 or 1873.
Q. Up to that time you had had the privilege, if you saw fit, of furnishing an extra amount of tobacco to your men?
A. Yes, sir ; sometimes the boys that did not use but a little tobacco would

have a surplus, and they would give it to me—say, here, I have got tobacco, take it and keep it for me if I want it, or if you know of a convict that needs it give it to them; I have done that; some men used but very little, others required more.

Q. In your observation of Mr. Morris, in his intercourse with the convicts, have you observed any want of evenness of temper and disposition of the treatment of them?

A. I can't say that I ever saw anything that showed ill-temper but once.

Q. What occasion was that on?

A. It was the occasion of his receiving the knife from Thurston; whether it was from excitement, or ill-temper, or passion, I know not.

Q. Did you ever see Mr. Morris indulge in any personal violence to the convicts except when they were receiving regular punishment?

A. I never have, sir.

Q. What were your opportunities for observing his personal intercourse with the convicts?

A. They were very familiar.

Q. Have you knowledge of any other facts other than what you have already mentioned that the committee should know relative to the discipline of the prison?

A. Well, I don't know that I do.

G. Nothing occurs to you as affecting the question, what was Mr. Morris' manner as to his subordinates, keepers and guards?

A. His treatment was always kind as a general thing, so far as my intercourse was concerned.

Q. Well, so far as you observed in his intercourse with others?

A. I never saw any thing that I considered out of the way.

Q. State whether the convicts that came under your observation were uniformly dressed, or whether some had advantages over others in that respect?

A. The shop men, so far as my observation went, some of the men working in very dirty shops, such as the trip-hammer shop, very dirty work, had an extra suit of clothes for the Sabbath.

Q. Well, did the men working in your shop have an extra suit of clothes for Sabbath?

A. There was, I think two or three that worked in the machine shop, one of my side shops, that had an extra suit of clothes, and I think one or two in the main shop, that was doing oiling, and that kind of work that got their clothes very greasy; I think they had extra suits, at least some did. Sometimes they were pretty shabbily dressed, in consequence of a lack of an extra suit of clothes.

Q. Well, was there any discrimination that came to your notice, other than for the reason of the character of their employment?

A. Not with shop men. Men around the halls were usually a little better dressed and cleaner than shop men, that was all.

Q. Did you see any distinction as to the make of the clothing, whether some was made so as to be more desirable than others?

A. Well, I have seen vests and coats made and cut a little different for some men. I don't think it was by the consent or knowledge of the Agent, however, and I think it was done by the tailors themselves, as near as I could ascertain by the convicts; that it was the tailors themselves that done this, and, perhaps, in so many men passing by that the Agent never did notice this particular convict, that they would prepare a coat or vest a little different.

Q. Any difference in the boots?

A. I have seen men with very nice boots on, whether they were furnished by the Agent or by themselves, I know not; I think sometimes men have been allowed to furnish themselves with boots; but still, this I don't know positively, understand; but only from convicts saying that they furnished them themselves.

Q. Well, do you know whether convicts were allowed to receive presents of clothing, boots or shoes, anything of that kind?

A. I think they were allowed to receive under-shirts and drawers, a portion of the time, from their friends.

Q. Did you observe other parts of the prison except in your own department?

A. I think the question that you are asking me now, in regard to those men— I think it was after I left the prison that there was so many men laying around; I had not the opportunity of running around the yard to see.

Q When you were there, any men that were laying about, apparently doing nothing?

A. I had no opportunity, unless they came out in front of the shop in the main yard—men from the hospital, that were able to get out and walk around the yard. I have noticed them frequently walking around the yard, my seat facing the yard, I could see them passing around the yard, but, as for their collecting in the State shops, etc., I had no opportunity of seeing it whatever.

Mr. Mellen:

Q. What time in the year was it that this punishment of Kincade took place, as near as you can recollect?

A. Well, it was in the spring of the year.

Q. What year?

A. I am not positive, but I think it was in 1871; I will not be sure.

Mr. Jones:

Q. After Mr. Morris was there?

A. It was after Mr. Morris was there. The punishment, I would like to state, with your permission—

Mr. Webber—Go on.

The Witness—Was not half as severe, in his case, as it ought to have been.

Mr. Webber:

Q. Which case is that?

A. Kincade.

Mr. Mellen:

Q. He was punished for reporting you, I understand?

A. Yes, or any punishment that I ever knew him to receive during my stay at the prison. He was a bad man; his conduct was very bad all the way through; and when I first went to the prison I was told by all the foremen—

Mr. Webber—It is not material what you were told.

The witness—Well, they simply gave me a history of his conduct before I took charge of him. That was all I was going to say.

Mr. Mellen:

Q. Had you reported him?

A. I had reported him under Mr. Bingham's administration; I think I never had under Mr. Morris' up to this time. But I was obliged to report him afterwards.

Mr. Webber:
Q. Did you conceive any dislike to him by reason of his having reported you?
A. I did not; convicts get all,—well, I won't say they get all they deserve,—because I don't think they have some of the time; but I will say this: they get the worst of it generally.
Q. Is it safe for a convict to report a keeper? Is it safe for the convict?
A. Well, that is the only time that I ever knew of a convict's reporting me. I think there was four of them got punished at that time on their own statements, either three or four.
Q. For reporting you?
A. For reporting me.
Q. Did you ever know of any other case where any other keeper was reported by convicts?
A. Well, I don't know; I had no means of knowing.
Q. What was the usage of the prison? If a convict was abused by a keeper, what was the usage of the prison with having his wrongs redressed?
A. Generally there was an investigation, if there was any reason to suppose that a convict had been abused by a keeper, that the Agent would investigate the keeper and see whether he had or had not abused such convict; that was the usual course.
Q. How was this brought to the Agent's notice?
A. It was brought to his notice from the keeper, and then by conversing with the convict; and I have known of his going and ascertaining from others the facts in the case, to ascertain the facts as near as he could. He did not wish to punish a man unjustly.
Q. Let me suppose a case. Suppose that you had conceived a spite against one of the men under your administration, under your care, and that you had exercised undue severity to that man, imposed harder tasks on him than on other men, and required him to perform them, how would that man obtain redress?
A. By application to the Agent.
Q. Would not his application be through you?
A. Not necessarily, because the Agent is usually about the prison; he can be seen at any time by applying to the guard.
Q. Did you ever know of a case where a convict complained of a keeper?
A. I never did; I never have known of any except this one, my own instance.
Q. Can you give the date when that complaint was made against you?
A. I can not.
Q. Can you give near enough so we can find it on the record?
A. It was sometime in the spring, I think the first year of Mr. Morris' administration.
Q. That would be in the spring of 1871?
A. 1871 I think. There was the case of Kincade and of Armstrong, I think both. Armstrong reported to me when he came back to the shop, that he had been crucified. That is the term that he used for being stretched on the cross. He was one of the men that reported me.
Q. Who were the others. You said there were three or four of them?
A. I have forgotten the other man's name. I think there was one other, if my memory serves me right.
Mr. Seager—I wish to read the record of this punishment. "May 18th, 1871, Thomas Kincade, John Armstrong, Fred Seifers, and Henry Simpson entered

into a compact not to go to their work, but remained in the dining-room and preferred charges against keeper Ayers. The courage of all except Armstrong and Kincade failed. They remained and were allowed to tell their stories in full, but failed completely to make any reasonable charge against their keeper ; and those two men were severely punished by several hours each upon the cross until they promised to return to their work, and perform their duties faithfully. The four men admitted to being in the plot, but Seifers and Simpson were let off with a sharp reprimand, from the fact that they did not make themselves very prominent in the matter, but simply encouraged it with talk and promises."

JAMES L. PERKINS RECALLED.

Mr. Webber—I would like to ask Mr. Ayers a question or two before we take up this other witness.

Q. Is this record that has just been read, the record of the case which you have spoken of?

A I think it is, sir.

Q. Do you remember whether you took this man from the cells that morning?

A. I don't remember now; we did not take all of our own men out in the morning from their cells. Understand, the men was mixed; but we took them from the dining-room in companies and marched them to their shops.

Q. Did you call this man at the dining-room that morning?

A. I called my company as usual, and this man wasn't marched out, and when we got to the shop that man was missing. Sometimes they stopped to get medicine, or something of that kind. If they are missing for any number of minutes, half an hour or so, we then send the lumpers to know where these men are, to notify the officers there that they are missing from their work. I got notice of this man being in the hall myself without sending for him.

Q How long after you got to the shop before you received that notice?

A. Well, sir, I can't tell you.

Q. Well, was it less than half an hour?

A. I should think not far from half an hour.

Q. What is the name of this man you called to send for them?

A. Lumpers, they are called. Each keeper has a man that is called a lumper to do running, bringing water, etc., for the balance of the men, and, if necessary, to go after the deputy.

Q. Is this lumper a convict?

A. This lumper is a convict.

Mr. Mellen:

Q. What legitimate opportunity has a convict for reporting their keeper?

A None, only as he sees the officers, that I know of; he would see the deputy twice a day passing through the shop, and generally the Agent about once a day.

Mr. Seager:

Q. Does he have any opportunity in the dining-room?

A. He has of seeing the deputy, not always the Agent.

Q. How does he report if he wants to call the attention of the deputy or the Agent?

A He calls the keeper's attention.

Q. How? By speaking to them?

A. Well, he may, or he will motion to him; if he nods his head he will go up and ask him what he wants; if he says to see the deputy, he has permission from the keeper to walk out and see the deputy; it is a very rare occurrence, however.

Mr. Jones—If he wanted to report a keeper, would he be very apt to call on the keeper for the privilege of reporting him to the Agent?

A. I should presume not; I don't know.

Mr. Mellen :

Q. Would that be his redress in that case?

A. He could do so, however, and the keeper would be obliged to make his request known, if he done his duty as a keeper, no matter if it was to report himself.

Q. What remedy would the convict have in case the keeper refused to notice him?

A. He would have to call on the Agent or Inspectors.

Mr. Morris—Is it customary for a convict to raise his hand as he is filing out past the deputy or Agent if he wants to see him,—if he is sick, or has any special favor to ask?

A. I think it is, sir; usually, if they are at the table in the dining-room the keepers are watching the men at the tables; if they want to leave their seat they call the keeper's attention to it; and then if they are marching out in the ranks they usually speak to the keeper,—at least my men do,—and then call the deputy's attention, and they have liberty then to pass out of the ranks.

James L. Perkins, examined by Mr. Bartow:

Q. Mr. Perkins, while you were at the prison were men punished without their punishment being recorded?

A. Yes, sir, I think they were.

Q. Can you give any reason why?

Mr. Seager—If the committee please, I would like first to have something shown as to this witness' knowledge of what he states here, that there was any punishment that was not recorded.

Mr. Webber—That can come out on cross-examination.

A. I knew men, or knew one in particular, that was punished several times by being showered and by being locked in a cell, and his time expired a few days before mine. We slept in a cell right close together, and where a man was put on the record he was not allowed to let his beard grow until after the Board had decided as to whether they would take away the time on the record or not, and this man supposed that he was on the record, but did not know whether he was or not; he had been punished several times, and he told me that he was going to inquire of Mr. Wood. Eight weeks was the time allowed for them to allow their beard to grow previous to the expiration of their time, and he was going to ask Mr. Wood and find out whether he had got to shave any more; his time was up,—that is, his short time,—and unless he was upon the record he was not obliged to shave any more; he went and asked Mr. Wood, and Mr. Wood went and examined the record, and he was not upon the record at all, and his beard grew from that time on until he went out. That is what I know about it in that case.

Q. What reason was assigned for the punishment not being on record in that case?

A. Well, I understood always,—I had heard from the officers and keepers, that where a man had committed any offense for which he was punished, if the punishment that was inflicted was considered sufficient for the offense he was not put upon the record at all, nor no record made of the punishment ; but, if

STATE PRISON INVESTIGATION. 187

in addition to that, the Agent desired the board to notice the case, and take his time away, that he puts him on record for that purpose, to bring his case to the attention of the board, and they had authority to take away, in addition to the punishment, a portion, or all of his time—what they term good time.

Q. Then the record seemed to be an additional punishment?
A. Yes, sir.

Q. Now, from your observation, and from your communication with prisoners, what seemed to be the most effectual punishment to subdue the party charged with offenses?
A. Well, sir, what I have seen and heard them say that they dreaded most was to get into the bare naked lock-up, or dark hole as they call it, until they had to come to time; I have heard a great many of them say that they had rather be punished in any other manner—that they had rather be whipped, and they had rather be showered than to go in a dark cell through the night after a hard day's work.

Q. Did they assign any reason for that?
A. They assigned the reason, if it was in the winter, very cold, no bed, no chance to lay down, and no supper, and pretty hard fare generally.

Q. Well, did they assign as another reason, that they hated to come down and acknowledge?
A. Yes; when they had got in there they could not come out until they had shown pretty conclusive evidence that they had got enough.

Q. You understood they were kept there until they would make acknowledgments and promises that was required of them; did you ever know of an instance where convicts were kept locked in what was called the dark cell after they had acknowledged their error?
A. No, sir; I never did.

Q. Was it understood among the convicts that they had not the right to report their keeper for what they considered a wrong?
A. It was understood that they had a right to do it, but that they got no redress if they did do it, nor any possibility of any redress, nor probability; that it was of no use; that the statement of the keeper was conclusive against the prisoner; he had nothing to say.

Q. Why were men around the yard with nothing to do, apparently?
A. Well, sir, there was quite a number of men that were at work in the yard,—masters' gang, loading teams, and doing other work about the yard; and then there were other men that were at work around in different places, doing different kinds of work; and there would be times when those men had nothing to do; the yard-master would not be there, and these men had nothing to do, and they came to the different shops around there, and at the same time there would be many times when this gang was having nothing to do in the yard, for a day or two, sometimes two or three days; there was another gang that was at work in the State lot more or less, sometimes quite a number, and for some reason they would not be employed for several days, and they would be all through the yard together, and laying around these shops.

Q. These men are men that were not engaged on contracts?
A. Yes, sir; these men were men that were not engaged on contracts. There is a large number of men, for quite a length of time, that have not been engaged on contracts.

Cross-examined by Mr. Seager:

Q. What was the name of this man that you speak of that was discharged just prior to you?

A. His name was Robinson.
Q. What was is his first name?
A. Charles Robinson.
Q. How many times do you know of his being punished, and what were the punishments.
A. I knew of his being showered once; he told me he had been showered several times.
Q. Showered once only?
A. Well, sir, it was while I was at the aslyum; that is, I did not see him showered.
Q. How do you know it was done?
A. Well, I only know it from hearsay.
Q. Did he tell you it was done?
A. Yes, sir.
Q. That was between one and two years ago; it was while you were at the asylum?
A. I think it was while I was there.
Q. Well, locate the date by what you were doing at that time?
A. Well, I don't know but it was while I was at work in the yard; I can't recollect the time.
Q. Well, what time in the year was it?
A. I think it was in the fall.
Q. Fall of what year?
A. I think it was in the fall that the shoe contract broke up there.
Q. What fall was that?
A. It was the fall of 1873, I think.
Q. Do you know of his being punished at any other time?
A. Nothing, only what he told me.
Q. How did he tell you that he was punished?
A. He told me that he had been showered two or three times, and I have seen him put into the dark hole, and kept in there through the night.
Q. When was that?
A. That was not more than a month before his time was out.
Q. When was his time out?
A. His time was out the 6th day of March.
Q. So, it was along some time this last February or January?
A. Yes, sir.
Q. This present year?
A. Yes sir.
Q. Who told you that punishments were made that were not put on record?
A. Well, sir, I understood it from what I heard the Agent say, and from what I had heard others.
Q. Mr. Morris?
A. Yes, sir.
Q. What did you ever hear Mr. Morris say about it?
A. I have heard Mr. Morris make the statement,—I forget now, what particular offense he was taking about, but that he would,—something; I can't recollect in particular. He made a statement in the dining-room that he would punish them, and in addition to that he would put them upon the record, and have their time taken away.

STATE PRISON INVESTIGATION. 189

Q. Did you ever hear him make any statement, that there was no punishment that was not put on the record?

A. No, sir, I never heard him say that there was none that was not put on record.

Q. Did you ever examine the record yourself?

A. No, sir.

Q. Never saw it?

A. No, sir; I never had anything to do with it?

Q. Did you ever hear anybody but Mr. Morris, at the time you speak of, say anything about punishment that was not on the record?

A. I have heard, and had conversation with freemen there, and keepers.

Q. Well, whom?

A. Well, with Mr. Wood.

Q. What did Mr. Wood tell you?

A. Well, sir, I don't recollect the exact conversation.

Q. Well, what did he say? I don't care for his exact language. What did Mr. Wood tell you about there being punishments that were not put on record?

A. The conversation was in relation to men being punished.

Q. Did Mr. Wood tell you that there were ever any men punished, whose punishment did not appear on the secord?

A. No, sir; I don't know that he did tell me that directly.

Q. Did he tell you that indirectly?

A. Well, from the conversation I had with him, I took it that men were not necessarily put upon the record because they were punished.

Q Well, did he tell you directly or indirectly?

A. No, sir; he did not tell me that directly.

Q. Or indirectly?

A. No, not in those words.

Q. What did he till you from which you drew that inference?

A. Well, the talk was in relation to the men having their time taken from them.

Q. When was this conversation?

A. It was two or three months before I came out.

Q. What did Mr. Wood tell you in relation to the men having their time taken from them?

A. Well, he told me that if a man was not upon the record, and that—something, in relation to his knowing—

Q. I want to know what he said, not *something*, but I want you to tell what Mr. Wood said?

A. I can't tell you what he said. We had a considerable conversation, and the conversation came up from another man's coming to him and inquiring of him as to whether he must shave any. He stood there at the door of the wash-room, the day that the men in the yard were shaving, and he inquired of this man if he was upon the record, and he said he did not know, he had been reported, and had been punished; and Mr. Wood said that he would look on the record. If he was not on the record he would not have to shave.

Q. What man was that?

A. He was a man that was driving the big mule team; I don't recollect his name.

Mr. Morris—How long ago, Mr. Perkins,—two months ago?

A. Yes, sir, it was two months ago that he was driving the team. He was driving the team when I came out.

Q. Did Mr. Wood ever say anything else in relation to that matter?

A. No, sir; not that I now recollect of.

Q. Who else ever said anything to you in regard to it?

A. Well, sir, I don't recollect now; I have talked with a great many about it; that is, with the men in there, and the foremen and the contractors. We had a great many discussions.

Q. How did the foremen know anything about it?

A. It was in relation to taking away their time.

Q. Don't you know that it is the board of inspectors that determines when a man is on the record, to determine whether he shall lose time for the punishment or not?

A. I so understand it,—yes, sir.

Q. That the fact that a man's time is taken away from him, is no proof that a man's name is not on the record, that is if the board of inspector consider the punishment inflicted sufficient; that the man's name may be on the record, and they not take away his time?

A. I did know that that was the case.

Q. Don't you understand that it is the board of inspectors that determine whether a man's time be taken away, or not?

A. Yes, sir, my understanding was, that if a man was put upon the record, that the board would notice it, and take away some time.

JESSE PARMENTER RECALLED.

Examined by Mr. Seager:

Q. What is the rule as to good time?

A. A man may be punished,—I know of two instances in my own experience there, men were punished when I was as much to blame as they were, because I was inexperienced; we got into a row, and he got licked. I was indiscreet and imprudent, and it resulted in a severe punishment. Well, when his time expired,—he had from that time behaved himself first rate,—he came to me and wanted I should go before the board and make an explanation, and I did so; I told the board that I was as much to blame as he was. Another case,—Joseph Henry. He was punished. He had been there five years and had not been reported. Henry got angry, and said some insulting things to me, and I reported him,—that was under Mr, Bingham,—and he was punished. I think it might have been obviated without any difficulty, if we had not each of us got mad. And when his time expired, he came to me and asked me if I would not assist him. And I went to the board of directors and told them I was as much to blame as he was. It is frequently the case that when men were punished, and made a matter of record, the board in reviewing it,—I think the board would testify to that, if there are any of them here,—would think that that was sufficient, if the man's conduct be good from that time up. It might occur when he had not been there over six months, and his conduct be good from that time until the expiration of his sentence, and he would be released, and get the full amount of his good time for good behavior.

Q. So that the fact that a man's name appeared on record that he had been punished, don't necessarily affect his time?

A. No, sir.

Mr. Webber:

Q. Now, Mr. Parmenter, isn't it sometimes the case, that the Agent, in making his examination of these reports, discovers that the keeper, or guard, is as much to blame as the convict?

A. Well, I should suppose he would.

Q. Did you ever know of an instance where he made inquiry enough to find the keeper or guard at fault?

A. I don't remember such an instance.

Mr. Morris—It is quite a frequent thing, Mr. Webber.

The Witness—Those two instances that I stated in my own experience.

Mr. Webber—Yes, I know those, but I am speaking as a general rule?

A. Well, it might have been, and I not notice it.

[The committee here adjourned to meet at Jackson Tuesday, April 13th, at nine o'clock in the forenoon.]

TESTIMONY TAKEN AT JACKSON, APRIL 13TH, 1875.

REV. GEORGE H. HICKOX, SWORN FOR MR. MORRIS.

Examined by Mr. Conely:

Q. You are chaplain of the prison, I believe?

A. Yes, sir.

Q. How long have you been such?

A. Two years and a half and thirteen days, when to-day is past.

Q. To what extent do the duties of your office bring you in contact with the convicts?

A. Why, they carry me to each man personally.

Q. With what frequency?

A. I intend it shall be regularly done once in four weeks. That is by calling at the cells during Lord's day afternoon. If the man is asleep, I don't wake him; otherwise I pass along and speak to him. Sometimes the conversation is somewhat extended, other times not at all.

Q. What opportunities have you had since you have been here, of observing the discipline of the prison?

A. Well, that is only casual, for the chaplain has nothing to do with that, only indirectly.

Q. Are you able to say, from what you have seen, whether the discipline of the prison has been lenient, or severe?

A. I have thought the intention—the rule to be lenient.

Q. Has your position been such that you have to any extent ascertained the feeling of the convicts themselves in regard to the discipline of Mr. Morris?

A. Why, to some extent I learned it.

Q. Well, to such extent as it has gone, how have you ascertained that feeling to be?

A. It is that the discipline is rational and lenient.

Q. Are you able to say what Mr. Morris is doing to further the intellectual improvement or culture of the convicts?

A. I should think it correct to say that he is doing what he can with the means at his command.

Q. What is being done by him, or what has been done by him by way of the introduction of magazines, or other reading for the benefit of the convicts?

A. I understood that magazines were introduced by him previous to my coming here. Since then, from time to time, that kind of reading has been increased, until it includes very generally the common magazines of the country, more or less of each, and a fair share of the weekly and a small degree of the daily issues of the press, except so far as they are sporting; or objectional in that.

Q. Are you able to say what Mr. Morris' habit has been in relation to the Sunday exercises that are carried on within the prison?

A. Yes, sir.

Q. I wish you would state, if you please?

A. He is uniformly there; it would be sufficiently correct to say he is always there. He leads the singing, and otherwise does as he can—as he may.

Cross-examined by Mr. Webber:

Q. By whom is the chaplain employed—the chaplain of the prison?

A. I don't know as I understand your question. The State, I suppose. I don't think I understand your question, Mr. Webber.

Q. Who made the appointment of yourself?

A. Oh, the inspectors appoint a chaplain.

Q. At whose pleasure do you hold the position?

A. At that of the inspectors, so far as I am informed.

Q. You have been here two years and a half you say?

A. Yes, sir; I commenced in October,—two years ago the first day of October.

Q. You say your duties carry you to each man,—do you have personal intercourse with each convict?

A. Yes, sir.

Q. Any one else present at the time of your conversation with them?

A. That is as it happens to be; I don't send any one away, and I have no secrets with any of the convicts.

Q. Are the convicts at liberty to talk with you freely and fully on any subject they choose?

A. I can't say, sir.

Q. Do convicts ever complain to you of anything concerning their treatment in the prison?

A. I would like to know what you mean by complaint. Do you mean whether they simply speak to me of it, or whether they enter complaints,—which is it?

Q. I mean to say, do they speak to you of it?

A. They speak to me of treatment,—yes.

Q. Are you at liberty to report what you may learn of the convicts to the Inspectors concerning their treatment?

A. I don't think, sir, I can answer that question. Yoy ask if I am at liberty to do so. It is a question I never raised; I never heard it raised. There is nothing said to me about it. I have uniformly understood that that thing was not expected of me, and for that reason have been silent.

Q. When convicts have spoken to you touching their treatment, I understand you that you have not mentioned it to the Inspectors?

A. No, sir.

Q. And have you mentioned it to any one?

A. No, sir.

STATE PRISON INVESTIGATION.

Q. State whether it is a common occurrence for them to speak to you in a complaining manner, as if they wanted something different or felt that something wrong had been done them?
A. Oh, no, sir. Permit me, if I may be allowed—
Q. Certainly.
A. Permit me to say, that such is my attitude, because of the view that I may take of the intention of the law and the government of the prison, and discipline of the,—as issued in a small pamphlet form,—such is my attitude to all matters of discipline, that they do not come to me. They don't expect me to touch that question at all; so that it is well nigh true,—it would be true, popularly speaking,—to say that they did not come to me with any complaints.
Q. I don't mean complaints, as though you had authority—
A. I understand you.
Q. To redress them.
A. No, sir.
Q. Or information that you may convey to those in authority?
A. No, sir; it is a very uncommon thing.
Q. But when you are complained to by any on that subject, what information did you convey to the convicts as to your attitude?
A. I tell them it is a matter of discipline, and I can't do anything with it, or I have no power in the matter, and that I suppose it is the intention of the inspectors that I should not have anything at all to do with it.
Q. In your intercourse with the convicts, did you have opportunities to discover whether they are all properly clothed?
A. The question embarrasses me a little, because if I say no, then it is understood that I have no such opportunity; if I say yes, then it would be understood that I was looking after that thing, or that I took notice of it specially whenever it occurred, or came before my eyes; a thing which I did not do. The clothing is not in my department, and from that I pay no attention to it. If a man speaks to me, and says: "see how my pants are torn," or, "see, my shoes want tapping," I say to them, "well, you know where to go, you know what to do;" and if they say no, I say to them, "I suppose that belongs to the hall master." That explanation will cover all in that direction, so far as it now occurs to my mind. May I be allowed to remark, for me to be prepared to answer questions right along in that line, I should regard as a thing against me in my position. Were I hall master, I should take different views, but I am chaplain.
Q. Without reference to your duty, or your ideas of duty in your official position, I desire to ask you, as a fact, whether any cases have come to your notice, where convicts have suffered by cold or otherwise, for want of sufficient clothing?
A. I can't answer that; I don't know. I did not know.
Q. You have charge of the education, so far as they are being educated, of the convicts, have you not?
A. Yes, sir.
Q. What proportion of the convicts are pursuing studies under your direction?
A. Three hundred would not be far out of the way, including those who write to their friends on each Lord's day. Throwing out that class it would drop down to about 200, perhaps; very near 200 would be sufficiently correct and as near as I could get to it.

Q. What is your rule as to who shall be permitted to engage in study and who shall not?

A. Those who need the benefit of study as it is given here, and of that class as far as I am able, at the time to instruct them. Those do not receive instruction who do not need it. That is the rule. There is a record kept in the hall master's office, so that I am able to know when a man applies to me for admission in school, whether he can read—whether he can write—whether he has any knowledge of figures. Before giving him a place there in school, I satisfy myself on those points.

Q. If he can read and write does he have an opportunity of coming into your school?

A. No, sir; because there are those who, so far as facilities are furnished me now, who can neither read nor write. There are those in sufficient numbers to cover all the ground that I can occupy with the means at my command.

Q. What studies are taught by you in the prison?

A. There is reading; commencing with the letters of the alphabet, even, in some cases. We intend to carry a man in that, if he is obedient and diligent, until he can read understandingly. We teach arithmetic until a man is able to do ordinary business as a laborer, and slightly as a mechanic, and there we leave them. In a few instances the grammar has been used, but that is because the men themselves wished to use it, and we have gratified them. It has not been the practice, so far, to instruct them in grammar. We regard it as too difficult to carry the men sufficiently into that study, with our advantages, to make it worth while. Occasionally the geography is used, but we have not purchased any grammars or geographies for prison use.

Q. What hours are devoted to study?

A. No hours; one hour, from half past eight on Lord's day morning until half past nine the same morning.

Q. And that is the entire time that is devoted to the teaching of this 200?

A. That is all the time. A reference to my report will show you that perhaps, at any time when you may be pleased to refer to it.

Q. How many teachers are employed during this hour?

A. I think at present, sir, there are twenty-three. It may not be precisely twenty-three. We increased two or three lately.

Q. In questions of that character it is immaterial about your being precisely correct; stating that it is approximate is sufficient.

A. You will appreciate, I presume, a reasonable caution in the matter.

Q. Are those teachers convicts or freemen?

A. They are both.

Q. About how many teachers are convicts?

A. About one-half.

Q. And who are the freemen?

A. The keepers; not all the keepers, but they are from the number of the keepers.

Q. Are there any studies given to those who are being taught for them to pursue during the week in their cells as they please?

A. They all of them carry the books used in class to their cells. They are all furnished with books,—spellers, readers, arithmetics, or bibles; we use the bible; we teach the bible by both convicts and freemen, or attempt to teach it.

Q. Have you more than one version of the bible in the prison?

A. No, sir.

Q. Which is that?
A. It is the common version. It is commonly called King James'.
Q. Are you ever applied to by the convicts for what is known as the Douay version?
A. No, sir; you refer to the one that is used in the Roman churches; no, sir.
Q. Are prayer books furnished?
A. They are not furnished by the state; prayer books are in use to some extent.
Q. What prayer books are in use?
A. Both Romanist and Episcopal.
Q. Are the convicts at liberty to have either one they choose?
A. Yes, sir; my report suggested that friends of the convicts send them prayer books, books of discipline, etc., as they pleased.
Q. I have read that; I am only inquiring those things that did not fully appear there. In what room is this teaching done?
A. In the dining-room.
Q. Have you ever witnessed any punishment of the convicts in the prison?
A. No, sir. What do you mean, may I ask you, by witnessing?
Q. Have you seen it with your eyes?
A. Yes, sir.
Q. What punishment have you seen or known of your own knowledge to be inflicted in the prison?
A. I have seen men locked in their cell, the cell they occupied; seen them locked in the bare cell; I have seen them wearing the clogg, the wire cap; under the hose; on the wooden horse; put on light rations, and, for a time when in bare cell, without any. While in bare cell, I don't think they have while there, because they are only there but a short time; they never have anything to eat or drink there; and some lighter things as simple resorts: for instance, if a man has been guilty of some infractions of the rules, he is forbidden his reading matter for two days, or ten days, or longer or shorter, as the time may be; not less, though, than two days—reading matter—something of that character. I do not think of anything more.
Q. When upon light rations, what is his ration?
A. I can only answer that I have heard it was bread and water.
Q. And how often is it given?
A. Permit me to say I do not speak from knowledge; I have simply heard "such a man is on bread and water;" I do not know how often it is given; I really ought not to have spoken of that, because it is simply what I had heard.
Q. How long a time have you known men to be confined in a bare cell, without food or drink; the longest?
A. Oh, I could not answer that with any degree of accuracy or definiteness. I see a man in bare cell, I speak to him, and sometimes ask him when he was put in, usually I do not; the next day I may see that same cell is occupied, and if I happen to recognize the man the next day I know he is the same man; otherwise I do not; I do not ask him if he is the same; I could not say how long the longest was.
Q. You say you have seen men punished by being under the hose. Have you ever witnessed an entire punishment from beginning to end?
A. No, sir.
Q. Can you state of your own knowledge for how long a time it is applied?

A. No, sir; strictly speaking, I would not say that I have witnessed the punishment under the hose, nor otherwise; I have only seen it in passing, while I could walk rapidly along, being obliged to pass in the discharge of my duty; in any other circumstances, or in any other way than that, I never witnessed the punishment under the hose.

Q. You speak of Mr. Morris' administration as lenient, as a rule. Explain what you mean by the use of that term or expression.

A. So far as I know it; and that I only know it as a general thing, as it has appeared to me from week to week and from month to month.

Q. Have you had such opportunities to witness the discipline of Mr. Morris as to enable you to speak from your own knowledge and say that it is lenient as a rule?

A. I think so, sir. So far as my knowledge extends, I think so.

Q. You qualify your answer by saying so far as your knowledge extends. I will repeat my question : Have you had such opportunities as to enable you to acquire a knowledge which would entitle you to say as a matter of fact, it was lenient?

A. Why, no, sir; not if you are carrying it into every department, to every hour, to every case, to all the incidents, persons, facts, words, and transactions, I wasn't there.

Q. Have you any means of knowing what complaints are made by convicts to Mr. Morris, and what his treatment of them is after receiving the complaint?

A. No, sir.

Q. Do you know by what rule punishment is dispensed?

A. No, sir.

Q. In the performance of your duties in the prison, have you known of any printed or written rule regulating punishment or prescribing the offense for which it should be inflicted?

A. To some extent those things are presented; that is, the punishment for any particular offense, so far as I know, is not prescribed; but certain offenses are declared to be subject to punishment, that is as far as I know of it.

Q. By what authority are certain offenses declared to be subject to punishment?

A. I suppose by the inspectors; I do not know, sir, where the authority comes from ultimately.

Q. Is there any rule declared by the inspectors which declares certain offenses subject to punishment?

A. That I do not know, sir.

Q. Is there any rule prescribed by the inspectors which declares the kind of punishment to be administered for the different offenses?

A. I do not know, sir.

Q. Has your opportunity of observing Mr. Morris in his intercourse with the convicts, been such as to enable you to speak knowingly as to whether his temper is uniform and even, and whether he always preserves an equanimity of temper in his treatment of convicts?

A. I could not answer that question : I do not know.

Q. You can answer the question if you will listen to it; I ask if your opportunity has been such?

A. Oh, no, sir.

Q. I did not ask what the usage was, but only whether your opportunity has been such?

A. No, sir.

Q. In your observing of Mr. Morris, in his treatment of convicts, have you ever seen him when he appeared excited or angry?

A. I do not know that I have.

Q. What is your judgment on the subject?

A. Oh, I should not feel justified in making any expression; he may be angry, and may treat men when in anger; he may not.

Q. On your direct examination I understood you to say that the general feeling among the convicts was that Mr. Morris' treatment and discipline was kind; now, how do you learn that fact?

A. I stated, so far as I knew it, and I learn it so far, by expressions which they make, and by their communications in their letters which they write to their friends.

Q. Do the letters written by the convicts to their friends all pass through your hands?

A. No, sir.

Q. Through whose hands do they pass?

A. Occasionally one passes through the Agent's hands.

Q. It is his right to examine every letter that is written by a convict?

A. Oh, yes, sir.

Q. And is it his duty?

A. I do not know, sir.

Q. Do any letters go from the convicts, directed to their friends, without going through his hands?

A. Yes, sir.

Q. Are convicts in any case at liberty to write and mail letters without their passing through his hands, or the hands of some officer of the prison, to be read?

A. Why, I suppose not, sir; the rules in their own cells, I think, forbid that.

Q. Are letters ever withheld because they contain matter which the officers think it not prudent to go out?

A. Yes, sir.

Q. State what kind of matter in letters is considered improper to send out?

A. Any thing that is vulgar, any thing that is profane, any thing particularly low, degrading, any personal abuse of their own friends, any profane language; things of that kind.

Q. If letters written by convicts are couched in proper language, but contain complaints of their treatment in prison, or contain complaints of officers about about the prison, are they permitted to be sent?

A. They would be, except I regarded it of sufficient importance to place the letter in the hands of the Agent.

Q. Did you ever pass any letters or allow them to be sent from the convicts containing criticisms on the officers?

A. Yes, sir.

Q. Without passing them into the hands of the Agent?

A. Yes, sir.

Q. State the nature of the criticisms that you will permit to pass?

A. I cannot do it. I have forgotten. I only remember the fact.

Q. Are such facts common?

A. No, sir; very infrequent.

Q. Is there any usage understood among the convicts that they are not at liberty to criticize the conduct of their officers?
A. I do not know, sir.
Q. State whether you have ever known of a convict being punished for having written a letter in which he indulged in criticisms on any of the officers?
A. I do not know of such a case. I do not remember such a case.
Q. If punishment should follow in such a case, would you be likely to know it?
A. I should rather answer that question negatively. I only learn of punishment incidentally; it happens so; and therefore I answer negatively in that case.
Q. Have the inspectors of the prison ever given you any instructions or directions as to what you should do in case of convicts speaking to you and complaining of ill-treatment?
A. No, sir.
Q. Are you ever advised with by the Agent as to what punishment would be proper to be inflicted in any particular case?
A. Yes, sir; sometimes; not often.
Q. Can you state any instance in which you have been advised with?
A. I can recall but one now, at this moment.
Q. State it, please?
A. And I shall only profess to state as I may remember, perhaps I shall not get the full details. This was the case of George Small or Smalley. For some offense—I understood this from the Agent—he had been locked in the bare cell. He was taken out of the cell for some purpose—perhaps to inquire into his case—I do not know the fact, so I should not have said "perhaps" at all. The bare cell was on the west side of the old central building, and his own cell which he occupied was in the east wing, while the bare cell was in the west wing. When released from the bare cell, he ran to his own cell, disregarding the direction given him and the order to stop, and went into his cell,—it did not happen to be locked, it was on the first gallery,—and refused to come out. This was at evening or near evening if I remember rightly, and what was done I do not know. He was left there, and in the evening the Agent sent for me to come to his sitting room. He asked me what I thought we had better do with George. Well, I said I thought I would not try to do anything with him that night; let him remain where he was. I said I thought there would not be any difficulty in managing the case the next day. I left the Agent, and that evening I talked with George in his cell and went up town. When I came back from the city the Agent was in his office, and as I came in the door he called me and I went in. I found that soon after I left, the convict sent for the Agent and wanted to see him, and I think the Agent told me the matter had been adjusted then when I returned. That is the only case I re-call, and that, so far as I remember, covers all my knowledge of the case.
Q. Did you understand that that case was adjusted without further punishment?
A. I did not know what was done, sir.
Q. The Agent did not inform you the manner of the adjustment?
A. Perhaps he did; I could not say he did not. I do not remember.

Re-direct examination, by Mr. Conely:

Q. I think you stated that you knew of no cases where punishment had been inflicted for sending letters criticising the officers. Am I correct in that?
A. I do not remember a case of the kind, sir.

Q. Do you know whether the convicts have any difficulty in making their wants known to the Agent?

A. I do not know.

Q. Do you know what the ordinary means are that are employed by the convicts whenever they wish to communicate with the Agent on any subject?

A. Well, I know some of the means.

Q. Will you state?

A. They are at liberty, I suppose, to call his attention to themselves and their wants or case when ever they meet him; whenever they are where he is. They are at liberty, I suppose, to communicate those things to their keepers, and ask them to speak to the Agent about it, and that is true, I suppose, of their privilege in this respect with all the officers. I have always done that myself. I found that I was requested to carry such word very soon after I came here. I asked the Agent if he wished me to bring to his notice such matters as I was requested by the convicts, and he informed me that he did, so I have always made it a practice. I suppose the same is true of the other officers.

Q. Has the Agent ever consulted with you in relation to the management of some of the more difficult cases of discipline?

A. Yes, sir.

Q. Can you give us some idea of the extent to which he has talked with you about cases of that sort?

A. No, I cannot.

Q. Can you say whether it is frequent, or only seldom, that he has talked with you about the management of difficult cases of discipline?

A. I should rather say occasionally.

Q. I wish you would give the committee, if you can, some idea of what aid the present Agent, Mr. Morris, has rendered to you with reference to religious exercises?

A. Why, the question seems to me a little general. I have found Mr. Morris always ready to furnish me every facility that I have asked, in my work as a religious teacher, and I have found him ready to aid in the work as far as I should expect any man would, who was not himself an experimental, active, christian man. I do not know as I have answered your question now.

Q. By an experimental, active, christian man, you mean a member of the church?

A. A man who calls himself converted and professes to be out in the work. Mr. Morris does not profess that, I suppose, but he has always shown a readiness to do what he could, and I should think all he could, in answer to that.

Re-cross examination, by Mr. Webber:

Q. What matters did you bring to the notice of the Agent, as indicated in one of your answers to Mr. Conely?

A. Principally little wants of theirs. I say little wants; they sometimes want this and want that; they want to purchase, it may be, a handkerchief; they are allowed a knife, and they might want to buy a knife; they might want to get some medicine such as they used to have, and they might want a bit of candy, they might want to purchase a book for reading, something they had seen advertised; they might want to purchase a school book such as we are not using; something outside of that.

Q. But I understood you, when I first examined you, that you did not consider yourself at liberty to bring to his notice complaints in matters of discipline?

A. Yes, sir; taking complaints in what I suppose to be the proper sense.

Q. Did you feel yourself at liberty to carry information which they might give you, either to the Agent or to the board, relative to the manner of their treatment?

A. No, sir; I did not. I gave you the reason.

Re-direct examination, by Mr. Conely:

Q. Is it a part of your duty, as a rule, to have the correspondence of the convicts pass under your inspection?

A. That is the rule, I think.

Q. Now, do I understand that you sometimes observed in those letters, unfavorable criticisms upon the conduct of prison officers?

A. Sometimes; not often. Very seldom; very seldom.

Q. Have you called the attention of Mr. Morris, at any time, to those unfavorable criticisms, that you remember?

A. I have placed in his hands all that I regarded as sufficiently objectionable to warrant my doing so, whether it were once or more. It is very seldom we find any such thing.

Q. In the letters that have come under your notice, have you found complaints in relation to Mr. Morris himself?

A. Yes, sir.

Q. Have you called his attention to those?

A. If they have been of any moment. A man might make a passing remark, which had, in my judgment, no weight, not even in the convict's mind, and not important, any way.

Q. Then do I understand you that you have exercised, yourself, some judgment about the matter that had complaints, to which you would call the attention of Mr. Morris?

A. Yes, sir.

Q. And do I understand you, that those that you regarded as serious, whether in relation to Mr. Morris, or to some other prison officers, you have brought to his attention?

A. Yes, sir.

Re-cross examination, by Mr. Webber:

Q. When you have passed letters, containing unfavorable criticisms of Mr. Morris, over to Mr Morris for his judgment, have you any information as to whether those letters were sent, or retained?

A. No, sir; I do not know what was done with them.

Q. If they were sent, would they be sent to you to be sent?

A. No, sir; not necessarily. I do not remember an instance of that kind. That is the rule that would be observed. I have an indistinct recollection of something of that kind having occurred, but I cannot recall it; I cannot bring it up; it is only before me, that I felt that I must answer the questions put to me as I have.

SOCRATES H. WOOD SWORN FOR MR. MORRIS.

Examined by Mr. Conely:

Q. You are hall master at the prison?

A. Yes, sir.

Q. How long have you been such?

A. One year.

Q. Have you ever had any other position in the prison?

A. Yes, sir.

STATE PRISON INVESTIGATION. 201

Q. What was it?
A. I was assistant keeper.
Q. When was that?
A. Something over two years before I was hall master.
Q. Just before?
A. Yes, sir.
Q. Any other prison experience?
A. No, sir.
Q. Then your prison experience is a little over three years last past?
A. Yes, sir.
Q. Did you know the man Thurston, the convict?
A. Yes, sir.
Q. Did you ever see him punished?
A. Yes, sir.
Q. When was that?
A. Well, I think it was in September, 1873.
Q. Do you know what he was punished for?
A. I think it was for having a knife and threatening to disembowel Mr. Morris and some others.
Q. Were you present at the time he made such threats that you remember?
A. No, sir; I was not present.
Q. Were you present at the time of the punishment?
A. Yes, sir.
Q. I wish you would state just what was done at that time.
A. That was at the time I was keeper,—had charge of a shop. When we came in at night we found Thurston sitting in the hall. After locking, and before the keepers were discharged, Mr. Morris asked him to produce a knife that he had. He hesitated, and after some little talk, he went to a spittoon filled with sawdust and dug it up and gave it to Mr. Morris. He was then taken down into the lower part of the yard, near the large shops, and punished.
Q. Did you witness the punishment?
A. Yes, sir.
Q. What was it?
A. He was flogged with a whip.
Q. What kind of a whip was it?
A. Well, sir, it was a common raw-hide, with the lash nearly worn off,—three-quarters of the lash gone and the pieces of buckskin was hanging.
Q. Who inflicted the punishment?
A. Mr. Morris.
Q. Who were present?
A. Well, the keepers of the yard, I guess, were nearly all present; I could not name them.
Q. How many in number?
A. I could not state.
Q. Half a dozen?
A. Yes, sir; a dozen or more.
Q. How long did the punishment continue?
A. Well, it was—I could not say; perhaps fifteen minutes; ten or fifteen minutes at spells.
Q. Do you know how many blows were given?

A. No, sir; I did not count; I should think perhaps between 40 and 50; perhaps 50; not over 50.

Q. What effect was observable on Thurston at the time, if any?

A. Well, along to the last of the punishment, he promised Mr. Morris that he would in the future, as long as he staid in the prison, he would behave himself. There was not much said at first

Q. What opportunity was given to him, if any, to make a similar statement to that, earlier in the punishment? Do you remember?

A. Well, Mr. Morris stopped several times in the punishment and talked to him.

Q. What did he say to him? Give the substance of what he said, if you cannot remember the language.

A. Well, I do not think I could.

Q. Do you remember the effect of what he said; what it was about?

A. I think—Well, I would not pretend to say.

Q After he had promised obedience, did the punishment continue?

A. No, sir; I think not. I think he got very little—was punished very little after he promised to behave himself.

Q. Do you know what his conduct was after that time in the prison?

A. Yes, sir; it was very good.

Q. How had it been before that time?

A. Well, sir, he was in my shop for four months; I considered him one of the worst men in the shop.

Q. In what respect?

A. Well, sir, he was desperate and tricky, and no dependence could be put on him. He was always getting into a quarrel with other men, and getting them into difficulty, if possible, with other convicts.

Q. Do you know whether at that time, Mr. Morris struck him with the butt end of the whip at all?

A. No, sir; I did not see it.

Q. Did you observe the whole punishment?

A. Yes, sir.

Q. Would you have been likely to see it?

A. I should think I should.

Q. What manifestations of any anger or of ill-temper were there at that time upon the part of Mr. Morris?

A. I did not see any; I saw determination.

Q. How frequently, to your knowledge, has the lash been used in the prison since you first came into it?

A, That is the only man that I ever saw punished with the lash.

Q. Well, have you some information on the subject, not derived from personal knowledge, as to the extent to which the lash has been used?

A. Very seldom that I have heard; I heard of some few men while I was in the shop. I had no chance of seeing them.

Q. Do you know what classes of offenses were punished in that way; or whether they were the more aggravated or less so?

A. Always for the aggravated cases; assaults on keepers or guards or something of that kind; some aggravated cases, and then, I believe, only on the worst men that were known to be.

Q. In Mr. Morris' intercourse, as far as you have observed it, with convicts, what is his temper?

A. I never saw him lose his temper.

Q. What opportunity have you had, in your two positions of keeper and hall master, to know what Mr. Morris' conduct is in that regard?

A. For the last year I have had as good an opportunity as any one about the institution, perhaps, with the exception of the deputy.

Q. What opportunity, under the prison, as managed, and as it has been managed since you have been connected with it, have the convicts had of making known their wants and complaints to the Agent in any particular, either against the officers or against the freemen that were employed about the prison?

A. There has been no,—I was going to say there had been no hour in the day when Mr. Morris was here when they could not have had a hearing from him.

Q. What is the method, as practiced, by which convicts get the ear of the Agent? For instance, suppose a convict has something to complain about to the Agent, what would be the way in which he would get the complaint to the ear of the Agent? I do not mean what is in the printed rules, but how is the thing done in the prison?

A. Mr. Morris is frequently in the yard, and convicts go to him at any time when they see him. They go to him in the dining-room; they come to him in my office when he is there; when he is passing through the yard; through the shops. I have noticed it in my shop a great many times.

Q. What hindrances or embarrassments or obstacles exist in the way of a convict complaining about the Agent or any prison officer?

A. I do not see any.

Q. Either to the Agent or to the Board. Do you know of any?

A. I do not know of any.

Q. Well, as the prison is managed, do the convicts have the largest opportunity to make known either their wants or their complaints to the inspectors?

A. I think they do have every opportunity that they could wish.

Q. Do you observe upon the part of the convicts any restraint about communicating their wants or desires to the Agent or to the inspectors?

A. No, sir; they will go to them with the most frivolous thing; go with the smallest matter.

Q. Has there any thing been held over the convicts by way of terror to them that operates to your knowledge to prevent them from making known fully to the Agent any thing they may wish to say against any prison officer?

A. No, sir; I never saw any such thing.

Q. Is there any similar restraint that prevents them, to any extent, from fully making known their wishes to the inspectors at the time when they meet here?

A. I do not know of any.

Q. Well, then, is the opportunity for intercourse between the convicts and the proper authorities perfectly and fully free?

A. I do not know why it is not.

Q. Suppose a case. Suppose I was a convict in the prison and had a fancy that I had a cause of complaint against the Agent himself, and desired to bring that to the knowledge of the inspectors, what would be my way of doing it as practiced at the prison? And I want you to state fully to the gentlemen of this committee in regard to this subject, and if there is any restraint operating in that, one way or another way, to prevent the convict from conveying his wishes to this board of inspectors, I want to know it. Now answer on that subject.

A. I have taken the names of the men in my shop and sent them here,—sent them to the office, where men have complained of Mr. Morris for withholding tobacco, and what other charges I do not know, and they have went from the shop and gone to the board of inspectors and seen them. I cannot speak, of course, only from my own—

Q. That is all. Now I will ask you another question: Whether in such cases there has ever been visited on the convict who has made complaint, any different treatment, so far as your observation has gone, from what he would have received had he made no complaint?

A. No, sir.

Q. Have you ever known of a case where a convict has been subjected to any worse fare or any worse treatment, or any indignity or punishment by reason or having made any complaint againt any prison officer?

A. No, sir, I do not believe such a thing has occurred since I have been here. I do not believe that any man has been treated any worse for it.

Q. Do the convicts know when the inspectors have their meetings?

A. Yes, sir; every man in the prison knows when the inspectors will be here.

Q. You have made mention of Thurston's punishment. Have you ever witnessed any other punishment?

A. Yes, sir, I have seen men showered.

Q. Whom?

A. I have seen several, but I do not know that I can—

Q. State whether in those instances of showering which you did see, whether there were any unpleasant or harmful physical effects?

A. I never saw any.

Q. Do you know at what season of the year that the showering has been practiced at the prison, or whether there has been any difference in that respect; are you able to say?

A. There has been very little through the cold weather this winter. There was more in the summer.

Q When you first came to the prison what stripe clothing was worn by the convicts; was it the same as is now retained?

A. No, sir; it was a broader stripe.

Q. Was it a more distinct stripe?

A. Yes, sir.

Q. Do you know who changed it, or caused it to be changed?

A. I have no means of knowing it for certain, but I suppose it was through Mr. Morris' instrumentality; I may be mistaken, but I suppose that was the case.

Q. Were you connected with the prison prior to the introduction of the magazines of the day?

A. No, sir.

Q. They were introduced at the time you came here?

A. Just introduced at the time, or a little after,—no, a little before I came here.

Q. Have you any knowledge through whose instrumentality they were introduced?

A. Mr. Morris'; I have had it from hearsay.

Q. But you have no personal knowledge on the subject?

A. No, sir.

Q. Do you know how often convicts were permitted to write to their friends when you first came here?

A. Well, they were allowed to write once a month when I first came here. Previous to that I understood they were only allowed to write once in three months.

Q. They are now permitted to write once a month, are they not?

A. Yes, sir.

Q. There has no change then, in that regard, been had since you came to the prison?

A. No, sir.

Q. I observe in the prison that some of the convicts wear a different sort of shirt from some other convicts. I wish you would explain to this committee how this happens?

A. Well, sir, in the first place, we have two styles or two colors of hickory shirting; one is a brown and the other a blue stripe; then when convicts come here, a great many of them have on colored shirting of different kinds; that is worn here. Those are—of course we never put on anything on to a man that he takes off on his coming into the prison. Those are taken, and as soon as I became hall master, rather than sell those shirts at two cents a pound, I asked Mr. Morris if it would not be as well that they wore them and save the shirts. A great many of them were good, and they are taken into the wash house and when a man's shirt would wear out, they are given out and worn.

Q. In the distribution of those shirts, what rule have you for the giving out of those shirts, if any?

A. Well, sir, I have in perhaps five or six instances, I have given boys that are connected with the halls, those shirts.

Q. Why have you done that? Why give it to those that are connected with the halls in preference to those that are doing some other kind of work?

A. Where they have got one, there are men in the shops that have got fifty.

Q. I do not understand you?

A. Well, the larger part of those shirts have gone into the shops, everywhere, only perhaps some of the boys about the hospital or main hall asked me for them, and I gave them to them; but not to exceed five or six cases; but they are worn all over the yard.

Q. What discrimination has Mr. Morris ever indicated to you should be made in the distribution of the shirts that might be regarded as a little better than the shirts that are given out?

A. Never; he never has given me anything.

Q. Has he ever given any such intimation in the way of other clothing?

A. No, sir.

Q. Have any of the men been measured for their clothing at all in the prison; any of the convicts, to your knowledge?

A. I measure nearly all of them. I have done that.

Q. Then did you select from the pile, or have them made to order by measure?

A. Have made them by the measure. I have done that for this reason: that clothes that fit a man passably well, he will take more pains with them and save them. I have done it as a matter of economy; but the men in the shops are measured as much as any other. I measure them whenever I can, without I can give a man a good fit. I take his measure for pants and vest and coat.

Q. To what extent have you observed that Mr. Morris has had "pets" or "favorites" among the convicts?

A. I never saw any of his pets or favorites.

Q. Would you have been likely to know it if there had been any such thing?
A. I think I should.
Q. Your intercourse with the convicts, as I understand it, is about as close as that of any other prison officer?
A. Yes, sir; perhaps more so.
Q. What complaints, if any, have you ever heard from any convicts in relation to Mr. Morris' having favorites among the convicts, or pets? Have you ever heard the thing spoken of at all?
A. No, sir; never heard it spoken of inside the prison walls.

Cross-examination by Mr Webber:
Q. What are your duties as ball-master?
A. I have charge—I take charge of the men when they come here—when we receive them into the prison; dress them, assign them cells; have charge of the wings, the bedding, clothing, and shoeing, of course, the shoe shop and tailor shop, etc.
Q. What hours do you employ in the service of the prison?
A. I work as long as—about an hour longer than the convicts do.
Q. Have you a regular hour for coming on in the morning?
A. Yes, sir; come on at the ringing of the first bell, which now is at 6.20.
Q. What time do you leave?
A. My last duty is to take the count at night, as keepers report to me, and know that every man is in his cell, or in his place, and accounted for.
Q. Does your duty call upon you to look after the provision that is purchased and brought into the prison?
A. No, sir; not only—I receipt for provisions that are brought here.
Q. Do you have anything to do with apportioning it out?
A No, sir.
Q. You say you saw Thurston punished?
A. Yes, sir.
Q. Were you present when he gave up that knife?
A. Yes, sir.
Q. How long after he gave up the knife before he was taken out and flogged?
A. Perhaps twenty or thirty mieutes.
Q. I understand it was in the evening that he gave up the knife?
A. It was after the ringing of the bell.
Q. And had it become dark?
A. No, sir.
Q. Was this his first or second flogging?
A. I think it was his second.
Q. Did you count the lashes?
A. No, sir.
Q. I understood you to say that they were not above fifty?
A. In my judgment.
Q. You heard of his first whipping, a week or two earlier than this?
A. Yes, sir; I presume I had.
Q. Do you recollect distinctly whether you did or not?
A. Yes, sir; I think I did; I think I had heard of the time that he was punished before.
Q. Do you recollect whether Thurston was showered in his cell before he was taken out to be whipped at that time?
A. I know he was not.

STATE PRISON INVESTIGATION.

Q. He was not showered in his cell?
A. No, sir.
Q. Did you time the whipping?
A. No, sir.
Q. Who did?
A. I do not know that any one did.
Q. When punishment was inflicted was it not usual to have it timed?
A. In cases of showering it is.
Q. In cases of flogging is it not usual to have some one count the lashes?
A. Well, I do not know that it is; I never saw but that one man flogged with the whip.
Q. Do you know whether any one was assigned at that time to count the lashes?
A. I do not know.
Q. Did you hear the number of lashes given him at that time spoken of, by any one who assumed to have control?
A. No, sir, I do not remember that I did.
Q. Did you examine Thurston's person after the whipping?
A. No, sir.
Q. Did you see any cuts through the skin, on his person?
A. I examined him when he went out.
Q. How long after that?
A. He went out in July; about the first of July, 1874.
Q. A year afterwards?
A. Yes, sir; when I dressed him I examined him.
Q. Did you not examine his body before, at any time?
A. No, sir; I saw him, but I do not know that I saw his body from the time he was punished until his time—
Q. If you stood by and saw him punished, cannot you tell whether you saw any blood as the result of that punishment?
A. I do not think there was any blood outside of the skin; there was red places where the lash hit him.
Q. Now, do you assume to speak from knowledge, or do you speak merely from your impresssion, standing at a distance?
A. I was not a great ways from him.
Q. Well, how far?
A. Perhaps six to twelve feet.
Q. Let me ask you whether you can speak confidently whether as a matter of fact any blood followed as a result of that flogging?
A. From what I remember now I should say there was no blood followed.
Q. Who did examine his person after the flogging?
A. I do not know, sir.
Q. Who took him in charge after the flogging?
A. I guess the—perhaps the hall master at that time.
Q. Who attended to putting on his clothing?
A. That I could not say.
Q. When he was whipped, how did Mr. Morris stand with reference to where Thurston was? Behind him or before?
A. I think he stood on different—sometimes on one side of him, and behind him, and different places.
Q. He changed about?

A. Yes, sir.
Q. How was Thurston tied to receive the flogging?
A. A rope was put around his wrists and tied to a post, up a little.
Q. Higher than his head, somewhat?
A. Yes, sir, a little; his hands were a little higher than his head; not much.
A. Made fast any other way?
A. No, sir.
Q. Now, how many times did Mr. Morris stop while inflicting that punishment?
A. That would be guess-work; I should say six or eight times.
Q. And how many blows do you think he gave at each time?
A. I could not say, sir.
Q. And you say he moved about, so as to take a fresh place every time?
A. Thurston moved about, and sometimes he was facing Mr. Morris and sometimes his back to him, and sometimes his side to him; I do not think Mr. Morris moved about.
Q. To what part of Thurston's body were these blows principally directed?
A. Well, I don't know as I could say.
Q. On what part of his body did you observe the greatest evidence of the flogging?
A. I should say around the middle portion of his body.
Q. In front?
A. Well, I could not say as to that; it was around his body.
Q. You cannot say whether it was on his back or in front?
A. I should think,—I do not know why they were not as much on one side,— in front as on his back.
Q. Did you observe any difference in the indications of the whipping on the front and on the back?
A. No, sir.
Q. Were the blows directed by a perpendicular stroke up and down, or were they sidewise, with a horizontal blow?
A. I should say they were horizontal blows.
Q. Was there any outcry made by Thurston?
A. Not exactly.
Q. In those outcries what did he say?
A. I do not know that I could repeat what he said.
Q. Can you repeat any thing that Mr. Morris said in the intermissions between the floggings?
A. No, sir; I do not remember what he said to him.
Q. You remember no question that he asked him? Let me ask you, did he ask him any questions, or did he use threats, or what did he say?
A. Well, he talked to him; I do not know as he threatened him any.
Q. This was the first and the only flogging you have seen in the prison?
A. Yes, sir, with the lash.
Q. Did not it make an impression upon you, the circumstances connected with it?
A. Yes, sir; I remember it.
Q. Can you tell any thing that Thurston said pending that flogging?
A. I do not think Thurston said much until along the last.
Q. What did he say when he did speak?

STATE PRISON INVESTIGATION.

A. He said that he would behave himself; he would be a good man after that, and told Mr. Morris that he would not have any cause for punishing him again.

Q. Did you observe whether Thurston had any blow upon his privates as the result of that flogging?

A. No, sir; I do not know that I did. He might have had; did not see any blow there; I did not know that he had any blow there.

Q. Now, you say that there is no difficulty in the way of convicts making known their wants to the Agent or to the inspectors. Did you ever know of a convict being punished for having complained of a keeper?

A. No, sir; I do not remember that I knew of it; I do not remember any such case.

Q. Suppose that a convict makes a complaint to Mr. Morris and Mr. Morris ignores it, how is the convict to make his want known to the inspectors?

A. He would inform his keeper.

Q. Suppose the keeper did not see fit to make the report?

A. If he did, I do not know; he would have to do some other way; but I never knew of a keeper's refusing to inform the deputy or the Agent if a man wanted to see the inspectors.

Q. If the keeper did make the report, who would he make it to?

A. Probably to the deputy, or if he would see the Agent, the first time he saw the Agent, to him.

Q. If he made it to the deputy, who would the deputy make it to?

A. I could not say. I know that men have been called out when I have reported to the deputy that such a man wanted to see the Agent or inspectors, or that they have gone there.

Q. What I want to get at is for you to tell me how, under the usages of the prison, a complaint against the Agent can be made, by a convict, to the inspectors. Your statement carries the complaint right back to the Agent. How is it to get to the inspectors unless the Agent sees fit to deliver it?

A. They see the inspectors themselves frequently. The inspectors are here and talk with them. They go through the shops. It is an occurrence of—

Q. Has the convict liberty to speak to an inspector when he sees him around without the permission of his keeper?

A. Well, sir, my men have told me when the inspectors were going through, and I have told them of it.

Q. Suppose you state to your man that he could not speak to the inspector, when he was going through, how then would he get his complaint known?

A. I never done any such thing; don't know that it was ever done.

Q. Is it possible that any such things should be done under the system?

A. I do not think it is.

Q. You have read the rules before?

A. Yes, sir.

Q. I will read you rule nine: "No convict shall be allowed to speak to the Agent or inspectors while in the shops, but can notify his keeper or guard if he wishes to speak to the Agent or inspectors." You knew of the existence of that rule?

A. Yes, I presume so.

Q. Now, having your attention called to it, I ask you, again, if the keeper does not see fit to report nor allow the convict to speak to the Agent or inspectors, how can a convict have a hearing under that rule?

A. I think that every man, if he wished to speak to the inspectors, would get permission to leave his place, and go directly to the Agent or—
Q. Let me ask the question, is this rule observed?
A. I do not think it is always.
Q. Have you known of others being whipped than Thurston?
A. Not of my own knowledge.
Q. Since you have been here?
A. Not of my own knowledge.
Q. You have seen men showered?
A. Yes, sir.
Q. Have you timed the punishments?
A. Yes, sir.
Q How long have you known that punishment to be inflicted at one time, at the longest?
A. Not beyond ten minutes.
Q. The most severe case of showering that ever came under your observation did not exceed ten minutes?
A. No, sir.
Q. Had you anything to do with keeping the record?
A. No, sir.
Q. When you made reports, while acting as keeper, were those reports in writing or oral?
A. Oral.
Q. Have you any means of knowing whether those reports which you made, always received attention?
A. From the deputy?
Q. From your superior officers?
A. Yes, sir; if I sent for the deputy he always came.
Q. Were you in the habit of sending for the deputy whenever you made a report?
A. Yes, sir; but for the last fifteen months I was in the shop I did not report a man out of my shop, so that the reports from me were not very numerous.
Q. Having charge of the clothing of the men, do they ever complain of being cold?
A. Well, some of the men have complained last winter.
Q. During the winter season what clothing are the men allowed?
A. They are allowed coats, pants, vests, woolen and cotton shirts; some men have cotton shirts and undershirts; other men have only a cotton shirt, others have a woolen shirt.
Q. Are they allowed drawers?
A. Yes, sir, they are, where their friends send them; or, on the order of the doctor, the State furnishes them.
Q. Not otherwise?
A. Well, I have given old men that went out doors and men that were exposed to the cold, I have furnished them, and most generally that were at work out doors in exposed places, drawers and undershirts.
Q. What do they have for stockings?
A. Good woolen stockings.
Q. But the mass of the men, as I understand you, have no drawers and undershirts, except they get them from their friends?

A. Well, the majority of the men have them, from their friends or from the State. I should say the majority.
Q. What proportion get them from their friends?
A. Well, I could not say; a good many; I have no means of knowing; I could not tell without going to the books of the wash-house.
Q. Do you allow convicts to receive presents of clothing from their friends of other articles except drawers and undershirts?
A. Handkerchiefs.
Q. Anything else?
A. Cotton socks in the summer.

Mr. Bartow:

Q. Supposing friends send underclothing, or means to buy underclothing, to the prison authorities here, would they be furnished with extra underclothing by the prison authorities, I mean?
A. They have; and we have had cotton flannel and made it up for them, they paying for the cloth only; giving the making, that is, the State made them.
Q. That won't really answer the question; the question is, supposing friends send extra underclothing here for convicts, would they be furnished in all cases by the prison authorities with extra underclothing?
A. Would they be given to these men?
Q. Certainly.
A. Certainly; every time.
Q. Supposing they sent means here to buy it for them, then would they be furnished?
A. That I cannot say; I have no means of knowing whether they do or not. I have never known of any one sending money here. I have no means of knowing when money comes to them.
Q. When complaints are made against the convicts by keepers or foremen, who are they made to?
Q. If complaints are made by the foremen they report to the keepers, the keepers to the deputy, and the deputy to the Agent.
Q. Now when the deputy reports to the Agent, is there any record kept of that report by the deputy?
A. That is not my—I have nothing to do with the records.
Q. You have the means of knowing?
A. No, sir; I only see the deputy have his book. He does his writing in my office a good deal of the time, but I never look at his books.
Q. You never noticed those records?
A. No, sir; I never look at them. I never look into his books, and I have no means of knowing.
Q. Do you know a man in the State prison by the name of Redwood, George Redwood?
A. Yes, sir.
Q. Do you know whether his friends sent him extra under-clothing or means to buy extra under-clothing, and that it was not furnished?
A. I do not know anything about it. I my memory serves me, I gave Redwood under-shirts.

Mr. Mellen:

Q. You think you gave Redwood extra under-clothing?
A. Yes, sir.
Q. Was that that you gave him from the prison shop?

A. I can explain that a little further by—in the spring or summer there is frequently men come here with nothing, perhaps, but an undershir on. He has one undershirt,—and those are sometimes saved; I receive the mall, and give them to that man or to some other man that needs them.

Mr. Bartow:

Q. Is not a man's private clothing that he owns before he came here, always kept for him?

A. Yes, sir, if he is under a year or fifteen months. Sometimes, a fifteen months' man, if he has a good suit of clothes, I retain them for him.

Q. What is done in other cases; in long time cases what is done with their clothing?

A. That clothing is given out to others as they go out. It is cleaned up and repaired, what there is—there is very little of it—coats, if they are coats, pants, and vests, it is all cleaned and repaired, and given to others that are going out.

Re-direct examination by Mr. Conely:

Q. Where was this George Redwood from, if you remember?

A. I think he was from Detroit, and I think he was sent from the recorder's court.

Q. Do you know what the so-called tobacco rule is?

A. I think I do.

Q. What is it?

A. That men that came here previous to July first, or along about the first of 1871, I think, are given tobacco, except to those who have given it up.

Q How is it about men that came since that time?

A. No man gets tobacco.

Q. Are some convicts supplied with better boots than other convicts?

A. We issue shoes, we do not issue boots except to men that are at work outside, and in the snow and mud in the fall. They are given cow-hide boots to work in the snow and mud.

Q. Is there any such thing as furnishing fine boots to any man?

A. No, sir, except on going out.

Q. Leaving the prison?

A. Yes, sir.

Q. In regard to the opportunity of any of these men seeing the inspectors, at their monthly meetings: do they have an opportunity so to do without disclosing to the Agent or officers, the purpose for which they wish to see the inspectors?

A. I do not think they are ever asked the question what they want to see them for.

Q. They simply make known that they want to see the inspectors, and when the inspectors meet here, the convict is sent for?

A. Yes, sir.

Q He does not communicate to the Agent or keeper the purpose for which he wants to see the Inspectors?

A. No, sir; I never asked a man.

Q. So, that if has any complaint to make against the Agent, he can make it to the Inspectors, without the Agent knowing anything about it?

A. Yes.

WILLIAM WEBSTER SWORN FOR MR. MORRIS.

Examined by Mr. Conely:

Q. You are interested in the wagon contract, I believe?

STATE PRISON INVESTIGATION. 213

A. Yes, sir.

Q. And your duties connected with the wagon contract are what—what position do you hold?

A. General manager of the whole business.

Q. To what extent does your business take you inside the prison?

A. Usually from eight to ten hours a day—according to the season of the year; at least I give my time through the working hours in the prison.

Q. How long has that been so?

A. Ever since I was connected with the wagon contract.

Q. How long is that?

A. I think it is about seven years.

Q. You were here then when Mr. Bingham was the Agent?

A. Yes, sir; I commenced here seven years ago last October.

Q. And have been here all the time that Morris has been Agent?

A. Yes, sir; I have been holding that position all the time. I have been away some of the time, but that was my business when I was here, at home.

Q. How many men are employed on that contract?

A. At the present time?

Q. Yes.

A. I should say about sixty-five or seventy men.

Q. How many have you employed—the highest number?

A. Since I have been connected with it?

Q. Yes.

A. As high as two hundred and over.

Q. What is the highest number that has been employed on that contract since Mr. Morris has been Agent?

A. I think at the time Mr. Morris came here, we were working as high as 160 or 175 men. That is my recollection of it.

Q. What price per day are you paying on that contract?

A. At the present time?

Q. Yes.

A. A dollar a day.

Q. What is the lowest price you have paid since Mr. Morris was Agent?

A. I would like to ask how long Mr. Morris has been Agent?

Q. He has been Agent four years last March.

A. The lowest priced men we employed at that time was fifty cents a day. We had three different classes of men on the contract when Mr. Morris came here, at 50, 65, and 76 cents.

Q. How does it happen that you are paying a higher price now than formerly?

A. Well, sir, I don't know as I am prepared to answer that question.

Q. I only care for it in this particular: Whether the discipline and management of the men, and their care, has made the men any more valuable than they were formerly?

A. If the discipline of the prison at the time this contract had been let was in such a state as it was at other times, I don't think I should have made such a bid for the men.

Q. At what time was the contract let,—how long ago?

A. A year ago last October.

Q. Then am I to understand that you are entirely satisfied with the discipline of the prison and at the time you took this contract you regarded it as of a high order?

A. Certainly; I should not have made such a bid as that if I hadn't.

Q. How has that dicipline been, so far as you have had knowledge of it, or so far as you have information in regard to its severity or leniency?

A. I don't know as I have a comparison to judge by. Do you mean in comparison with other administrations since I have been here?

Q. You might do that without specifying any particular one?

A. That is the only thing I can judge by of course.

Q. Yes?

A. I should say that the discipline of the prison was very much more lenient than it was previous to the time Mr. Morris came here, while I was connected with the prison. I don't know anything about it previous to that.

Q. What manifestation, if any, of unevenness of temper on the part of Mr. Morris, have ever been brought to your attention in his intercourse with the prisoners?

A. I never have seen Mr. Morris in his intercourse with the prisoners very much. 1 never found him very variable in his temper, so far as his intercourse with me is concerned.

Q. What is the disposition of your men, so far as you can tell, as to their cheerfulness in the shops,—their general disposition?

A. I never have seen or heard any of my men that have evinced any sour disposition. There is of course, some cases in the position and way I have contact with these men in the raising of their work. Of course men here don't like to work very well, and if they raise their work they may be dissatisfied with me, and sour from that cause.

Q. That is, you increase the labor that they are required to do, in a certain amount of time,—is that it?

A. Yes, sir; the work is varied at the various seasons of the year.

Q. What is the disposition of the convicts, in relation to Mr. Morris' treatment of?

A. I never have found, or heard of a case where there was any fault found from any cause. That is, as far as his treatment is concerned.

Q. In the early part of Mr. Morris' administration, Mr. Webster, I would ask you whether there was any insubordination of any sort in your own shop or whether there was any dissatisfaction among the convicts there calling for more than ordinary treatment?

A. I don't understand what you mean. If you mean convicts attempting to escape—

Q. Anything of that sort, yes?

A. There was some men went out of my shop once over this wing here. I think that was about the commencement of Mr. Morris' administration. I may be mistaken; it may have been before that. Aside from that, I don't recollect any trouble.

Q. How many men were there that went from your shop?

A. I think there were four or five.

Cross-examined by Mr. Webber:

Q. I understood that you are paying a dollar a day to some of the men?

A. I am, sir.

Q. How many men do you have in your employ?

A. We are working about 60 men—from 60 to 70; I don't know the exact number.

Q. You pay a dollar a day for each man?

A. Yes, sir; that is the contract price.
Q. If you increase the number, does your contract give the same price?
A. That depends altogether on the arrangement we make with him in regard to the men. I did not mean to have you understand me that we paid a dollar a day for every man in the shop, because some men are not able to do a day's work. Of course we only pay what they are worth.
Q. How many men do you pay a dollar a day to?
A. That I don't know, sir. The books will show that.
Q. How many men are you under contract to employ at a dollar a day?
A. Fifty men.
Q. You are at liberty not to take any more if you are a mind to?
A. They cannot oblige us to take any more, sir.
Q. Now, who selects that fifty?
A. The men are awarded to the contracts as they come in; as new men come in. That is at the disposition of the Agent and board of inspectors. The priority, I believe, is given to the old contracts.
Q. Speaking of your contract,—state whether your contract gives you the right of selection of your fifty men.
A. No, sir; it does not.
Q. You have no right of selection over other contractors?
A. No, sir.
Q. How long has this contract to pay a dollar a day been in force?
A. A year ago last October.
Q. Do I understand you that that contract was made because of the special discipline of the prison?
A. You understood me to say that we made this bid for these men, at that high figure, which you are well aware is much higher than was ever paid in any prison. On account of that, we were satisfied with the discipline of the prison, and satisfied with the management. At all events, we should not have made so high a bid unless we were satisfied.
Q. How long a time does this contract continue?
A. Ten years.
Q. What assurances have you reserved to yourselves, in the contract, that the same management shall continue?
A. We have no assurances, sir. That is one of the things that we have got to take our chances on.
Q. Is it not a fact, that the men that went upon your contract in the first instance were men who were skilled in that particular department?
A. They were men that had worked on the contract, sir.
Q. So that they became somewhat skilled?
A. Yes, sir.
Q. In that branch of the work?
A. Yes, sir; could not very well be otherwise. We had to take our men from the old contract; that was from the larger number.
Q. That first contract was for a larger number?
A. Yes, sir.
Q. In selecting the first fifty men for this new contract, were you at liberty to select from the old men?
A. We took fifty men from the old contract to commence the new.
Q. Who made the selection of that fifty from the old men?

A. Well, I presented the names to the Agent. I was governed a good deal by the foremen in my shops.

Q. And he ratified it. Did he find any fault with the list of names that you presented?

A. The Agent?

Q. Yes.

A No, not that I am aware of. No, sir. Our bid specified that we should have that privilege. When they accepted the bid they accepted the terms.

Q. That is what I supposed, but that is not what you stated a little while ago.

A. You spoke then of men that were being put on to the contract, new men that came in. We have no priority among the men that come in. Of course men are coming in all the time.

Q What I meant was, do you not have priority in the contract to the extent of your fifty men at the commencement of it?

A. This is at the commencement of it. I did not understand that you meant that. I thought you meant men that were coming in. We had over 120 men to select from.

Q. You speak of the men being cheerful in the shops. What opportunity have you to judge of their cheerfulness?

A. The best opportunity in the shops. I am in the shops every day, and always with them.

Q Are you talking with them?

A. If I have any business with them?

Q. Do you converse with them on subjects other than what they are at?

A. No, sir; that is not my business. I have enough talking to do to get work without conversing about any thing else.

Q How do you define cheerfulness as used in connection with the men in these shops?

A. When a man don't find fault. That is the only means I have of knowing whether they are cheerful or not.

Q. When they don't find fault then you consider them cheerful. Now, what right have they to find fault to you? If they wanted to find fault ever so bad, have they any right to mention it to you?

A. Certainly.

Q. In what particular?

A. More particularly in regard to their work, the amount of work required, and the manner of doing it, and how I am to accept the work.

Q. Suppose they find fault with the general discipline of the prison, have they any right to mention it to you?

A. I suppose they have a right to do so.

Q. Have they ever done so?

A. No, sir.

Q. Do you understand that the rules of the prison would allow you to speak to the men, or they speak to you on the subject of the discipline of the prison?

A. I don't know as I know any thing about the rules in that respect.

Q. Have you ever read the rules of the prison in that respect?

A. So far as it applies to my position I have.

Q. Have you ever read the rules of the prison so far as applies to the discipline of the prison,—to their treatment?

A. I learned it more from experience than from any rules. I don't know as I ever read the rules through.

Q. Now, you speak of the increase of labor in the shops. Do you give every man his daily task?

A. As far as it is possible, I do so, with the kind of work they are employed at.

Q. And when that task is finished they are at liberty to quit work?

A. Yes, sir.

Q. Even if it be before bell?

A. Certainly.

Q. Does it lie within your province to fix the days' work?

A. No, sir.

Q. Who fixes the task for the day?

A. I ask the authorities for the amount of work that I think is right, then they investigate the matter and pass judgment upon it.

Q. What authorities do you ask?

A. I come first in contact with the keeper in the shop. All my business with the authorities is done through him, if I can do it satisfactory.

Q. Has the keeper authority to authorize you to increase the work of your men?

A. He notifies the men that I wish such and such work. That only applies to cases where the men don't do the amount of work.

Q. I am speaking now about fixing what the task shall be. With whom does it lie to fix the task?

A. With the authorities of the prison, the deputy and the Agent.

Q. You make known to them your desires, and if they assent to it they direct you to increase the task accordingly?

A. Yes, sir.

Q. I understood you to say that you never had heard of a case where a convict had found fault with Mr. Morris and his treatment?

A. To me, I said.

Q. To you?

A. Yes, sir.

Q. Have you ever heard of a case where convicts had complained to others of Mr. Morris?

A. No, sir.

Q. Now, I don't understand that under the rules of the prison the convicts had a right to find fault to you of Mr. Morris?

A. No, sir; I don't know any thing about that, I say; I have never read the rules in that respect; the subject has never been brought to my attention; of course I never thought any thing about it.

Q. The most of your men are quite orderly?

A The majority of them are.

Q. What percentage of the men working under you really require any strict discipline to keep them in order?

A. That is a question I can't answer, sir.

ULYSSES FOSTER SWORN FOR MR. MORRIS.

Examined by Mr. Conely:

Q. You reside in Jackson?

A. Yes, sir.

Q. And are now foreman of the wood shop on the wagon contract, are you not?

A. I am not actually in that capacity now; I am overseeing the machinery in the department now. I have been on the wood department up to five or six weeks ago.

Q. How long have you been engaged on the wagon contract?
A. Well, since October, 1846.
Q. Your employment since October, 1846, to the present time?
A. Except nine months, I have stopped in that shop.
Q. What length of time do you spend in that employment?
A. Well, it makes fully ten hours a day to me during the year.
Q. In the summer is it more than that?
A. Oh, yes, it is more than ten hours in the summer time; but the average through the year is about ten hours. As severe a winter as we have had this one, I have had to be there a good deal more of the time than what the men are. I have been nights and mornings,—at night after they left.
Q. Into how close contact with the prisoners does your employment bring you?
A. Well, to instruct them about their work; show them about the tools, and in every respect, showing them how to use them, how to care for them, and various ways. We have nothing but apprentices, you might say, from the commencement of one year to the end of it all the way through.
Q During the administration of Mr. Morris, how has the management of the prison been as to efficiency, so far as you have knowledge of it?
A. Well, sir, so far as our wood-shop is concerned, we have not had but very little trouble; in the blacksmith shop, we have had some trouble, for some reason another; whether because there was different men, I can't say what was the cause. The men in the wood-shop have all done very well all through the administration thus far. We have had some instances of hard men in there that have to be dealt with somewhat.
Q. Do you remember any specific cases?
A. Well, I recollect one,—the case of Wilson, while he was at work in our shop.
Q. What was there about that case?
A. He refused to work; he stated the night before that he had got through work there. That is, he told me, about the time they were washing up, that he had got through work, and my reply was to him, says I, I am sorry; says I, Wilson, I wan't your work, and it will be bad for you to refuse, I think. That was all I had to say to him; I passed right on; I never had a great deal of conversation with the man because he came there first, rather a desperate man when he came in.
Q. Do you remember what he was sent for?
A. I don't.
Q. Do you remember where he came from?
A. He came from Detroit.
Q. What reason did he give, if any, why he stopped work?
A. Well, he had formerly worked at shoemaking, and his work in the wood-shop was standing at the bench, and he complained of his leg; one of them had been shot, I think he said; he had a lame leg, and it troubled him. I don't know how his leg was, or anything about it.
Q. Did he go to work afterwards?
A. He came up the next morning, did not go to work, and was sent inside, and the next thing that I saw of him was when he was brought back to the shop. He had been punished and sent back, and he went to work.

Q. How has Mr. Morris' administration been as to kindliness towards the convicts, so far as you have observed?

A. Very kind, sir, in every respect, so far as it come under my observation; and so far as my previous experience has been here with the different Agents that have been in, it seemed to me, that after five or six weeks after he had been here, that he was in my mind, and the movement of things, it seemed he was altogether too lenient. There would be so many that would take advantage of it, that it rather let the discipline down. Its tendency seemed to be a little in that direction for a time, but they soon got over it.

Q. Do you know John Driscoll, "Silver Jack," as he is sometimes called?

A. When he first came here he was in our shop; he was in our shop six weeks, or two months. I don't know what shop he is in now.

Q. What was his character and disposition while in the wagon shop?

A. Pretty wild. There didn't seem to be any such thing as taming him in any way. He would laugh and make fun, and want to scuffle with the men, even in the shop. There did not seem to be anything there only his perfect kind of tricky meanness. There did not seem to be anything very malicious about him there in the shop.

Q. Did he attempt to escape?

A. Yes, sir.

Q. How long was he gone?

A. I think he was gone four or five hours.

Q. How soon did he return to the shop?

A. I don't recollect.

Cross-examined by Mr. Webber:

Q. What opportunity have you had, Mr. Foster, to observe the manner in which Mr. Morris treats the convicts?

A. Well, the way that I observe that, is this: the men, from time to time, as they come into the shop they repeat what is said to them, and tell what they have, and the difference that they see in the prison from the past; that they speak of in my presence; it is done repeatedly.

Q. Is it a common practice for the men to indulge in your presence, in criticisms on the management, or discipline of the prison?

A. Well, there is some few of them that speak of it, when there is anything very special turns up; every-day occurrences, I don't know any more about that from them than if I was not here.

Q. Are you at liberty to converse with them concerning the discipline and management of the prison?

A. No, sir, I never did that.

Q. Have you any other means of judging of Mr. Morris' treatment of convicts, except by what you hear the convicts say?

A. I have from a man that has been punished, or when he has been reported for certain things and not punished. I know when a man has been punished when he comes back to the shop.

Q. You know that from what he tells you?

A. Oh, no, sir; not always.

Q. You have seen punishment inflicted, haven't you?

A. Since Mr. Morris has been here, I think I have seen one or two cases whilst they were administering the punishment. I was passing through the hall in one case, and the other case was when they were showering a man down to the old wash-house. That is the only punishment I think that I have seen inflicted since Mr. Morris has been here.

Q. Then, except in those two cases, all you know is from what the men told you?

A. No, sir.

Q. What else?

A. I can tell by the looks.

Q You see them?

A. Yes, sir.

Q If a man has been showered, can you tell it?

A. I can tell very near, when he is sent right down to the shop.

Q. What do you discover that makes you think that he has been showered;

A. He is generally chilly; he comes up showing that he is not very comfortably warm, and asks permission to go to the stove when he is sent to his bench by the keeper. I tell them that I have no control over them at such a time; they must stay where the keeper puts them.

Q Do you discover any other indication, except chilliness?

A. When they have been showered?

Q. How recent have you had one come to your shop that had been flogged?

A. I don't think I have any in the wood-shop since Mr. Morris has been Agent.

Q. In any of the shops under you?

A. I think there was a man flogged that worked in the blacksmith shop, may be eighteen months ago.

Q. What means had you of knowing that he had been flogged?

A. The foreman told me that.

Q. You did not examine his person?

A. No, sir.

Q. Did you ever examine the person of any of the convicts that had been flogged since Mr. Morris has been here?

A. No, sir.

Q. Are you at liberty to speak outside of the prison of what you observe or what is stated to you inside the prison?

A. I suppose I am, if I choose to; there is no rule here that deprives a man of that, that I know of.

Q. And no such rule ever been applied in your case?

A. No, sir; not that I know of.

Mr. Conely—Have you known of any showering to have occurred this winter?

A. No, I don't think I have—not in our department.

Mr. Webber—Did you ever have any men in your shop wearing the wire cap?

A. I don't think there has been any in the wood shop since Mr. Morris has been there. I don't know as there has on the contract in any of our shops. I don't know but Silver Jack did wear the wire cap a day or two.

Mr. Bartow—Is this Wilson that you speak of, one that is known as James Wilson?

Mr. Morris—William Wilson; James Wilson is on the cigar contract.

Mr. Webber—Do you know what he was punished for?

A. At that time?

Q. Yes.

A. Well, he was sent up, and he was punished quite severely. I suppose it was for his obstinacy, in some shape; at least that is what the Agent told me when he brought him back at the shop. He showed that he had had some pretty rough handling.

Mr. Bartow—The question was, do you know what Wilson was punished for, and what he had done?

A. Oh, at the time he was sent in, when he refused to work that morning. He told me the evening previous that he had got through work.

G. Did he go to work immediately after punishment?

A. Yes, sir.

Q. Were you in the shop when Thurston was punished—were you in the prison then?

A. I don't recollect.

Q. Were you here when Driscoll, or "Silver Jack," as he is called, was brought back to the prison?

A. Well, I was in the yard; I don't recollect whether I saw him that day or not.

Q. Did you hear any conversation between him and the Agent about his capture?

A. No, sir.

HON. WILLIAM S. WILCOX, RECALLED FOR MR. MORRIS.

Examined by Mr. Conely:

Q. I want to ask you as to the opportunity convicts have of making known their complaints to the board of inspectors, against officers or freemen. I want to show to what extent the intercourse is hindered or trammelled; if any are obstructed in any sort of way; whether through fear of punishment, or any other fear. I want you to state it to this committee fully, all there is on that subject.

A. I had supposed that every convict that had any grievances, that he deemed of sufficient importance to take notice of, felt at liberty to ask the privilege of going before the board of inspectors and making known those grievances. In the six years that I have been here, in passing through the yard, I never have repulsed a convict in a single instance; but have, as patiently as I could, heard what he had to say. Without referring to the printed rules, specially, it is my understanding that any convict can reach the board of inspectors at their meeting through their keepers.

Q. Do you know whether or not convicts have come before the board of inspectors personally and made their complaints known in cases where those wants have not previously been known to the Agent himself?

A. Please state the question again.

[The question read by the stenographer.]

A. There have been instances where convicts have wished to see the board without having the Agent present, and they have made known their wants, but they were not wants that the Agent did not know about.

Q. Where they desired to see the board and to have the Agent absent, have their wishes been granted in that regard?

A. Wish to have the Agent absent?

Q. Yes.

A. Yes, sir; their wishes have been granted in every case, because we should not feel at liberty not to do it.

Q. Do you know of the existence of any fear or threats or any other things existing in the prison to prevent the convicts from communicating freely to the board of inspectors any thing they may wish to say?

A. I don't know of any thing, but I can imagine there might be.

Q. Please explain why you may imagine that?

A. Well, I can imagine that a convict might feel that the Agent was arbitrary, and even if he felt a grievance, that it would be better for him to bear his grievances than it would to have it known that he had come before the board of inspectors with his grievances.

Q. That you imagine as incident to the system, rather than as incident to the particular incumbent of the office?

A. Yes, sir; I think I have a plan in my mind that will obviate that thing, because there is no such thing existing; I don't know that there is to-day. I have a plan in my mind that will obviate that entirely.

Q. Have you discovered upon the part of Mr. Morris any indisposition whatever to allow the convicts to come before the board whenever they have desired it?

A. Oh, no, sir; in cases of infraction of the rules he has brought convicts before us,—requested that they come before us and state their own case. In some places where he thought there might be blame attached to the keeper, and they were provoked to commit an infraction of the rules.

Q. You have heard a considerable of the testimony that has been had before this committee since it began its labors at Lansing, haven't you?

A. Yes, sir; I have heard and read it very near.

Q. You have heard the testimony in relation to different sorts of punishment that have been employed. I wish you to state whether the employment of these various methods of punishment have been to any extent experimental on the part of the board of inspectors?

A. Well, now, they have.

Q. Why was that?

A. We would seek to control the men with the mildest punishment that was possible to control them with; and the most humane.

Q. With that idea in view, what punishment did you undertake to use?

A. When Mr. Morris came into the prison it was the understanding that we disapproved of the lash only in the very last emergency; and as a partial substitute for that—or rather I might say that he agreed with us in regard to that, and I think he thought he could run the prison without it—he introduced the cross; I never understood that the board approved of the cross; I think as soon as Mr. Morris understood that the board did not approve of the cross, for various reasons, that it was gradually left out of the punishment; we have criticised from time to time, as the record book has been read, we have criticised various kinds of punishment, and we calculated that our opposition to severe punishment, and especially to any thing that would be brutal, was such that it would have all the influence upon Mr. Morris that any resolutions could have.

Q. That is oral criticism?

A. Yes, sir; oral criticism; it was very difficult for us, and in fact we could not define what we would do for insolence, because you cannot define insolence, it runs along on a scale way up, and, of course, if you attempt to meet insolence with comparative punishment, it would be difficult to prescribe; and so in respect to other things—other modes of punishment; the shower bath, or rather the hose, is an experiment.

Q. So regarded by you now, even?

A. Yes, sir; it is an experiment now; I am anxious to know—I have made frequent inquiries—I am anxious to know whether it had better be abandoned;

whether there is anything to take its place ; whether it is really injurious ; as soon as any member of the board were convinced of that the others would drop it ; we have had no contention of the board in regard to those matters since I have been here ; the clog we found in use when we come here ; I have seen six of them walking around here.

Q. Before Mr. Morris' time ?

A. Yes, sir ; I have gone with Mr. Colliar and ordered them off ; I don't like them at all ; I should never have put one on to a man's leg ; I have not seen anything—I have read about one or two, but it has been my understanding that they were on but a short time ; the cap is an experiment ; it is a mark of disgrace ; and it has rather been my understanding that it is used mainly with men that attempt to escape ; I don't like the cap very well ; men hate to wear it because it is a mark of disgrace ; it is a mark of disgrace when strangers come in to see them ; I have seen them in other prisons—a net of wire, and just a mouth-piece ; I would not consent—if I should see one of them—to have it worn in the prison ; but this is very much less objectionable than any cap that I saw in prisons at any other place ; they were made like a net that you get to keep horses and cows from eating corn, in other prisons ; the strap is an experiment, that in my mind is a substitute for the whip ; and if you are going to inflict any punishment at all, perhaps that is as good a substitute for the whip as anything that you may apply to a convict ; the dark cell was in use when I came here, and we ordered the plank off from the door ; I had rather be punished myself with a whip than to have my fresh air taken from me ; we took the plank from the door, so that the cell is a bare cell.

Q. Stripped of furniture?

A. Stripped of furniture, and the man put in it. I do not just approve of the bare cell, under some circumstances. There are times when, perhaps, a bare cell works well,—I think there is, sometimes. The locking of a man in his cell, and putting him on short rations, is really, to me, the most humane punishment that we have in the prison ; shutting him up there with the understanding that he is to remain there until he sends for the Agent, and is willing to come out and behave himself. Well, you can accomplish all that, but just as soon as he begins to take on his food again, and gets strong again, he begins to feel good and kick. You can bring him to at the time, but they don't seem to be afraid of it. Still, it seems to be the most humane punishment that we have. The next, and best punishment that I like, is a good square talk with the convict, after you both of you get cool and deliberate, and try to convince him that it is a great deal better to be a man,—to try to be a man, and be a good convict, and save his good time, than it is to be constantly violating the rules, and getting the prison down on him in that way. I know a good many men here have been saved by that, by Mr. Morris' talking to them, and by the inspectors. It seems to me the whole of it is pretty much a system of experiments.

Q. When men are talked to in that style, although they may be reported by the keeper for an offense precisely similar to what some other man may have been reported for, if he shows that he is tractable, on being talked to, and the indications are that he is likely to be a good man, you would not, without a proper exercise of discretion, punish him under those circumstances, would you ?

A. No, sir.

Q. Then it may happen sometimes, that in a wise and proper administration of prison discipline, that one person would receive punishment for an offense, while another person, guilty of the same offense, would not receive the same punishment?

A. Yes, sir.

Q. And in that way, the good time of the convict is saved also, is it not?

A. Yes, sir ; we have convicts in the prison that I have promised, and Mr. Colliar has promised, that if there is no further reports against them, that they shall have our influence left here, on record, asking the inspectors that decide upon their case, a long time hence, if there is no further record against them, not to take any good time from them. One of them has run four years, and he has not been reported since. We took a clog off from him when he supposed it had been put upon him for him to wear during his stay here ; and he has not been punished since.

Q. Are there not difficulties in the way of establishing a tariff,—a specific punishment for specific offenses, in your judgment?

A. I don't see how you can do it any more than you can establish a regular tariff, one in which you will govern your children.

Q. In the proper administration of punishment, is it not right the special infirmities of temper, particularly of convicts, etc., the fact that different convicts have different dispositions ?

A. Certainly.

Q. And have had different training in early life ?

A. Yes, sir; it is one of the most important duties, I think, for the Agent to become acquainted with the peculiarities of his men, and treat them accordingly.

Q. And in the dispensing of punishment, and the determination of the character of the punishment is there not necessarily required a large amount of discrimination and discretion ?

A. Oh, yes, sir; and of good temper.

Q. Have you seen in Mr. Morris' administration, any indication that in the administration of punishment, he has been guided by any motive other than the good of the prison, and the good of the convict ?

A. I never have discovered in Mr. Morris any disposition to be vindictive towards a prisoner.

Q. That covers it. Do you know Mr. Cook, the man that was sworn as a witness in the early part of this investigation ?

A. I do.

Q. Did he ever make any complaint to you at all about the things he has testified to ?

A. No, sir.

Q. Did you talk with him about the business of the prison from time to time ?

A. I talked with him in November or December, at our November or December meeting. It is my judgment it was November.

Q. What year ?

A. 1873.

Q. What, if anything, did he say in relation to the subjects about which he has testified ?

A. They were not referred to, the subjects about which he testified.

Q. I was not myself present at the examination of Mr. Cook, and don't know really what he did testify to. I understand that he testified to some specific acts of cruelty. Did he ever bring those to your attention ?

A. No.

Q. Did he express himself at all in regard to the management of the convicts, or in regard to the manner in which they are treated ?

A. Perhaps I might make a brief statement that will shorten the matter : In

STATE PRISON INVESTIGATION.   225

November I was there, and went to the hall-master's office and looked at his supplies; talked about the quality of the goods, particularly the Clinton cloth; noticed some of the shirts, and showed me the shoddy. I asked him what provisions were made—if they were ample to supply the whole of the convicts with undershirts; what the character of the clothing was that was in his possession ready to distribute. I asked him if Mr. Morris was as solicitous about the outer man as he was the inner convict. He stated that Mr. Morris had never offered any objections nor placed any obstacles in the way of his giving out clothing to the men as his judgment dictated. I said to Mr. Cook that you are situated here so that you can judge better of the administration and government of this prison than any other man except the deputy. The keeper is confined to his squad of men. It is the hall-master's business to overlook every man that comes in. His position was such that he would know every man. Every man would have to go to him that went to the hospital, and come to him when he came from the hospital. In brief, he said that he thought Mr. Morris had introduced a great many improvements. That ain't just the word that I want to get hold of, but that carries with it the idea,—a great many improvements; I cannot use his language exactly—but he approved of the discipline of the prison. Before I came to another meeting he wrote a long letter, covering four pages of foolscap, asking an increase of salary. The hall-master gets a keeper's salary. When I came here the next time I made the best inquiries I could in regard to the duties of the hall-master, and found that he was not doing any more for his pay than others, and I never spoke to him about it. That is the substance of my conversation with Mr. Cook.

Q. Was Mr. Cook discharged to your knowledge?
A. He was discharged.
Q. Do you know why?
A. For neglecting his duty.
Q. You live at Adrian?
A. Yes, sir.
Q. How far are you from Rome Center?
A. I am nine miles.
Q. Do you know J. L. Perkins?
A. Most certainly.
Q. His home was at Rome Center, was it not?
A. Yes, sir.
Q. Were you acquainted with his reputation for truth and veracity there?
A. Yes, sir.
Q. Was it good or bad?
A. Bad.
Q. Do you know how many times he has been in here to prison?
A. Twice.
Q. Do you remember for whot offense he was sent the first time?
A. I would not like to state.
Q. The last time he was sent for forgery, was he not?
A. Yes, sir.
Q. Do you remember that there was a civil trial involving the same merits as the criminal trial for forgery?
A. At the time?
Q. Yes, or just before that.
Mr. Webber—We won't go into that matter; that is not legitimate.

Mr. Conely—I don't want it.

The witness—I could not state anything about that.

Mr. Mellen—Did any convict ever complain to you when he was before you that a request that he had made to the keeper had not been reported to you of his grievances?

A. I think there has been, but not for the last three years. When we learned that we thought we had made a rule that would prevent that. I think the keepers understand, I think the Agent understands that if the board should find that a keeper had been requested to give us notice that a convict wanted to see us, if the keeper or Agent failed to do his part towards giving the notice us we would dismiss him.

Cross-examined by Mr. Webber:

Q. Do the inspectors practically exercise any supervision over the employment or dismissal of a keeper or guard?

A. I ought to be able to answer that question. I have canvassed it in my mind a good many times. We do, and still we don't.

Q. Explain that paradox.

A. We think you know that the employes of the prison must be in harmony with the Agent in order to make the discipline and the running of the prison a success; and we have stated to him that we wished he would dismiss a keeper, and he has done it. We have commenced criticising a keeper for being lazy, or indifferent, or any other fault, and he would very soon disappear. We haven't any idea but what if we should say to Mr. Morris we don't believe that keeper is a good keeper for you but what, if we were to give any reasons at all, or even not, that he would soon disappear.

Q. Have you made any rule on that subject?

A. No; we have got the law.

Q. Can you refer to a place on your records for the last two years where a deputy keeper or guard has been discharged by the board?

A. Yes, sir.

Q. Has it been the practice?

A. November 20 there was one discharged.

Q. I desire to call your attention to section 8097 of the Compiled Laws, which reads as follows: [Reads.] "The assistant keepers shall preserve proper discipline among the convicts under their charge, and may punish them for misconduct in such manner and under such regulations as shall be adopted by the board of inspectors, and any such keeper shall as soon as the next day after inflicting punishment upon any convict deliver to the agent or deputy keeper a written memorandum thereof, signed by him, stating the offense committed and the kind and extent of the punishment inflicted." Calling your attention to that statute, I would ask if the board of inspectors have ever made any regulations as to the manner of punishing convicts for misconduct?

A. I do not remember that they have placed on record any specific manner of punishing convicts.

Q. Calling your attention to the further provision of the statute which says that "the next day"—

A. Wait a moment, please; let me explain; the facts are that we have not made any specific directions what punishment to use or how to do it, I mean, and placed it on record.

Q. Again calling attention to the statute which requires such keeper "as soon as the next day after inflicting punishment upon any convict deliver to the Agent

STATE PRISON INVESTIGATION.

the agent or deputy keeper a written memorandum thereof, signed by him, stating the offense committed and the kind and extent of punishment inflicted," I would ask whether the board has taken care to see that that provision of the statute was observed?

A. No keeper has been allowed to inflict any punishment upon a convict since I have been an inspector. As one of the inspectors I believe that that law is impracticable, and if we should undertake to carry it out in the prison, we would have an insurrection in the prison within a week.

Q. Has this rule, which requires the officer inflicting the punishment to deliver a written memorandum thereof, signed by him, stating the offense committed, and the kind and extent of the punishment inflicted, been observed? What I wish to ask is whether a written report signed by the officer inflicting the punishment has been recorded.

Mr. Conely—Does not his other answer cover that, that no punishments have been inflicted. That statute only applies to cases of punishment inflicted by assistants.

Mr. Webber—If you object to my question, you might best object at once.

Mr. Conely—Well, I will object to that question. And my objection is this: That that statute does not apply to either the Agent or deputy; it only applies to men in charge of the shops; and that the witness has already answered that no punishments are inflicted by the men that have charge of the shops. And I think I may say that there has not been for 20 years—that punishments have been inflicted by assistant keepers. The punishments have been inflicted by the deputy keepers and by the agents. Under the practical administration of things here, the assistant keepers have never inflicted punishment, consequently this statute does not apply, and has no force here, and the witness' previous answer, if I mistake not, shows that.

Mr. Bartow—It occurs to me, as one member of the committee, that the reason you give why the question should not be answered, is not a valid reason; that while the question is a proper one, the reason you give for its not being a proper one, is a good reason, or might be a good reason, for its not being done, but not a good reason why the question should not be answered.

Mr. Conely—The reason that I urge is, that it has been already answered by a former answer.

Mr. Bartow—Well, perhaps that might be true, but not materially affect the question now at issue. The question is now, whether it is a proper question that should be answered; and while I regard that it is a proper question that, should be answered, the reason that you give for its not being a proper question might be a good reason for its not being done—your objection might apply and be a good reason for its not being done, and yet not be a good objection to the question. If it is a proper question then it should be answered. It seems to me that it is a proper question.

Mr. Conely—With the intimation from the chairman, I will withdraw the objection, only I felt that those of you who came here as strangers, did not fully understand the scope and the effect of the statute.

Mr. Bartow—I am willing to admit that as one member of the committee, but the question here at issue is, whether the question is a proper one to be asked. I think it is.

[Question read by the stenographer.]

A. All the reports that have been required are in those conduct record books.

Q. And those are written up at the end of the month by the Agent, from memoranda, furnished by the deputy, and are not signed by one?

A. Yes, sir; there may be instances where they have been written up before the end of the month, but it is my observation that it has been the rule to write them up ot the end of the month.

Q. Now, if the authority to punish convicts for disobedience of the prison rules is not found in the statute which I have read, will you tell me where the board claim it to exist?

A. I should have to hunt for the law before I could answer that.

Q. Is there any other statute within your knowledge on the subject?

A. I am not prepared to answer that. I have read all the law connected with the prison, but of course I am not a lawyer, and I do not remember. I supposed that the board were acting in accordance with the law when they were placing the discipline of the prison in the hands of the Agent under their direction.

Q. Have you any clear idea as to the source of the authority of the Agent to inflict punishment on the convicts for breach of the prison rules?

A. My impression is that he has power from the board of inspectors, in a humane and proper manner, and rules that we may make for him.

Q. That hardly answers my question. I would like the question to be read. [Question read by stenographer].

A. Not distinct enough so that I am prepared to make the answer now, without investigating, nor clear enough.

Q. You spoke of punishments being experimental on the part of the board; is there anything on the records to show any rules or regulations relative to those experimental punishments?

A. I do not think there is.

Q. It all rests in parole instructions and advice given the Agent by the board?

A. Yes, sir.

At this point, on motion of Mr. Webber, the taking of further testimony was adjourned until to-morrow morning at nine o'clock.

WEDNESDAY A. M., APRIL 14, 1875.

HULBERT PERRINE, SWORN FOR MR. MORRIS.

Examined by Mr. Conely:

Q. You reside in Jackson?
A. Yes, sir.
Q. And are employed in the prison?
A. Yes, sir.
Q. What is your business?
A. Assistant keeper.
Q. How long have you been such?
A. It is nearly ten years since I first came here.
Q. You have been here continuously ever since Mr. Morris has been here?
A. Yes, sir; well, I guess perhaps about four weeks I was away after he come.
Q. Were you present at the punishment of Thurston, the convict?

A. Yes, sir.
Q. Do you remember when it occurred?
A. I could not exactly tell the time; no, sir.
Q. Were you present at more than one punishment inflicted upon Thurston?
A. No, sir.
Q. Do you recollect about hearing about any other?
A. I do not know but I did.
Q. Can you say whether the punishment that you were present at was the first or second that he received, from what you heard?
A. Well, I should think it was the second from what I heard.
Q. Where did it occur?
A. In the lower end of one of the shops in the back part of the yard.
Q. Go on in your own way and state all you know about that punishment.
A. When I came in at night I saw Thurston sitting on a bench in the hall that was known as the hall master's hall; when we locked up, the deputy did not, as usual, say it was all right, and then we could go home; but the Agent said he wished we would remain a few moments, and he called up Thurston, or told him to bring him that knife he had concealed there, and Thurston rather reluctantly got it out, I think out of a spit-box, and brought it to Mr. Morris. I do not know that I examined the knife or looked at it very particularly, but I should think it was four or five inches long, dirk fashion, made in that style. Mr. Morris told him then that he should flog him. Then he took him to a shop in the back part of the yard, tied his hands together, and tied him up so his hands were a little above his head, and Mr. Morris commenced to whip him, and perhaps gave him four or five blows at a time and then talked with him. He did so until he was through flogging him. [A knife was here produced and shown to witness]. I should think that was the knife; it looks very much like it. [The knife produced was made from a steel putty-knife, the blade just three inches long, breadth at the widest part 11-16 of an inch, sharpened on both sides].
Q. You had got along in your narration to where you said Mr. Morris stopped and talked with him?
A. Yes, sir; he gave him perhaps four or five blows at a time and stopped and talked with him until he got through flogging him; then they untied him, I believe, and brought him to the hall. That is the last I see of him. They were untieing him when I came out of the shop.
Q. What did Mr. Morris say to him at these intervals?
A. I think that he asked him if he would behave himself in the future, and he promised him that he would.
Q. How soon in the course of the whipping did he promise him that he would behave himself?
A. I do not know that I remember that, but perhaps after he had whipped him may be five minutes.
Q. How long did the whipping continue?
A. I should not think it exceeded over ten or twelve minutes.
Q. Was there any whipping done after the man gave up and promised good behavior?
A. Not much of any, I should not think, although he begged, and after all I guess he did not come down and say that he would do just what was right until it was nearly through. They most all will beg before they are punished much.
Q. Do you know how many blows were inflicted?

A. I do not know exactly.
Q. W re they all given by Mr. Morris?
A. I believe they were, yes, sir.
Q. Upon what part of his person were they inflicted?
A. Why, around his body, from his shoulders down.
Q. How low down? any about his legs?
A. I did not notice; I do not think he struck him around his legs, that I remember of.
Q. Were any of them inflicted upon the front of his person or upon his sides, can you say?
A. I could not say, no, sir. I think he was tied in such a way that the most of it would come on his back.
Q. Can you describe the whip?
A. Well, it was a whip that was worn a considerable, I should think, from the looks of it, I believe that perhaps a foot or ten inches from the lash it was broken down,—dropped down before they commenced using it. I noticed it when it was brought down.
Q. Can you tell of what the whip was made?
A. Well, 1 could not, no, sir.
Q. Was it like any sorts of whips that are on sale?
A. Well, yes, sir; I should judge it was one of that kind.
Q. Any wire in it?
A. I did not notice any.
Q. Did you know the whip so that you could describe it, having seen it at other times?
A. I do not know that I have seen it before or since.
Q. What appearance did Mr. Morris present, of being in anger or out of temper?
A. Well, I thought he was pretty cool when he talked to him, and he talked to him in about the usual tone; I think he might have been a little angry at the time he took the knife away from him; he might have spoken a little faster than common, but at the time when he was punishing him I thought he was in his usual temper, about as he always is.
Q. How is that, angry or otherwise?
A. No, sir; he talked to him very moderate.
Q Can you say what was the number of blows?
A. Well, I could not exactly, no, sir.
Q. Can you approximate it? Can you within a range not exceeding so many and not less than so many?
A. Yes, sir; I should think it might be between forty and fifty blows.
Q. Did you ever see any other punishment inflicted in the Prison?
A. Yes.
Q. Whom?
A. Well, it was before Mr. Morris' administration.
Q. I speak only with reference to Mr. Morris' administration?
A. I do not remember; I might have seen them showered; I think I did one night, see a boy—two boys showered.
Q. Do you remember who the boys were?
A. I think they were boys that worked on the cigar contract.
Q. Did you see the entire punishment?
A. Yes, sir, I believe I did.

Q. Were there any ill effects to the boys attending that punishment?
A. I think not; the next morning they were in their places in the shop. I was keeping the shop at that time.
Q. To go back to Thurston: did you observe at the time, or have you ever observed since that time, the effect of any of those blows upon his person, as to producing marks or drawing blood, or anything of that kind?
A. I did not see any blood at the whipping.
Q. Or gashes, or anything of that sort?
A. No, sir.
Q. Have you seen his body since?
A. I have not; no, sir.
Q. Did you know Thurston before the whipping?
A. Yes, sir.
Q. What was his character as a convict within the prison?
A. Well, he was a pretty obstinate fellow; what we term here a pretty hard case. I had charge of him on the lockup that we had, I should think for nearly a year; I unlocked him mornings and locked him in at night.
Q. Can you say how that hardness of conduct manifested itself in him?
A. Well, he was very obstinate; in case the keeper spoke to him he would not answer his question; pretty insolent sometimes. A number of times I had occasion to report him for talking in the ranks. He would deny it immediately, but I knew very well that he did talk, and still he would deny it to the deputy.
Q. What do you know about Mr. Morris' temper in his intercourse with the convicts and in his management of the prison?
A. I do not know that I have ever see him out of temper much. Usually about the same.
Q. Manifests some warmth sometimes, I suppose?
A. Yes, sir.
Q. Did you ever see any act of his that indicated that he was actuated by any vindictive or revengeful motives?
A. No, sir.
Q. So far as your knowledge extends, how has his administration been as to severity?
A. I should think not very severe, from what I have seen a number of times.
Q. Do you know what his reputation is in that regard among the prison employes as for severe or lenient discipline?
A. Well, it is generally calculated that he is very lenient. Used the men as well as could be expected under the circumstances.
Q. Do you know how he is viewed by the public,—the community here at Jackson in that regard?
A. Well, I should think, take it from the general tone of the papers, that they thought he was rather lenient.
Q. How is it so far as conversation extends among the people here at Jackson; do they regard him as lenient or severe?
A. Yes, sir, that's the general opinion.
Q. Which way?
A. That it was rather lenient.

Cross-examination by Mr. Webber:

Q. Were you ever employed in a prison before you commenced here as assistant keeper under Mr. Morris?
A. Yes, sir.

Q. Where?
A. I was employed as guard under Mr. Winton's administration.
Q. How long ago?
A. That commenced, I believe, if I am not mistaken, in 1865.
Q. How long did you continue in the employment of the prison at that time?
A. I guess about between three and four years under Mr. Winton and Mr. Bingham's administration; I think I came here in June, 1865, and went away in February, 1869.
Q. At the time when Thurston was punished, when you saw it, it was in the evening?
A. Yes, sir; after the rest of the men were locked up, just before sundown.
Q. You think in June, 1873?
A. When this whipping occurred?
Q. Yes?
A. I guess that is about the time; I could not say exactly as to the date.
Q. Thurston was in his cell when you first had your attention called to his case that evening?
A. No, sir.
Q. Where was he?
A. He was on a bench in the old building as we came in at night; in the main building; sat on a bench usually set out there for men that are dropped out there for any misdemeanor through the day; they are reported there at night for the deputy to take care of, whatever he sees fit to do with them; he sat on the bench when I came in that night.
Q. Did you know how long he had been sitting there?
A. No, sir; I could not say.
Q. After you saw him there how long before his case was called up for attention?
A. I should think not more than ten minutes.
Q Who addressed him in the first instance?
A. Mr. Morris.
Q. What did he say?
A. I think he asked him to bring him the knife that he had there.
Q. After the knife was handed to Mr. Morris, what did he then say to Thurston?
A. I think he told him that he should flog him for it.
Q. Do you remember the language that he used to convey that idea?
A. No, sir; I do not; not the exact language; I could not say.
Q. To what place was Thurston taken to be flogged?
A. To a shop in the back part of the yard; in the lower part of one of the shops.
Q. Did he go on receiving the order voluntarily, or was he carried?
A. He went on his own accord, I believe.
Q. Was he hand-cuffed at this time?
A. I think not.
Q. Who removed Thurston's clothing previous to his whipping?
A. I think he did it himself.
Q. State whether Thurston indulged in any conversation while going from the hall to the place of punishment, or in removing his clothing?
A. I think I heard him whilst we were going to the shop using some threats, but what it was I cannot say.

Q. Were you near enough at the time to understand what he did say?
A. No, sir; I was a little behind him; I heard him talking in a low tone, as though he were threatening, or kind of growling like to himself.
Q. Was Mr. Morris nearer to him than you in going to the shop?
A. I think not; I think Mr. Morris was behind me.
Q. Who tied up Thurston to receive punishment?
A. I think the hall master done it, Mr. Cook; I am not certain about it.
Q. What was he tied up with?
A. With a small cord.
Q. To what was the cord attached?
A. To a post in the shop.
Q. How high from the floor was the point to which the attachment was made?
A. I should think about six feet from the floor, perhaps.
Q. Did you measure it?
A. No, sir.
Q. State whether he was tied up or whether some one held the other end of the cord?
A. Well, I should think he was tied; could not very well hold the other end of the cord without receiving some of the punishment, I guess.
Q. Was he made fast in any other way than by the hands?
A. No, sir, I believe not.
Q. Did you time that punishment?
A. I did not, sir.
Q. Did any one?
A. I could not say that they did; no, sir.
Q. Did you count the number of blows given?
A. I did not; no, sir.
Q. Did any one?
A. Not that I know of, no, sir.
Q. How near did you stand to Thurston when he was receiving the punishment?
A. Well, perhaps fifteen feet from him.
Q. Did you stand near enough to see the effect of the blows upon his person?
A. Yes, sir.
Q. After the first few blows and at the time of the first intermission, did any one step up to see what the effect of the blows already given had been on his person?
A. I don't remember that there did; no, sir.
Q. How did Thurston stand, with his back or his face to Mr. Morris when receiving the punishment?
A. Well, I think he stood rather with his side to him the most of the time.
Q. Which side?
A. Either his left or his right side, I could not say, he was tied to the post and Mr. Morris stood off here.
Q. How many blows were given before Thurston commenced begging?
A. Well, perhaps eight or ten, although he said all the time that he was not so bad a man as they represented, or something of that kind. He did not get right down and beg until he had given him maybe eight or ten blows.
Q. To whom did he say that he was not as bad a man as had been represented?
A. To Mr. Morris.

Q. That was before the punishment commenced?
A. Well, about that time, I guess, that it commenced.
Q. Did he state any grievance that he had that had induced him to break tho rules?
A. I don't remember that he did; no, sir.
Q. At the time of the first intermission, then, I understand you, that he fairly yielded, and got right down and begged?
A. Well, it might have been at the second intermission.
Q. Now, cannot you tell how long it was that Mr. Morris was engaged in giving the whipping, up to the first intermission?
A. I do not think that I understand the question.
Q. From the time the flogging commenced, to the first intermission, how many minutes?
A. It might not have been more than a minute or two minutes; somewhere there.
Q. Did the blows fall rapidly or with deliberation?
A. Well, quite moderate, I thought.
Q. How long was the stock of the whip?
A. Well, I should think it was over three and one half or four feet—the stock.
Q. How long was the lash?
A. Well, I should think perhaps about ten inches or a foot; down to where it was laid down; something similar to that. It appears it was broken.
Q. How long was it from the break down to the end?
A. I should think about ten inches or a foot.
Q. Do you mean that the entire length of the lash was ten inches or twenty inches or two feet?
A. No, sir; I should think from where it bent down it was ten inches or a foot.
Q. How far was it from the stock to where it bent down?
A. Oh, three feet and a half or four feet, as near as I could guess at it now.
Q. Either you do not understand me or I do not understand you. What is the entire length of the lash from the stock to the tip of the lash?
A. It is possible that there might have been some of the stock broken off. It was laid down and broke.
Q. What kind of a stock was this?
A. I did not examine it close. It might have been oak or it might have been ratan.
Q. Was it a braided whip?
A. 1 could not say as to that; I should presume the lash was.
Q. The stock I am speaking of. Had it a braided cover?
A. Yes, sir, it might have had; yes, sir, I should presume it did.
Q. Did you ever have that whip in your hand?
A. No, sir.
Q. Can you speak with any certainty in describing that whip, then?
A. Well, from my recollections is, and what I saw of it that night—
Q. Your attention was more particularly directed to the individual receiving the punishment than to the instrument with which it was administered, was it not?
A. Well, I might have looked at them both as far as that—
Q. Can you swear positively that the entire number of blows given on that occasion was less than sixty?

STATE PRISON INVESTIGATION. 235

A. I should think it did not exceed fifty.

Q. Have you any means of knowing how many blows were given except a mere guess?

A. That is all; I did not count them; I could not tell exactly.

Q. Now, how many of these intermissions were given in that punishment?

A, There might have been five or six; I could not tell exactly.

Q. Did you look on the lower part of the abdomen of Thurston after the punishment was ended to see the effect of it on that part of his person?

A. I did not, sir.

Q. You say that Mr. Morris is generally considered lenient by the employes of the prison?

A. Yes, sir.

Q. Whom do you mean by the employes?

A. I mean the keepers and guards at the prison.

Q. Is Mr. Morris' administration a subject of criticism by the employes in their conversation with each other?

A. I believe not; no, sir.

Q. Do you consider yourself at liberty to criticise the administration among yourselves?

A. Yes, sir; if we have any fault to find, why we go to him or the deputy.

Q. True; but can you complain to each other of it without going to him or the deputy?

A. I suppose we could; yes, sir.

Q. Is it your practice to do so?

A. No, sir.

Q. Then how do you get at the general reputation for leniency among the employes?

A. If there is any such thing occurs it might be spoken of or mentioned.

Q. And from the fact it is not spoken of you infer the reputation?

A. Yes, sir.

Q. Now, you say that he is generally considered as lenient by the community at Jackson,—what do they know about his administration of the prison?

A. Well, I do not know as they know any about it only from hearsay.

Q. Have they any means of obtaining accurate information concerning his administration in the prison?

A. Well, I do not think they have in particular.

Q. The employes about the prison are not in the habit of going up town and talking about the administration of it, are they?

A. No, sir; that would be against one of the rules of the prison.

Q. What means have you of knowing that the community regard it as lenient?

A. I have frequently had men speak to me in that way in regard to the prison; business men in the town.

Q. Did you hold conversation with them on the subject?

A. No, sir; not of any amount.

Q. Whom did you ever have speak to you on the subject?

A. I don't remember exactly.

Re-direct examination by Mr. Conely:

Q, I ask you whether, during the punishment of Thurston, Mr. Morris struck him with the butt end of the whip?

A. I did not see him do it, sir.

Q. Did he strike him on the head?
A. I did not see him do it.
Q. Would you have been likely to have known it if such a thing had occurred?
A. I think I should; I stood in the shop all the time.

Re-cross examination by Mr. Webber:
Q. Do you know the form of the oath that you took as a keeper?
A. Well, I have taken it.
Q. Do you remember its form?
A. I do not remember it exactly; I could not state it.
Q. Was it written, and did you sign it?
A. Yes, sir.

DR J. B. TUTTLE, SWORN FOR THE COMMITTEE.

Examined by Mr. Webber:
Q. You are the physician of the prison?
A. Yes, sir, at present.
Q. How long have you been acting in that capacity?
A. This present term, it will be three years the second day of May; I was here before that, three years.
Q. In what years were you here in your first employment?
A. In a part of 1859, 1860, 1861, 1862, and a part of 1863.
Q. Will you state generally your duties in the prison?
A. Well, my duty is to visit the prison once a day and examine all that are sick, prescribe medicine for them such as I think they need, and give them such other treatment as they need, according to their sickness, and direct somewhat whether they shall go to work, or sit in the hospital or go to their cells. At present we are so situated for hospital room that we cannot retain those who are not able to work,—we cannot retain all of them in the hospital, so we send those that are not very bad to their cells, and let them lie on their beds or sit up, as they are disposed. When a man comes to the hospital for treatment, I examine him and find out whether he is sick enough to be excused; if he is, 1 excuse him; if not, I give him some medicine and send him back to his work.
Q. Is it any part of your duty to examine and direct as to what clothing they shall wear?
A. Well, I suppose that as I have somewhat the superintendence and supervision of the health of the prison, it would come under my—it would devolve upon me to take some notice of that. If a man is suffering from a want of clothing, and was sick in consequence of it, or was feeble in health and needed a little more clothing than another, it would be my duty to direct it.
Q. Have you authority to direct that additional clothing if in your opinion it is proper?
A. I understand that I have.
Q. I notice that in your report for 1874, that you use the following language: "The convicts, in general, are well clothed; but I feel it my duty to call your attention to the necessity of furnishing the men with sufficient warm clothing, both for wearing and bedding at the beginning of cold weather in the fall. A multitude of diseases are introduced by taking cold, and in that way much more is lost by sickness than would purchase many pairs of drawers and undershirts." What did you observe in the management of the prison that led you to that recommendation?

A. The change from summer clothing to winter clothing, sometimes is not made in season, as a cold snap comes on, and a person with the common summer clothing on would feel it materially, and if they did not change, would perhaps, take cold. Our men come in and say their bedding was not sufficient. In the summer-time they sleep simply on the canvass; they do not have anything under them; in the winter-time they have something under them to keep the cold from coming in under, as it will come from under as well as from over; and have had them complain to me that their cots were too thin; nothing to put a top of them,—the straw beds have not been put on,—and sometimes they cover them with a blanket to lay on first; they get onto that, and then they put their clothing over them. The idea I thought to convey in the report was, that these changes might be made in time to prevent these colds.

Q. When the change is made from summer clothing to winter clothing, is a sufficient amount of clothing, in your judgment, furnished to protect the health and comfort of the convicts?

A. Well, that depends upon whether it is a prisoner or a freeman.

Q. Suppose it was a freeman, would it be sufficient to keep him comfortable?

A. It would not be sufficient for me.

Q. What is the winter clothing for the bed?

A. They usually have a straw tick filled with straw.

Q. About how thick?

A. Oh, it is thick enough; I could not tell; it is of sufficient thickness, and sheet over that, then these blankets.

Q. How many and how heavy?

A. I do not know as I ever counted the number of blankets they have; some of them more, some of them less. Some require more and some require less; two or three blankets, three or four blankets. I have been called to go and see convicts in their cells when they have not been able to come to the hospital; find them covered up with clothing enough to smother a man, almost. How they got it I do not know. Some seemed to have more than others at times.

Q. Can you speak advisedly as to the regular supply to those that are not on the sick list?

A. I don't believe I do know how many blankets they do have. They have a sheet under them, a sheet over them, and then two to four blankets, I guess, in the coldest winter weather.

Q. Now, what are the extremes of the temperature in their cells, in the winter?

A. Well, I have known it to be 70°; and I don't know but I have been in the wings, at times, when the heat has been on pretty high,—that it has been over °; and I have known it to be down very cold; not in the night-time; I am not there much in the night,—very seldom in the night,—but I am speaking of the day-time now. Usually the steam is shut off after the men go to their work, and the halls are sometimes quite cool; but when the steam is on the heat is sufficient to keep them comfortably warm.

Q. What is the ventilation in the wings through the cells; how long would it take to have the cold air that might accumulate during the day in a cell be replaced by warm air, which should be made from the steam pipes, when the steam is again put on?

A. No; I could not state.

Q. Have you ever given any attention to see whether the warm air does get to the cells?

A. Well, it does get in; I do know exactly how soon or what time in the afternoon they let on the steam; but they do it, I suppose, so as to give the men proper warmth when they go to their cells.

Q. Have you ever satisfied yourself from examination, or from official information, as to whether the temperature of the men's cells, in the winter, is such as to make the men comfortable in that regard?

A. Well, many times I have thought they were not comfortable, so comfortable as I would like to be myself.

Q. Now, as to the air in those cells, is there sufficient ventilation, so that the air for the convict to breathe, towards morning, is pure?

A. Well, I do not think the ventilation is proper; I do not think the cells are well ventilated; but you are aware that 250 or 300 men shut up in a wing like one of ours here, the air would become somewhat vitiated before morning. In the old wings the cells are not ventilated at all. The east wing was made with the view of ventilating the cells,—very poor at that.

Q. Now, as to the clothing for the convicts: when they dress in the morning for cold weather, and after the winter clothing is given them, what clothing have they, the general run of convicts?

A. They have a pair of pantaloons, vest, shirt, and round-about.

Q. Stockings and shoes?

A. Stockings and shoes and cap or hat.

Q. The bulk of the men have no under-shirts and drawers?

A. I guess not.

Q. In your opinion, as a physician, have they sufficient clothing to be comfortable in cold weather?

A. Well, as I said before, it would not be comfortable for me; it might be for a prisoner.

Q. Does your knowledge as a physician lead you to believe that a man's nature changes by being put in prison?

A. I guess not much.

Q. In your official capacity have you informed the inspectors of your views in this regard otherwise than in your report?

A. I have not.

Q. Have you held conversation with them on this subject?

A. No, sir; I think I spoke to Dr. Bliss about it, not in an official capacity though.

Q. At what time in the fall of 1874 was the change made from summer to winter clothing?

A. I do not remember when it was.

Q. When the change was made was it general as to all the convicts at the same time?

A. Well, it was intended to be general, but they could not get the clothing as fast as was necessary; there was some difficulty in getting the clothing made fast enough to make the change all at once.

Q. Have you ever noticed anything in the food furnished the convicts to criticise professionally?

A. No, sir; the food is good, sufficient, and wholesome, so far as my observation goes.

Q. Do you remember the case of a man named Budlong in the prison?

A. I know a man by the name of Budlong in the prison.

Q. In what department of the prison is he now?

STATE PRISON INVESTIGATION. 239

A. It seems to me he is in the tobacco factory, in the cigar shop; I am not sure.

Q. I allude to the one who claimed to be insane, or at least who acted as though he might be insane; do you remember such a case as that?

A. No, I do not; this man that I have reference to is a simple sort of man; does not know but very little.

Q. When a convict acts in a strange manner, as an insane person might be supposed to act, and as insane people do act, state whether you are called upon by the agent to assist in determining whether the insanity is real or feigned?

A. Well, I do not know of any case occurring in which I was not counselled in regard to it; I do not know of any case of insanity where my judgment has not been asked—my opinion has been asked in regard to it.

Q. Is a person ever sent to the insane department of the prison without your certificate?

A. Yes, sir.

Q. By what authority are they sent there if not by yours?

A. I do not know.

Q. You have known of persons being sent to the insane department of the prison where you have not been consulted in regard to it?

A. Well, perhaps I do not understand you; I have not been consulted in regard to their being sent there; I have, perhaps, been consulted in regard to their insanity, but have nothing to do with their going to the asylum.

Q. Then I will repeat my question: have you ever known of the case of a convict sent to the insane department of the prison until after you had examined and given an opinion as to the sanity or insanity?

A. Well, I guess there is one there that I never had anything to say about, but I think he was sent by the judge directly there.

Q. You think that is the only one?

A. I think so; I do not remember of any other.

Q. How often do you visit the insane department of the prison?

A. Only when I am sent for to go there.

Q. The same as to other convicts?

A. Well, I visit the hospital every day, but I do not always go to the asylum. I go there if they send word or leave an order for me to go there. If there is no order for me, I do not go.

Q. How many convicts are there now in the insane department of the prison?

A. I have not counted them lately; I think there is in the neighborhood of ten. I do not know the exact number.

Q. Is the treatment which they do receive in the prison suitable, in your opinion, for persons in their condition?

A. No, I do not think it is; I do not think it is possible to treat them properly in their condition; I think they receive as good treatment as is possible under the circumstances.

Q. What suggestions would you make in that regard, with a view to improving their condition?

A. In the first place, I would have the asylum surrounded by a wall so that they could be let out into a yard, and not be liable to escape, so they could treat them with some degree of humanity.

Q. Are they now each permanently confined in a cell?

A. Pretty much so. I do not know but there is one or two that have liberty to go out into the hall. Some of them are not vicious; but, as a general thing, they are enclosed in a solitary cell.

Cross-examination by Mr. Conely :
Q. The treatment of insane persons is a specialty, is it not?
A. I believe it is.
Q. You never have had any practice in that regard at all, have you ?
A. No, sir. I have some ideas in regard to it, but little practical knowledge.
Q. Very little practical knowledge?
A. Yes, sir.
Q. The ideas that you have have been gained, I suppose, incidentally, and not by reason of any special study that you have given to that subject ?
A. Yes, sir.
Q. The things that are lacking, that you judge may be, and perhaps are, necessary in the treatment of insane persons are, to what extent, due to Mr. Morris ?
A. I do not understand your question.
Q. You spoke, in your direct examination, that the treatment of the insane convicts was not such as was warranted upon considerations of humanity,—substantially that.
A. That is the idea.
Q. I wish you would state to this committee to what extent, if any, the Agent is responsible for any lack of proper treatment of the insane convicts.
A. I do not think he is responsible at all. I think his treatment is as good as is possible under the circumstances. I wish to correct my former testimony, given before the inspectors. The question was asked me by the inspectors if I knew of any of the convicts being injured by punishment so that they needed any treatment, that came under my observation. I think I made the statement that I knew of but one, and that was simply sore-throat,—a little sore-throat from showering. But I since have recollected of one case which, as that statement has been published, I would like to state and have it corrected.

Re-direct examination by Mr. Webber:
Q. State that case?
A. A man by the name of Rushing came to the hospital some time in November,—the first of November, with his hip, and leg, and side somewhat bruised, and he was laid up with it for about ten days; I asked him what caused it, as I had no other means of knowing what caused it, except what he said himself ; he said the Agent struck him with his cane.
Q. That was November, 1874?
A. Yes, sir; I think he came into the hospital about the 1st of November. He had been feeble. He had been complaining before that, and was locked up in his cell. He went to his cell to remain there during the day, and after this he remained in the hospital for a few days. He complained of being very lame. I did not think he was as lame as he pretended to be. He was bruised some, and what we call black and blue.
Q. Describe this man Rushing in his physical appearance?
A. Well, he is a spare, slim man, about five feet eight inches, perhaps.
Q. Weigh about —— ?
A. Weigh about,—well, he is very spare and poor in flesh, I should not think he would weigh more than 140 pounds.
Q. Age?

A. He must have been between 50 and 60. He has got a son here that is over 20,—25 I think.
Q. Is his son in the Prison?
A. Yes, sir; a convict.
Q. Could you tell by the appearance of this man's person how many blows he had received?
A. Well, I should think about three from the bruises. One was up on his hip, or a little above, and the other was along on his thigh, and one was down on his ankle. How many blows he received in each place I could not tell.
Q. Did you learn the offense for which that punishment was inflicted?
A. Yes, sir; I afterwards learned it.
Q. From whom?
A. I guess from different ones. Mr. Morris told me himself of it; I think he told me.
Q. State what Mr. Morris said to you on that subject?
A. He said, for exposing his person through the grates as visitors were passing through the hall.
[The conduct record is here handed to Mr. Morris, and he is requested to point out the entry of the punishment spoken of by the witness.]
Mr. Morris—October 29th, the record is made.
[The following is the record.]
"Oct. 29, 1874. Robert Rushing, locks in 44 east. As a party of ladies and gents were passing through the wing, one of the ladies lagged behind. When near Rushing's cell, looked up, and he shook his privates at her. Watered until his amorous affection had left him."
Q. Does your duty call upon you in any manner to decide as to the punishment to be inflicted, or to be present at their infliction?
A. I do not understand it so.
Q. Have you ever been present and witnessed the effect of the punishment upon a convict or anything of that kind?
A. I never have seen full punishment on any convict. I have been passing through when they have been showering men—I have had them come directly to the hospital and have a good sweat.
Q. What is the effect upon the system of a severe showering?
A. Well, I have never seen any evil effects from it, except in that one case that I have stated. It caused a little inflammation of the tonsils,—sore throat for a day or two, and that may have happened if he had not been showered; I could not say as to that. Those that I have seen directly after being showered —I have had several cases where they have been sent up into the hospital after being showered; that was when the old hospital was in existence,—and all the effect it had on them, it would produce an abundant perspiration, and they would stay there and sweat it out for half a day, and they would go to their work the next morning. I never saw any evils from it; I have always been afraid of it, nevertheless.
Q. What induced that fear?
A. It looks to me as if I should not like to try it myself.
Q. Well, as a punishment?
A. I have been afraid that the reaction, the chill, the great shock that it would give nature, would produce evil effects.
Q. Have you ever been advised with by the Agent as to whether there were any convicts whose physical system would be particularly liable to such injury?

A. I never have.

Q. Has Mr. Morris, while acting as Agent, ever advised with you as to the propriety of inflicting any particular punishment in any particular case?

A. Never.

Q. Did you know Driscoll, who attempted to escape and was shot?

A. Yes, sir.

Q. Did you extract the ball?

A. Yes, sir.

Q. Was Mr. Morris present at the time the ball was extracted?

A. Well, I couldn't say; I do not know whether he was in the hospital, I do not know but he was; I know there was several in there. The hall master was in and came and wanted the bullet after I had extracted it, because he said it belonged to his pistol. I do not remember any other individual who was in there.

Q. Have you any information from Mr. Morris how far he stood from Mr Driscol when he shot?

A. No, sir, I don't know anything about it.

Q. Have you any knowledge from Mr. Morris as to whether Driscol spoke to him before he fired?

A. I have not.

Q. Or whether he spoke to Dri-coll?

A. I have not.

Q. What opportunity have you had since Mr. Morris has been Agent, to observe his intercourse with the convicts; and his manner with them generally?

A. I have not had much opportunity, sir. I am here once a day, go to the hospital and attend to my business and right away.

Q. And frequently he is not about at the time?

A. I very seldom see him.

Q. Have you ever observed sufficiently so that you could state whether as a general rule, his temper is equable and uniform in the treatment of convicts?

A. I never saw him out of temper as I know of, in my life, except he may have got a little provoked at me one time. I think he did, but not very bad.

Re-cross-examination by Mr. Conely:

Q. Did Rushing state to you how the injuries came upon his person?

A. He is the only one that stated to me, and the only means I had of ascertaining.

Q. What did Rushing say about how these injuries came to be inflicted?

A. He said Mr. Morris caned him, I believe.

Q. Did he say why he did it?

A. No; I did not ask him.

Q. Did he tell you?

A. No, sir.

Q. Did Mr. Morris state anything to you in relation to that when he told you about punishing him? How the injuries came?

A. Mr. Morris said to me that he hallooed when he was showering him, I think, and that was the reason he struck him, to stop his noise.

Q. I want to ask you a little in relation to the clothing. Have you ever called Mr. Morris' attention to the fact that, in your judgment, in some seasons of the year, the men were not sufficiently clothed?

A. All that I have ever had to say to Mr. Morris about it, was in consequence of my speaking to the hall master about furnishing the men more clothing, as

STATE PRISON INVESTIGATION. 243

I understand it, under Mr. Morris' direction, of course; and if there is any person needs extra clothing in consequence of their health, they could come to me about it for directions. If I say "such a man must have a shirt, another shirt," or something of that kind, he usually gets it. But through the fall of the year, and through the winter too, men will complain about their clothing; not having sufficient, and they will come to the hall master, and the hall master sends them to the physician, and I have no right to order clothing except to those who specially need it in consequence of their health. I understand that so, and when they are not sick, and need clothing in consequence of that, I send them back to the hall master. We had got in the habit of sending them back and forth in that way, and finally I went to the hall master and told him that there was so much complaint made for the want of clothing, that I wondered that he did not get some clothing made up at once and furnish them, and not have them complaining all the while, and he thought I was meddling, I suppose, with something that was not my business, and the Agent spoke to me about it.
Q. That was the time you spoke of when he seemed to be out of humor?
A. Yes, sir.
Q. Do not men feign symptoms frequently?
A. They do, very frequently.
Q. Do not the men oftentimes make complaints when there is no ground for the complaint?
A. Very frequently.
Q. Sometimes they deceive you, I suppose?
A. Yes, sir; they would deceive the very elect sometimes.
Q. Can you rely upon their statements of their symptoms?
A. Never; that is, I take them just as far as I think they are reliable, and no farther.
Q. You like to have confirmation from what you may observe yourself?
A. Yes, sir.
Q. Either from the pulse or tongue, or something else?
A. Yes, sir.
Q. In that, your practice inside the prison, I take it, must differ very materially from what it is among persons outside?
A. Very materially.
Q. Ordinarily, outside of the prison, you could rely upon the person's statement of his own symptoms?
A. Yes, sir; and yet there are cases outside where people think they are a little sicker than they are.
Q. How is the rule inside, as to the deceptions practiced by convicts in the statement of their own symptoms,—what is the rule about that, do you expect that they ordinarily tell you just as it is?
A. Yes, sir; I expect that they do.
Q. At the same time you exercise more caution about receiving their statements than you would from a person outside?
A. Yes, sir.
Q. The shirting, of which you speak, that these men wear in the winter, is it made of wool?
A. Well, they are not all woolen shirts.
Q. In the winter?
A. No; I guess it is intended that they all shall have woolen shirts, but they have not all had them.

Q. Well, those that had cotton shirts, have not they all had woolen shirts?
A. No, sir.
Q. Do you know to what extent that has been?
A. No, I do not.
Q. Do you know how many men there are in the prison that to-day have two shirts on?
A. I do not.
Q. You know that some of them have?
A. Yes, sir; I cannot say to-day; I think there has been prisoners having two shirts on during the winter.
Q. Describe the shirting that is worn by the convicts generally.
A. The cotton or woolen, or both?
Q. Describe them both.
A. The cotton shirting is a coarse,—I do not know the name of the goods,— it is a checkered or mixed sort of shirting; pretty substantial heavy goods,— thicker than factory. The woolen is pretty coarse woolen goods. I should think some of the cloth they had last winter was very poor, and some of it was better; I think the second lot was rather better. It is a brown and grey mixed goods, coarse, very coarse, and pretty substantial and strong.
Q. These men work in a heated shop during the day, I believe?
A. Not many.
Q. What is the temperature of the shops?
A. The shops are not many of them very warm; not too warm.
Q. Do you know what temperature?
A. No; I do not.
Q. Or about what?
A. They would not range to 70 by a good deal, except some blacksmith shops and cooper shops, where there is a good deal of fire; and even in some positions in the trip-hammer shop they are exposed to a draft that is very severe, sometimes.
Q. What is the distance that they travel out of doors, to go from the halls to their shops,—what is the extreme distance?
A. I never measured it.
Q. Give some estimate of it.
A. Some go further, and some not so far; some have to march from the dining-hall to the back side of the shops; I don't know what the distance is; I never measured it; I should think it was twenty rods, nearly, and I don't know but more; some get into the shops near the end of the wing, and don't have to go so far.
Q. Do you know how much of the time during the day these men are obliged to go out of doors, in going from the halls or the dining-room to their shops?
A. Not much time, I guess. Just as quick as a man can walk from the shop to the dining-room, and from there back again; two to three minutes. They sometimes stand a little while, forming ranks to march in; sometimes one rank has to wait for another a little while.
Q. In regard to the bedding, do you speak from personal knowledge when you speak of their sleeping on a cot without anything under it, just upon the canvass?
A. Yes, sir, I do; in the summer time; I don't think they do in the winter time.
Q. Do they do that as a matter of choice?

STATE PRISON INVESTIGATION. 245

A. I suppose so.

Q. Did you ever hear any complaints from any of the convicts in regard to the insufficiency of the bedding?

A. I have.

Q. How frequently.

A. Well, in the winter time, in cold weather, they complain a good deal; very frequently. Some men require more bedding than others; some men complain while others do not.

Q. In answer to questions on your direct examination, you have spoken of this by saying that certain things would not be sufficient for yourself. Your occupation takes you out of doors a good deal, does it not?

A. Yes; of course.

Q. You are naturally a thin blooded man, are you not, sensitive to the cold?

A. Well, I will change that; the clothing of the prisoners is not what citizens require, as a general thing.

Q. There is no difference between them and the prisoners, in regard to keeping them warm, is there?

A. I suppose not. I don't know as it is possible to give them any other clothing; I don't know anything about that; but I know that the prisoners are not clothed as the citizens are outside.

Q. Is the clothing such, in your judgment, as it ought to be, leaving out of consideration the fact that they are prisoners, or that ought it to be, to keep them reasonably warm?

A. I don't think it has been.

Q. Have you any idea as to where the defect is, whether it is in the prison management, or in the construction of the prison, or what. Have you formed any judgment about that?

A. No; I don't know as I have. I think it is all together; it is from a lack of entire prison management from the Legislature down to the Agent.

Q. There has been difficulties, during the past year or two, on the subject of keeping the men warm, that have arisen in consequence of the building that has been going on within the walls?

A. I suppose there has been a great deal of difficulty in consequence of that; we have been put to a great deal of inconvenience in consequence of that.

Q. Has that inconvenience made it more difficult to keep the halls of the proper temperature in extreme weather?

A. The west hall, I think it has; and the putting of new pipes and heating apparatus has had something to do with it. They have not learned to manage it as well as they will in a little while.

Q. Have you in your judgment, at any time, or do you now regard that there have been any faults in the distribution of clothing, or in the care of prisoners, in the matter of clothing, on the part of Mr. Morris?

A. No, sir; please repeat the question.

[The question read by the stenographer.]

Q. What I want to get at is, if Mr. Morris has been at fault in his prison management I want to know it. If the fault has been from difficulties that have arisen by way of the building that has been going on, or whether it is his?

A. I don't know how much authority Mr. Morris has with regard to the dispensing of clothing; I supposed, however, that he had a right to give out such clothing as he was a mind to; and if he had, why, it all devolves upon him to furnish him the necessary clothing.

Q. Have you discovered that the men have become sick at all by reason of the insufficiency of the clothing, so that they have had to come under your care?

A. Well, in the fall of the year, when the cold weather begins to come on, there are a great many men that commence complaining about colds, and complaining also of an insufficiency of clothing. I can't say but what they would have had a cold if they had had other clothing.

Q. You find that the changes of the seasons that people outside of the prison take cold more than at other times?

A. Yes, sir.

Q. It is quite difficult sometimes to tell how one takes cold?

A. That is true.

Re-direct examination by Mr. Webber:

Q. I would like to ask you what criticisms, if any, Mr. Morris indulged in, in consequence of your speaking to the hall keeper as you did about clothing?

A. Well, he wrote me a letter and sent it to the hospital. I don't know as I can word the letter.

Q. Have you that letter?

A. No, I have not; I did not see fit to keep it.

Q. State the substance of the letter as near as you recollect it.

A. Well, the letter stated what was not true. He charged me with talking to the prisoners about the hall master not furnishing them sufficient clothing, or the Agent,—I don't remember exactly how it was worded,—but it was communicating with the prisoners, or finding fault with Mr. Morris to the prisoners about their lack of clothing, which is not true; and I simply went to him to correct that matter, and he seemed to be a little excited and talked pretty severe to me. I did not say anything to any prisoner about it; I simply spoke to Mr. Wood, and the deputy was present. I said: "If you are going to furnish the prisoners clothing when it is severely cold, why not give it to them now? If you have got clothing on hand, get it made up as quick as you can; they are complaining, bitterly complaining, about the want of clothing." I don't know but there were some prisoners present; there are always helps around the different offices; there might have been at that time.

Q. And I understand you that Mr. Morris at that time spoke very sharply to you in consequence?

A. Well, he was pretty severe.

Q. State wherein he claimed you had done wrong?

A. Well, he thought there was no truth in the matter; he thought there was no occasion for any complaints; he thought the prisoners were well clothed, and had sufficient clothing; he said he never mistrusted that there was any such thing until he saw my report; that there was no need for any complaints at all.

Q. Can you remember any expression Mr. Morris made use of?

A. I don't believe I can; I have a miserable memory; I don't think I can remember them.

Q. You don't care to remember them?

A. Why, yes, I would like to if I could; if I could, I would remember them.

Q. Speaking of this man Rushing—I understood you to say to Mr. Conely that you conversed with Mr. Morris concerning his being in the hospital, and that you asked Mr. Morris something about why he was struck?

A. No, I guess you did not get my meaning; I never spoke to Mr. Morris about it until a few days ago, and I told him then that I should have to correct my statement, and told him why; then Mr. Morris told me why he struck him.

Q. What reason did he assign for striking him?
A. Because he halloed when he was watering him; he struck him to stop his hallooing.
Re-cross-examination by Mr. Conely:
Q. Prior to that communication to Mr. Morris, had you ever complained to him in relation to the clothing that brought it to his attention that the men were complaining to you?
A. I don't think I have; I don't know as it was my duty, so far as the hall-master dispenses the clothing under Mr. Morris' directions.
Q. I simply wanted to know if you ever had?
A. No, sir; I don't think I ever did.
Q. This note assumed that you had been talking to the convicts improperly?
A. Yes, sir.
Q. And so far as the letter indicated, if it indicated anything, it indicated that Mr. Morris was under that apprehension at the time?
A. It seemed so.
Q. Mr. Morris, with the single exception that you have named, has always been courteous to you?
A. Yes, sir.
Q. There has been entire harmony between you and him as to the administration of your duties?
A. Perfectly, sir, perfectly.
Q. He never has thrown any obstacles in your way, has he?
A. Never.
Q. And so far as you know you have had his co-operation in anything that you desired?
A. I have.
Q. I will ask you one thing further, Doctor, as to his conduct among the sick. Whether it is marked by humanity, kindness, gentleness, etc.?
A. Very kind, sympathetic, and humane toward all the sick, when we are both of us satisfied they are sick. There are some men that have played off on both of us,—puzzled us very much.
Re-direct examination by Mr. Webber:
Q While settling the question of sickness, state Mr. Morris' manner in the treatment of the convict, before the question is settled as to whether he is sick, or as to whether he is merely playing off?
A. Well, he usually leaves it almost entirely to me, until,—sometimes intimates that he thinks I am deceived in regard to such a convict, and that he is playing on me, and that I had better watch him pretty close. And sometimes I have ventured to him that I thought such a convict was feigning sickness, and I had a notion to send him to the shop; and we consulted in that way. Sometimes I have counseled with the deputy. He would come to me and say that such a man was in the shop, and he thought he was feigning sickness, and I had better watch him.
Q. Did a case ever occur where a man, claiming to be sick, was sent to the shop, and it was afterwards found out that he was actually sick?
A. Yes, sir; I have sent men to the shop, when they would come in to get medicine, and state they were sick, and I was not fully satisfied that they were sick enough to lay off, and I would send them back to the shop, and perhaps the next day they would not be well, and I would let them stay in. I would have to use all means, and every discretion and prudence to manage those

things. It is a very difficult thing to manage. I never have put a man to work any length of time, when he has been feeble, unless he has done it at his own request. Some men will work when other men will not. Many men, I have marked in, as you call it, at the hospital,—excused them from work, and they would say : "Oh, I had rather go to work a great deal, than to be shut up ; I don't want to stay in the hospital, the time goes so slow. I want to work." And he would work, when another man would not work at all.

PATRICK O'NEIL SWORN IN BEHALF OF MR. MORRIS.

Examined by Mr. Conely :
Q. Where do you reside?
A. Detroit.
Q. How long have you lived there?
A. My life-time.
Q. What is your business?
A. Detective on the metropolitan police of Detroit.
Q. How long have you been engaged in that business?
A. Ever since my boyhood.
Q. How old are you now?
A. 25 in May. Ever since I was 12 years old.
Q. Do you know the two boys named Jacobs and Fairfax?
A. Yes, sir.
Q. Convicts?
A. Yes, sir ; I know them.
Q. Do you know when they were sent here?
A. I don't remember the date.
Q. Well, about how long ago?
A. I could not tell you.
Q. Do you remember the offense for which they were sent?
A. I do, sir.
Q. I don't want any details about it, but just state what it was for?
A. Burglarly and sneak-thieving.
Q. Were you present in the prison at the time when any punishment was inflicted on them ?
A. I was there, sir.
Q. What was that ?
A. Showering.
Q. By whom was it administered ?
A. Mr. Morris.
Q. Had you known the boys before that time ?
A. I did, sir.
Q. Do you know how the punishment came to be inflicted ?
A. I do, sir.
Q. I wish you would just state to this committee all you know about it.
A. I came out with two prisoners, I don't remember their names, I asked Mr. Morris if I could see Fairfax and Jacobs ; he asked me what I wanted to do that for, and I told him.
Q. State just what you told him.
A. I told him I wanted to see them to see if I could not get some information of some goods that they had stolen, a part that I had not got, and about some pawn tickets that I found in the lining of a satchel, which I did not find when

I arrested them ; and he sent for them, and they came, and I saw Fairfax ; he admitted that the tickets belonged to Jacobs—the pawn tickets he admitted belonged to Jacobs ; I then saw Jacobs, and Jacobs denied it, so I then went over to where Fairfax was ; I had them separate then ; Mr. Morris was not with me then, and did not hear what was going on ; I went to where Fairfax was, and told him that Jacobs denied it ; well, he says, they belong to him ; so then I could not get any more information from them, and I started up towards where Mr. Morris was, going out, and they had left where they was, and Mr. Morris asked me what I found out ; I told him I did not find out anything ; that this Jacobs was too old a head for me ; would not say anything ; afraid that it would make him trouble again when he went out ; so Mr. Morris says, " What does Fairfax say about it?" I told him, says I, "Fairfax says the tickets belong to Jacobs, and Jacobs denied it ;" well, he says, "Come back, I will talk to them ;" so he talked to Fairfax, and Fairfax told him that the tickets belonged to Jacobs ; Mr. Morris then saw Jacobs, and he denied it; so Mr. Morris says, "How is that, Fairfax?" Fairfax says, "Yes, they belong to Jacobs ;" and Morris says, "What did you lie to me for?" he didn't give any particular reason ; Mr. Morris says, "I don't allow any prisoner to lie to me ;" so then we talked there a few minutes longer, and Mr. Morris ordered them to be punished.

Q. Did you see the punishment?
A. I did, sir.
Q. What was it?
A. Water—showering.
Q. How long did it continue?
A. Not any longer than two minutes ; that was the longest.
Q. Where was the water applied?
A. On the hip ; about there ; around the legs.
Q. How did the boys behave after that?
A. While he was showering them Jacobs hollered out two or three times, "I will never tell you a lie again ;" hollering to Mr. Morris ; I believe he said it twice, and then Mr. Morris—I was in a kind of a hurry ; I wanted to see Morris before I went away ; and they no more than said that twice, then Jacobs said he would not lie again, and Mr. Morris quit ; so they went into another room with them ; into the other room there was some towels, or something ; then they dried themselves, and Mr. Morris waited—
Q. Had you ever done any business of any kind for the Agent, or for the State prison, in the way of obtaining information as to the whereabouts of escaped convicts, or anything of that sort?
A. I have, sir.
Q. State what you have done?
A. Well, Gleason, I think, was a pickpocket that got out. I went to Toledo, and I went to Cleveland to get trace of him for Mr. Morris, and gained that he was in Toledo, and Cleveland, but could not get him out of Cleveland, because the police force there they set in with the thieves,—the police did, and we could not get him out of Cleveland at all, and I went down to Toledo, then I was at Toledo twice, and could not get him out of there at all; then I went another time to Buffalo, and I went to Toledo again, on another prisoner.
Q. Did you ever go to Canada, at all?
A. Yes, sir, I have been to Winsor, at different times.
Q. Across the river?
A. Yes, sir.

250   STATE PRISON INVESTIGATION.

Q. What remuneration have you ever received for such services?
A. I travel on my passes, and trip passes. I never received anything from the State.
Q. Or from the prison authorities?
A. No, sir; only from information I would get sometimes from Mr. Morris, in the prison here. It would pay me well.—I have got some information from him which has paid me well.
Q. Then the only remuneration that you have received has been in favors that you have received in that way?
A. Yes, sir.
Q. Had you rendered any of these services before you desired to get this information from the two boys?
A. Oh, ever since Mr. Morris has been appointed.
Q. You expected some remuneration from the people for whom you are at work about the pawn tickets?
A. Yes, sir; a very little about the two pawn tickets, because there was not any money up but for two coats; I wanted to get them back for the people, not that I expected to gain anything, because there was no reward offered; and they were only pawned for small amounts, and I wanted to get them back. Not because there was any reward for these two articles, because there was not.
Q. Did you understand that in the seeking this information from the boys, that Mr. Morris was doing you a favor?
A. Yes, sir.
Q You had formerly done favors for him?
A Yes, sir; I have, or tried to.
Q. Do you know Redwood?
A. Yes, sir.
Q. Convict?
A. I do, sir.
Q. Do you know what he was sent up for?
A. Embezzlement.
Q. Do you know whether he was ever in the house of correction?
A. As near as I can recollect, I think he was; I would not be positive. He was sent out collecting money for Farington and Campbell,—a grocery house,—and he lost it in this Louisville and Kentucky lottery.
Q. Do you know Rushing?
A. Yes, sir.
Q Do you know what he was sent for?
A. Yes, sir.
Q. What was he sent for?
A. Cattle stealing and burglary.
Q. Do you know what his son was sent for?
A. His son was for burglary at Pontiac, in a harness shop, I believe. They were all implicated in cattle stealing, and tried on it, and for burglary.
Q. Do you know whether Rushing had any lameness about him before he was sent here?
A. If you will allow me to tell the conversation: I came out and told Mr. Morris about this Rushing. I told him to look out for him, that he was desperate; that he got out of the Pontiac jail there, and when they got him back they had to keep him in irons; and that he complained a great deal of sickness; and the night that I arrested him—that myself and Detective Bishop and several of

STATE PRISON INVESTIGATION. 251

us arrested him, it took him quite a time there to change his clothes, because he pretended to be very sick, and had to take some medicine and rub himself quite a while. And I was in the room while he changed his underclothes, and I noticed some sore on his back while I was in the room. His back was marked, and he then took a plaster off of it. He had a plaster on his back, and one on his breast, and I noticed it all blue and marked.

Q. You don't know what was the cause of it?
A. I did not, but I afterwards asked him what was the cause of it, and he did not—

Mr. *Webber*—We don't care about what Mr. Rushing may have told you.
Mr. *Conely*—We don't care about it.

Cross-examination by Mr. Webber:

Q. You say you are connected with the metropolitan police in Detroit?
A. Yes, sir.
Q. And have acted how long in that capacity?
A. I have worked for the force ever since I was about—I have been regularly appointed somewhere about four years as a detective.
Q. You received your appointment from the—
A. Police commissioner of Detroit.
Q. And are governed by the rules of the force?
A. The metropolitan force under the metropolitan law.
Q. And the rules of the board?
A. Yes, sir.
Q. This Jacobs and Fairfax were colored boys, were they not?
A. Yes, sir.
Q. You say they had been convicted for being burglars and sneak-thieves.
A. They had been convicted of burglary. We had complaints against them for sneak-thieving, they plead guilty to, and there were two sentences on burglary.
Q. What court sentenced them?
A. Recorder Swift.
Q. How long had they been out here when you came out to interview them?
A. Well, it was from three to five weeks—three or four weeks probably.
Q. Did you bring them out?
A. Yes, sir.
Q. Originally?
A. No, I am not positive now whether I brought them out or not. I brought two out when I came out to see them.
Q. Did you bring these boys out, when they came out?
A. I think I did, I am not positive.
Q. How old are the boys?
A Well, 19 and 21.
Q. You say you interviewed them first, and then Mr. Morris took it up for you?
A. I interviewed them, and then Mr. Morris talked to them after, right before me.
Q Those pawn tickets were some that you found in the satchel when the boys were arrested originally, there in Detroit?
A. Yes, sir; inside the lining of the satchel.
Q. Did you have the pawn tickets with you when you came out here to see them?

A. Yes, sir.
Q. Did you show them to Fairfax?
A. Yes, sir.
Q. And he said they belonged to Jacobs?
A. Yes, sir.
Q. You saw the boys punished yourself?
A. Yes, sir; I stood right there, because I was waiting to see Mr. Morris.
Q. Did you time it?
A. There was—I forget the man's name now that came out, and I asked him what time it was when he came down the steps. A gentleman that came up from the hotel. I came up, and he wanted to go through, and he thought that by coming up with me, they would get a chance to go through. And then before we came down—we could see them from where we were standing. I forget now, whether it was thirty-five minutes past, or half past one, and from the time that I came down and went back again, it was not any longer than two minutes' time by the watch.
Q. You looked at the watch to see how long you were gone?
A. No, in coming down—before I came down, I asked him the time.
Q. Was that just when the punishment was about to commence?
A. No, sir; he stood right there.
Q. When was it with reference to the infliction of the punishment?
A. When I commenced talking—when I started out to go to them, and came back, I think Mr. Morris stood there with the hose in his hands.
Q. And then you asked what time it was?
A. Standing right along on the steps I asked him what time it was.
Q. Where the boys stripped?
A. Yes, sir—naked.
Q. Both?
A. Yes, sir.
Q. And was there more than one stream thrown on them?
A. Well, there was three or four—probably four or five streams.
Q. Through how many different nozzles?
A. Through one nozzle.
Q. Then there was but one stream thrown?
A. One stream; yes, sir.
Q. And were they standing close together—the boys?
A. Yes, sir; right close up together.
Q. And which got the most of it?
A. Jacobs. One would turn around—Jacobs would be on one side, and he would come around and Fairfax would get it again. But Jacobs got the most.
Q. Did you get any further information from them after that water was applied?
A. I never spoke to them afterwards; they were right in the other room.
Q. You say that Fairfax told you the truth in the first instance, and owned up?
A. Yes, sir.
Q. Tell me, if Mr. Morris punished them for lying, why did he punish Fairfax?
A. He punished Jacobs.
Q. But he punished Fairfax, too?
A. Yes, sir.
Q. What did he punish Fairfax for, if he punished Jacobs for lying?

STATE PRISON INVESTIGATION. 253

A. I suppose he spoke to Jacobs—they were both standing there, and Jacobs muttered a good deal before he would say—Fairfax muttered a good deal before Morris came up. He did not tell me what he told Morris. He kinder muttered a long time about telling Morris. He intimated as much he would not tell him right out. Fairfax did before Jacobs.

Q. You are sure that it did not exceed two minutes?
A. Not any longer, sir; I am quite positive of that.
Q. And it was all thrown on Jacobs' left side?
A. Well, Fairfax got around once or twice. It was kinder rounding where Jacobs was standing, and Jacobs got his foot kinder fastened in there, and the other fellow behind him, and he held him right there, so Morris then quit.
Q. You say you got information of Morris which was valuable to you. Tell me what value it was?
A. I did not get any information of Morris at that time.
Q. Well, other times?
A. In getting information of stolen property.
Q. What value was that to you?
A. It is getting people back their property.
Q. And securing the reward?
A. I never secured but two rewards.
Q. How large rewards have you ever secured?
A. I have secured twenty-five dollars and ten dollars.
Q. Was that the extent of the value of this information that Mr. Morris had communicated to you?
A. No, sir.
Q. In what further respect was it valuable?
A. In arresting criminals. When we were arresting one, there would be others in the mob, and in getting the others.
Q. Do you mean to be understood that it was a personal favor to you?
A. Well, I don't know how to reply to that question.
Q. I mean, was it personal to yourself?
A. Yes, sir; of course the rewards would be when I would get them. I would get eighty per cent of the rewards. Twenty per cent goes to the police force.
Q. How long has that been a regulation in that force, that eighty per cent goes to the detective?
A. Ever since I have been on there.
Q. Don't you know that the regulations of the metropolitan police force don't give the detective a cent, except in the discretion of the police commissioners?
A. No, sir.
Q. When you went to Cleveland and Toledo, did you go on your own expense or were you under the daily pay of the metropolitan police force of Detroit?
A. Well, I was under daily pay—and then if we want to go anywheres, we ask the chief, and he lets us go.
Q. Then it was nothing personal with you—it was a matter connected with the police force that called you to Toledo and Cleveland?
A. And for Mr. Morris.
Q. Yes, but it was the metropolitan police force that did the service, and not you. You merely went for the force?
A. Well, the force didn't know anything about it.
Q. But your chief did?
A. He knew when I went to Toledo.

Q. Did not he know when you went to Cleveland?
A. No, sir, because I did not see him before I went away.
Q. And you are sure that this was not over two minutes—that punishment.
A. Yes, sir; quite positive.
Mr. Bartow—Where was this stream directed on Jacobs?
A. Along the side and legs; they would twist around.
Q. When they would twist around it would not strike them on the side?
A. No, but it would strike the other on the side, because they would keep from Mr. Morris.
Q. Did they front him during any portion of the time the stream was on them?
A. No, sir.
Q. Was the stream continuous from the time it commenced until it ended?
A. Yes, sir.

The committee here took a recess until two o'clock, P. M.

AFTERNOON SESSION.

On the assembling of the committee Mr. Conely read the following statement:

"John D. Conely, Counsel for the Agent, then stated that as such counsel, he conceded that there was no legal justification for the punishment of the two boys, Fairfax and Jacobs; that he was desirous simply to bring to the attention of the committee that what was done by Mr. Morris in connection with the boys was not accompanied by circumstances of severity, and that it was an effort on the part of Mr. Morris to make some requital for favors which the State had received from the police force."

SOCRATES H. WOOD RECALLED FOR FURTHER CROSS-EXAMINATION.

By Mr. Webber:
Q. Have you charge of the distribution of newspapers and magazines to the convicts?
A. Yes, sir; they pass through my office, all of them.
Q. How are those newspapers procured for the convicts—at whose expense?
A. They are procured at the expense—so far as I know, the expense of the convicts or their friends.
Q. How many newspapers weekly are distributed through the prison?
A. Well, I don't know that I could answer that; I have not kept any record of any kind, and I might not—
Q. Give an approximate estimate?
A. To preface a little, there are a great many that come irregular; their friends send them one paper this week and another one next week—papers, after they have read them they come, and others, possibly, have subscribed from here, and I could not come anywheres near it, but I should think there were three hundred, and perhaps more, that get them regularly.
Q. As often, say, as once a week?

A. As often as once a week; that would be my opinion, still I might vary from the facts.

Q. Are all newspapers that are sent permitted to go to the hands of the convicts?

A. No, sir.

Q. What class are excluded?

A. The Illustrated Police paper, Police Gazette, Day's Doings, any sporting or disreputable papers.

Q. But all papers, aside from those of that general class you speak of, are permitted to be taken and received by the convicts?

A. Yes, sir; so far as I know.

Q. How many convicts are taking magazines?

A. Well, I don't know that I could approximate that; I would not want to say, because I could not come anywhere near the truth.

Re-direct examination by Mr. Conely:

Q. I will examine Mr. Wood upon a branch of the subject that is indicated by Dr. Tuttle's testimony in regard to clothing. What do you know about the convicts at any time having insufficient clothing,—I mean insufficient for the purpose of warmth?

A. Well, sir, it has been my aim that there should not be any when it is brought to my notice, so far as I am able.

Q. Has there been any time when you haven't been able, for any reason, to supply the convicts with clothing suitable for the weather—if you can call to mind any?

A. Well, yes, sir, there has; we did not get our woolen or flannel for shirts as soon as we needed it.

Q. Can you remember when that was?

A. I cannot, sir.

Q. When the flannel came first, was that accepted?

A. No, sir.

Q. Do you know why it was not accepted?

A. Yes, sir; because Mr. Morris didn't think it as good as they had agreed to furnish.

Q. What delay did that occasion as to the time, if you remember?

A. I should say that it delayed us six weeks; I think it did that; and after we got it Mr. Morris told me to hold on and not use any of it until the board saw it, for it was miserable cloth, and he did not like to use it; he thought the board might reject it then; and he did not like to use it; that they might censure him if he done so.

Q. What can you say about the supply of bed clothing in the winter season: has that at any time been insufficient?

A. Well, I think that the bedding has been sufficient; I have called on Mr. Morris several times for blankets and got them. Sometimes when it was extremely cold, the men some of them complained of not sleeping warm, especially in the west wing; because they could not heat the wing sufficiently.

Q. Were there any complaints from the east wing?

A. Well, not so much—not but what it could be sometimes. I have had a man's blanket wear out, and he would come to me and complain that he slept cold. As a general thing we could warm that wing, so the men have been warmer, and been better satisfied.

Q. What have been the difficulties about warming the west wing?

A. After they took the old flat roof off from the wing, there was a good deal more space, and the heat, of course, went up into the ridge, and we could hardly heat it with the steam.

Q. Whenever you called Mr. Morris' attention to matters connected with the clothing, how has he endeavored to meet it?

A. He has always done everything that he could. I never called on him for bedding without he ordered it.

Q. Do you know of his telegraphing at any time?

A. Yes, sir; he has telegraphed two or three times for clothing, or for different articles,—for sheeting and blankets.

Q. Have the complaints which you have heard upon that subject been long continued, or were they temporary in character?

A. They were temporary, during the extreme cold weather.

Q. Do you know anything about the temperature of the wings at night during the past winter?

A. No, sir; I don't know that I could tell.

Q. Your duties require you to be here at night, do they?

A. No, sir; I am not here in the evening.

Q. Do you know any thing about a letter that passed from Mr. Morris to Doctor Tuttle in relation to this matter of clothing?

A. No, sir.

Q. Do you know any thing about Doctor Tuttle having spoken in the presence of convicts about the insufficiency of the clothing?

A. Yes, sir; he came into the office at one time and complained about it; can't say exactly now what he said. I remember his coming in there and speaking about the clothing.

Q. Was that in the presence of the convicts?

A. Yes, sir.

Q. Do you know how many were present?

A. Well, I can't say.

Q. Did you communicate that to Mr. Morris, do you remember?

A. I did.

Re-cross-examination by Mr. Webber:

Q. Can you state what month it was that this flannel came that was rejected?

A. No, sir.

Q. Can you state the year?

A. I think it was in 1874.

Q. But you are not sure as to that?

A. I am pretty sure.

Q. Was it the supply of flannel that was ordered for last fall?

A. Yes, sir.

Q. Was it in warm weather when it came, or cold weather?

A. I think it was cold weather, sir.

Q. Do you know how long it was after that order was given before it came?

A. No, sir; I don't know when it was ordered.

Q. Do you know where it was ordered from?

A. I think from Flint.

Q. In this State?

A. Yes, sir.

Q. How long after that was sent back before other flannel came?

A. It was not sent back.

Q. Why was it not sent back?
A. Well, I think that the reason that it was not sent back was because the manufacturer came up and met the board and made some arrangement in reference to the State keeping the flannel.
Q. At a less price?
A. I think at a less price.
Q. You speak of it as flannel. Was it all wool?
A. No, sir; we call it flannel.
Q. How much of it was wool?
A. A small portion of it.
Q. How large a quantity was there of it?
A. I think about 2,000 yards.
Q. For what garments was it designed?
A. For shirts.
Q. And after the board concluded to accept it it was worked up into shirts for the convicts?
A. Yes, sir.
Q. Now, how many blankets are allowed in a cell as a winter covering for the beds?
A. Two double blankets.
Q. What kind of blanket are those?
A. Those are army blankets.
Q. Regular army blankets?
A. Regular army blankets; yes, sir,
Q. That is, four thicknesses of cloth is allowed them?
A. Yes, sir.
Q. And each cell has that allowance?
A. Yes, sir; some old men or sick men have more.
Q. Where men are locked in a bare cell in the winter time have they any blankets furnished them?
A. Yes, sir; sometimes.
Q. In whose discretion does that rest whether they will have them or not?
A. It is in the Agent or deputies.
Q. Is there any general rule on the subject?
A. No, sir; I think not.
Q. How many men are locked in the bare cells—in the same cell at once—the most you have known in one instance?
A. I don't think that there has been since I have had an opportunity to know anything about these matters—there may have been three or four.
Q. At one time, in the same cell?
A. Yes, sir.
Q. What conveniences are furnished men in bare cells for answering the calls of nature?
A. A bucket.
Q. How often is that removed?
A. It is removed generally twice a day, if a man is in there.
Q. Is there a cover to those buckets?
A. Yes, sir.
Q As to underclothing—have there been any complaints from the convicts to you that they had not underclothing to keep them warm?
A. Yes, sir; sometimes.

Q. Is the complaint any ways general—has it been?
A. Well, there are a good many that come to me for undershirts and drawers.
Q. And what do you do in such cases?
A. I always furnish them so far as I can.
Q. What is the limit of your ability?
A. Well, sir, I judge as to where a man works; whether he is in a cold part of the shop; or whether he is an old man or a young man, or whether he is unwell; whether he is sick; if there is anything wherein I think he needs underclothing, I manage in some way to get it for him and give it to him. I have made it out of flannel; I have made drawers out of sheeting, before I got the flannel. I made some drawers out of flannel, and given out other undershirts that came in, and supply as fast as is in my power. All men that are at work out of doors that are exposed, have been supplied.

Q. Do you mean to be understood that all men who work out of doors, and in the colder part of the shops, have been supplied with undershirts and drawers during the past winter?
A. Yes, sir; or woolen shirts.
Q. With two shirts?
A. No, sir.
Q. Then they have had only one shirt on at a time?
A. Yes, sir; but a good many have a cotton shirt and a woolen shirt; others have a woolen shirt and drawers.
Q. Have you applied to Mr. Morris for any undershirts and drawers, when they have not been furnished?
A. I have not gone to Mr. Morris.
Q. You haven't applied to him for them?
A. No, sir.
Q. You speak of Dr. Tuttle complaining about clothing in the presence of the convicts. This was in your office?
A. Yes, sir.
Q. What convicts were there?
A. Well, there were two men that were with me in the office at the time.
Q. Working in the office?
A. Yes, sir; and there was one or two in the hall just outside; I don't remember who the others were.
Q. They were convicts that were habitually employed in and about the office and about the hall?
A. No, sir; I think they were some men that came down from the hospital.
Q. Did he speak then in a loud tone to you?
A. Yes, sir; he spoke so they could hear.
Q. What reply did you make?
A. I told him that we had two thousand yards of cloth—of flannel to shirt these men with, and I made the remark to him that I had been to him before and requested him to give orders for any men that he thought needed woolen, and let me know, and that we were making just as fast as we could—supplying all that I thought was necessary. I was using my best judgment to supply every man that I thought needed it, and I had asked him to do the same, and I did not know what further I had to do. That was about the substance of the reply I made.

Q. When these convicts come to you and ask for additional clothing to keep them warm, do you then pass judgment on their case as to whether they need it or not?

A. I find out, if I don't know where they work, whether they are going out doors, or if they are in a cold part of the shop ; find out in what part of the shop they are and use my best judgment; yes, sir.

Q. Can you give an approximate estimate of the number of men in the prison during the past winter, that have been furnished with the common prison apparel, and in addition thereto, an undershirt and drawers?

A. I don't know that I could; I have not kept any record of it all.

Q. Can you tell how many pairs of drawers and how many undershirts you have given out this winter?

A. No, sir; I have kept no record of that whatever.

Q. As to the temperature of the wings—there is four tiers of cells in each wing, is there not?

A. Yes, sir.

Q. How many thermometers are kept in each wing to indicate the temperature?

A. I think there is one in each wing.

Q. Where is that thermometer placed?

A. It is hung generally on the first gallery, perhaps six feet from the base—from the floor.

Q. About six feet from the floor?

A. Yes, sir.

Q. How far is that hung from the steam pipes?

A. Well, I should judge it was ten or twelve feet, perhaps more; perhaps fifteen feet.

Q. What is the average of the temperature as indicated by that thermometer at each hall as kept?

A. I could not tell you.

Q. Whose business is it to keep watch of the thermometer and see that the wing is kept properly warmed?

A. It is, I suppose, the engineer's. He has the heating or seeing to the heating of the wing.

Q. Can he leave the engine and go to the wing at any time he pleases?

A. Yes, sir.

Mr. Conely—I would like the stenographer to minute that special attention is called to page 2220 of the compiled laws of 1871, being a joint resolution providing for the letting to the lowest bidder contracts to supply the State Prison and State Reform School with goods manufactured in this State, composed of wool, or partly of wool and partly of cotton.

FRANKLIN S. CLARK SWORN.

Examined by Mr. Webber:

Q. You reside at Jackson?

A. Yes, sir.

Q. And are acting as clerk of the prison?

A. Yes, sir.

Q. How long have you been acting in that capacity?

A. It will be three years the first day of May next.

Q. State your duties as such clerk?

A. My duties are to keep the records and accounts; the record of the men as they come in and go out,—enter upon the records,—enter up the papers as they come in,—the commitments; discharge them, and make the discharge on the record; and to pay all claims that are presented here, and that are due from the prison.

Q. Do you keep the accounts between the State and the contractors?

A. Yes, sir; I keep all the accounts here.

Q. Are you charged with the duty of keeping an account of the punishment inflicted for an infraction of the rules?

A. At the first of every month, or the close of the month, I make up what I call a discharge list for the coming month, and on that I make the abstracts from the convict record, and the men that go out on that month, and make the charges against them from the record.

Q. What record?

A. From the convict record,—the daily convict record, where we take the description of the men,—his height, his weight, the court from which he came, the length of time, and when his time expired, etc.

Q. Does your business give you any opportunity to observe the intercourse between the Agent and the convicts?

A. Very little; very little indeed, sir. I am rarely inside except on some special errand.

Q. As I understand, you are charged with no duties as to making the original entries in what you term the convict record?

A. No, sir; that record there, I have nothing to do with; I barely post that into my convict record.

Q. But that posting is done after those entries are made in this book?

A. Yes, sir.

Q. Who makes these records in this convict record, as you call it?

A. It is sometimes by the Agent, and sometimes by the deputy. I see some in the handwriting of Mr. Morris, and some in the handwriting of the convicts.

Q. Are those records kept in the same office that you occupy?

A. Yes, sir; they are kept in the vault.

Q. And when they are written up they are written up in the same office that you occupy?

A. I could not say that, sir. No, sir; they are not written up there. The deputy takes them and has them written up where it is most convenient probably. I don't know where it is done.

Q. When supplies are purchased for the use of the prison are you charged with keeping account of them?

A. Yes, sir.

Q. From what do you make your entries?

A. From the original invoices.

Q. Do you see the goods themselves when they come in?

A. Very rarely, sir.

Q. It is not a part of your duty to check off the goods?

A. None at all; that is the hall-master's duty.

Q. By the invoices?

A. Yes, sir.

Q. When these goods are distributed about and used for the purposes of the prison, or the contractors, or otherwise, whose duty is it to check them off?

A. The hall master; he has the entire control of it, for manufacture and distribution.

Q. Have you an account on your books with Mr. Morris, the Agent?

A. No further than as an employe.

STATE PRISON INVESTIGATION. 261

Q. Do any goods go for his use, or the use of his family, which were purchased by the State?

A. Some; the account is rendered to him every month by the hall master. Whatever of the State supplies goes to the house of the Agent, they are charged up to him and deducted every month.

Q. And you enter them on your books?

A. I do not keep any account except a memorandum account, and settle with the Agent as I do every other employe, by pay-roll; make up their accounts on an envelop, and make whatever deductions there may be and put the account in with the money.

Q. The charge made is cash, with what supplies he has had?

A. Yes, sir; and credit that particular account, whatever it is, whether meat, or whatever it my be, as so much money received from different sources.

Mr. Conely—I am not prepared to cross-examine Mr. Clark now; I will reserve the right to cross-examine him, and call him to-morrow morning, if the committee shall meet.

HENRY L. WOODARD SWORN FOR MR. MORRIS.

Examined by Mr. Conely:

Q. Where do you reside?
A. I reside in Tompkins.
Q. That is in this county?
A. Yes, sir.
Q. You formerly lived in the city here?
A. Yes, sir.
Q. And were connected with the prison in some capacity?
A. Yes, sir.
Q. How long were you keeper?
A. I do not know as I can tell exactly; I came here in the fall; I was a guard and keeper about three years and a half; it may vary a little, but not a great deal.

Q. How long a time under Mr. Morris?
A. Somewhere about two years; I would not say for certain; it was fully two years. I do not recollect the time I come here first.

Q. How long since you moved into Tompkins?
A. Two years ago; I left the prison two years ago the first of this month.

Q. Did you ever see Mr. Morris administer any punishment upon any convicts?
A. Yes, sir.
Q. State when and who it was?
A. I could not tell the name nor when; I have seen him shower several; never saw him whip a man.

Q. Did you ever see any other kind of punishment administered except showering?
A. No, sir; except locking in a cell.
Q. Did you ever see any ill result attend upon the punishment of convicts?
A. No, sir.
Q. What was the general course of the treatment while you were here?
A. It was kind. I thought a good many times perhaps it was too kind in some cases.

Cross-examination by Mr. Webber:
Q. When you say Mr. Morris' administration was kind, you speak of it as a general rule?
A. Yes, sir, I do.
Q. Did your duties call you to witness all the punishments that were administered?
A. No, sir.
Q. What proportion of the time that you were here, either as guard or as keeper, did you have an opportunity to observe his personal intercourse with the convicts?
A. Well, I do not know as I could answer that question, because some days there would be an hour or two in a day and sometimes not as much. He would be out and in a good deal, and where the showering was done in the lower hall at the time I was here, and if there was to be showering or showering any one there, why I would notice it as I went through.
Q. Where did your duty call you to be stationed?
A. The most of the time in the cabinet shop.
Q. Was there any showering done in that shop?
A. I do not know but what there was one; I would not say for certain; I know that I kept that shop under Mr. Morris; I won't say positive, but it was a little over a year, without reporting a man; I did not find it necessary.
Q. How many men did you ever see showered under Mr. Morris' administration?
A. Not more than two or three.
Q. And were you there during all the time of the punishment of that two or three?
A. No, sir; I was there during the time of two.
Q. Do you remember their names?
A. No, I do not; I did not get acquainted with the names of any of the convicts only those under me.
Q. They were not men that were under you?
A. No, sir.
Q. And it was merely accidental that you happened to be there to witness it?
A. Yes, sir.
Q. Did you time the showering?
A. No, sir.
Q. Did you ever see any instance of severity on the part of Mr. Morris in his treatment of the convicts?
A. No, sir, I never did.
Q. Did you ever witness any indications of anger on his part when he was speaking to the convicts?
A. No, sir; never saw him angry in my life.

[The memorandum book kept by the deputy on which infractions of the rules are noted from day to day by him, and from which it has been the practice at the end of the month to write up the convict record, so called, and also the convict record or conduct record, for comparison. The memorandum book now presented is one which was kept by deputy Winans.]
The following is a copy of an entry on the deputy's book:
"Jan. 5, 1874. Jesse W. Barker, for stealing cigars; cold water, severely."
From the convict record:

"Jan. 5, 1874. Isaac W. Barker, for stealing cigars from the debris of the cigar shop and hiding them in several places about the yard; took two full boxes and several hundred in loose lots about the yard. Denied it at first, and only came down and owned up after severe watering."
From the memorandum book:
"Jan. 8. Reason Webster, for having a can of molasses in his cell; cold water on his feet five minutes."
From the convict record:
"Jan. 8. Reason Webster, for stealing and carrying a can of molasses from dining room to his cell; watered his feet five minutes."
Same date, from the memorandum book:
"John Mapes, for talking in ranks; watered on feet five minutes."
From the record book:
"John Mapes, a constant violator, for talking in the ranks; watered on feet five minutes."
From memorandum book kept by deputy Winans, date June 3, 1873:
"David, *alias* Drayton Thurston, by superintendent Donough, for throwing tools around; when spoken to about it by deputy was impudent; and when told by deputy that if he did not look out and take care, he would get whipped, said: 'By God, I am good for it now; I can take it now as well as any time;' and after being brought to the hall by deputy refused to go into the west wing and be locked up. Said he was going to work and would not go into the west wing; said he would knock hell out of the first man that put a hand on to him. Deputy called gate-keeper with a revolver and he then went into bare cell, but continued to talk insulting all the time, saying: 'You damned cusses! I would like to lick about a dozen of you!' Afterwards, as gate-keeper went by his cell, said: 'You d—d son of a bitch, I will wring your own neck for you when I get out of here.' And said to conductor, when conductor told another man to stop talking: 'Go to hell, you big bugger! I would snub your mouth for you if I was out there.' Also said 'he would wring the neck of any d—d son of a bitch that undertook to whip him.' Also told guard 'he was put in bare cell for whipping deputy, and by Jesus, he would whip any G—d d—d son of a bitch that punished him; will not live to punish any other man.' Told keeper Bedford that 'he would run a knife through any G—d d—d man that dared lick him.' Told Agent that he would 'fix the man that put a whip on his back.' Called Agent 'a d—d cur,' and a good many other names that I do not remember."
Then, after several other entries comes the following:
[Entered in the handwriting of Mr. Cook, who was acting as deputy that day.]
"June 13, 1873. Convict Drayton Thurston, reported for having a dirk or dagger in his possession. Flogged, and kept in the bare cell 12 hours, and sent to his work."
Immediately following is another entry, under date of June 14:
"Convict Charles Simmons, reported for giving a dagger to convict Thurston. Flogged and sent to shop."

CAPT. JAMES D. HINKLEY, SWORN FOR THE COMMITTTEE.

Examined by Mr. Webber:

Q. You are now acting as deputy-keeper of the State prison?
A. Yes, sir.
Q. How long have you occupied that position?

A. Since the 27th of August last.

Q What punishments have been in use since you have been in the prison?

A. We have used the clog, the wire cap, the hose, bare cell, and strap.

Q. Wooden horse?

A. No, sir.

Q. You have also, as a lighter punishment, deprived men of lights and reading matter?

A. Yes, sir.

Q. Any other kind of punishment that you think of?

A. We have handcuffed men together; that had slipped my mind. That is usual in cases where they have a fight.

Q. Have you been present to witness the most of the punishments since you have been here?

A. Every punishment since I have been here, unless it was when I have been absent. I have been absent two days in that time, perhaps.

Q. Has the strap been used since you have been here?

A. Yes, sir.

Q. Do you remember how many men have been strapped since you have been deputy?

A. I do not remember of but four.

Q. Have you ever administered the punishment by the strap yourself?

A. Yes, sir.

Q. In how many cases?

A. One case.

Q. How many blows?

A. I gave eleven blows.

Q. Upon what part of the body?

A. Well, I intended to hit them around the base, mostly. They squirm; you cannot always tell where you will hit a man when you strike at him.

Q. After giving these eleven blows, did you examine the person of the convict flogged to see the effect?

A. No, sir.

Q. Do you remember the name of the convict?

A. I do.

Q. What was it?

A. It is Isaiah Bajley.

Q. About what date?

A. It was on the morning of the 19th of last month. The record there was commenced on the 18th; that is the time the punishment commenced, but the punishment was finished upon the morning of the 19th.

Q. Did you count the straps?

A. I did.

Q. Who reported Bajley to you?

A. He was reported by keeper Holt.

Q. After giving his report, what investigation did he make as to the truth or falsity of it?

A. I reported to the Agent and the man Bajley was brought in here and examined by the Agent and Mr. Bliss, one of the inspectors, who happened to be here from Detroit, and Mr. Holt was sent for and came in and made a statement.

Q. Who decided on the measure of the punishment?

A. Mr. Morris.
Q. Did he tell you how many blows to give?
A. Yes, sir.
Q. What was the instruction as to the severity of the blows?
A. There was nothing said about it.
Q. Was any further punishment inflicted upon Bajley?
A. He was confined in a bare cell the day before.
Q. After the strapping or before?
A. It was before the strapping; when he was first reported.
Q. He was put in the bare cell and received his strapping the next day?
A. Yes, sir.
Q. After receiving the strap, where did he go?
A. He went into the dining-room, got his breakfast and went to work.
Q. What work is he employed at?
A. He is employed on the tool contract.
Q. How old a man is Bajley?
A. Well, he stated that he was thirty years old. I should think he was somewhere in that neighborhood; 28 or 30.
Q. You made no examination to see what the effect of the blows were on his person?
A. Not until seven or eight days afterwards.
Q. Did you then?
A. Yes, sir.
Q. What did you find?
A. I found a little black and blue streak on his back, perhaps three inches long.
Q. Nothing further?
A. Nothing further.
Q. What is the usual course that is pursued when a convict is reported for breaking discipline; I mean as to investigating into the truth or falsity of the charge?
A. If it is nothing very serious the keeper's statement is the basis of punishment—for little infractions of the rules.
Q. If it be serious?
A. There is an investigation of the affair; give the convict a chance to make his statement. Well, in all cases the convict has a chance to make his statement; but where it is just the convict's word against the keeper's word, the keeper's word is taken. If it is more serious, we get at the truth of the matter.
Q. Usually, what length of time after the report is made before punishment follows?
A. Well, they are very often reported through the day, and ordered to step out of the ranks as they go in at night, when they are locked up in a bare cell, and punishment usually comes afterwards; that was the practice when I came here, and we have followed it up since.
Q. Have you ever become satisfied that the report of the keeper was mistaken, and that the convict was not guilty of the charge laid against him?
A. I never found it so since I have been here.
Q. Do not foremen sometimes report men for infraction?
A. Yes, sir.
Q. And in such cases do they report to you?
A. They report to the keeper and the keeper reports to me.

Q. What is the practice when the report comes from the foreman. I mean as to investigation?

A. Well, it is investigated the same as if the keeper made the report correct.

Q. If the question is as between the foreman's word and the convict's word, which is taken?

A. The foreman's word.

Q. The complaints of the foremen usually are for short work, are they not?

A. Yes, sir; usually that is the character.

Q. And sometimes for not doing good work?

A. Yes, sir; sometimes for threats.

Q. Made by the convict to them?

A. Yes, sir.

Q. Is it possible with the supervision that is exercised here for foremen to use improper language to a convict and the keeper not hear it?

A. Yes, sir, it is possible; he may be in another part of the shop.

Q. Are the opportunities for such improper language frequent?

A. The foreman is in one part of the shop and the keeper usually stands or sits near the center of the shop.

Q. So that such opportunities are, as you may say, frequent,—almost constant?

A. Let me understand the first question now.

Q. Are opportunities for a foreman to use improper language to a convict frequent?

A. The opportunities are frequent; yes, sir.

Q. Are complaints ever made by convicts against the foremen?

A. They are, occasionally.

Q. What is the character of those complaints when made, usually?

A. I do not remember but one or two instances where they said the foreman swore at them; cursed him.

Q. And what is the practice of the prison authorities in such cases?

A. Well, if that should be found out that the foreman was in the habit of doing that, he would be shut out of the yard, I suppose; I have never seen a case of the kind since I have been here.

Q. Such cases have been reported since you have been here?

A. I think there was a case reported from the cooper shop. On an investigation we found no truth in the statement at all.

Q. What investigation did you make in that case?

A. From the convicts that stood around where they could hear what was said.

Q. Then what was done with the convict who made the report which you found to be false?

A. That convict was punished.

Q. Have you ever known of a case where a convict complained of a freeman where the truth has been found to lie with the convict?

A. I do not recollect where there has been a report made by a convict against a freeman except in this one case.

Q. Since you have been in the prison has any instance come to your knowledge where a convict complained of any keeper or guard or any of the officers of the prison?

A. I do not think of any case.

Q. In the intercourse of Mr. Morris as Agent, with the convicts in the pris-

STATE PRISON INVESTIGATION. 267

on, have you ever observed any unevenness of temper in administering discipline or in speaking to the convicts?
A. No, sir, I have not; I have seen him earnest.
Q. Have you ever seen him excited?
A. I do not think I ever saw him excited; I have seen him earnest and bound to get at the facts.
Q. What is your practice as to making a record of infractions of the rules in the prison?
A. Well, if they are reported at night as they come in, I set it down the next morning and make out the record on my scrap book.
Q. Do you not make any entry until the next morning after the report?
A. Yes, sir; if it happens through the day I very often make the report at the time.
Q. The same day?
A. Yes, sir.
Q. But do you ever allow more than the next day to elapse before you make the entry?
A. No, sir.
Q. When do you carry these memorandum book entries to the Agent?
A. Well, it has always been left in his reach every night; that is, until I commenced having the entries taken there. You can see the difference in the handwriting. Since that I have kept it myself.
Q. Now, how are these entries transferred from your book to the convict record, or conduct record, as it is indiscriminately called?
A. They are transferred; the language may vary a little, if on the investigation we find that the language may need a little altering.
Q. Well, I ask you to describe the manner in which they are transferred; who does that?
A. It is done by one of the convicts.
Q. I mean who did it when you first came here?
A. Mr. Morris.
Q. How was it done?
A. Well, he has the book laid right before him and copies from that.
Q. Mr. Morris copies right from the book?
A. Copied from the book, and at the same time he had an understanding of every case, I think, as he was present at every punishment.
Q. Did you read from your entry for him to copy?
A. No, sir.
Q. Was there, so far as you know, any comparison between the record as made and the entry made by you?
A. No, sir.
Q. Were all the entries which you made on your memorandum book transferred to the convict record, or were some omitted?
A. I think some were omitted.
Q. Why were they omitted?
A. Well, for reasons that the Agent could explain, perhaps, better than I could.
Q. I will read from the memorandum book, and also from the record book, under date of Sept. 1, 1874, the memorandum says: "Charles Simmons, reported for striking one man in his shop with a hammer, bare cell 36 hours." The record says, under the same date, that Charles Simmons received 48 hours in

bare cell without food or drink. Will you explain that deficiency between the 36 hours and the 48?

A. It might have been,—well, it was in this way: that the punishment was to be 36 hours, I suppose, but the punishment was longer than that, when that was copied off it was put down correct. As I had just commenced then, the Agent told me in that case in particular—and I guess you will find others through the book—that all I need mention was the case itself, as he and I were both present, and he knew the whole case through—all I need do was just to minute it down, just to bring it to his memory.

Q. Under the date of Sept. 6, I find simply the words, "Jack Shorey," and in the record I find a page concerning the case?

A. That was by order of the Agent, to just put the name down, as he knew all about the case. Both of us understood it, and he would write it down.

Q. And he wrote it out at the end of the month?

A. No, sir; he wrote it out,—I don't think it run to the end of the month. It has not been usual for him to wait until the end of the month to write up those records. I have seen him writing on the records as often as once a week or once in two weeks.

Q. Why are entries which are entered on your memorandum book, omitted on the record book?

A. Well, it is for some good reason.

Q. State if you are governed by rules?

A. All I can say is in my own case.

Q. You are governed by rules in this matter, are you?

A. Yes, sir.

Q. What is the rule by which you omit to make upon the convict record, the same entries which you made at the time of the breach of discipline?

A. It very often happens that a new man—perhaps he has been here one or two weeks—will violate a rule and be reported by the keeper. We will reprimand the man and send him back to his place and no report made of it, and it may be set down on the book, and when we come to draw it off at the end of the week, make up our minds that it ought not to go on the record.

Q. In other words the Agent and the deputy exercise their discretion as to what cases shall go on the record?

A. We do as far as that is concerned.

Q. Have you any general rule on that subject that is applicable to all cases, or is it a matter of discretion in each case?

A. I do not think there can be any general rule for all cases.

Q. Well, then, you will answer my question how?

A. Will you please state it again?

[Question read by stenographer.]

A. I can say we have no general rule; that answers the first part of it.

Q. What does determine whether the entry on the memorandum book shall go on the record?

A. I do not know how I can answer that, unless it is to determine by good sense and judgment.

Q. Of the Agent and deputy also?

A. Yes, sir.

Q. Have you heard any complaints during the winter from any of the convicts directly, or through their keepers, or the hall master, in reference to their clothing?

STATE PRISON INVESTIGATION. 269

A. Yes, sir; through the severest weather we had men complaining of the cold.
Q. State generally their complaints, and whether they were frequent?
A. It is in the hall master's department where the clothing is.
Q. He is under your direction?
A. Yes, sir, partly, although I hardly ever interfere with his line of duty; whenever a man complained of an insufficiency of clothing we would try to see that he was clothed.
Q. It is a part of your duty to see that the hall master performs his duty, is it not?
A. I suppose that is a part of it.
Q. Now, what personal examination have you made in any of the cases of complaints, to see whether more clothing was needed?
A. I have examined the men as they stood before me.
Q. Well, to see whether they were cold or not, do you mean?
A. To see whether their clothing was sufficient or not.
Q. Have any of the men desired undershirts and drawers?
A. Yes, sir.
Q. When they did not get them?
A. I presume they have desired them when they did not get them; yes, sir.
Cross-examination by Mr. Conely:
Q. This book that you call the conduct record is not intended to be a precise record of the memorandum that you make, is it?
A. No, sir.
Q. This book, the conduct record, is more amplified?
A. Yes, sir.
Q. Than the original entry you make yourself?
A. Yes, sir.
Q. And in this conduct record, the person making it—Mr. Morris, when he has made it, gives a larger amount of detail than you give in the memorandum book?
A. Yes, sir; and uses his own language, knowing all the circumstances of the case.
Q. I think you stated that some of the convicts have desired more clothing when they did not get it?
A. I did not really mean to be understood in that way; we tried always to supply them with clothing when they called for it and the hall master thought they needed it.
Q. Has it not sometimes happened that they have called for clothing when they have not been furnished with it?
A. Yes, sir; I presume it has.
Q. In what cases has this happened?
A. Well, it may have happened in cases where the men have worked outside of the shop; may be exposed to the cold; we have had a very bitter winter, and it would be a wonder if men with just a jacket and vest on would not suffer, even if they had under-clothing on.
Q. So far as you know, if a man has expressed a wish for more clothing he has been furnished it in those cases where clothing was necessary?
A. Yes, sir.
Q. The cases where such clothing has been denied then, I understand to be where you have regarded that they did not need the extra clothing?

A. Yes, sir.

Q. Is it not true that in the management of the prison you find some men, perhaps quite a large number of men, who make a point of asking for things that they do not need?

A Very often done.

Q. Then the statement of a convict that is made to you on such a subject you do not place so much reliance on that you would to the same statement made by a person outside?

A. Well, in regard to the clothing, a person can by their own eyes see a good deal about that; and a man's statement, even if he made no statement at all, you could see whether they needed any clothing or not.

Q. Do you know of any cases that have occurred here in the prison of suffering in consequence of a lack of a sufficient supply of clothing?

A. No, sir; I have not heard of even a finger being frozen in the yard.

Q. Do you know of any one suffering in consequence of being poorly clothed?

A. No, sir.

Q. Do you know of any of the men suffering at night in the wings in consequence of cold?

A. They have reported to me that they have suffered some.

Q. What measures have been taken to prevent that?

A. Well, that was before the steam works were connected so that they could heat the wings properly.

Q. I will ask you then, if in your judgment the reason of that arose from the insufficiency of the arrangements for heating at that time?

A. Yes, sir.

Q. Has that been remedied?

A. It has in a measure. I do not think the west wing can be heated sufficiently when there is a strong, cold wind blowing; there is too much space in the roof, and perhaps too much leakage in the shingles there. I do not know where the heat escapes.

Q. Something is needed to make the heating arrangements in the west wing perfect?

A. Yes, sir. I was trying to think how low the thermometer had been down; I do not know, but I heard of it being down to 47 at one time.

Q. 47 below zero?

A. Yes, sir; 64 I think is the point that they try to keep it at.

Q Something has been said to you about some persons' names being omitted from this conduct record; were the cases that were omitted trifling in character?

A. I can only state that so far as I have drawn the record off from my book, they were.

Q. I suppose there has been no rule about it, but when you came to a case— came across a trifling case that you thought ought not to go on the book to a man's prejudice, you have left it off. I suppose that is about as it has been?

A. Yes, sir.

Q This conduct record is used by the inspectors to see and determine whether a man shall be allowed his good time or not?

A. Yes, sir.

Mr. Bartow:

Q. Is that conduct record, or a sort of ledger that is kept before the convicts, the record that determines whether their good time shall be taken away from them or not?

A. This is the only record that determines that.
Q. This is the only record?
A. Yes, sir.

Mr. Webber:

Q. I find in this memorandum book, which commences with Jan. 6, 1875, two entries following dated Dec. 9. Is that intended for Dec. 9, or Jan. 9?
A. That should be Dec. instead of Jan.; no, it is Jan.
Q. It should be Jan. 9 instead of Dec. 9?
A. Yes, sir; it should be Jan. 9.

Mr. Webber—The memorandum under date, as written, of Dec. 9th, reads as follows: "Richard Lane, Thomas Cooper, and Charles Addelson, for howling as they came down stairs from the cigar shop, bare cell six hours."

As recorded in the conduct record under date of Jan. 9th, it is as follows; "Thomas Cooper and Charles Addelson, of the lower cigar shop, were reported by keeper Howel for hallooing in the ranks while marching from the shop to dinner; bare cell six hours."

Q. Calling your attention to this omission of the name of Lane from the record, and this case from the memorandum, what explanation do you offer for that omission?
A. When we come to investigate the case, these men are both out at night as the last bell rings. They are ordered to stop and see the deputy. I find out from the keeper what the complaint is and act accordingly, by going in and notifying the Agent of what has been done. I usually put them in the bare cell and step in and tell the Agent what has been done, and the time is fixed for them. I state the case as near as I can find out without losing my supper. [Don't know as it is necessary to put that in, though.] After investigating them next morning it was found that the keeper was not sure in Lane's case, but of the other two boys he was positive about; and rather than have Lane lose his good time, besides the punishment, I left his name out.
Q. In such case where you become satisfied that a man has been punished without just cause, what is your practice with reference to that man?
A. Well, there is no way to give him back his bare cell that he gets, of course.
Q. Do you inform him of the fact that you have become satisfied of the fact that you have punished him improperly?
A. Yes, sir.
Q. And have you any practice by which you tender him, in the way of light work or otherwise, any compensation for the punishment that he has received?
A. No, sir.
Q. What is the rule of the prison with reference to the keeper that shall make such mistakes and who is found in fault, as in this case of Keeper Howell?
A. Well, he was sure of two men, and the other he was not so positive about, but still thought that he was right at the time he made the report.
Q. Is the rule as to the benefit of the doubt reversed in these cases? In other words, if the keeper was not sure about Lane, why should he have been punished by the bare cell until the question was settled satisfactorily?
A. I do not know really how to answer that, unless it was that he had the punishment before the record was drawn off.
Q. Is there not a large percentage of moisture in the air in these wings in which the cells are contained?
A. Not of moisture. I guess there is a large percentage of foul air, so Prof. Kedzie says in his analyzation of it.

Q. Have you ever seen the walls of the cells in either wing wet by condensation?
A. I do not think I have. I have seen them wet by the water leaking through the east wing roof. It does now into some of the cells so that we frequently have to take the men out at night. If there should come up a shower, we should have to take some of the men out and put them in the hall.
Q. Have you examined the cells in the wings sufficient so that you are able to say whether the walls of the cells are ever wet by condensation?
A. I never noticed anything of the kind; never had my attention brought to the subject.

Re-cross-examination by Mr. Conely:
Q. As to Lane, I wish to ask whether at the time the offense was reported, and before the infliction of punishment, at any time, any doubt was expressed as to Lane having participated in the conduct?
A. No, sir.
Q. Then the doubt arose after the punishment had been inflicted?
A. Yes.

Mr. Webber:
Q. Do you know whether keeper Howell was discharged for that error?
A. He was not.
Q. Is he still in the prison employ?
A. Yes, sir.
Q. Do you know whether that mistake of his was reported to the Agent?
A. I do not think it was. I think you can lay that all on me.

Mr. Conely:
Q. Do you think it is possible to run an institution like this without some mistakes?
A. No, sir.
Q. What do you pay these assistant keepers?
A. They are getting $60 a month.
Q. There are no perquisites connected with the office of assistant keeper?
A. No, sir.
Q. It is of course the rule that the keeper's word is taken in preference to the word of the convict?
A. Yes, sir.

REV. ROYAL C. CRAWFORD SWORN.

Examined by Mr. Webber:
Q. State your age and residence?
A. I am 58 years old, sir, and reside at Allegan.
Q. Were you formerly acting as chaplain of this prison?
A. I was.
Q. At what time did such employment commence?
A. I have served at two different times. I suppose it is in regard to the last time.
Q. Give the first and then the second.
A. My first service as chaplain was commenced—I am not positive now what year it was—under the administration of Mr. Hammond; Mr. Hammond was Agent of the prison. It was about 1858; I was here in 1857, I know; I think it must have commenced in about 1856.
Q. And continued about how long?

STATE PRISON INVESTIGATION.

A. Continued two years and a half and a little over, and run into the administration of Mr. Leaton.

Q. Did you commence again?

A. I commenced again five years ago last fall, in September.

Q. That is, September, 1869?

A. Yes, sir.

Q. And continued until when?

A. Continued until two years ago last fall. That would be 1872—two years last October since I left.

Q. Do you remember when Mr. Morris commenced acting as Agent of the prison?

A. My impression now is that it was in the month of April, four years ago this present month.

Mr. Morris—March.

A. I was not certain whether it was March or April—in the spring of 1871.

Mr. Morris—I took up the reins the 17th of March, 1871.

Q. Therefore about a year and a half you were acting as chaplain under Mr. Morris' administration?

A. Yes, sir.

Q. During that time what were your duties under the prison regulations?

A. My duties were, sir, to preach the gospel to the convicts once on the Sabbath, and oversee or superintend what we call our prison Sunday school in the morning; to have charge, or had charge of the library; see that the convicts were supplied with books; and also to read the correspondence of the convicts —all that was received, and what was sent out. Those were most of the duties devolving upon me.

Q. Did you have occasion to witness any punishment inflicted on convicts while you were here, after Mr. Morris took charge of the prison?

A. No, sir; I don't remember to have witnessed a single case of punishment after Mr. Morris came to the prison; I am not positive, but I think my impression is that I did not witness a single case.

Q. Did you know of any cases of severe punishment in the prison after Mr. Morris came here?

A. No case of what I would call severe punishment.

Q. Is there any feature of Mr. Morris' administration of the discipline of the prison that you consider open to criticism?

A. Well, there were some features of it that to my mind were open to slight criticism; and that was the exceeding humanitarian system adopted by him in the management of the prison. I thought when he first commenced that he opened a little too liberal in the manner of his treatment to convicts, and expressed myself to some of my friends that I was fearful that we would be under the necessity of drawing a tighter rein at some future time. I don't know that I ever stated it to him, but I hoped in the meantime that he would be successful; but I was afraid it would not be, having as much knowledge as I had of the prison in former times.

Q. Did you discover any want of equanimity of temper in the administration of the prison by Mr. Morris?

A. I can't say that I ever did; I don't know that I ever saw Mr. Morris, in a single instance, exhibit anything otherwise than an even temper, in his management of the convicts.

Q. What was the cause of your leaving the prison as chaplain?

A. I resigned, sir; I had been here three years, and I did not desire to remain any longer; I wanted to get away, and left for that reason.

Q. Was there any change in your duty after Mr. Morris took charge?

A. No, sir.

Q. In other words, were there any duties which he assumed to take charge of which had formerly been assigned to you, and which by the regulations of the inspectors belonged to you as chaplain?

A. I think not, sir; I have no recollection of any such change.

Q. I wish to call your attention particularly to the distribution of reading matter to the convicts. Was not that by the rules made your duty?

A. The circulation of the prison library was made my duty; aside from that Mr. Morris adopted the magazine distribution system here, as a matter of reform; and in order to get the men to quit using tobacco, proposed to give each man a magazine for a year that would quit the use of tobacco, and give them to a certain day to make up their minds and report; and a number of men that had entered into the contract to receive the magazines, in place of tobacco, made their report and their names were taken, and Mr. Morris ordered the magazines. Those magazines were distributed by Mr. Morris' order; I had nothing to do with that; they never were assigned to me as a part of my duty by the inspectors, and consequently I had no supervision over that at all.

Q. In this arrangement with the convicts about their magazines, was there any promise that the magazines should be furnished them for more than one year?

A. No, sir; only one year; that was the contract, that he would give each man a magazine for one year; that is the distinct understanding, as I remember it.

Q. Supposing they thought they would have the magazines as long as they did not get the tobacco?

A Well, I don't know what they thought; I don't know what idea they got of it; I know that was the understanding that I had of it, and I never had a convict express himself, as expecting that he was going to receive a magazine any longer than a year.

J. R. BENNETT, SWORN ON THE PART OF MR. MORRIS.

Examined by Mr. Conely:

Q. You are the United States Marshal for the Eastern District of Michigan?

A. Yes, sir.

Q. Situated at Adrian?

A. Yes, sir.

Q. How far are you from Rome Center?

A. About six miles.

Q. Do you know James L. Perkins?

A. Yes, sir.

Q. That was a convict here?

A. Yes, sir.

Q. He lived at Rome Center, at one time, did he not?

A. Yes, sir.

Q Are you acquainted with his reputation for truth and veracity in that community?

A. I think I am.

Q. Is it good or bad?

A. Very bad.
Q. From what you know of his reputation would you believe him under oath?
A. I would not.

Cross-examination by Mr. Webber:
Q. How long has he lived there?
A. It as been some time since he lived there. I brought him to State prison here twenty years ago, I guess, or eighteen; perhaps fifteen. That was the first time; and I attended court when he was sent here the second time for forgery. Both cases were for forgery.
Q. Has he ever resided at Adrian since his first conviction there?
A. I am not certain; I think he did for a while. Well, I am not positive about it; he has been there, anyway.
Q. He has been there enough so they kept his acquaintance, did they not?
A. I guess so.

Re-direct examination by Mr. Conely:
Q. Do you not remember that he had resided at Adrian until a short time before he was arrested on the last charge?
A. Well, I don't remember; I think he did.
Q. He was admitted to the bar and practiced law, did he not?
A. I heard so.

ESAIAS WARNER SWORN ON THE PART OF MR. MORRIS.

Examined by Mr. Conely:
Q. Where do you reside?
A. I reside in Jackson.
Q. Are you connected with the prison in any capacity?
A Yes, sir.
Q. What is it?
A. Guard.
Q. How long have you been here?
A. Three years the first of next month. No; I have not been guard that long. I came here in May, but I went on guard duty permanently—that is, I have been here three years the 20th of July coming. I have been here three years the first of May. It will be three years in July since I began guard duty.
Q. What salary did you get?
A. I got fifty dollars a month.
Q. Do you know John St. Clair, the convict?
A. Yes, sir.
Q. Did you know him on the 7th day of July, 1873?
A. Yes, sir, I think I did.
Q. Did you know of his being punished at that time, or about that time?
A. Well, yes, sir; I think it was about that time; I could not say; it was either in June or July; I think it was in July.
Q. Did you see the punishment?
A. I did not.
Q. Do you know the circumstances that led to the punishment?
A. Yes, sir.
Q. What kind of work were you engaged in at that time?
A. Digging a cellar under the new dining hall.
Q. Were you on guard at that time?
A. Well, yes; I was drawing guard's pay.

Q. Were you in the employ of the State at that time?
A. Yes, sir.
Q. And not in the employ of private persons?
A. Oh, no.
Q State just the circumstances that led to the punishment of John St. Clair?
A. Well, sir, Johnny St. Clair was working in my gang at the time; I was running about ten wheelbarrows, I think; he was wheeling at the time, I think, and he changed off with Thurston. I guess you have all heard of him. He changed off with Thurston; he took the shovel and Thurston took the barrow. They was going to change for a rest,—kinder rested them you know. St. Clair, when the other men had their barrows full, ready to go out, his was not half full, and we had to run them on one plank, you see, because there was no other way to get out and in, so I spoke to him about it; he was resting. I told him to fill the barrow, and when the men was gone out they could rest; and he worked very slow,—kinder killing time. The other men was waiting with their barrows. And he come in the second time, and he done the same thing right over,—worked just as slow as he could. His barrow was not half full when the others were out. I spoke to him about it again, and he did not do any better. And the next time they came in Thurston says: "I will shovel, I can fill the barrows as fast as the rest." So he took his shovel and stepped down into the pit, and filled the barrow. Just then one of the men spoke to me something in regard to the work,—about his working, and I looked around to see what he wanted, and when I looked back, the shovel was coming for me just as tight as he could drive it with both hands. He struck at me three times with the shovel, and then he threw the shovel at me, and threw two brick-bats at me besides. I sent for the deputy, and Mr. Morris and the deputy both came.
Q. Did any of these things, the shovel or the brick strike you?
A. Yes, sir; struck my arm.
Q. Which?
A. The shovel.
Q. How many times did he strike you with the shovel?
A. Twice.
Q Did the brick strike you at all?
A. No, sir; I dodged them.
Mr. Webber—It was St. Clair, I understood, that struck you?
A. Yes, sir.
Mr. Conely—
Q. Did you strike him at all?
A. I did not; I never touched him in the world.
Q. Did you strike at him with your cane?
A. I did not.
Q. Or punch him?
A. I did not.
Q. What did you say to St. Clair when he declined to go on with the work?
A. He did not decline to go on; there was nothing said about it. He did not say whether he would go on or not; nor I did not suppose he was angry; nor I did not speak to him harshly; the first warning I had was the shovel.
Q. Before you said a word to him?
A. Oh, I spoke to him about filling his barrow, and then they could rest.
Q. What did you say to him?

A. I says: Johnny, fill up your barrow, and then you can rest while the men are gone out.
Q. Did he make any reply?
A. He did not.
Q. How many times did you tell him so?
A. I think he filled two barrows; yes, he only filled two barrows. I told him both times.
Q. And did he obey you?
A. I would not know what you would call it. He went to work, just killing time. He took about a third of a shovel full, but I did not know at the time that he intended to strike me, because I did not speak cross to him.
Q Did he strike you angrily?
A. Oh, indeed, yes, sir; he tried to kill me.
Q. How?
A. Yes, sir; he tried his best to split my head open.
Q. How near did he stand to you when he struck at you with the shovel?
A. Oh, I was then so he could reach me with the shovel; three or four feet, sir.
Q. Was this a long-handled shovel?
A. Short-handled shovel; we don't use no others.
Q. Had you had any difficulty with St. Clair at any time previously?
A. No, sir; I never had.
Q. How long had he been at work under you?
A. Well, I think he was in my gang when I first took the gang; I had the gang about five weeks before this occurred.
Mr. Bartow—What reason did he assign, if any, for making this assault upon you?
A. Not a word, not a particle of anything; he never spoke to me, only he stepped right out of the pit with his shovel, while this other man was calling to me to see about his work, and when I turned to look back again the shovel was coming as tight as he could send it with both hands; I threw up my hand and it struck my wrist, so that I could not use it for two weeks; he struck twice I am certain, and threw three brick bats.
Q. Did you ever know of any cause for it?
A. I never did.
Q. Was he considered a malicious man?
A. I never heard anything spoken of him more than the rest of the men; he had been running a barrow previous to this; in fact I did not have the gang but a short time before that.
Re-direct examination by Mr. Conely:
Q. Are you on duty at night?
A. Half the time.
Q. Were you so during the winter?
A. Yes, sir.
Q In the halls?
A. Yes, sir.
Q What has been the temperature of the halls during the past winter?
A. Sixty-five has been Mr. Morris' orders; that was what was understood.
Q. How near to that have you been able during the severe weather to maintain that temperature?
A. When do you mean?

Q. What is the lowest it has run down at any time at night?
A. Fifty-one is the lowest that I have seen.
Mr. Mellen—Was there any complaint by the men in their cells during the cold weather of being cold nights,—sleeping cold?
A. Well, yes, sir; it seems to me I have heard them talk something about it; speaking about being chilly last night, or something, but nothing serious; they never said they wanted to see the Agent, or anything about it; that was this winter.

Cross-examination by Mr. Webber:
Q. What was your duty?
A. Guard at that time in the hall; I am on the wall half the day and inside half the night.
Q. Which wing are you in?
A. I was in both wings; I have been in every place in the prison.
Q. I mean in the winter?
A. I have been in both—they change around from pillar to post.
Q. Was it any part of your duty to keep watch of the temperature?
A. Yes, sir; we always do watch that.
Q. How many times in the course of the night would you look at the thermometer?
A. Oh, my goodness! I should say fifty times in half the night—passing at all times.
Q. Did you look to see what the temperature was?
A. Yes, sir.
Q. Fifty times a night?
A. I should think so—I guess I saw—
Q. And you never saw it lower than fifty-one?
A. Fifty-one, I think, is the lowest.
Q. Are you sure?
A. I ain't certain, but we are very apt to notice such things, because we are in there ourselves, and when it is cold we feel it.
Q. When you have been there as guard, what clothing have you had on to keep you comfortable during a winter night?
A. A greater part of the time in my shirt-sleeves, sometimes with this coat on.
Q. During the winter?
A. Yes, sir.
Q. Do you wear a woolen under-shirt?
A. Yes, sir.
Q. And then you had a shirt over that?
A. Yes, sir.
Q. And then a vest?
A. Yes, sir; then when I did not have a coat, that is all.
Q. You usually wore pants, I suppose?
A. Oh, yes; but they don't reach up over my body.
Q. And with drawers?
A. Yes, sir.

Re-direct examination by Mr. Conely:
Q. Cotton or woolen drawers?
A. Woolen drawers.
Q. Of course when you went to bed you took off some of this clothing?

A. Yes, sir.

Mr. Webber:

Q. Did you ever wear an overcoat when you were on guard, out in the wings, in the night time?

A. I don't think I ever did, when I was well.

Q. Have you been ill?

A. There was sometimes that I did not feel well, you know. I have been sick; I was pretty careful of myself, and kept my over coat on.

Q. When you were well enough to do guard duty, you have sometimes worn an overcoat in those halls?

A. When I would be sitting down in the hall, you know, sometimes take my overcoat over my shoulders.

Q. Well, you have worn an overcoat?

A. Oh, I have had an overcoat on in the wing, but the other guard did not.

Q. How many nights during the past winter have you found it comfortable to to have an overcoat on?

A. Not but a very few.

Q. Have you worn it ten nights?

A. I could not say; perhaps I did. I have been sick a good deal during the winter.

Q. You have been sick a good deal?

A. Yes, sir; that is, not feeling well.

Q. But well enough to do guard duty?

A. Yes, I can't help myself; I can't get off.

Re-direct examination by Mr. Conely:

Q. The times when you wore your overcoat were times when you had not been well?

A. Yes, sir.

Q. And you wore it for that reason?

A. Yes, sir.

Q. Did the other guard wear an overcoat?

A. I don't think he did.

The further examination of witnesses was here adjourned until nine o'clock to-morrow morning.

THURSDAY A. M., APRIL 15, 1875.

CHARLES H. WELTON, SWORN ON THE PART OF MR. MORRIS.

Examined by Mr. Conely:

Q. You are employed within the prison?

A. Yes, sir.

Q. On what contract?

A. Furniture contract of Henry Gilbert & Sons.

Q. How long have you been so employed?

A. Thirteen years.

Q. Then for the last thirteen years your employment has been within the prison?

A. It has been within the prison.
Q. In what capacity?
A. General charge of the furniture contract; the entire time.
Q. You have known Mr. Morris' administration here ever since it began?
A. I have, sir.
Q. Did you ever witness any punishment inflicted by him?
A. Well, occasionally, as I have been passing through the hall, I have seen the water used; I have a great deal of running out and in; sometimes I stop and look and sometimes I pass along.
Q. Does your position enable you to judge of the influence of any particular discipline upon the prison?
A. Well, somewhat.
Q. Does it enable you to judge of the influence of discipline on the men upon your own contract?
A. Do you mean the punishments?
Q. I mean does it enable you to judge of its effect upon the men; I don't mean have you seen a particular punishment—and are you able to judge from the conversation of your men; from their conduct, deportment, and expression of feeling, or otherwise, while under your control; are you enabled to say what the influence of any particular administration may be upon the men?
A. I think I have.
Q. What, in your opinion, has been the influence of Mr. Morris' administration upon your department?
A. It has been entirely since Mr. Morris has been here very quiet.
Q. Are you enabled, to some extent, to form an opinion as to whether the administration has been lenient or severe?
A. Well, with the experience I had previous to that, it has been, I should say, very lenient.
Q. Why did you come to that conclusion,—in other words, on what is your judgment based, previous agents?
A. Previous administrations.
Q. That is you compare it in your mind with the administration of former agents?
A. Yes, sir.
Q. How are you able to do that, when, as a rule, you did not witness the punishments?
A. From the effect upon the men; their common talk; I am where any of our own men can speak to me at any time during the day, or they can send for me to see me, and often they broach these subjects of their treatment, after punishment, etc., when there has been any of it going on—any punishments that have been talked about—and make some remarks about it.
Q. It is against the rule, is it not, for them to told about it?
A. Well, I think it is.
Q. Is that rule habitually violated or not?
A. I should say not, sir.
Q. Well, they do talk about about it to some extent?
A. They do to some extent with freemen that are not regular officers. I often check them in talking, or commencing to talk. I often have to do that—tell them I don't want to hear about it.
Q. Not to give encouragement to such kind of talk?
A. I don't endeavor to do that.

Q. Do you know LaMountain?
A. I do, sir.
Q. He is at work on the Gilbert contract is not?
A. Yes, sir.
Q. What sort of a man is he?
A. Well, we call him smart—keen.
Q. Is he particularly so?
A. Well, he does not never say much to me about anything except his work, that he attends to properly, and he is making a fine workman.
Q. Is he a man of particularly bright intellect in that direction?
A. Yes, sir, he is.
Q. Do you know of LaMountain making any keys?
A. I have heard so; I don't know personally.

Cross-examination by Mr. Webber:
Q. How many men are employed on the furniture contract?
A. At present, one hundred.
Q. How many have been employed on an average, say for the last four years?
A. Say—one hundred—let's see—four years. Our contract is three years old. Say an average of one hundred. It is only 107 or 108.
Q. And you have charge and supervision of all these men?
A. Yes, sir.
Q. State whether it is a common occurrence for men on your contract to be called away from work for punishment?
A. It is not, sir.
Q. What percentage of your men are punished—say monthly?
A. It would bother me to figure that out, I guess; but to the best of my recollection I should not say they averaged two a month, out of a hundred; I don't think they averaged that. I know occasionally of men being called out and punished.
Q. You say that as compared with previous administrations, Mr. Morris' administration, you consider kind and lenient?
A. I do, sir.
Q. Have you found it any the less efficient?
A. No, sir.
Q. From what you have seen then of the administration, it would be your opinion, that a lenient treatment would be, if firm, equally efficient with a severe treatment?
A. Yes, sir, in most cases; there are cases that require different treatment.
Q. How is it as to the men working?
A. Will they accomplish more work in the same time, under a lenient treatment than under a severe one?
Q. I don't think they do, but they do it more cheerfully?
Q. How is it as to the quality of work, as compared with the two treatments?
A. I never claimed that had anything to do with it. It depends entirely upon your foreman over them. A convict will slight unless you watch them—most of them; and some of them will do fine work, any way; they are a little ambitious.
Q. You are sometimes a little crowded for work?
A. Once in a while.
Q. What course do you pursue, in case you are crowded for work, to get extra work out of the men?

A. Well, we ain't crowded except occasionally we have men that are idle—that are not hurried, and we hurry them up a little.

Q. Do you ever offer the men any inducement to hurry up a little?

A. I do, sir; that is general.

Q. State what that inducement is, if it is general?

A. We give our men a month's work—sometimes give them a job that lasts two to three months; I say to the men, "All your work will be booked that you do from the time you come in until you go out, and we have a set task in some case on the bench, and if when your time is out you have done beyond your task we will pay for it;" but I don't tell them that I employ them to do over-work at any time; but when their time is out if they have been good men and work what work we give them, we will pay them the contract price for it—that is the per diem, the same as we pay the State.

Q. Is it a common occurrence for them to get over-time?

A. Not much; there is a few men that are more rapid, and others ambitious; when they get started it is an easy matter for them to make, say a few bureaus or something of that kind extra a month, or two months, and at the end of a year or two they perhaps have from ten to twenty or thirty dollars; we have not encouraged it at all the past year and a half in no way.

Q. Do you ever put out tasks as a day's task, so that each knows what he has got to do every day?

A. We do on one or two machines, for instance on bureaus and extension tables; you may call it a task, a day's work; we give 275 feet of extension tables, after the machine work is done, for a month's work, which will be in the neighborhood of 16 feet a day, and we give 25 bureaus of one kind a month, and 30 of another kind, and so on; it can be reduced to a day, but our jobs are such that a man can't make one piece in a day, and finish it; it is to be carried on by a general process, a dozen or a dozen and a half at a time.

Q. Has it ever come to your knowledge in the shops about the prison, where contractors offer extra inducements to the men to get them to increase their work,—their daily task, and then, after a week or ten days, require them to do as much work as they have been doing under this extra inducement, without continuing their extra compensation?

A. I have heard of such things only; I don't know anything about it personally, and my information is simply upon convict information. I never heard of it through freemen.

Q. Is there any particular shop from which those rumors come more than any other?

A. Are you speaking under Mr. Morris' administration?

Q. Yes?

A. I never heard of it under his administration.

Q. I desire to confine my examination entirely to his administration?

A. I never heard of it under his administration.

ALEXANDER SMITH SWORN ON THE PART OF MR. MORRIS.

Examined by Mr. Conely:

Q. You are the engineer within the prison?

A. Yes, sir.

Q. How long have you held that position?

A. Eighteen months to-day.

Q. What is the line of your duty?

A. My duty is to attend to the heating apparatus, take care of the boilers and engine, and everything pertaining to it—or rather in the State prison; that is, for the State, not on the contracts.

Q. By that last remark you mean that the contractors for prison labor furnish their own steam?

A. Yes, sir.

Q. You have nothing to do with that?

A. Nothing whatever.

Q. You furnish the steam and the heat that is used for the State authorities?

A. Yes, sir.

Q. Do you know anything about the temperature of the wings as it has been kept during the past winter?

A. Yes, sir.

Q. At night as well as by day?

A. Yes, sir; it is reported to me in the morning by my assistant.

Q. Who is your assistant?

A. His name is Charles Wells.

Q. Is he a convict?

A. Yes, sir.

Q. What is the lowest temperature that you have heard about in these wings during the past winter?

A. The lowest that has been reported to me is forty-eight. That is as near as I can remember.

Q. Have you any recollection of any temperature lower than that?

A. I have not.

Q. At the time when that temperature was reported to you as the lowest that you remember, do you remember how low it was outside?

A. Yes, sir.

Q. How low was it?

A. It touched at twenty-eight degrees at my house.

Q. Above or below?

A. Below zero.

Q. And the report that you gave of the thermometer inside is above zero?

A. Forty-eight is the lowest above zero that it has fallen in the prison to my knowledge.

Q. Are there some practical difficulties in the way of heating up the west wing?

A. Yes, sir.

Q. I wish you would state what those practical difficulties are.

A. Well, the central building is not complete; and in the manner that it was all exposed in the fore part of the winter. There was a partition between the central building and the west wing, and that was taken down to get—I don't understand the reason why; and when that was taken down the roof was raised to a great extent, and it was a hard matter to heat the wing. The east wing we have no trouble whatever with.

Q. Then the space that requires to be heated in the west wing is a larger amount of space than in the east wing?

A. Yes, sir.

Q. That arises from the difference in the roof?

A. Yes, sir.

Q. And the shape of the roof?

A. And the shape of the roof.

Q. In the construction of the heating apparatus, as I understand it, the steam that you use passes through the central building before it reaches the west wing?

A. Yes, sir.

Q The central building is pretty large, isn't it?

A. Yes, sir; I would state in answer to that question, that the main pipe runs through the basement of the center building, and it was not covered—the center building was not covered—it was all open; consequently the steam was reduced to a great extent in going that distance.

Q. Then there was a great loss of heat?

A. Yes, sir.

Q. Do you know whether those things have been remedied or not?

A. Yes, sir, they are remedying them now.

Q. Do you know whether Mr. Morris manifested any desire, or made any efforts to remedy or paliate the difficulties that existed through the winter in regard to the west wing?

A. Yes, sir.

Q. I wish you would state to the committee just what interest he manifested in that, and what efforts he made?

A. I called his attention to it, and told him the difficulty with it in heating the west wing, and he investigated the prison himself; went through the wing, probably the same morning that I reported to him; I ain't certain; and I showed him a great many holes in the wall, where a good deal of air got through, and he called Mr. Donough's attention to it—the superintendent of construction here, and he had it all closed up. And there were several doors that were left open in the center of the building at night. He had them also boarded up, so that there would be less cold coming into the building.

Q. What, if anything, have you ever observed on the part of Mr. Morris, that evinced a disposition to neglect anything that was essential or desirable for the health or comfort of the convicts?

A. I never saw anything that came under my jurisdiction. If I reported to him, he always attended to it right away. I never saw anything in my passing around the prison that would lead me to think otherwise.

Q. Were you present at any time, when any of the men had been showered?

A. Yes, sir, several times.

Q. Do you know the nozzles that they used at the end of the hose?

A. Yes, sir.

[The witness is here shown two nozzles.]

Q. Are either of these the nozzles?

A. Yes, sir.

Q. Are there any others in the prison?

A. Not except the fire nozzles. I presume the contractors have nozzles, but I don't know anything about that.

Q Did you ever know of a fire nozzle to be used in the showering of convicts?

A. No, sir.

Q. Have you ever known of any others than the ones you now hold in your hands?

A. I know this [referring to the one shown him]. I have known that to be used, yes, sir.

B. But the one you now hold in your hand is the one generally used?

A. Yes, sir.

STATE PRISON INVESTIGATION. 285

Q. I wish you would give to the stenographer the extreme length of that nozzle?
A. It is 20½ inches.
Q. The diameter of the orifice where it joins the hose?
A. One inch.
Q. The diameter where the water comes out of the end of the nozzle?
A. A fraction over 3-16, as near as I can get at it with my scale; I could not call it much over.
Q. I wish you would give the extreme length of the other nozzle?
A. Eleven inches.
Q. The diameter of the orifice where it joins the hose?
A. One inch.
Q. The diameter of the hole at the end of the nozzle where the water comes out?
A. A quarter of an inch.
Q. These nozzles are the brass nozzles that are ordinarily used for watering lawns and street washing?
A. Yes, sir; I presume so.
Q. Such as you have seen used?
A. Yes, sir.
Q. Do you remember how many men you have seen showered in this way?
A. No, sir; I could not tell exactly how many I have seen.
Q. Was it part of your business to prepare the hose and get it ready.
A. Yes, sir.
Q. Can you say whether or not you have seen showered all that have been showered?
A. No, I have not. There may be one or two that I have not seen when I have been attending to my other duties around the prison.
Q. As a rule you have seen them showered?
A. Yes, sir.
Q. What is the effect, if any, upon a man; have you ever observed as the result of showering?
A. I never seen any ill effects from it at all.
Q. After the showering has been done, what is usually done with the men?
A. If the men seem chilly, Mr. Morris or the deputy would bring them into the boiler room until they got warm, and then send them back to their shops; that is all that I ever seen done with them.
Q. Has there been the same watchfulness on the part of the person administering the showering to notice whether the man needed to go to the boiler-room or not?
A. Yes, sir; it seemed to me that there was watchfulness in that respect.
Q. Do you know whether any of the men have gone to the hospital or not after being showered?
A. I never knew of any in my knowledge.
Q. Have you ever, at any of these times, or at any other time, seen any manifestation of ill temper, or malice, or vindictiveness on the part of Mr. Morris?
A. I have not, sir.
Q. So far as you have observed in his intercourse with the convicts and with officials, how has his temper been? has it been even or otherwise?
A. As far as I have observed, his temper was always even.
Q. Have you ever been engaged in any other prison?

A. No, sir.
Q. The business of engineering,—is that your trade?
A. Machinist and engineer; yes, sir.
Q. How long have you lived in Jackson?
A. I have been in Jackson three years next July.
Q. Who did you work for before you came into the prison?
A. I worked for the foundry down here about eight months before I went down here, and I put this machine up in this rolling mill up here. That is all the work I have done in town.
Q. By the machine shop, you mean the Jackson foundry and machine company?
A. Yes, sir.
Q. On Mechanic street?
A. On Mechanic street.

Cross-examined by Mr. Webber:

Q. As employe of the prison, how many hours do you spend on duty?
A. My hours are varied. I am often called up through the night. I am here, keep the heating apparatus in order, and if any thing gets out of order at night I am called; my hours vary; generally ten hours, but sometimes a little more, sometimes a little less.
Q. Where do you live?
A. I live on Oak avenue.
Q. How far from here?
A. About one mile.
Q. Do you go home over night?
A. No, sir.
Q. How many assistants have you?
A. I have only what I call an assistant, and then there are two firemen and one boy for keeping the boiler-room clean and in good order.
Q. Are they all convicts?
A. Yes, sir.
Q. Is your assistant a practical engineer?
A. No, sir.
Q. You leave the heating apparatus in his charge when you are away?
A. Yes, sir.
Y. How long has he been acting as your assistant?
A. Since I have been in the prison—eighteen months.
Q. Always found him reliable?
A· Yes, sir.
Q. Do you know how many thermometers there were in the two wings?
A. Yes, sir; one in each wing.
Q. How frequently have you had occasion to examine these during the past winter?
A. I examine them frequently; I go through the wings every evening before I leave, and there are no men in there in the day time, except probably a sick man or two. I examine them probably three or four times a day to see the temperature, so that I can arrange it for the evening. I generally look to it in the evening, before I go home, to see that it is all right.
Q. How does the temperature in the day time compare with the temperature in the night?
A. It is somewhat colder, for the reason that the windows are raised up for

ventilation, and it ranges probably as low as forty-five; somewhere in that neighborhood.

Q. Have you been in the habit of shutting off the steam during the day time?
A. Yes, sir; when the weather permits.
Q. What would be the temperature outside, that would allow you to shut off steam from the wings?
A. When it gets about summer heat.
Q. Give me the degrees.
A. Well, about 65 or 68.
Q If it was 65 or 68 outside, then you would shut off the heat?
A. I would shut off the most of it; I would leave one coil on for men in each wing that were sick.
Q. Suppose the temperature outside stood at forty, would you run steam in the day time in the pipes in the wing, just the same as you would in the night?
A No, sir; I would not; I would probably leave one coil more; for instance, in the night in very severe weather, I would put all the coils on, and in the day time I would leave one coil on, if the weather was moderate, and if the weather was severe—that is winter weather, I would put two coils on. I have to use my judgment, of course, as to the weather.
Q. You speak of seeing men showered,—was it any part of your duty to give that showering attention?
A. Yes, sir; a part of my duty to connect the hose to the pump.
Q. Anything beyond that?
A. No, sir; well, putting on the nozzle, that's a part of my duty.
Q. Did you ever time the showering?
A. I never did.
Q. Who did time the showering when it was done?
A. I have seen Mr. Morris time it; I have seen Mr. Hinkley time it.
Q. Did you ever know of showering being done when it was not timed?
A. I don't think I have to my knowledge.
Q. What is the pressure put on the hose?
A. About ten pounds to the square inch.
Q. How heavy a pressure can you put on?
A. Probably I could put on about fifteen or twenty pounds.
Q Don't you know more definitely than that?
A. I could know, but I have no means of knowing; we have no gauge. I know we have no more, because the hose would not take the water away from the pump.
Q. Then I understand you that the—
A. The pressure on the tanks is ten pounds to the square inch.
Q. Were you at liberty to criticise whatever you saw going on there?
A. Well, I presume so; it is a free country; I can talk if I will. I don't know as I have any right to criticise the administration; I don't know whether I have any business to criticise the administration.
Q. Were you at liberty, under the usages of the prison, to speak outside of the showering which you saw?
A. I presume so, yes, sir.
Q. Were you in the habit of doing so?
A. No, sir; I was not.
Q. Do you remember any particular cases where parties were showered severely?

A. I never saw one showered severely.
Q. You never saw one showered severely?
A. No, sir; what I call severely.
Q. What time did you arrive at your work in the morning?
A. Generally at first bell, before the convicts are out.
Q. What time do you go away at night?
A. At the last bell at night.
Q. And you remain here all through the day?
A. Yes, sir.

Re-direct examination by Mr. Conely:

Q. In the showering which you have seen within the prison, have they been continuous, or has it happened that Mr. Morris would have the showering stopped and then renew it again in some cases?
A. Yes, sir; I saw it frequently. Perhaps Mr. Morris would want some explanation, and they would not give it, and then he would stop to give them an opportunity to make the explanation, and then if they would not do it he would probably give them a little more.

Cross-examination by Mr. Webber:

Q. Do you remember any particular case where you can state the conversation that took place between Mr. Morris and the convict when the showering was going on?
A. I could not state any particular case.

CALVIN T. BEEBE, SWORN FOR MR. MORRIS.

Examined by Mr. Conely:

Q. You have been employed within the prison a good many years?
A. Yes, sir.
Q. How long?
A. Twenty-eight years ago last fall, I think, I came in here.
Q. And your employment has been here at the prison ever since you came here?
A. Yes, sir.
Q. What has been your employment?
A. I was foreman about 22 years, and since I have been forging and repairing.
Q. Upon what contract?
A. First with Pinney, Connable & Co., and then I have been with Webster, and then I commenced with Withington & Cooley, and I have been with them ever since.
Q. How many men do they have on their contract now?
A. I believe it is about 150; I do not know exactly; it does not come under my supervision.
Q. Have you had any occasion at times to observe Mr. Morris' conduct and demeanor within the prison?
A. I have.
Q. So far as you have observed, how have they been?
A. Well, I can explain it in this way: that he has been more lenient, took more pains to have the men contented, and gave them privileges more so than any man has done which has been agent since I commenced; there has been ten or eleven since I commenced.

STATE PRISON INVESTIGATION.

Q. To what extent has Mr. Morris' leniency, that you speak of, interfered with efficiency?

A. Well, I don't know as it has any.

Q. Has it had any visible effect to decrease or increase the product of labor in your opinion?

A. I should think not; of the two, we have thought sometimes that he was a little too lenient and easy with the men; we have not found any fault otherwise than that.

Q. What I want to get at is this: whether you think the kindness which he has manifested has had any effect to lessen the amount of labor that the men have done, or interfered with the good order and firm discipline that is essential to be maintained in such an institution?

A. No; I think not.

Q. Have you ever observed upon the part of Mr. Morris, and if so what indications, of unevenness of temper?

A. I never have seen anything of it at all.

Q. Or of undue severity in particular cases?

A. No, sir.

Q. Or as a general thing?

A. No, sir.

Cross-examination by Mr. Webber:

Q. What opportunities have you had to observe Mr. Morris in his intercourse with the convicts?

A. He goes through the shops very frequently, and I see his intercourse towards the men in the shop; I very often go through the prison here, and I see it there; and sometimes, when there is anything going on up to the hall, like music or speaking, to interest the men, I go up there then; I never have seen anything but what was very kind and respectful to the men; that is the opportunity I have.

Q. What do you mean when you say you sometimes think his treatment is too lenient?

A. I mean by that that he is very often in the habit of giving papers and reading to the men, and getting music here and getting speakers here to interest them, and very often he takes a good deal of pains in that way, and we old men that have been here so long think it is carrying the joke a little too far; it would be as well if he did not do it; we are a little more severe than he is.

Q. In other words, do you think because the men are convicts they should not have newspapers and hear music?

A. I have no objections to hearing music, but I do not believe in setting the men up a great deal higher and ahead of civil citizens, that is murdering and robbing in the highway.

Q. You would have the imprisonment become practically a punishment?

A. I would have it so that men would be sick of coming four or five times; if he got out I would make it so they would hate it instead of like it.

Q. Have you had experience so that you can say whether any larger percentage return, from a lenient treatment, to the prison, where lenient treatment is the rule?

A. I cannot tell anything about whether that is what induces them to come back, but one would naturally suppose that treatment would induce them to come back sooner than severe treatment. That is the only opportunity I have of knowing anything about.

Q. You have no personal intercourse with the convicts in the shops yourself?

A Have been with them all the time; in every shop my business calls me.

Q. Are you foreman?

A. I have been about 22 or 23 years. For six or seven years I have been doing the forging and repairing.

Q. Now, do you sometimes think that at a man don't do a full day's work?

A. Sometimes they don't, I guess; I don't have charge of their days' work now; they did not when I was foreman.

Q. You have not had charge of their days' work at any time under Mr. Morris?

A. Since Mr. Morris has been here?

Q. Yes.

A. No, I think not.

Q. Have you such opportunities as to know what is said and done by the foremen in the shops?

A. Yes, sir; reported to me most every day if a man fails in doing his work, in case he does.

Q Do they ever use any inducement to get man to do a little extra day's work?

A. I have done it, years ago; I guess they over-work.

Q. I have tried to confine it to Mr. Morris' administration?

A. No; there has been no over-pay, I guess,—no pay for extra work since Mr. Morris has been here; it was stopped when Mr. Bingham was in.

Q. Do you know whether there is any rule allowing or prohibiting foremen or contractors from giving extra pay for extra work?

A They are not allowed to pay them for extra work, not even tobacco.

Q. There is a rule prohibiting it?

A. I don't know any such rule, only it has been generally understood they were not to give them any tobacco for over-work.

SANFORD HUNT SWORN FOR MR. MORRIS.

Examined by Mr. Conely:

Q. What is your occupation?

A. Reporter on the Daily Patriot.

Q. Have you been in the habit of visiting the prison a considerable?

A. Yes, sir.

Q For some time past?

A. I think I have been here daily for the last six months.

Q. On Sundays as well as other days?

A. I have been here Sundays, although not every Sunday.

Q. With considerable frequency?

A. Yes, sir; I think for the last two months I have not missed only about two Sundays,

Q What is your object in visiting the prison so often?

A. Well, partially to ascertain anything in the line of news items that may transpire here during the day, and also particularly for the sake of getting acquainted with the convicts.

Q. You have assisted some in the singing at church services, have you not?

A. Yes, sir.

STATE PRISON INVESTIGATION. 291

Q. What has been the nature of your intercourse with the convicts?
A. With many of them it has been intimate.
Q. Have you supplied them with books or papers, or read to them, or anything of that sort?
A. Yes, sir.
Q. That you do, I suppose, because you take an interest in the subject?
A. Yes, sir; I do not do it indiscriminately.
Q. Have you had the opportunity to any extent to learn the feeling of the convicts, from their manner or otherwise, in relation to the administration of Mr. Morris—whether they regard it as severe or otherwise.
A. I think I have.
Q. How have you done that?
A. I have conversed a very little with convicts in the prison upon that subject; but after they were discharged I have conversed with a number of them, and as a rule they seem to think it very lenient.
Q Have you heard the administration of Mr. Morris within the prison commented upon by the people here at Jackson?
A. Yes, sir.
Q. So far as you have heard it, what has been the expression of opinion as to its severity or leniency?
A. The general opinion, so far as I have been able to ascertain it, was that it was lenient—perhaps to a fault.
Q. I suppose you never have witnessed any punishments?
A. Nothing except the wire cap, or something of that kind.
Cross-examination by Mr. Webber:
Q. When you have been making your daily visits, through what part of the prison do you go?
A. I generally pass through the east wing to the hall-master's office, and frequently go into the engine-room, dining-room and other rooms.
Q. Do you go through the shops?
A. I have occasionally; I do not daily.
Q How often do you go through the shops?
A. Not far from once a week.
Q. Do you go alone through the prison?
A. Not very often; no, sir.
Q. Who attends you generally?
A. There is no particular one; sometimes I go with the deputy, sometimes with Mr. Morris, and sometimes with the conductors.
Q. You speak of being intimate with the convicts; how many convicts within the prison are there that you are intimate with?
A. I think more than ten or a dozen that I can call myself intimate with.
Q. How many are there that you are what you may say familiarly acquainted with?
A. Oh, perhaps double that number.
Q. What is the class of convicts that your acquaintance is more particularly confined to?
A. I do not know that I can answer that question; I do not know as they are confined to any particular class, although they are most of them the better behaved convicts.
Q. You have not given any special attention to those that are more troublesome?

A. No special attention; no, sir.

Q. In your passing through the prison are you at liberty to indulge in such conversation with convicts as you choose?

A. I do not regard it so; no, sir.

Q. Are you in the practice of indulging in conversation as you go through?

A. I have conversed with a great many men out of the shops; I never have done it in the shops.

Q. You do this by special permission, or is it a usage of the prison?

A. I do not know whether it is the usage or not; I know I had permission.

Q. How many different convicts do you suppose you have spoken to in the prison during the last six months?

A. I could not give the number.

Q. I mean that have spoken to you also?

A. I could not remember; generally when I speak to a man he speaks back. I speak to a great many men Sundays; sometimes not more than two or three words.

Q. What is the special object of your interesting yourself in these convicts?

A. Well, I have taken a great deal of interest in the subject of prison reform.

Q. And it is by reason of that interest that you are acquainting yourself with convict life?

A. Yes, sir.

Q. How many have you spoken to after their discharge, about the discipline of the prison?

A. I could not answer that; I do not know.

Q. Any considerable number?

A. Oh, not a great many; no, sir.

Q. A dozen or fifteen?

A. I should think there was more than that; it could not be very far from that.

Q. Do you know what their sentence had been; how long they had been here?

A. It varied; some of them two, and five, and other terms; I do not know exactly.

Mr. Bartow:

Q. You stated that in your communications with discharged convicts, I think, they had generally,—or had said that Mr. Morris' treatment generally, was kind and lenient?

A. Yes, sir; I believe I did.

Q. Have you heard them also state individual cases of severity?

A. I do not think I ever did; I do not know unless it was in one case. A man that was discharged from the wagon contract claimed that his day's work was doubled.

Q. You did not hear them speak much of punishment?

A. I heard some of them.

Q. Some of these discharged convicts?

A. Yes, sir.

Q. Have you heard them relate instances of severe punishment?

A. They don't seem to regard it as severe.

Q. They don't?

A. No, sir; one or two said they deserved all they got.

STATE PRISON INVESTIGATION. 293

Re-direct, by Mr. Conely:

Q. A newspaper office is in the habit of receiving a large number of newspapers, by way of exchange, are they not?

A. Yes, sir.

Q. Have you, to any considerable extent, been in the habit of bringing down newspapers received at the Patriot office by way of exchange, and distributing them among the convicts?

A. Yes, sir.

Q. You had that permission, did you?

A. Yes, sir.

Q. You are a member of the Episcopal church here in Jackson?

A. Yes, sir.

Q. And in addition to the work that you have been doing here, at the prison, you have been engaged in some other work connected with the mission church and Sunday school connected with the Episcopal church, in the northwest part of the town?

A. Yes, sir.

Q. You have been in the habit of attending that school Sunday afternoons?

A. Yes, sir.

CAPT. HINKLEY, RE-CALLED FOR MR. MORRIS.

Examined by Mr. Conely:

Q. At the time when men had been showered, have you ever taken pains to ascertain the length of time that intervened from the beginning of the showering to its conclusion?

A. Yes, sir.

Q. What has been the most; what has been the largest time, in your recollection, in which such showering has been done.

A. There had never been a man showered over ten minutes, to my knowledge.

Q. What opportunity, if any, during the showering, has Mr. Morris given the convicts to relent?

A. He has given them all the opportunity that is necessary. He has frequently stopped the showering and asked them if they were willing to go on and do their work and behave themselves, or whatever questions were necessary in that case.

Q. Did you see Rushing showered?

A. I did.

Q. Who held the hose?

A. I think Mr. Morris held the hose.

Q. Do you know whether Mr. Morris struck Rushing at any time during the progress of the showering?

A. He did.

Q. With what?

A. With his cane.

Q. Do you know why it was?

A. Yes, sir.

Q. Why was it?

A. He struck him for setting up such a howl; making so much noise.

Q. Do you know how many times he struck him?

A. Well, it might have been three times.

Q. Did you discover any ill effects from the striking;
A. No, sir, I did not.
Q. Do you know whether Rushing had been lame before that or not?
A. It is my impression that Rushing has been lame ever since I have been in the yard; that it is my impression.
Q. Do you know for what offense Rushing was punished?
A. Yes, sir.
Q What was it?
A. For showing his privates to ladies as they were passing in the wing. He was confined in a cell.
Q. Do you known to what extent the matter was investigated to ascertain whether it was true or not?
A. I know that this report came one day, and it was the next day before he was punished. I know we took particular pains to investigate the case, and find out the truth of the matter.
Q. Did you hear Rushing's statement in regard to the matter?
A. Yes, sir.
Q What was his statement?
A. Well, his statement was that he might have been using the bucket just as they passed.
Q. Was this his statement in relation to it, when first inquired of?
A. The first statement he denied any knowledge of it; doing anything like it; he denied it; I will state right here, perhaps it might throw a little light on the subject; that after we had found out the truth of the statement, he was brought out and taken into the wash-house, he pretended not to know what he was to be punished for. Mr. Morris did not tell him what he was to be punished for. After the punishment commenced, perhaps three or four minutes, Mr. Morris had stopped to question him two or three times, and asked him if he knew what he was being punished for; finally he said that it was probably for using the bucket when ladies were passing, and showing his privates. So that he had in his own mind that he knew was he was being punished for.

Cross-examination by Mr. Webber:

Q. How did you settle the truth of the charge when Rushing denied it?
A. We settled the truth of the charge by getting Mr. Lander's statement from his wife. In the first place, she reported it.
Q. She reported it?
A. She reported it to him, and he reported it to the hall-master, and the hall-master reported it to me. I went over to the shop and saw Mr. Lander, he told me all the circumstances, and I told Mr. Morris about it.
Q. Was Mr. Lander with his wife in passing through the hall?
A. He was with his wife, but he said, some 12 or 14 feet ahead, he was walking along, and she happened to be behind the rest of the party, looking along and looking in the cells, and happened to look up on the first gallery, and just as she got opposite the cell she looked up and he was there.
Q. Mr. Lander did not assume to have any personal knowledge of the subject?
A. Only his wife's statement.
Q. Did you have any personal interview with Mr. Lander on the subject?
A. I did not.
Q. Did Mr. Morris?
A. I do not know whether he did or not.
Q. Did you hear of his having any?

A. No, sir.

Q. Then the truth of the matter was settled by taking Mr. Lander's statement of what his wife told him?

A. Yes, sir; so far as I know.

Q. Now, what assurance had you that she was not actually looking through the door, when he was using the bucket?

A. Well, it is Mr. Lander's statement, that she was simply passing in the hall,—she was passing along the hall,—and he showed his privates, and shook it at her, right close to the cell door, no bucket in his hand.

Q. How long was the showering?

A. He was not showered to exceed ten minutes.

Q. I understand you to say that you never have known of a case of shower-over ten minutes?

A. No, sir.

Q. Do you usually time it yourself?

A. I do.

Q. When the record states, as I observe it does frequently, that they were severely showered, what does that mean?

A. That would be about ten minutes' showering. From eight to ten minutes.

Q. Is there any difference in the severity of the showering, as to the manner of applying the hose, as to the part of the person to which it shall be directed?

A. I presume it would hurt less on the bottom of the feet than it would on the face.

Q. I do not ask for your presumption. I ask for the fact, as to the mode of the punishment?

A. Well, there never has been any particular part of the body to direct the stream on that I have seen.

Q. When you used to punish a man severely by showering, do you not find practically that you can make the punishment more severe by directing to some part of the body than others?

A. I presume it would hurt worse in some parts of the body than others.

Q. I do not ask your presumption; I ask what you find by experience?

A. Yes, sir.

Q. You have found that it does affect them more in some parts of the body than others. Now, in this case, you say that Rushing was put under the hose without telling him what he was to be punished for?

A. Yes, sir.

Q. And that after he had been showered a little while, Mr. Morris inquired of him if he knew what he was being punished for?

A. Yes, sir; gave him a chance to make a statement before he commenced punishing.

Q. Is it a common practice to put men under the hose without informing them what they are to be punished for?

A. No, sir.

Q. It has been mentioned several times that punishment by showering was quite light, and with some men it did not seem to amount to much. I think you stated so when you were on the stand before. Now, what makes them scream so if it is not severe?

A. So as to get rid of the punishment.

Q. Are they any more likely to scream and writhe when the hose is directed to one part of the body more than another?

A. I don't know that they are; some will commence making a fuss before there is any punishment given.

Q. What part of the body do you find most vulnerable in the use of the hose?

A. Well, I cannot answer that, but I suppose around the body would be worse than on the legs.

Q. Your practical experience?

A. Yes, sir; as far as I can tell you.

Q. You have seen a great many men showered?

A. Yes, sir.

Q. And must have some knowledge on the subject from your experience?

A. Yes, sir; it would hurt a man more about the bowels than it would about the legs.

Q. How long a time is the stream directed ever to any particular part of the body, the stream playing right along?

A. Well, I don't know as I ever saw it directed on any one particular part of the body for any length of time. It is generally showering all over.

Q. Is the stream directed directly against the person, or is it above them and falls on them in a spray?

A. Directly against the person.

Q. What kind of a noise did Rushing make when he was showered?

A. He made an outcry; I do not know that I could describe the kind of noise that he made.

Q. As though he was in pain?

A. As though he would like to get rid of the punishment.

Q. What kind of a cane was this that Mr. Morris struck him with?

A. It was a common walking cane.

Q. Hickory?

A. I could not tell; I presume likely hickory; most of our canes are hickory.

Mr. *Morris*—I will produce it if it is necessary.

Q. Did he say any thing to him before he struck him?

A. Yes, sir.

Q. What did he tell him?

A. He told him to stop his noise or hollering.

Q. And then because he did not stop he struck him?

A. Yes, sir.

Q. Did you notice where the blows hit him?

A. They hit him on the side of the leg here somewhere. I don't know but they hit him on the stern.

Q. Can you give the exact words that Mr. Morris used to him at the time, or just before he struck him?

A. No, sir; I don't know as I can; my impression would be that he told him to stop his noise.

Q. You have no recollection of the words?

A. I could not tell the words exactly.

Q. Did he stop his noise after he was struck?

A. He did.

Q. Was there any showering done after he received the blows?

A. I think there was.

Q. Did he receive all three of those blows at one time, that is, one following right after another?

A. Yes, sir.

STATE PRISON INVESTIGATION.

Q. There was no showering intervened between the blows?
A. No, sir.
Q. Did he make any outcry while being showered after having received the blows?
A. No, sir.
Q. Now, do not you know that the conduct record shows frequent entries of showering fifteen and twenty minutes each?
A. No, sir.
Q. Is it always the case that either you or Mr. Morris holds a watch and times the showering?
A. Not always the case; a very light punishment the watch would not be held.
Q. When you speak of ten minutes showering, do you mean ten minutes actual flowing of the stream, or ten minutes including the intermissions?
A. That includes the intermissions.
Q. Are you in the habit of making your record show the length of time the water has flowed when showering?
A. It is the habit, yes, sir; there is cases there where the time is not put down.
Q. Have you witnessed all the punishments by showering that have been administered since you have been deputy?
A. Yes, sir; I have been absent two days in the time, and there was no punishment during those two days while I was absent; no record of it.
Q. Has there been any flogging since you have been here?
A. Yes, sir.
Q. With the whip or the strap?
A. Strap.
Q. I find an entry under date of October, 1874, where George Hall was tied up and given ten lashes?
A. That was a mistake; that was the strap; I put down lashes when I first commenced the entries there, and I found out it made a difference as to whether it was "strap" or "lash;" it is strap in every case; I never have seen a whip since I have been here.
Q. I see under date of October 20, 1874, where Nathan Ross is charged with "having borrowed a knife and traded it off with John Seaton for to get one of his own, and being a lover of tobacco, he traded the knife again with Smith for some contract tobacco; that Ross denied all knowledge of the transaction, but finally owned up after being well wattered." Was it the custom,—has it been the custom since you have been here to put men under the hose to induce them to own up?
A. Yes, sir; that is if the facts are traced to them, and we know to a certainty that they do know it.
Q. When you know that they have knowledge, that is, when you make up your mind that they have knowledge concerning some transaction which they deny, it is the practice to put them under the hose in order to induce them to tell what you have concluded they know?
A. Yes, sir.
Q. When you get their statement, made after being "well watered," as this record states, do you regard that statement reliable so that you can act under it?
A. Yes, sir.
Q. Do men ever complain of cold from this watering?

A. Yes, sir; they appear cold; I do not know as I ever heard them complain of being cold.

Q. When men are punished by showering in what do you consider the punishment to consist; in the cold, in the shock, or how otherwise?

A. Well, I suppose it consists in both.

Q. What is the particular in which the severity consists in your judgment, from your knowledge and experience?

A. I should think probably in the shock.

Q. Do you know the reason why the fact of those three blows given to Rushing with the cane were not entered upon the record as a part of the punishment?

A. No, sir; it was through neglect of mine; it was no fault of Mr. Morris.

Q. Mr. Morris knew that the blows were given?

A. Yes, sir.

Q. And he has the supervision of the making up of this record, has he not?

A. No, sir; not that part of it there.

Q. Has he not had the supervision of the record since the date when he ceased to make it up himself?

A. He has had a chance to look at the book and examine.

Q. Did you ever know another instance where a man had been struck to make him stop his noise or for any other purpose while being showered?

A. There have been other cases, but I cannot call them to mind in particular.

Q. In such cases has the fact of such striking been put down on the record as any part of the punishment?

A. No, sir; not to my knowledge.

Q. Did you ever strike any one to make him stop his noise while watering?

A. I don't think I ever did; I don't do the punishing generally.

Q. How many such cases do you remember where Mr. Morris has used his cane to have them stop their noise while they were being showered?

A. I cannot think of more than one or two cases, and I could not call to mind who they were.

Q. I think you said yesterday that Mr. Morris was uniformly free from anger in administering punishments?

A. Yes, sir.

Q. Do you wish to be understood that he has taken his cane, and without any anger, struck men to make them stop their noise while showering?

A. Well, I punish my children without being angry, very often—strike them with a strap. I did not consider that he was angry at any of these times. I never saw him angry when he was punishing a man.

Q. Did you ever know of a stream of water directed to the mouth of a convict to prevent his making his noise?

A. Yes, sir; I have seen it directed all over their person—to the mouth, or anywhere else, wherever it might hit.

Q. It can be carried to any particular part, in the will of the operator?

A. Yes, sir.

Q. Then, I ask you again, have you known, for any purpose, a stream of water directed at the mouth?

A. No, sir; I have known it to be directed, not at the mouth, but at any part. A person has a chance to dodge the stream there, and we generally don't put the stream on to the face.

Q. Have you ever known the stream to be directed to the mouth?

STATE PRISON INVESTIGATION. 299

A. Yes, sir.
Q Was that at a time when they were making a noise?
A. Well, I don't recollect any particular time when they were making a noise and the stream was put on to their mouth.
Q Do you remember the punishment of Michael Shannon, on the 20th of February last?
A. Yes, sir
Q I notice that the record states that he was given ten lashes, and the word "lashes" is erased with pencil, and the word "strap" written in.
A. "Straps" is correct.
Q. It was done with a strap?
A. Yes, sir.
Q. Do you know when the change was made in the record?
A. It was made—well, a short time ago; I guess it was since this investigation commenced.
Q. You think this change was made since the investigation commenced?
A. Yes, it was made by my order.
Q. But it is made by Mr. Morris, isn't it? [Showing witness book.]
A. That is made by Mr. Morris, yes, sir; but I guess you will find one other case there, of Thomas.
Q. How many straps have you ever known to be administered to a convict?
A. Fifty.
Q. At one time?
A. Yes, sir.
Q. To more than one?
A. No, sir.
Q. Is that the highest number?
A. That is the highest number.
Q. That was on the case of Benjamin Thomas, on the sixth of March last?
A. Yes, sir.
Q. How long after his offense before that punishment was inflicted?
A. I think it was the next day; I am not sure but it was the same day in the afternoon.
Q. I notice that in addition to the fifty straps he had ten days on bread and water?
A. Yes, sir.
Q. Was that in a bare cell or in his own cell?
A In his own cell.
Q Did he receive the straps before he was locked up for the ten days?
A. Yes, sir.
Q. Do you know whether the attention of the prison physician was called to him after receiving the straps?
A. I do not know.
Q. Did you examine his person after receiving the straps to see what the effect was of that punishment?
A. I examined while he was being whipped and while he was putting his clothes on.
Q. Was the skin broken?
A. No, sir.
Q Do you know whether any of the skin was killed or sloughed off in consequence of those blows; did you examine to see?
A. No, sir.

Q. Do you know whether the effect of that punishment was such as to disable him for work?
A. I know that it was not.
Q. He could have gone to work if you had felt disposed to send him to work?
A. Yes, sir.
Q. How old a man is this Thomas?
A. I should think he was a man between 30 and 35.
Q. What part of the body were these straps administered?
A. On his back and shoulders down.
Q Entirely on the back part of his person?
A. Yes, sir.
Q. Has there been any change in the general manner of punishment since you came in the prison?
A. I could not say.
Q Is not locking in the bare cell resorted to more frequently than it was when you came?
A. Yes, sir, I think it is.
Q. Practically how do you find it to work as an inducement to better behavior?
A. It works well in a great many cases.

Re-direct examination, by Mr. Conely:
Q. What contract is this man on now?
A. On the Withington & Cooley contract.
Q. How long has he been on that contract?
A. Since the 16th of last month.
Q. What contract was he on before that?
A. He was on the cigar contract.
Q. Do you know why he was changed?
A. Yes, sir.
Q. Why?
A. The foreman said he would not work in the shop with him. In justice to the prison authorities,—I do not know as I have a right to dictate, but we should show that these men that are chilled have a right to warm themselves—that is, they are ordered to go and get warm.
Q. State what you know about that?
Mr. Bartow—We have that evidence.
Mr. Conely—There is probably no dispute about that.
Q. Is the opportunity given them to go either to the hospital or to the boiler room?
A. Yes, sir.

Mr. Webber:
Q. How long a time is given them to warm up?
A. We give them all the time they need. We do not limit the time.

CLARK COLE SWORN FOR MR. MORRIS.

Examined by Mr. Conely:
Q. Were you present at the whipping of Thurston?
A. I was, sir.
Q. What is your business?
A. At the present time I am keeping the big gate.
Q. What was your business at the time that Thurston was punished?
A. I was keeper in one of the shops.

Q. How long have you been connected with the prison.
A. Well, it is about 30 years, I think.
Q. I want to barely ask of you one or two questions connected with that punishment. How many blows were given?
A. Well, I did not count them. I judged them to be between thirty and forty blows.
Q. Did you observe any ill effect from the punishment that was given Thurston?
A. I did not.

Cross-examination by Mr. Webber:

Q. How near did you stand to where Thurston stood while he was being punished?
A. I could not state; within ten or fifteen feet.
Q. Were you then acting as a keeper?
A. Yes, sir.
Q. That was his first or second whipping?
A. That was the only whipping I saw him get.
Q. Did you know of his having another one about a week or ten days from that, either before or after?
A. I did not.
Q. What time of day was this?
A. This was at night, after we got through locking up, about six or half past six.
Q. Thurston was stripped naked?
A. His clothes were taken off with the exception of his pants.
Q. His pants were left on?
A. Yes, sir.
Q. And on what part of the body was the punishment administered?
A. Around the shoulders mostly, I should judge.
Q. Do you not know?
A. Well, there were marks in other portions of his body; probably around the sides.
Q. Across his abdomen, here?
A. I did not notice any in that particular point.
Q. Did you notice any on his breast?
A. I think there was some that came around on his breast.
Q. Did you step up to look at his body after the whipping was concluded?
A. I did not go very near him.
Q. Did you take any particular observation to see?
A. I looked at him as he stood there.
Q. Did you time the punishment?
A. No, sir.
Q. You did not count the blows?
A. I did not count them.
Q. How many intermissions were there, if any, in that punishment?
A. Well, there was two or three; three I guess.
Q. How long were those intermissions?
A. I could not tell exactly; Mr. Morris talked to him after he struck him eight or ten blows. He talked to him, and he did not seem to be very penitent and he applied the rod again.

Q. Then when he spoke to him at the second intermission, how did seem to appear?

A. Well, he said he wasn't so bad a man as they took him to be. Think that was the remark that he made. The keepers were all standing around there,—most of the shop keepers,—and we were talking among ourselves, and Mr. Morris at the same time was talking to him, and I could not distinctly understand what he did say.

Q. Can you remember any thing that Mr. Morris said to him? any particular expression?

A. Well I don't bring just to mind particularly just now; it was in relation to a knife that he had to use on the person of Mr. Morris.

Q. That knife had been already taken away, had it not?

A. He took it away before we started to go down to the shop to punish him.

Q. Then Mr. Morris, you say, spoke to him about that knife after he got down there?

A. In regard to his intent, what he was going to do with the knife, and the consequences of having such a knife about him.

Q. You think Mr. Morris asked him what he intended to do with the knife at those intermissions?

A. I think he asked him in the entry here where we started with him to go down to the shop. I think he asked him what he intended to do with the knife.

Q. I am talking about what took place after the punishment commenced. Do you remember any thing that was said in the first intermission of the punishment?

A. I never have charged my mind with it since, but I know he was talking to him about this transaction; he mentioned something about the knife and the characteristics of a man using such threats.

Q. Can you recollect any of the terms that Mr. Morris used in characterizing a man that would have such a knife.

A. I do not bring any thing particularly to mind now what he said in regard to that.

Q. Do not you know that at the first intermission Thurston begged for mercy and promised that he would behave himself thereafter?

A. He did towards the last of his punishment.

Q. Did not he at the first intermission?

A. I think he made some remarks that he would behave himself; I think that was the remark that he made: "I can behave myself." I think that was the remark that he made. "I think I can behave myself." I think that was the remark that he made.

Q. Are you sure that was the remark?

A. I ain't positive; I never made any record of it. I think that is the remark that he made.

Q. Then at the third intermission what did he say?

A. Well, he requested Mr. Morris to stop punishing him.

Q. And made promises of better behavior?

A. Yes, sir.

Q. Did the punishment then stop?

A. Yes, sir.

Q. No more punishment after that?

A. No, sir; I did not witness any more after that.

Q. Then there really was two intermissions in the punishment only?

STATE PRISON INVESTIGATION. 303

A. Well, short intermissions; Mr. Morris talked to him twice or three times, I think.

Q. When Mr. Morris stopped whipping him to speak to him, did he step up nearer to him to speak to him?

A. Nearer to Thurston?

Q. Nearer to Thurston.

A. I think he stood in about the same position. He might have stepped up to him.

Q. He spoke loud enough so that you could hear all that he said, if you had given attention?

A. Mr. Morris?

Q. Yes.

A. I do not know that he did; we were a'l talking there among ourselves, and Mr. Morris was talking.

Q. The keepers were talking among themselves?

A. Yes, sir.

Q. So that they were not giving strict attention to what Mr. Morris was doing?

A. We stood there looking on and making observations, and did not pay much attention to what Mr. Morris was saying, only he told him that he could not tolerate such actions. I heard that remark made to him by Mr. Morris.

F. S. CLARK RECALLED.

Examined by Mr. Conely:

Q. I want to ask you whether Mr. Morris has, to any extent, made it his habit to consult with you in relation to the matter of punishment in extreme cases, or difficult cases?

A. He does very often. I will not say in all cases; he does in very many cases.

Q. Are you able to say that the dispensation or punishment is, with him, a matter of considerable deliberation?

A. Well, I think it is, as a rule.

Crosss-examination by Mr. Webber:

Q. What leads you to that opinion?

A. Why, observation from day to day.

Q. Does he not often receive information of offenses against the prison discipline, and cause punishment to be inflicted, without coming in the office at all after he gets the information?

A. Yes, sir.

Q. In such cases you have no opportunity to know whether there is deliberation?

A. No, sir.

Q. Do you mean to be understood that Mr. Morris is in the habit, when this information is brought to him in the office, of advising with you as to what would be the proper punishment in that particular case?

A. He very often does that, and I think his punishments are generally administered after mature deliberation, and the examination of the case.

Q. Has the extent of the punishment usually been settled before he leaves the office?

A. No, sir; I cannot say that it has.

Q. Is the character of the punishment to be inflicted settled before he leaves the office?

A. I cannot say that it is thoroughly settled; definitely settled, whether it is best to punish the man with the hose, the strap, or something other. He thinks the case requires a certain kind of punishment.

Mr. Conely—This is all the testimony that we shall ask the committee to hear at Jackson, unless there should be something developed to-day that would make it necessary.

WILLIAM M'DONALD, CONVICT, PRODUCED AT THE REQUEST OF THE COMMITTEE, AND SWORN.

Mr. Morris—I have only this to say to you, William, under the circumstances: knowing you are a convict and under my charge here, I do not want you to take the stand here with any sort of fear or intimidation of any treatment you may hereafter receive at my hands.

The Witness—You need not go to the trouble of telling me that, sir; that is something I do not fear of man. I know that I have got to face you here for six years more, but still the truth shall come.

Mr. Nelson—I would like to state that this is a majority of the committee, not the entire committee, that calls this witness.

Mr. Bartow—While that is true—that can appear in the report of course—this is the decision of the committee just as much as an act of the Legislature is an act, although it is opposed by some of them.

Mr. Nelson—I wish it to appear that it is done by a majority of the committee, and not by the whole.

Mr. Morris—Under the circumstances, I guess I will retire.

The Witness—I would rather that Mr. Morris would be present and hear all that I have to say as far as I am concerned.

Mr. Conely—You may as well retire, Mr. Morris.

[Mr. Morris here retired from the room.]

Witness examined by Mr. Webber:

Q. Where were you born?

A. I was born, sir, in county Galway, Ireland; I believe it is on the prison books as in Springfield, Mass., but I am under oath now.

Q. What was your age when you came to America?

A. Well, I was very young; I could not say what it was.

Q. And in what place did you first settle?

A. Springfield, Mass.

Q. How long did you remain in Massachusetts?

A. I remained there, sir, as near as I can remember, until I was between 13 and 14 years old.

Q. And then to what place did you remove?

A. Well, I was of a rambling nature and took to the water and went to sea.

Q. At what time did you first come to Michigan?

A. I came to Michigan, I think it was—to stay in Michigan—to settle in Michigan?

Q. Yes, to stay in Michigan?

A. Not until 1865 or 1866.

Q. In what part of the State did you then settle?

A. Monroe.

Q. From what place were you sent here?

A. Monroe.

Q. On what charge?

STATE PRISON INVESTIGATION. 305

A. I was a butcher there; I had a license, and was charged with taking three head of cattle—larceny.
Q. At what time were you sent here?
A. I was sent here—I arrived here on the 14th day of September, 1869, the last time.
Q. What was the term of your last sentence?
A. Fifteen years.
Q. You say you were sentenced for fifteen years?
A. I do.
Q. Have you ever been punished?
A. I have.
Q. In the prison?
A. I have, sir.
Q. What punishments have been inflicted on you?
A. Under whose administration?
Q. Under Mr. Morris?
A. I was tied on the cross.
Q. Do you remember when?
A. I do, well.
Q. Give me the date.
A. I was tied on the cross on the 6th day of July, 1871.
Q. By whom were you placed there?
A. I was placed there by deputy Martin.
Q. Was any one else present assisting him?
A. At the time I was first put up?
Q. Yes.
A None but him and me alone.
Q. For what offense were you placed there?
A. Well, sir, I am under oath now, and I cannot tell you; I will tell you the circumstances that took place, and you can come to whatever conclusion you please.
Q. State the circumstances.
A. I was taken sick, which I think the hospital records will show, if they ain't destroyed, about the middle of June, with the bloody diarrhea, and lay in the hospital, bed-fast there, until the 3d day of July; it was so near the 4th, and I was anxious to get out of the hospital to get down to see the performance in the dining-room, that I left the hospital before I was really able; and it was the habit then, if a man was able to get out of the hospital and get around, he was able to work, that is, I thought that way; I was working in the cigar shop, where my work was light, and I went to the cigar shop the next day after the fourth, and fell short of my day's work, the task that was allowed me, thirty-three cigars; the keeper comes to me the next morning, and said he, "McDonald, you did not do your day's work yesterday;" here this 33 cigars—I only had it from a convict—I did not count my day's work; but the man that counted it come to me the next day, and tells me that it fell short 33 cigars—I do not swear positively to this number—I think Mr. Hollingsworth's books will show; the keeper comes to me, and says he, "McDonald you do not do your day's work yet;" says I, "sir I made all I could; I am just out of bed, and I am not able; I worked from bell to bell, faithfully and diligently;" says he, "that makes no difference; you must do it;" says I, "I will if I can; I shall work to-day from bell to bell, and if I don't do my day's work, send in and tell them to hold

39

on until I get through; this was what took place—the conversation between me and the keeper; well, he stood and talked awhile, and finally I told him to go away and let me alone; says I, "I am sick; I am doing the best I can;" and the words that we had after that—that was the substance of it, I cannot recollect, but there is other men in the prison that was sitting there listening to the whole thing; he sent for the deputy, this deputy Martin, and the deputy comes up to me, and says he, "Mac. put on your coat and come with me;" I done so; he took me into the hall in the central building—the old hall; took his bludgeon down--the cane—and says he, "come on in there ;" I went in according to directions, and he took me into the upper solitary, in No. 13, if I remember ; I think it was No. 13, but I would not be positive ; I think there was 24 cells in there, I would not be positive ; I think it was 13 that he took me in ; opened the door and there I seen a cross ; I should judge the top of it was about six feet eight inches high, the top, or perpendicular part of the cross ; he told me to turn my back to it ; he held the club in his hand, and says he "turn your back to it ;" I turned my back to it, and on the left arm—there was two straps, one on each arm, and on the left arm of the cross there was a strap that run around it twice ; well, he told me to put my left hand up first ; got the arm to the left arm of the cross and rove the strap through and pulled it tight ; I knew the kind of man he was, and I knew there was no kind of use of saying anything that it hurt me, because I thought he would take a delight in it to know that a person was in misery ; he fastened my other arm, but the other strap was not so long, it did not go around only once, consequently he could not get so tight a purchase on it ; he left me and went down, and I do not exactly know the time—this was, I recollect, between 8 and 9 o'clock in the morning of the 6th of July ; sometime in the forenoon he brought Mr. Morris up ; they both came up together ; and Mr. Morris came up and says he "you are here ;" this was about the conversation, I could not recollect all that took place there—says he, "you are here," said I "yes, sir," something to that effect, and he went on and said—asked me several questions, and I was about to tell him the misery I was in, and says he "Oh, shut up, who is keeper, you or Mr. Wing ?" well, it was not granted me the privilege of telling him the misery I was in, and he talked to me awhile and went away ; sometime in the course of the day he brings a visitor, a freeman,—I did not know the gentleman, I never seen him before nor since, that I know of ; he steps up to the small door—there was an iron door inside of a wooden door ; there was a shutter for the iron door, and there was a hole, small hole, I should judge about four inches square, with a slide in it—he steps up to the small door.; he kind of grabbs it in this way, (illustrating), and he points in this fashion ; I think he asked me " what is your charge ?" this was asked, whether it was that time or not ; I seen what he meant, I understood his meaning ; says I "thieving ;" " behold," he points to this visitor, says he—he may be here in the crowd for all I know—he pointed to me and showed him, as if it was a child pointing to a toy—something he felt tickled over, showing the visitor me on the cross; the man, whoever he was, whirled around in disgust, and walked away; he could not look at it ; he stuck his head in, and says he, "I would rather do any work in the yard than stand on that cross half an hour;" said I, " so would I;" I staid there until night; this was Mr. Morris that I am speaking of coming up to the door; I staid there until night; till after the bell had rung, and Mr. Martin came up and untied me ; when he took off the straps, said I to him, " hold on a minute;" when my arms dropped, the first the blood rushed to my head—the first that I felt of this misery, when put on the cross, was a kind of tingling sensation in my fingers; this is the position I was in [showing], I was standing on the balls of my feet, and my arms extended in this way, my arms drawn out, and by the strap being drawn tight, this tingling in my fingers, and gradually it came up into my arm and into my body, which caused a numbness; after it got up into my body I could not feel the pain much, but I was in misery.

Q. What time did you say they took you off?

A. It was after the bell at night. When he let my arms drop the blood rushed into my head and I was dizzy, and braced myself against the cross. Says I, "Hold on a minute and let me get a little steady." He got behind me and he pushed me out; I went through the door—there was a gallery around the solitary and surrounded by a railing; as I went out he came up and gave me a shove, and that railing saved me from going down to the lower floor; he came up to me and gave me another shove, and took me to the door—it was a double door, one was open and the other shut; I think it fastened in some way; I come to the door and staggered out on to the platform, and there were iron stairs and an iron bannister that led down into the old solitary building; they were then using it for cutting meat up, packing barrels away, and had scales in it, and one thing and another; I got on to the railing; I could not use either hand; could not get my hand to my head, they was so numb; I fell on that railing and kind of slid down to the bottom of the stairs; by the time I got down there he was after me and gave me another shove until he shoved me out; by that time my head began to get steady and the blood to circulate so that I could keep my feet; by the time I got to the door of the east wing I could walk; there was a guard in there by the name of Henry; he was doing guard duty; I do not know whether his surname was Henry, but they called him Henry or McHenry; and I went down the hall and he comes up to me; says he, "Mac, what is the matter?" "Well," says I, "I have been on the cross; I have just got off the cross; let me sit down here a minute, I cannot walk; let me sit down here until my head gets steady." Says he, "Certainly, sit down." I sat down on the stone, the old stone steps leading into the gallery of the west wing; I sat down and he sat by me there somewheres, I should judge about five minutes; and, says he, "sit there until you get ready to go." And I sat there, and finally says I, "I will go to my cell now;" he started with me and goes up and unlocks the door; he throws the cot down that I sleep on, and goes and gets me a drink of water—I asked him to—and I threw myself down on the cot without taking my clothes off; I could not take my clothes off; my fingers were so numb and stiff that I could not unbutton my clothes; I lay there until about twelve o'clock at night, and by that time, rolling, I got the blood circulating in that arm so that I could handle them to unbutton; but I did not take off my clothes; I came out in the morning with my company and went to the dining-room and got my breakfast; went from the dining-room into the hall and found Mr. Morris sitting on the hall-master's table; I goes up to him and tells him the condition I was in; he laughs at me. "But," says I, "I want something done for that arm; some liniment put on it, or something." Says he, "go to the hospital and tell the steward that I sent you up there to have him rub some liniment on your arm, or something;" I went up to the hospital, and the steward he rubbed some liniment on it, and I came down. "Now," says he, "go to work;" says I, "my arm is numb; there is no feeling in my fingers;" and I drawed it out that way and showed it to him; and it was dark, kind of blue, as if you bind something around your finger and the blood settles in the end of it; well, I forget his answer, but he told me, at least, to sit down; I sat down on a bench, and sat there until the doctor come; I believe the doctor that was here then was Dr. Smith; I think it was; this was in 1871; you can easily ascertain by the hospital record. He says, " Mr. Martin, take this man up to the hospital and see what ails him."

Q. Who said that?

A. Mr. Morris; Mr. Martin took me up to the hospital and said nothing about my being on the cross the day before or anything of the kind; I goes up to the doctor, and says he, " Doctor, examine this man and see what ails him." The doctor looked at me, and says he, "All I can see about him is a little unnatural heat in his arm." " Come on, Mac," says he; I followed him down; Martin goes down to the Agent and he says, " The doctor says there is nothing the matter with this man; " says he, " there is nothing the matter with him;" " Well," says he, "go to the shop;" I started to put this coat on—this is the same coat, I have worn it ever since he has been here—I was pulling it up, or a man went to assist me to put the coat on, and he turned around and says he, " Put him on the cross again, Mr. Lane."

Q. Who directed that?

A. Mr. Morris directed Mr. Lane; says he, "Put him on the cross again." Mr. Lane starts with me and takes me up into the solitary and puts me on the cross. This is Mr. David Lane here in town. He took me up to the cross and put me on it, and when he put me on he was humane enough for to take my shirt sleeves,—that is, the straps,—around in a way that it did not bind my flesh on the wrists. Well, I was not in so much misery, and, in fact, then that arm had got beyond that. I staid there from the time the doctor came in the morning until,—well, the bell rung as I was going into my cell. Recollect that this was the 7th of July that Mr. Lane put me on the cross.

Q. That was the next day.

A. Yes, sir, that was the next day. I went to my cell and came out the same as usual with my company in the morning; went to the dining-room and got my breakfast and went to the hall and sat down on a bench. Mr. Morris came down the stairs and he walks up. I was sitting on a bench in about this fashion. Mr. Morris walks up and looks at me,—" Ah, you cannot get that down here,"—and walks away. I did not speak to him; did not make any reply. Mr. Lane in an hour or so,—I would not be positive as to the time,—comes to me and says he, " Mac., go to the hospital." I started and went up to the hospital; I went up to the doctor; he looked at me and said, " go and sit down." I come out the next day,—I would not be positive whether the next day was the Sabbath or not,—but the next day I walked out from the cell and went to the hall again, and says Lane, as soon as he saw me, " Go to the hospital, Mac." I went up. The doctor saw me and looked at me and says he, " Go and sit down." I went and sat down. This was repeated three or four days, until the fourth day, I think, he was busy writing a prescription. The hospital,—the doctor's stand,—was then surrounded by a sort of banister about so high [showing.] I goes up, being the next man to him, and puts my hand on the banister. While he was writing he discovered a kind of disagreeable smell; says he—he told me—" Pugh, what smells so?" and looked around at my hand; says he, "Pugh, put some carbolic wash on that hand; it stinks!" The steward then noticed my hand and examined it. The steward went according to directions and put the carbolic wash on. He got this,—this small round box that is filled with pins,—the pins project with a spring, and they filled that with croton oil,—I think they called it croton oil,—and went to puncturing it with this croton oil; but they did not raise a blister, only when they got up here, outside of the breast and on the back. They then practiced that, I should judge, for over a month without any effect whatever. Well, the hand began to smell bad; in fact it was so bad that I could not sit in the dining-room; a man could not sit by me. I have went into the wash-room when the thermometer was below zero, and the men would rush out of the wash-house and the smell would cause them to spew as quick as they got out. This is known all over the prison. I went to Mr. Morris, and says I, "Mr. Morris, the men are finding fault with my sitting in the dining-room." Says he, "Is that so, Mac.?" Says I, "Yes, sir." "Well," says he, "then don't go near there." I went out; I used to sit out in the yard while the men would go in and eat, and then I would go in and get my meals after they went out. It was so bad that a man could not stay with me, using this carbolic wash all the time. Well, that went on so for quite a while. I used to go to the doctor for a quite a while, and finally says he, "McDonald, there is no use in your coming to me any more. All I have to say is this: I have done for you every thing in my power, and I cannot do any more, and I will tell you you cannot do any thing for that arm unless you can get something to strengthen it, and I do not know of any thing that will do it." So I kept using this carbolic wash on it. I went and got weak lye, and took about one-third lye and water and washed it, just, you know, so that it felt slippery. That did not seem to do any good; that did not affect the smell in any wise, nor any thing else. The carbolic wash would drive the smell away while it was on, that is, for a short time, and it has been going on just so until this Mr. Tuttle come here. I was taken down very low and sick and bad, and felt it working into my body. My breast is bad here yet. And I meets him here in the hall; I was crawling out of my cell; I weighed 102 pounds, and my natural weight is 145. He comes up to me and says he, "what is the matter?" I told him "I do not know what is the matter; I do not feel sick, but," says I, "I feel just as if I was dropping away." Sometimes the blood would rush into my head and I would have to whirl over; if I threw my head over this way when the barbers were shaving me I would have to throw it around this way. "Well," says he, "come up to the hospital." This was the first conversation I ever had with the doctor. I goes up to the hospital, and says he, "Let me see your hand." I took the cloth off, I undone it. Mr. Tuttle and Mr. Croker, the old hospital keeper, were sitting there, and Dr. Tuttle turns around to him and says he, "this is awful, Mr. Croker." I do not know what his reply was, but he shook his head and kind of turns around. Mr. Croker could never look at it; he told me often "It is a thing I don't want to see." Says he, "I cannot look at it." There was a man in the hospital by the name of Thurston.

Q. What was his first name?

A. I do not know; I think he was here some 17 years.

Mr. Wood—David.

Mr. Conley—A freeman or a convict?

A. He was a convict; I do not know what conversation took place between him and Mr. Thurston and Mr. Croker; but finally Thurston comes to me and says he, "Mac, do you want that arm cured?" Says I, "I would do anything to have it—it—anything done with it to have it cured." Well, says he, "The doctor has given me charge of this, and I am going to cure this arm." "Very well," said I, "you can do so." "Well," says he, "submit to my treatment, don't growl or find any fault, and I will fetch it out all right." "Very well," said I, "proceed." There is a man here now that was a witness to the whole thing; he goes and gets a pail of hot water, boiling water, and he gets a little mustard; he takes me into a little place that was used as a dispensary,—this old hospital was all in one room; I could not describe the place, but he takes me off into this northeast corner of the hospital and begun his operations; there is a man in here that saw him; I believe he told me the other day that he even felt the temperature of the water; said he, "put your arm in there." I did, but when putting the other arm in with it, I felt the heat before, and I would not put it in; he gets a rag with this water and sulphur and places the rag on my arm and puts the water on it.

Mr. Nelson—Do you mean mustard or sulphur?

A. I am wrong, yes, sir; it was mustard and water; he puts the rag on top of my arm, and it was saturated with this mustard and water and raised a blister; I am under oath and I can positively swear with a clear conscience that I believe that this is all that saved my life; the blister that was started on my arm it run, and there was chunks fell out of it; it run and has been running until a year and a half, until that has saturated clothes for the last year and a half with the exceptions of six weeks that I have had to change them every morning; this hot water, recollect, the rag was placed on top of the arm and pressed down until it raised a blister, until it burned the flesh, and in fact there was chunks of flesh fell out of it the size of a silver dollar; the conversation that took place, as I said before, between the doctor and this Thurston I know nothing about, only he said the doctor had given him full charge of this arm; but I do say one thing that I heard the doctor tell him; says he, "don't aggravate that arm any more."

Q. That was Dr. Tuttle?

A. Yes, sir; that was Dr. Tuttle. Says he, "don't aggravate that arm any more;" says he, "there is no life in that." I did not catch the rest of it. This was what Dr. Tuttle said to Thurston. Thurston then got a little bran-bag and opened my fingers out, [shows his hand,] and drawed the fingers out and placed the bran in there, and gets another bag and puts it under my arm here; now, says he, "I have got it running, I am going to do the best I can; your shoulder is stove in," says he, "like an old sweeneyed horse," something to that effect. Well, he kept on until my health began to improve. I could not get a passage; I lay there in the hospital for 22 days, right on my back, until this matter had discharge so that it would relieve me. I do not know what ailed me; I do not know that it is down on the hospital record. I was not sick; I could not tell what ailed me. May be I was in such misery that I did not know what did ail me. It kept on so, and it has been running since. Well, gentlemen, there has since that occurrence, since I was here before the board of inspectors, there is one thing that I wish to state and that is this: there was three witnesses came out here,—I cannot swear to this, but I read it in the papers,—I suppose it is all right,—and one states that he furnished me lye and potash to put on this arm. You know that lye and potash will leave a mark; it will be apt to. I think, but won't be positive, that the paper stated further, that this man furnished me lime and potash, or something to that effect, shortly after this took place. Now this man's name is LaMountain. I wish that this committee would be kind enough to find out the time that this man came here, and then refer to the time that this arm was hurt, and see how his oath will corroborate with the time this thing took place.

Mr. Bartow—Do you say that it was not true?

A. His statement? I positively say that this is a man that I did not know anything about; he come to me at the time it was stated he tried to get out;

me come to me, and says he, "have you got a piece of brass?" says I, "what kind?" "One about four inches long," I think he said, "an inch and a half wide, and one-eighth of an inch thick. I said "no, you will find an old file or something." Says I, "what do you want for." He gave me some answer that I could not recollect what it was now. He told me so, and that was the last I had heard; I did know the man; I never seen him, never spoke to him but that time. I might have spoke to him, but did not know him, until after I got to work in the cabinet shop awhile ago. Well, now, gentlemen, this man, I understand, has been getting men into trouble right along by lying on them. He has tried to make his escape, so I understand, and furthermore, there has been other men in the shop that he has got into trouble for stealing money for them, and I learn from these men that Mr. Morris has come around and apologized to them for punishing them upon his word.

Q. Before you were placed on the cross was there any other charge against you for which you were placed there, except what you have stated?

A. Nothing that I know of; and I have got certificates from Mr. Morris stating that my record is clear from the time that I come into this prison,—I have got them, that is safe.

Q. From what time?

A. From the time he used these tickets. I have got a receipt for my good conduct from June 1871, until—I forget the time that those tickets were withheld. I have got them right along every month, and have got them to show.

Mr. Bartow—That was your first punishment?

A. This was my first punishment under Mr. Morris.

Q. Have you ever been imprisoned before?

A. I have, sir.

Q. In what prison?

A. I was imprisoned in Columbus, Ohio.

Q. For what term?

A. Three years.

Q. On what?

A. Being that I am asked that question, I am under oath now, I will give the particulars.

Q. Just name the charge?

A. I would rather—

Mr. Bartow—Just give the charge?

A. It was for burglary; but I would rather they would know the particulars of it, being that I am under oath, I do not know but what you want to get a charge of perjury against me.

Q. Do you know where Dr. Smith is now?

A. No, sir.

Q. Do you know where this man Croker, that was hospital keeper, is?

A. The last I seen of him, he was here in this prison.

Q. Do you know what Croker's first name was?

A. No, sir; I do not.

Q. You do not know the name of the visitor that came to your cell?

A. I do not; I never saw the man since nor before, to my recollection. The man that seen them apply this hot water to my arm, is in the prison; yes.

Q. What is his name?

A. His name is Austin.

Mr. Bartow—Is he a freeman?

A. No, sir; he is a convict.
Mr. Bartow:
Q. For anything that you know, was that arm as well as the other one, up to the time you were put on the cross?
A. I can prove it by two men that seen me perform on the gymnastic pole,—that was Everts, that was keeper here. He kept the kitchen a while; he was keeper in the cigar shop in 1870.
Q. Did you ever use that lye or potash on your arm for any disease before you were put on the cross?
A. Never, never, sir; nor any of it after, only to see if it drove the smell away. That was the only thing that I ever have used besides this carbolic wash that they gave me.
Mr. Nelson—Have you been punished under Mr. Bingham's administration?
A. I was punished once, and I had the iron collar on once.
Mr. Bartow—Such a collar as that? [Referring to one lying on the floor.]
A. No, sir; that is nothing to be compared to it. The one I had on weighed 21 pounds.
Q. What were you punished for?
A. I was punished once for quarrelling in the shop; that is having a wrangle with one of my comrades; and another time for writing a note. Not about any one in the intitution, or any thing in it. They may have the note yet; I do not know.
Mr. Webber:
Q. How has your treatment been since 1871?
A. Well, sir, I cannot complain since that time of my treatment; I wish that every one else in the prison could say the same thing.
Q. Do you know that they could not say the same thing?
A. Oh, yes, sir; I am satisfied that they could not say the same thing. I know that. Yes, sir; I know it.
Mr. Mellen—Can you move that left arm?
A. No, sir; I cannot. I cannot move it a particle.
Q. Is your shoulder withered much?
A. Oh, it is smaller than the other one. Men that have seen it tell me that it is about a third smaller than the other.
Cross-examination by Mr. Conely:
Q. How old are you?
A. I was 33 the third day of last September?
Q. How old were you when you came to America?
A. I could not say; I was very young.
Q. Can you say about how old?
A. I could not tell positively. I do not think I was more than four or five years old.
Q. Where did you live?
A. After arriving here?
Q. Yes?
A. Springfield, Mass.
Q. How long did you live there?
A. Until I was 13 or 14.
Q. Where did you move to then?
A. I went to sea.
Q. What vessel did you go on?

A. The first one?
Q. Yes?
A. The first one that I went on was the Creole.
Q. What port did you sail from?
A. Boston.
Q. What trade was the vessel in?
A. She was in the West India trade.
Q. Making short voyages?
A. Yes, sir.
Q. How long were you with her?
A. Only to New Orleans. We just went to New Orleans; she was bound for New Orleans.
Q. You left her at New Orleans?
A. Yes, sir.
Q. What position did you have on board ship?
A. Well, I was a kind of cabin boy; a kind of scullion.
Q. What did you do after you left New Orleans?
A. I went into rafting on the river.
Q. How long did you remain in the employment?
A. Only that winter.
Q. What did you do then?
A. I went to sea then.
Q. From what port?
A. New Orleans.
Q. What trade were you in then?
A The trade was New York; I came to New York, but I think the vessel was the Silas Green.
Q. Did you make more than one trip in her?
A. No, sir.
Q. What did you do when you arrived at New York?
A. I came west.
Q. Have you ever been to sea since that time?
A. Yes, sir.
Q When you came west at that time, to what part of the west did you come?
A. I came to Buffalo.
Q. Did you go on the lake?
A. Yes, sir.
Q. How long did you remain in that work?
A. I have remained in that work nearly all the rest of my life. I went once in a vessel called the "Silas Green;" I have made several voyages from New York since that, and I have sailed in a vessel called the "Silas Green."
Q. Then your sea-faring life, since you reached Buffalo, has been two or three voyages since then?
A. No, sir; I have made many voyages; I shipped in the ship "Yankee," once, bound for Port Burwell.
Q. How long did you remain in that?
A. I was aboard that vessel all winter, and kept ship in her in Port Burwell that winter; I would not say positively—it was in the time of the Russian war.
Q. When you got through with her, what did you do?
A. I left the "Yankee" in Port Burwell and came overland to Chatham?
Q. Did you go to work in Chatham?

A. Yes, sir.
Q. What did you do there?
A. I worked at several things there; I went into a machine shop to learn the trade.
Q. What trade?
A. Machinist.
Q. How long did you remain at it?
A. I could not say positively.
Q. Was it one year?
A. No, sir.
Q. Was it six months?
A. I think it was.
Q. Less than three months?
A. Oh, it was more than three months.
Q. It was somewhere from three to six months, and you learned the trade of machinist?
A. I did not; I went there with the intention of learning it, but I did not stay there long enough, you know.
Q. Did you ever work at that trade after that?
A. I never did.
Q. What made you leave Chatham?
A. I took a notion to go somewhere else.
Q. Where did you go?
A. I went on the lakes.
Q. What kind of a craft did you go in on the lakes?
A. Sailing craft.
Q. How long did you remain at that?
A. I remained at that, off and on, until the time that I came here, with the exceptions of two years and eight months.
Q. Where did you spend the two years and eight months?
A. Columbus, Ohio.
Q. Ever in any prison besides the Michigan prison and the one at Columbus?
A. No, sir.
Q. Ever in prison in Wisconsin?
A. No, sir; never in my life.
Q. No other place but that?
A. No other place but that.
Q. When was it you went to Columbus?
A. I went there in March, 1861.
Q. Fourteen years ago, and you are now 33?
A. Yes, sir.
Q. You were then in your 19th year of age?
A. Yes, sir; about that.
Q. And remained there two years and eight months?
A. I would not be positive; it was somewhere in the neighborhood of eight months.
Q. In your direct examination by Mr. Webber, you say that you were not ashamed of having been in the Columbus prison; what did you mean by that?
A. I say that charge was a thig—
Q. What was the charge?
A. It was burglary.

Q. I want to know why you were not ashamed?
A. It was because I was justifiable.
Q. Why is it justifiable?
A. I came from Cincinnati that winter, and I worked for a man in Toledo; my clothes was at a washerwoman's, and I could not get money enough to pay the woman, from the man that I worked for; I was about to ship in a vessel that was lying there, and I could not get my clothes, and I went and took provisions enough to get $3, and paid my washerwoman's bill, and was arrested and sent to Columbus for three years.
Q. What was the charge?
A. Burglary.
Q. Did you break into a house?
A. No, sir; I raised a latch on an outhouse and went in.
Q. What had you been doing in Cincinnati?
A. I had not been doing anything at Cincinnati; I had been at work at White's packing house, in Louisville, Kentucky.
Q. Did you work in Cincinnati?
A. No, sir; I worked in a packing house in Louisville.
Q. When you came out from Columbus what did you do?
A. I went out into the country; it was in the fall.
Q. In what part of the country?
A. In Ohio.
Q. On a farm?
Q. Yes, sir.
A. What did you do?
A. Yes, sir; I was doing choring and helping to chop wood.
Q. And you came out from Columbus in the fall of 1863?
A. 1863.
Q. And worked in Ohio during that winter?
A. During that winter.
Q. That would take it to the spring of 1864?
A. Yes, sir.
Q. What did you do then?
A. I went on the lake.
Q. In what vessel?
A. Well, I did not go in a vessel; I went in a yacht.
Q. What is the name of it?
A. The "Juliette."
Q. Was it a private yacht?
A. I bought her myself in a place called China on the river St. Clair.
Q. What did you pay for her?
A. I do not remember now.
Q. About how much?
A. I think it was $100.
Q. Where did you get the money?
A. I worked for it and got it.
Q. The earnings of that winter?
A. Yes, sir.
Q. What did you do with that yacht?
A. I went down to this side of Sandusky to what they call Ottawa.
Q. Did you use her for any purpose of making a living?

A. I went down there according to agreement.
Q. For what purpose?
A. Taking a man up to Windsor, or men up to Windsor.
Q. Was it during the war?
A. Yes, sir, it was during the war.
Q. Taking the men from where?
A. From Moore's Peninsula.
Q What kind of men were these?
A. Soldiers; one man was dressed in uniform.
Q. United States soldiers?
A. No, sir.
Q. British?
A. No, sir.
Q. What was the uniform?
A. It was a Confederate uniform; I could not say—they had a Confederate uniform on under their clothes.
Q. And this peninsula, what was the name?
A. It is a place on lake Erie what they call the old starch factory.
Q. Is it on the American side or on the Canada?
A. It is in the State of Ohio.
Q. And you were engaged in taking these men from there over to Windsor?
A. Yes, sir.
Q. How much did you do of that sort of business?
A. I never made but one run, that is, just the one trip. Went down alone and got them and fetched them to Sandwich.
Q. Where was that agreement made?
A. That agreement was made in the town of Windsor.
Q. Did the men furnish you with the money to buy the yacht?
A. Not all of it.
Q. Did they any portion of it?
A. I do not wish to enter into the particulars of that. I got the yacht and paid for her.
Q. I do not care about the amount that he furnished or the conversation. Did he furnish you with any portion of it?
A. He furnished me enough to satisfy me.
Q. He did with some portion of it?
A. With a small portion. I went and bought the yacht and took her down to this Ottawa, got these men and took them up.
Q. To Sandwich?
A. To Sandwich, yes, sir.
Q. And left them there?
A. They were there the last I seen of them. All but one of them.
Q. How long did you remain there?
A. Where?
Q. At Sandwich?
A. I did not stop at Sandwich.
Q. What became of the yacht?
A. She was seized by the government.
Q. Which government?
A. The United States Government.
Q. What did you go to work at then?

STATE PRISON INVESTIGATION. 317

A. I was out west.
Q. What did you go west for?
A. I was arrested on the Canada shore, taken by force of arms, and taken by the British Government. Lord Lyons demanded my release. I was released on this condition: that I joined the Union army.
Q. Did you do so?
A. I did so.
Q. How long did you remain in the army?
A. I was in the army at the close of the war.
Q. In active service?
A. I was at the taking of Mobile.
Q. What time did you enter the army?
A. I entered the army in 1864.
Q. Where?
A. At Detroit; but I did not stay with that regiment.
Q. What regiment was that?
A. I was an eastern regiment. I joined the 19th regiment at Detroit.
Q. The regulars?
A. Yes, sir.
Q. Who had command of that?
A. I could not tell you.
Q. Who was your captain?
A. That I could not tell you. I was there only two days and one night. Went from Fort Wayne to Canada with nothing on me but my shirt and boots. I run three lines of pickets, jumped the banks, got to the river, and got into an old skiff and went into Canada. And that is all I can tell you about the 19th regulars.
Q. When did you join the army after that?
A. I joined it, sir, in Vermont.
Q. How long after that?
A. I could not say positively.
Q. About how long?
A. It was the next spring.
Q. What time was it you deserted from Fort Wayne?
A. I thing it was in August.
Q. What did you do from August until the following spring?
A. I was out west, through the Western States.
Q. What States?
A. I was in Indiana, Illinois, part of Michigan, and into Missouri.
Q. Traveling?
A. Yes, sir.
Q. What business were you engaged in?
A. The business that most any traveler has that has no particular business.
Q. What was it?
A. That you can answer about as well as I.
Q. No, I was not there; what were you doing for a living?
A. I was traveling.
Q. What were you doing for a living?
A. I got some money for giving up the claim that the British had, and got some money while I was through the West.
Q. Did you have that money with you when you deserted from Fort Wayne?

A. I had part of it.
Q. How much?
A. I forget.
Q. As much as a hundred dollars?
A. Oh, yes, sir; I was paid $100 the night I enlisted.
Q. Did you have as much as $200 when you deserted from Fort Wayne?
A. No, I did not.
Q. You must have had to earn something between August and the following spring?
A. I lived in kind of an economical way.
Q. Did you earn anything?
A. Oh, yes, sir.
Q. How did you earn it?
A. By working for it.
Q. What sort of work?
A. I was on the Mississippi.
Q. What kind of work did you do that winter on the Mississippi?
A. I was unloading flat boats.
Q. How long a time were you engaged in that?
A. Something over a month.
Q. Were you engaged in any other work that winter?
A. No, sir.
Q. What pay did you get for that work on the flat boat?
A. Forty cents an hour, while I worked.
Q. How much did your pay amount to that you got from that service?
A. I could not say.
Q. About how much; was it as much as $20?
A. Yes, sir; sometimes I worked two or three days at a time, and other times I did not work for a day or a week; I could not tell, any way.
Q. Did you make as much as a hundred dollars?
A. I don't remember; I was working quite a while.
Q. Did you get $125?
A. I won't positively say how much.
Q. Did you get any money from any other source that winter?
A. Oh, yes.
Q. What other source?
A. That I could not tell you.
Q. Why?
A. I do not think it has any bearing.
Q. Oh, you have the privilege to say that to answer it, would subject you to a criminal prosecution.
A. No, sir; it will not.
Q. Why do you decline to answer?
A. Becaus I think it is out of place.
Q. If it exposes you to a criminal prosecution I do not want to press it.
A. I do not think it does.
Q. Why don't you want to answer?
A. I went to Joliet and enlisted in an Illinois regiment; went to Springfield and left the camp and went to Quincy, Illinois.
Q. You deserted again, then?
A. I deserted again.

STATE PRISON INVESTIGATION. 319

Q. Have you deserted from the army at any other times than the two that you have named?
A. No, sir; I went right down then to Vermont and enlisted in a Vermont regiment and went south and staid until the close of the war.
Q. Did you get pay at this time you enlisted in Illinois, or bounty?
A. I did.
Q. Did you at Vermont, also?
A. No, sir; I did not.
Q. What time did you enlist in Vermont?
A. I could not be positive as to the time.
Q. What year?
A. That I could not tell you.
Q. What time were you mustered out of the service?
A. I got to Cairo the 4th day of July.
Q. Were you ever mustered out regularly?
A. Yes, sir; I was mustered out at New Orleans.
Q. Of the same year that you enlisted?
A. Yes, sir; I enlisted in Vermont, joined the conscript camp, went from there to Dolphin Island, then started for New Orleans, and got into the fight at Mobile, and that was the only battle I was in; no, I was in a skirmish after that with Dick Taylor's cavalry. I was mustered out between the middle of June and the 4th of July, 1865.
Q. What did you do after that?
A. I went home.
Q. Where was your home?
A. Springfield, Mass.
Q. Are your parents living?
A. My mother is living yet; my father died a year ago last April.
Q. How long did you remain at home?
A. I remained at home about a month, I believe.
Q. Did you engage in any work at home, or only visit?
A. I went to work.
Q. What kind of work?
A. I went to chopping stove wood and helping around generally.
Q. Did you work for strangers?
A. No, sir; I did not.
Q. Where did you go when that month ended?
A. I went back onto the lakes.
Q. What kind of work did you get into there?
A. Sailing a vessel.
Q. What position did you have on the boat?
A. I was master.
Q. Did you own the vessel?
A. No, sir.
Q. Who owned the vessel?
A. A Cleveland firm.
Q. What time did you begin as master?
A. I got home some time in August or the latter part of July; I arrived in Cairo on my way home from New Orleans in July; I went to Chicago and came down on the propeller Young America, and I went to Springfield, and while there I received a letter asking me if I would take charge of some vessel that was

to be sold at Port Colburn if they should buy her, and if such was the case, to come to Buffalo at a certain time; as soon as I got that I went there, and we went to Gravelly Point; it is known as Port Colburn, and the parties bought her.

Q. About how many tons was this vessel?
A. I think she registered 30 tons.
Q. What, if anything, was she engaged in?
A. She was engaged in smuggling.
Q. How long were you engaged in that business?
A. I was engaged in that, for the Cleveland company, for a year in her, then.
Q. Were you engaged in any other vessel in smuggling?
A. Yes, sir.
Q. What vessel was that?
A. The "Champion."
Q. Where did she sail from?
A. From Buffalo.
Q. When was that?
A. That was that fall, along before freezing up time.
Q. Which fall?
A. The fall of 1865.
Q. That was the same season you engaged on the other vessel you spoke of?
A. It was.
Q. What was the name of the one you got charge of at Gravelly Beach?
A. I do not propose to tell the name of it; the United States authorities has been after me and offered me my freedom if I would turn State's evidence on that company; and I do not propose to do it.
Q. You told the name of the "Champion;" you are at perfect liberty to say, at any time in the course of the examination, that if any question that is asked to answer it would expose you to a criminal prosecution—
A. It would not; because the United States government knows all about this at this time.
Q. What objection is there to telling what you know about the one at Port Colburn?
A. Simply this: I have relatives that knows that I took charge of that vessel, and seeing it public, they would know all about it.
Q. What time did you get it?
A. In August, 1865.
Q. When did you get the "Champion?"
A. I got it just after I lost the other; I was ordered to wreck her.
Q. When did you wreck her?
A. Just before freezing up time.
Q. I understood you to say you were a whole year with this vessel?
A. I say that I smuggled for that company a year; but you did not understand me to say that I was in that same vessel a whole year.
Q. Well, you were for that company, but you were not in one vessel all the time?
A. No; I smuggled for a year in contraband goods from Canada.
Q. Have you been engaged in that business for any length of time except that year?
A. I stated about a year altogether.
Q. Did you ever smuggle for any other company?
A. I never did.

Q. Were you ever engaged in that business at all except for that time you have named?

A. Only this far: when I was aboard that vessel doing business I have accommodated other parties by their request on my own hook.

Q. That brings you down then to what time in 1866, when you left this Cleveland company?

A. It brings me down to about May.

Q. May, 1866?

A. May, 1866.

Q. What were you engaged in then?

A. I came here to Jackson.

Q To the Jackson prison?

A. Yes, sir; engaged as a cigar maker.

Q. That was the first time?

A. Yes, sir.

Q. What were you sent for?

A. I was sent for running contraband goods; the charge was larceny.

Q. Where were you tried?

A. I was tried at Ann Arbor.

Q. In the Washtenaw circuit?

A. Yes, sir.

Q. In the circuit court?

A. I could not tell you.

Q. Who was the judge?

A. Judge Lawrence.

Q. What is the lengh of time for which you were sent?

A. Two years.

Q. Do you remember the time you came?

A. I do not; I was sentenced the 21st day of June, but did not arrive here until some time after that.

Q. That was in 1866?

A. Yes, sir.

Q. And you were sent for how long?

A. For two years.

Q. And remained how long?

A. I remained until the expiration of my sentence, with the exception of the time I was out on a writ of *habeas corpus.*

Q. Where did you go to?

A. I went to Detroit.

Q As a witness?

A. Yes, sir.

Q. You made some good time?

A. I was not reported while I was here the first time.

Q. You went out in February, 1868, did you?

A. I forget the time.

Q. It was in the early part of 1868?

A. Yes, sir.

Q. What did you go at then?

A. Well, sir, I went to Monroe, and went from there out west and went to work driving team, and went from there home.

Q. How long did you remain at home?

A. I remained there the most of the summer.
Q. That would be the summer of 1868?
A. Yes, sir.
Q. Where did you go to then?
A. I came west again.
Q. Whereabouts west?
A. To Michigan.
Q. What did you do?
A. I went into the butchering business.
Q. Where?
A. At Monroe.
Q. Did you continue there until you were arrested?
A. I did.
Q. Continue in that business?
A. Off and on; I did not stay there steady; I was there off and on.
Q. What were you sent for the last time?
A. For three head of cattle.
Q. Stealing three head of cattle?
A. Killing and stealing three head of cattle.
Q. Was it all one offense?
A. No, sir.
Q. Were you convicted on each?
A. I plead guilty to one.
Q And had a trial on two?
A. Yes, sir.
Q. Were the convictions all had at the term of court?
A. Yes, sir.
Q. Tried at Monroe?
A. Yes, sir.
Q. Before coming to the prison the last time had you ever had any lameness in your arm?
A. I have, once.
Q. When was that?
A. That was in 1861.
Q. What was it?
A. I got the shoulder jerked out of joint.
Q. Where?
A. At Columbus.
Q. In prison?
A. Yes, sir.
Q. How long were you laid up in consequence of that?
A. I was laid up for three months. Bed-fast. I used to have those night sweats.
Q. Was it the same arm that is now injured?
A. Yes, sir.
Q. Did you ever at any other time have any injury to that arm?
A. No, sir; never.
Q. Were you experiencing any inconvenience from that arm at the time you say Mr. Martin put you on that cross?
A. Not in the least. I done my work in the cigar shop, and men that seen me perform on the gymnastic pole could tell you that. I could lift myself up—

Q. You say you had been sent to the hospital before the time that this occurred?
A. Yes, sir, some time in June.
Q. What time in June did you go to the hospital?
A. I could not say, but you will find it there if you have got the hospital record.
Q. How near can you state to it?
A. I could not say. I think I was in the hospital previous to the 22d.
Q. Do you remember what you said on your direct examination?
A. Yes, sir.
Q. What did you say then?
A. About the middle of June?
Q. What was the matter with you then?
A. Bloody dysentery.
Q. Was that the first thing for which you were sent to the hospital?
A. I believe it was; I might have went there to see the doctor.
Q. Did you ever go for rheumatism?
A. I do not remember.
Q. Did you ever have the rheumatism?
A. I have had rheumatism in my hip.
Q. When was that?
A. Why, I felt it now and then; I could not say.
Q. Did you ever go to the hospital for rheumatism?
A. I could not say.
Q. Did you ever go to the hospital for rheumatism?
A. I don't know but I have.
Q. You don't know whether you ever did or not? Do you know whether you entered on the 15th of June for rheumatism?
A. I don't know.
Q. You don't know whether you did or not?
A. No, sir.
Q. Did you enter the hospital for anything else?
A. I do not remember anything else but this bloody dysentery.
Q. Did you complain of anything else to the doctor?
A. Not that I know of.
Q. Did you have the rheumatism before you came into the prison?
A. Yes, sir, I had it before, when I was on the lakes.
Q. Did you ever have the catarrh?
A. Yes, sir.
Q. Did you ever go to the hospital for that?
A. Yes, sir; I have went and got catarrh snuff.
Q. Did you go to the hospital at any time through that June for catarrh?
A. I could not say.
Q. Do you know whether the doctor prescribed anything for you about the 15th of June?
A. I could not say; I know that he always prescribes when a person goes there sick, or did at that time.
Q. Did you remain in the hospital from the time you were taken sick?
A. I was to bed—
Q. Did you remain at your cell at all?
A. I may have been sent to my cell a few days; there was two of us taken

down with the bloody dysentery, and one of them died and the other one got well.

Q. Do you remember whether you staid in your cell?
A. I may have staid there a few days.
Q. Do you remember about it?
A. I do not.
Q. Can you say whether or not on the 15th day of June you represented to the doctor that you had rheumatism and that he prescribed for you?
A. I do not remember anything of that kind.
Q. Can you say whether or not on the 16th day of June you staid in your cell?
A. I cannot.
Q. For rheumatism?
A. I cannot.
Q. Did you stay in your cell at all for rheumatism?
A. I don't remember ever staying in my cell; I don't remember of it. I may have staid there a day.
Q. Can you say whether on the 17th of June the doctor treated you for rheumatism?
A. I do not think he did.
Q. Why?
A. Because I don't think it; I think it was about that time that I was lying bed-fast in the hospital with the bloody dysentery.
Q. Do you remember of going to the hospital on the 20th of June?
A. I do not.
Q. Do you remember that you worked on the 18th and 19th of June?
A. I don't think I did.
Q. Do you remember being treated for catarrh on the 20th of June?
A. No, sir; I do not.
Q. Do you remember that you were in the machine shop and worked on the 20th of June?
A. I do not; I do not think I was.
Q. Do you remember that you worked on the 20th and 21st of June?
A. No, sir.
Q. What do you think about it?
A. I think the contract books would show that.
Q. What is your opinion about it?
A. I think I was sick in the hospital at the time with the bloody dysentery.
Q. The 22d of June, do you think you were sick with the dysentery?
A. I think I was.
Q. Do you remember that you were treated on the 22d day of June for rheumatism, and that you were in the shop?
A. No, sir; I do not.
Q. Do you remember that you were in the shop on the 23d day of June, and labored half a day?
A. I do not remember.
Q. Is there such a thing as putting men on half labor?
A. Yes, sir; I have been on half labor myself.
Q. Were not you put on half labor on the 23d day of June?
A. I do not remember.

STATE PRISON INVESTIGATION.   325

Q. Is not it true that on the 23d day of June you only complained of rheumatism?
A. No, sir; that is not true.
Q. Did not you work in the shop on the 24th and 25th of June?
A. I do not think I did.
Q. Is it not true that the first complaint of dysentery that you made was on the 26th day of June?
A. I could not say with regard to the date; but I think it was some time along about the middle of June.
Q. Is not it true that, on the 28th of June, instead of being abed, that you spent a portion of your time in your cell?
A. No, sir, because I remember being put in the hospital and getting up July third.
Q. Is not it true that on the 29th of June you spent your time in your cell and not in the hospital?
A. I cannot remember anything of that kind. I tell you now positively, that I think it was sometime about the middle of June that I was taken down with the dysentery, and remained in bed until the third of July.
Q. I ask you if it is not true that on the 29th of June you spent your time in the cell?
A. No, sir, I don't think it was.
Q. Is not it also true that on the first day of July you spent a part of your time in your cell?
A. I cannot remember anything about it.
Q. Did you spend your time in the cell and take your meals at the hospital?
A. No, sir; I am satisfied I did not. My memory is good enough to serve me.
Q. Your memory is positive?
A. I do swear that on the third of July I got out of bed.
Q. Did not you spend the most of your time in your cell, taking your meals in the hall on the first day of July?
A. I think not.
Q. On Monday, the third day of July?
A. That is the day I got out of bed.
Q. Were not you treated for rheumatism?
A. No, sir.
Q. Did not you spend your time in the shop on the third of July?
A. No, sir; I spent it in the hospital, and went down to the dining room on the fourth of July.
Q. I am simply asking you whether you did not spend your time in the shop, on the third of July? and go to the doctor to represent that you had the rheumatism?
A. I don't remember nothing of that kind, on oath.
Q. Do you remember whether you did or not?
A. I remember that I did not.
Q. On the fourth of July did not you spend your time in the cell and take your meals in the hospital?
A. No, sir.
Q. On the fourth of July did not you spend a portion of your time in your cell?
A. Yes, sir.

Q. And part of the day in the hospital?
A. I spent the morning, until the performances began, in the hospital, and then went to the dining room.
Q. Were you under the treatment of the doctor that day?
A. I think I was.
Q. Did you represent that you had the dysentery?
A. I think I did; I had nothing else.
Q. You say you did not take your meals at the hospital that day?
A. I took it in the dining room.
Q. On the sixth day of July you say you were all day—
A. I was from eight o'clock in the morning the sixth day of July—
Q. Until the ringing of the bell?
A. On the cross.
Q. In the solitary?
A. I was, for a fact; that I positively swear to.
Q. Now the sixth day of July did you go to the doctor at all?
A. I did not.
Q. You are sure of that?
A. No, sir, I do not think I did; I might have went in the morning but I do not think I did.
Q. If you did go to the doctor, what did you go for?
A. Well, it must have been the dysentery.
Q. Did not you go on the sixth of July to the doctor for rheumatism?
A. No, sir.
Q. What time in the day does the doctor visit there?
A. From seven to ten o'clock in the day; sometimes eight.
Q. If you saw the doctor at all on the sixth day of July, you must have seen him before eight o'clock in the morning?
A. I was put on the cross between eight and nine.
Q. You must have seen him earlier than that?
A. If I seen him; but I am satisfied that I did not.
Q. Did not you complain to the doctor on that day, of rheumatism?
A. I did not, sir.
Q. On the seventh day of July did you see the doctor?
A. I did not.
Q. Are you sure of that?
A. I am sure positively, that it was—no, the seventh? yes, sir; that is the day they took me and examined me, and the doctor said he did not see anything but a little unnatural heat in the arm.
Q. Where did you spend your time that day?
A. On the cross.
Q. Did not you take your meals at the hospital that day?
A. I took no meals out of the dining-room. I had breakfast in the dining-room and spent the rest of the day on the cross.
Q. Did not you spend any part of your time in the cell?
A. Not until after the ringing of the bell.
Q. What did the doctor order that day,—the seventh of July?
A. I was taken up there to be examined by the doctor; Martin took me up there, and says he, "What ails this man?" He looked at me, and says he, "All I can see is a little unnatural heat in the arm."
Q. Did he order any thing that day?

STATE PRISON INVESTIGATION.

A. I believe not.
Q. Did you apply anything?
A. I applied some liniment, sent by the Agent in the morning.
Q. Did the doctor apply any thing?
A. I believe not.
Q. You think the Agent sent it up?
A. The Agent sent me up from the hall.
Q. Did you apply to the Agent for some liniment?
A. I did.
Q. Why did you apply to him?
A. I did not have the privilege of going to the hospital.
Q. Are you in the habit of applying to the Agent for those things?
A. I went in and told him the condition that my arm was in, and applied for something to rub onto it, and he told me to go in and tell the steward that he sent me up there.
Q. But the doctor did not order any thing?
A. I think not.
Q. On the eighth, where did you spend your time?
A. In the hospital.
Q. Did not you spend it in your cell?
A. If Sunday was the eighth, I spent it in my cell.
Q. Now, you did not state why you were put on the cross?
A. You think I did not?
Q. Yes?
A. I think I did.
Q. What was the reason you were put on the cross?
A. The circumstances, were the—
Q. I do not want all the particular circumstances; what did you understand the particular charge against you?
A. I did not understand any particular charge; I simply related the conversation that took place between me and the keeper.
Q. Were not you informed of why you were punished?
A. I was not.
Q. By any body?
A. No, sir; by no one; I told you all the dispute that me and the keeper had, and was taken from there to the cross.
Q. Taken right there from the shop?
A. Taken right from the shop and put on the cross in the morning.
Q. Of July sixth?
A. Yes, sir.
Q. Can you say whether on the sixth of July you had been to the hospital?
A. I don't think I had; if I went to the hospital it was before then.
Q. Did you go to the shop when the other men did?
A. I won't be positive; there is this: when I went to the shop I found another man in my place; I had been away from the shop two weeks, went back and found another man in my place, and I went to the keeper and asked him where I should work.
Q. What dispute was there between you and the keeper on the morning of the sixth of July?
A. No, the fifth I worked in the shop, and the dispute arose on the sixth.
Q. What was the dispute on the morning of the sixth?

A. That I did not do the full day's work the day before.
Q. How soon did that dispute arise?
A. Shortly after the time for coming into the shop.
Q. What was the time for coming into the shop?
A. I should judge we were unlocked at half-past six at that time; I remember nothing but the conversation.
Q. You do not remember a thing that occurred that morning except that?
A. I might have went up to the hospital after coming from the dining room, but I do not remember.
Q. Coming from your breakfast?
A. Yes, sir.
Q. You don't remember that you did?
A. No, sir.
Q. Mr. Martin came there, did he?
A. Yes, sir; he did.
Q. And ordered you to the solitary?
A. The conversation that took place between the keeper and Mr. Martin I do not know anything about; he came to me, and said he "get your coat and come with me;" I followed him; he took and put me on the cross; he came and took his cane and put me on the cross.
Q. What did you mean by bludgeon?
A. I do not know any difference between a bludgeon, a cudgel, and a cane.
Q. When you speak about his club, do you mean his cane?
A. Yes, sir; in fact, when you come down to that, it was not a natural cane.
Q. Was it an unnatural cane?
A. Yes, sir.
Q. What sort of a cane was it?
A. It was one that I should judge was about an inch and a half in diameter, or nearly so, a very unnatural bludgeon for a man to carry.
Q. Was it a cane that he was in the habit of carrying?
A. Yes, sir—I would not be positive.
Q. Did anybody assist him in putting you on the cross?
A. No, sir.
Q. Was anybody present?
A. Not the first time.
Q. Did he ever put you on the cross but once?
A. No, sir.
Q. What do you mean by the first time?
A. It was the first time.
Q. Did he come to you during the day?
A. Him and Mr. Morris come together.
Q. You swear positive?
A. Yes, sir, I do.
Q. You don't remember about that particularly?
A. I do, and I will as long as I live.
Q. What did Mr. Morris say to you?
A. He came up and says, "you are here?"
Q. What else did he say?
A. I wanted to tell him the misery I was in, and says he, "shut up."
Q. Who said that?
A. Mr. Morris.

STATE PRISON INVESTIGATION. 329

Q. Was there anybody with you there in the solitary at all during the time?
A. No, sir.
Q. And they only when they came to see you?
A. There was a stranger with Mr. Morris.
Q. Was it before or after he and Martin came together?
A. It was after.
Q. What conversation was had there between you?
A. He looked in at the door and said he, after taking the visitor—
Q. I am not speaking of the time he and the visitor were there, but the time he and Martin came there.
A. Yes, sir.
Q. I want you to confine the conversation to the time he and Martin came there together.
A. There was no one came to see me until the time that he and Mr. Morris came there together.
Q. I want the conversation at that time?
A. The conversation was simply this: "You are there, are you?" Says I, "Yes, sir." He went on and asked me several questions; I cannot recollect them all.
Q. Recollect part of them?
A. He asked me several questions, I could not say what, but said he, after I was about telling him what misery I was in, says he, "shut up; who is keeper, you or Mr. Wing?"
Q. Mr. Morris said that?
A. Yes, sir.
Q. And Martin was present?
A. Yes, sir; I remember then he asked me how long I come for, and I told him 15 years. "What was your charge?" I told him. He looked at me. Said he. "Do you mean to say that you were sent here 15 years for larceny?" Says I, "Yes, sir."
Q. That is the whole of that conversation?
A. Yes, sir, as near as I can remember.
Q. How long had you been on the cross at that time?
A. I had been on,—this was some time in the forenoon.
Q. And Mr. Morris and the visitor came after that?
A. Yes, sir.
Q. What occurred then?
A. He came up to the door with the visitor. The first I knew anything about any person they came up to the door, and there was a wooden door that kind of hid the grating of the solitary. He opened the wooden door and he pointed to me. I won't be positive with regard to whether he asked me what my charge was or not, but he asked me what my charge was there or before that. I won't be positive but the charge was mentioned, but he pointed with an indignant look. The visitor turned and walked away.
Q. Did he make some expression? "Behold!"
A. He said something; "see," or "behold." The expression was made when the finger,—the arm was extended.
Q. Are you sure about the expression?
A. I could not be positive.
Q. You testified in your direct examination that he said "behold?"
A. "Behold," or "see;" it conveys the same meaning.

Q. Are you positive those are the words he used?
A. I could not.
Q. He pointed then to the cross?
A. Yes, sir.
Q. Who took you down from the cross?
A. At night?
Q Yes.
A. Mr. Martin.
Q. Did you ever complain to Mr. Morris at all about your arm?
A. I did not.
Q. Did you ever to the board of inspectors?
A. I did not.
Q. You knew you had the opportunity to complain to the board of inspectors?
A Yes, sir.
Q. I want to know your reason for not complaining to the board of inspectors?
A. That is just what I wanted you to ask. The reason why I have never complained to the board of inspectors was this : I have been in this prison now going on nine years altogether, and I have never known it to fail, a man that would go before the board of inspectors with regard to anything, but that was punished afterwards. That, sir, is my explanation.
Q. I wish you would give an instance of that, sir?
A. I can refer to no particular points; but—
Q. I do not want you to refer to any particular points, but just give me the name of any man that went before the board of inspectors and was punished afterwards?
A. I cannot under Morris.
Q. Anybody else?
A. Yes, sir, I can.
Q. You can under somebody else?
A. I can remember several cases under Bingham.
Q. Can you under this administration?
A. Not to be positive; I have heard men say that when they went to the board of inspectors that they got no satisfaction and was punished afterwards for some trifling offense. When a man went before the board of inspectors with a complaint against Mr. Morris, there was always some trifling offense brought up against him.
Q. I want you to refer to one case that has occurred here since Mr. Morris has had charge here?
A. I will tell you one; I remember one instance where a man went to the board of inspectors with regard to not receiving socks; and I remember that he was flogged in a day or two afterwards.
Q. What was his name?
A. I cannot refer to it. This was not under Mr. Morris.
Q. I am asking you about Mr. Morris; I want you to give an instance.
A. I cannot give the name; but it has been the impression that the board of inspectors sanctioned the acts of the Agent.
Q You never heard of one being ill-treated in consequence of going before the board of inspectors since Mr. Morris took hold?
A. No; not to be positive.
Q. Now, Mr. Lane put you on the cross the next day?

A. Yes, sir.
Q. Anybody assist him?
A. Yes, sir.
Q. Who was it?
A. It was Lane's son.
Q How long did you remain on on that day?
A. I remained from the time the doctor came that morning until the bell. The bell was ringing about the time I left the solitary to go in tne cell.
Q. From what time in the morning?
A. I cannot say; it is some four years ago; it will be four years in July, and I cannot recollect the hour. It was as soon as the doctor came.
Q Was it in the morning?
A. Yes, sir.
Q You remained there without dinner.
A. Yes, sir.
Q. Were you taken down?
A. I was taken down once during the day.
Q. How long did you remain away from the cross then?
A. Not more than five minutes.
Q. Where did you go?
A. Down into the central building.
Q Did he put you on again?
A. Yes, sir; and his son was with him.
Q. The second time?
A. Yes, sir.
Q Who took you down at night?
A. I think it was Lane.
Q. Was his son with him?
A. No, sir.
Q How soon after that did this trouble come on in your arm about this smell?
A. It could not have been over three or four days; I think three or four days; not outside of that.
Q. That smell was offensive?
A. Yes, sir.
Q. Had there been any sore on your arm before that?
A. None whatever; the blood had apparently stopped circulating.
Q. When did that smell business cease?
A. It has not ceased yet; you can smell it yet.
Q It continues from that time until now?
A. Yes, sir; with the exceptions only of when this discharge is dried up. After it is dried up for two or three weeks this disagreeable smell occurs. It is here to speak for itself.
Q Was there any sore on the arm?
A. Yes, sir.
Q. That summer?
A. No, sir; there was not.
Q. When did it first begin to run?
A. After Dr. Tuttle came here. I think it will be two years next August.
Q. And yet there was a very offensive smell about it?
A. There was a very offensive smell.

Q. It did not begin to run until after mustard was applied?
A. You asked me about a sore; when the fingers was drawn down in that way [showing], there was a kind of sore in the cracks of the fingers where the fingers was drawd down, but not what you would call a sore on my arm.
Q. When did you first see that?
A. That was the same time that this was done. Dr. Smith was here at the time, and he told me, says he, "keep them fingers out as much as possible," and I kept a rag in there.
Q. When was this that Mr. Morris told you you could go to work?
A. That was the 7th of July, in the morning.
Q. Where were you then?
A. I was in the central building, in the hall.
Q. What did he say to you?
A. After coming down from the hospital after seeing the doctor, Mr. Martin told him, says he, "There is nothing the matter with this man." I came down, and says he, "put on your coat and go to the shop." I started to put on the coat; another man went to assist me, and says he, "Come back; come back; put him on the cross again."
Q. Who said that?
A. Mr. Morris.
Q. What did he say about your going to work?
A. He told me to go to work; I told him I was not able.
Q. That was it?
A. Then he sent me to the hospital to be examined by the doctor; the doctor looked at my arm, not knowing anything about my being on the cross, and said he, "I cannot see anything the matter with the arm, except a little unnatural heat."
Q. That was the day after Martin had put you on the cross?
A. That was the day after the first day I was on the cross.
Q. When was this carbolic acid applied?
A. That was about four days after.
Q. At that time there was no running sore?
A. No, sir.
Q. And yet they applied carbolic acid?
A. Yes, sir; it smelled so bad that they applied carbolic acid—carbolic wash; not acid, but wash.
Q. Have you ever put potash on your arm, at all?
A. No, sir; I have used weak lye, but that was but three times.
Q. Have you ever put potash on your arm?
A. No, sir; I never have.
Q. Did you get any potash from this man La Mountain?
A. I never did; I never spoke to him only once in my life until here the other day; I asked him when this conversation took place between him and I; he looked at me in surprise, and says he, "what do you mean?" there was other men came around, and I walked away; I never had no conversation with him; I knew nothing about him; did not know the man's name.
Q. You spoke at one time about being in the hospital 22 days?
A. Yes, sir.
Q. When was that?
A. That was when this potation was applied to my arm.
Q. When the blister was made?

A. Yes, sir.
Q. When was that?
A. I think it will be two years next August.
Q You spoke about not having any discharge for a long time there?
A. Yes, sir; I did.
Q How long were you without any discharge?
A. I could not say positively.
Q. How many days, probably?
A. I should think five or six weeks; that is only "think," I "think;" it was only about that.
Q. In standing with your arms attached to the cross, how closely were your feet to the ground?
A. I was standing on the balls of my feet.
Q. What was the keeper's name in the shop?
A. His name was Wing.
Q. Were you on the cigar contract that season?
A. I was.
Q. Were you on the cigar contract when you came into the prison when Bingham was here?
A. Yes, sir.
Q. Have you ever been on any other contract?
A. No sir; I was put on the cigar contract before Bingham was here.
Q. Have you ever worked on any other contract?
A. Not to be marked; I have been on other contracts; what they call a "lumper" here.
Q. Were you not a lumper before that?
A. I have been since I got this arm hurt; I am yet.
Q. You are now?
A. Yes, sir.
Q. Did you ever hear Mr. Morris say to the prisoners that any convict could confer with the board of inspectors if he desired?
A. I have, and I have heard of him locking them up for wanting to see them, or something that they wanted to show this committee.
Q. When did you hear that?
A. The other day.

F. S. CLARK RE-CALLED.

Mr. Conely—Mr. Clark, read the record in the case of the convict La Mountain?
A. "Napoleon La Mountain, *alias* Leo La Mount, recorder's court, Detroit, Nov. 13, 1872, for seven years. Charged with breaking and entering a store in the night time with intent to commit larceny.

The committee here adjourned to meet at Lansing at the call of the chairman.

TUESDAY, APRIL 20th, 1875.

Committee met in Chaplain's room at prison at 9 A. M.

PHILIP LADEAU, SWORN.

Examined by Mr. Conely:

Q. Mr. Ladeau, where do you reside?
A. At Monroe.
Q. What is your business?
A. I am not doing anything at present; was formerly sheriff of Monroe county.
Q. How long have you resided in Monroe?
A. I was raised there.
Q. Do you know William McDonald, a convict in the prison?
A. Yes, sir.
Q. Did you know him at Monroe?
A Yes, sir.
B. How long have you known him?
A. Six years, I think.
Q. What business was he engaged in when you knew him?
A. Well I never knew; he was peddling, or trading and butchering, something of that kind.
Q. Did you know of his being under arrest?
A. Yes, sir.
Q. What offense was he charged with?
A. Stealing cattle.
Q. Anything else?
A. Well, what I arrested him for was stealing cattle.
Q. Did you know him before his arrest?
A. Yes, sir.
Q. Did you know his reputation for truth and veracity?
A. Yes, sir.
Q. Was it good or bad?
A. Bad.
Q From what you know of his reputation, would you believe him under oath?
A. No, sir, I would not.
Q Were there other warrants out for him besides the one or ones for cattle stealing, that you spoke of?
A. Yes, there was three warrants for cattle-stealing, and there was some charge of smuggling against him.
Q You heard that?
A. Yes, sir.

Cross-examined by Mr. Webber:

Q. How long did you say you knew McDonald?
A. I think I knew him in 1864–5, some three or four years before I arrested him. I arrested him in 1869.
Q You say his reputation was bad?
A. Yes, sir.

STATE PRISON INVESTIGATION. 335

Q. For truth and veracity or for general cussedness?
A. He bore a bad name for truth and veracity. I found this out afterwards. His reputation was bad.

CHARLES KIRSCHGESSNER SWORN.

Examined by Mr. Conely:

Q. Where do you reside?
A. At Monroe.
Q. How long have you lived at Monroe?
A. Twenty-five years.
Q. Do you know this McDonald?
A. Yes, sir.
Q. Did you know him at Monroe?
A. The first time I was acquainted with him I put hand-cuffs on to him when I had him arrested.
Q. Did you know his reputation in that community as a man of truth?
A. Yes; and his reputation was bad.
Q. From what you know of his reputation, would you believe him under oath?
A. I would not.

Cross-examined by Mr. Webber:

Q. Did you say that you did not know him personally until you put hand-cuffs on to him?
A. I knew of him—knew his reputation—and he was a terror to the whole community.
Q. You knew his reputation before you hand-cuffed him?
A. I heard about his reputation as a bad man.
Q. For truth and veracity?
A. Yes, sir; I heard about it, and that it was bad.
Q. Did you learn his reputation afterwards for truth and veracity?
A. Yes, sir; after we had him in jail.
Q. How did you ascertain it to be?
A. Bad.

HENRY D. SPAULDING SWORN.

Examined by Mr. Conely:

Q. Where do you reside, Mr. Spaulding?
A. I reside at Monroe.
Q. What is your business?
A. Well, I have been deputy sheriff and deputy United States marshal.
Q. Did you know this McDonald that is in prison?
A. I never was acquainted with him until after he was arrested; I was after him, but never got sight of him.
Q. Did you know his reputation in that community?
A. Yes, I did.
Q. Did you know it before his arrest?
A. Yes, sir.
Q. Did you know his reputation for truth and veracity?
A. Well, I have heard men say that he was bad—I never was personally acquainted with him.
Q. That is not necessary; I only want to know his reputation for truth and veracity.

A. Bad.

Q. Well, from what you know of his reputation, would you believe him under oath?

A. No, sir.

DAVID LANE, SWORN.

Examined by Mr. Conely:

Q. Mr. Lane, where do you live?
A. My residence is in this city.
Q. What is your business?
A. Manufacturing spring beds.
Q. Whereabouts are you carrying on that business?
A. In Kalamazoo.
Q. Have you ever been employed in any capacity in the prison?
A. Yes, sir.
Q. When?
A. I was employed here from March, 1866, to December, 1872.
Q. In what capacity?
A. First as guard, afterwards as keeper, and then hall keeper.
Q. Did you know the convict Wm. McDonald?
A. Yes, sir.
Q. Do you remember at any time of his having been punished within the prison?
A. I do; yes.
Q. When was that?
A. I could not fix the day, but it was soon after Mr. Morris' arrival here; within a few weeks I should think.
Q. Do you remember what he was punished for?
A. My recollection is that he was punished, at least he was reported for refusing to do his work, and for insolence to the keeper in the cigar contract.
Q State the circumstances connected with the punishment, as far as you know them.
A. My memory is not very distinct in regard to the matter; I remember the report and the punishment; he was punished by being fastened on an instrument called the cross.
Q. By whose direction?
A. That I could not say; Mr. Martin executed the punishment; Mr. Martin was deputy at that time.
Q. State what you witnessed of the punishment.
A. I accompanied Mr. Martin, and witnessed his being fastened to the cross, but left immediately after.
Q. Did you hear anything said to him by Mr. Martin at the time?
A. I have no recollection of the conversation, if any.
Q. Did you take any part yourself in attaching him to the cross?
A. No, sir.
Q Do you know the name of the keeper by whom he was reported?
A. I think Mr. Wing, of the contract at the time.
Q. At what time of day did this occur, as near as you can recollect?
A. It was somewhere in the forenoon; it was before noon, I remember; the particular time I could not fix.
Q. In what room or part of the prison was the punishment inflicted?
A. It was in the cell of the old solitary—so called.

STATE PRISON INVESTIGATION.

Q. How long did you remain there at the time it occurred?
A. Probably not over five minutes.
Q. Were you there at the beginning of it?
A. At the time of his being fastened on the cross?
Q. Yes, sir.
A. Yes, sir.
Q. Did you see him again during the day?
A. I don't remember seeing him at all during the day.
Q. Was your son there at the time?
A. He might have been there at that time; I hardly think it, but my memory is not distinct in regard to that.
Q. Do you remember whether he came immediately from the cigar shop or from some other place?
A. Not positively; my impression is he did.
Q. Do you know of his being punished a second time in a similar way?
A. I do not.
Q. Do you know of his being punished on two successive days?
A. I do not.
Q. Did you ever hear of his being punished on two successive days?
A. Only as I read it in the newspaper,—the report of his testimony,—I never heard of it.
Q. Do you remember the precise duty or kind of duty you were performing at the time of this punishment, whether as guard, keeper, or hall keeper?
A. I was hall keeper at that time.
Q. What is the nature of that duty?
A. It is so various it would be hard to describe. I had a general supervision of the State supplies, provisions, clothing, etc.; the men at work in the halls were under my charge; also in the State shops, blacksmiths, carpenters, etc. in a general way.
Q. At the time of this punishment did anything occur to indicate to you that the same punishment had been inflicted the day before?
A. No, sir, there didn't.
Q. Were your duties at the time such that if such a punishment had occurred on two successive days you would have been likely to have known of it?
A. I should have been likely to have known of it.
Q. Do you know how long he remained upon the cross that day?
A. I can't determine, no, sir.
Q. Have you any reason that leads you to think it was in the forenoon?
A. No definite reason, simply an impression.
Q. Have you any recollection as to whether it occurred early in the forenoon or late in the forenoon?
A. I have not.
Q. Who was physician at the prison at that time?
A. My impression is that Doctor Tunnicliff was doctor at that time; it is merely an impression.

By Mr. Conely:

I desire to correct that, Mr. Lane, and say that Dr. John E. Smith was physician at that time.
Q. Do you know, Mr. Lane, what time Dr. Smith usually got here at the prison?
A. Well I should think between 9 and 11 o'clock in the forenoon usually.

Q. What time did Dr. Tunnicliffe usually get here?
A. About the same range of time I should think.
Q. Was Dr. Smith in the habit of getting here earlier than 9 o'clock at any time, do you remember?
A. I couldn't state; I have nothing to fix those dates in my mind as to the hour.
Q. Do you know where Dr. Smith resided?
A. He resided on First street in this city.
Q. How far is that from here?
A. Very nearly a mile I should judge.
Q. Have you any recollection as to how late that day McDonald remained on the cross?
A. No, sir; I have not.
Q. What is the latest time that he was on the cross that you remember?
A. I don't remember seeing him on the cross after he was put on in the morning.

Cross-examined by Mr. Webber:

Q. Can you tell in what month he was put on the cross.
A. I could not; no, sir.
Q. How long did you remain at the prison after that occurrence?
A. I remained at the prison until December 6, 1872.
Q. And this you think was in the summer of 1871?
A. I think so; yes.
Q. You went with Mr. Martin when McDonald was put on the cross?
A. Yes, sir.
Q. But you didn't assist him in making his hands fast?
A. No, sir; I did not.
Q. Do you know whether the strap that went around the left wrist was put round once or twice?
A. I do not; I didn't examine.
Q. Did you ever make a man fast to that cross?
A. Sometimes; yes, sir.
Q. Do you remember whether the strap for the left-hand wrist was longer than the one for the right-hand wrist?
A. I do not recollect now.
Q. Do you remember whether he was put on the cross before or after the men went to the shops that morning to their work?
A. No, I cannot fix the time.
Q. Do you know who directed him to be placed upon the cross?
A. I have no recollection now; don't know that I ever knew.
Q. Do you know whether McDonald had been to the hospital that morning?
A. I don't know whether he had or not on that morning.
Q. Do you know whether McDonald had been in the hospital for some days before this?
A. Well, my recollection is that he had some time previous.
Q. Do you recollect for what diseases?
A. No, sir; I never knew.
Q. How soon again did you see McDonald,—did you see him again the same day he was put on the cross?
A. I have no remembrance of seeing him.
Q. Do you remember seeing him afterwards?

STATE PRISON INVESTIGATION.   339

A. I don't remember that my attention was called to him after the occurrence for some days, perhaps weeks.

Q. When your attention was first called to him after this occurrence, what called it?

A. He came to me and said his hand was injured, and wanted I should look at it.

Q. In what condition did you find it?

A. I found his hand was tied up,—bandaged, and the fingers contracted, bound down. I requested him to remove the bandage and he did. There were sores in the palm of his hand and between his fingers that seemed to discharge, and had a very offensive smell, and I sent him to the hospital.

Q. This you think was about a week after?

A. My impression is it was several weeks.

Q. Several weeks?

A. Yes, sir.

Q. I would be glad to have you fix the time as near definite as you could.

A. It is impossible for me to fix it with any degree of definiteness.

Q. Do you remember whether this was while the warm weather still continued?

A. I think it was in the summer, or perhaps the fall.

Q. You say then you took him to the hospital.

A. I sent him to the hospital—told him to go.

Q. You didn't go with him?

A. No, sir.

Q. When McDonald showed you his hand did he tell you how it had become injured?

A. He said it was injured by punishment upon the cross.

Q. Did you report that statement to any one?

A. I mentioned it to Mr. Martin.

Q. What reply did Mr. Martin make?

A. He said it could not be possible.

Q. Did you mention it to Mr. Morris?

A. No, sir.

Q. Do you know any reason why no record was made of that punishment?

A. I do not; no sir.

Q. When the deputy was with you in administering the punishment, I understand it was no part of your duty to report the punishment?

A. No, sir; not at all.

Q. Now, did you keep any track of McDonald after he went to the hospital with the sore hand?

A. No, sir; not with reference to the hand.

Q. You had not known whether he was on duty or not, before he showed you the hand?

A. Well, if I had known he was off duty, I should probably have known it in a general way.

Q. But you have no recollection?

A. I have no recollection.

Q. Is it possible he might have been off duty and you not remember it?

A. It is possible he might have been off duty and I not remember it the first time.

Q. I understand you paid no further attention to the case after it went to the hospital?
A. I did not.
Q. And you can't tell what the result was?
A. No, sir.
Q. Do you know where Dr. Smith is now?
A. I do not.
Q. Can you tell how many weeks Mr. Morris had been in charge as Agent when this punishment was inflicted?
A. I cannot fix any time.
Q. I would like to have you state again, Mr. Lane, your best recollection as to who was acting physician for the prison at that time.
A. My impression is the same as it was before; still I may be at fault; I don't assert it as a fact.

Re-direct by Mr. Conely:

Q. Have you any recollection how soon after this punishment occurred that you first saw his hand was sore?
A. The instance I mentioned is the first and only time I remember having my attention called to it; I cannot fix the time.
Q. Well, was it at the time that you saw his hand was sore, and he made the statement to you that it was occasioned by the punishment?
A. Yes, sir.
Q. Do you know whether Mr. Morris knew of the punishment at the time?
A. I do not know.
Q. Do you know whether or not Mr. Martin ever inflicted punishments without the knowledge of Mr. Morris?
A. No, sir, I do not; I had no means of knowing whether he did or not.
Q. Mr. Lane, how high were McDonald's hands elevated at the time of the punishment?
A. At right angles with his body.
Q. What was the position of his feet?
A. He stood freely on his feet; there was nothing to prevent.

Mr. Bartow—Was that the first day that he was speaking of?

Mr. Conely—Mr. Lane's statement is, that he knows nothing about any other than one day. We assume that he never was punished except the first day.

[Mr. Conely here produced the hospital prescription record—also a book called the check book for labor.]

MR. MORRIS SWORN.

Examined by Mr. Conely:

Q. Mr. Morris, in whose handwriting is this first page of the hospital prescription record?
A. I recognize it as Dr. Tunnicliffe's, formerly physician and surgeon in the prison.
Q. Whose handwriting is this under date of May 21, 1871?
A. I recognize this handwriting only by the fact that Dr. Smith followed Dr. Tunnicliffe immediately. I am not sufficiently acquainted with Dr. Smith's handwriting to identify it.
Q. At what time does Dr. Tunnicliffe's handwriting end?
A. It ends May 20, 1871.
Q. Do you remember the fact that Dr. Smith acted as prison physician and surgeon in 1871?

A. Yes, sir, for a few months. He began in May, right after Dr. Tunnicliffe left.
Q Do you know how long he continued to act?
A. I don't recollect exactly.
Q. Who succeeded Dr. Smith?
A. Dr. Tuttle.
Q. Do you know Dr. Tuttle's handwriting?
A. I saw it frequently, but don't think I should recognize it outside of the prison. Dr. Tunnicliffe's I would.
Q. This other book, the smaller book, is what?
A. It is what we call the check book, and is used by the keeper for keeping a tally of the time during the month that each man labors in the shop.
Q. The names in the first column are written by whom?
A. They are usually entered by the clerk from month to month.
Q. Who keeps these marks opposite the days?
A. The keeper; he makes the entry each day.

Crss-examined by Mr. Webber :
Q. In this check-book for labor kept by the keepers, what does a single mark mean?
A. It signifies that he was present that day and labored.
Q. What does the letter "P" marked on that day mean?
A. It indicates that he was out of the shop under a penalty or punishment.
Q. What does the letter "S" mean?
A. Sickness.
Q. And where a fraction is used, it indicates what?
A. Half time.

By Mr Conely :
Q. I now call your attention to an entry of Nov. 30, 1870, in the check book, relative to Wm. McDonald. What is the mark under that date?
A. That is for half a day's labor.

By Mr. Webber—I take the check-book for labor, and turn to June, 1871. It shows that Wm. McDonald worked every day during the first half of June; that he was sick on the 16th of June; that he worked half a day each, on the 17th, 19th, and 20th; worked a full day on the 21st of June; was sick on the 22d of June; worked half a day on the 23d and 24th each, and was sick the balance of the month.

I turn to July, 1871, and find that McDonald was sick the 1st, 3d, and 4th days of July; is marked as working on the 5th day of July; is marked as punished on the 6th of July, and is marked as sick during the balance of the month.

I turn to August, and find that he is marked as sick on the first day of August, and the balance of the month is left blank.

I turn to September, and find he is marked sick on the first day of September, and the balance of the month is left blank.

I turn to October, 1871, and find he is marked sick on the 2d, and the balance of the month is left blank.

On the next page, entered in pencil, I find that McDonald is marked as working half time, commencing with the 2d to and including the 12th of October, and then is marked as sick for the balance of the month.

JEROME H. HOWARD SWORN.

Examined by Mr. Conely :
Q. Where do you reside, Mr. Howard?

A. Jackson.
Q. What is your business?
A. I am not in any particular business just now.
Q. Were you ever employed in the prison?
A. I was.
Q. In what capacity?
A. As hospital keeper.
Q. During what time?
A. From May, 1871, I think, till September, 1872.
Q. What were your duties?
A. I was to keep order in the hospital and see that the men had proper care.
Q. Did you have anything to do with making entries on the register?
A. No, sir; I never made any entries; I was always by when the physician was there?
Q. Had you anything to do with administering medicines?
A. Yes, sir; I was there sometimes before the doctor came, and when I deemed it necessary would administer some simple remedies.
Q. Do you remember the convict Wm. McDonald?
A. I do.
Q. Did you know him when you first went into the prison?
A. I don't remember him when I first came here.
Q. How soon after going there do you remember McDonald?
A. Well, I could not say; perhaps not until along in June or July. I presume I had seen him; I have no doubt I have seen him in the hospital, but there were so many there, and all strangers to me.
Q. Where do you remember first seeing him?
A. I do not know whether it was in the hospital or outside of it. I think it was in the hospital. I saw him many times out in the yard.
Q. Do you remember what he complained of at first?
A. No, sir; I do not.
Q. Do you remember his having a lame arm?
A. Yes, sir.
Q. Do you know what his complaint was with reference to his arm—what he said about it himself?
A. No, I do not remember what he did say about it. The most that I remember about his arm was that it became unmanageable to him; he hadn't much use of it.
Q. Did you ever hear him state what occasioned it?
A. No, sir; I do not remember that I ever did. I do not remember him saying what did cause it, or what he thought caused it.
Q. I will ask you to repeat now when you stopped acting as hospital keeper?
A. I think it was the first of September, 1872.
Q. Do you know what treatment his arm received?
A. Well, sir, I cannot state what the treatment was, it is so long ago.
Q. Do you remember whether or not he ever made any statement in your hearing or presence as to having been punished on the cross?
A. No, sir, I do not remember that he ever did.
Crosss-examined by Mr. Webber:
Q. I understood you to say that you sometimes dealt out medicine in the absence of the doctor?
A. Yes, sir.

STATE PRISON INVESTIGATION. 343

Q. When you did so, was any entry made on the hospital record?
A. No, sir; only what the physician entered in the morning when he was there.
Q. Did you make a statement to the physician when he came of what you had done?
A. Sometimes I did.
Q. And did he make entries of your statement on the record?
A. I think not.
Q. You can't speak positively on that?
A. No, sir, I cannot; it is my opinion that he did not make such entry.
Q. Then in cases where you dealt out medicines in the absence of the doctor, no record was made of them?

Re-direct examination by Mr. Conely:

Q. How would you know what to give?
A. I would examine the patient sometimes; frequently have done so in the absence of the physician; and I would give them some remedies until the physician came. When he did come, I would tell him what I had done. If the convict was sick in the hospital afterwards I told him what I had done for him; but I don't think there was ever any entry made of it. There were some few remedies that I had some little knowledge of.
Q. What were those remedies?
A. Oh, there were quite a good many: aconite, belladonna, iris, and some others I don't now remember the names of.

By Mr. Bartow:

Q. Did you ever know of that medicine killing anybody?
A. No, sir.
Q. I suppose the remedies you gave were in common use in families?

By Senator Mellen:

Q. Were you ever in the habit of dealing out medicines before you went there?
A. No, not a great deal, but I have seen a great deal of sickness—our people were sick a great deal at home.
C. You never practiced medicine?
A. No, sir.

By Mr. Conely:

Q. Had considerable experience as nurse?
A. Yes, sir; a great deal.

GEO. E. RANNEY, M. D., SWORN.

Examined by Mr. Conely:

Q. You reside at Lansing?
A. Yes, sir.
Q. What is your business?
A. Physician and surgeon.
Q. How long have you been in practice?
A. I have been in active practice since March, 1863; previous to that I was engaged as hospital steward in a regiment of cavalry during the war.
Q. How long were you engaged in that service?
A. I was acting as hospital steward, or acted rather as assistant surgeon, but only ranked as hospital steward, for nearly a year.
Q. Are you a graduate of a medical school?

A. I am.
Q. What school?
A. University of Michigan.
Q. You are a brother-in-law of Mr. Morris?
A. I am; I will state further in regard to the length of time I was engaged in the army, in June, 1863, I went back to my old regiment, and was afterwards made surgeon, was chief operator of our division, and subsequently surgeon in charge of the hospital cavalry corps, military division of the Mississippi.
Q. Are you a member of the State medical society?
A. I am.
Q. Did you hold any position in that society?
A. I am Recording Secretary, and have been since its organization.
Q. How long is that?
A. It was organized in 1866, I believe.
Q. I think you stated you were a brother-in-law of Mr. Morris?
A. I am.
Q. Married your sister?
A. Yes, sir.
Q. Have you seen the convict McDonald?
A. Yes, sir; I saw him this morning for the first time.
Q. Have you talked with him?
A. I have.
Q. On what subject?
A. Well, his previous health and his recent condition.
Q. Was your talk with him and observance of him this morning sufficient to enable you to form a definite opinion as to his mental condition?
A. I didn't make the examination with special reference to that, but with partial reference. It was not, perhaps, as thorough as I would like. I would have asked him more questions if I had expected truthful answers. If I can rely on his own statements his mind is very much confused at present.
Q. I wish you would give to the committee, at not too great length, the circumstances which led you to that conclusion. What was said or done by him this morning that leads you to the opinion that his mind is confused at present?
A. He says that he has had vague notions; one in reference to some man, whose name he mentioned, supposing that he came to his cell and told him that he had the covers of saints' hearts and wanted him to take some; said that he had ate cart loads of them.
Q. Did you examine his arm?
A. Only partially. I pulled the glove or mitten off and I saw it was badly shrunk away and partially paralyzed.
Q. Can you state whether that particular form of paralysis has any definite name in the profession?
A. It is recognized as a form of creeping paralysis.
Q. Give, as far as you can, some of the known causes that produce that form of paralysis.
A. I believe it is attributed to lesion of the brain or nerve centres of the brain and spinal cord.
Q. State whether, in your opinion, that form of paralysis is ever occasioned by any external injury to the hand or arm, or can be.
A. Not originally; it might be an exciting cause, I think. I have seen a great many gun-shot wounds in the extremities and different portions of the body,

but have never seen paralysis follow a point nearer the spinal column or brain than the point of injury. The nerve force is generated at the nerve centres, but they supply the muscles as far as the nerve is intact, or at least so far as it is healthy.

Q. Then I am to understand that in case of an injury the paralysis would be further removed from the nervous centres than the point of injury?
A. Yes, sir.
Q. And not between the point of injury and the nervous centres?
A. Except in rare cases from reflex action, and these are generally of short duration. It might result from indigestion, disease of the kidneys, or bladder, or urethra, or constitutional syphilis, or other causes.
Q. What connection, if any, is there between paralysis of this character and mental insanity?
A. It is sometimes a precursory symptom of mental insanity,
Q. Where such paralysis is accompanied or followed by mental insanity, what would be your conclusion as to the nature of the injury which produced the paralysis?
A. I should infer that it was as I stated before, a lesion of the brain or nerve centres.
Q. Have you heard any of the testimony that has been given in this investigation?
A. Yes, sir.
Q. Have you heard the testimony detailing any of the circumstances connected with McDonald's punishment?
A. I don't think I have; I have read it in the paper.
Q. What paper did you read it in?
A. The Post, if I remember.
Q. Suppose a person were fastened by his wrists to a structure in the form of a cross, with his arms elevated, not directly above his head but diagonally some distance above his head, and maintained there a period of eight or ten hours with his wrists fastened to the cross-piece of the cross, and no fastening upon the arm between the fastening at the wrist and the trunk—state whether in your opinion in such a case such a punishment would cause a paralysis of the whole arm?
A. As I understand you, he would have ability to move his muscles a little. I have no hesitancy in saying that unless the arms were extremely stretched, it would not produce paralysis in a healthy subject.
Q. Suppose a man were standing easily upon his feet, and his arms extended with right angles to his body, in such a case would paralysis of the arm result?
A. Not in a healthy subject would that be the result. I will state an instance: In plastic operations, sometimes where part of the nose has been lost, it is necessary to dissect a portion of the integument from the arm and transplant it to the nose, and in doing that the arm is brought up before the face, and the partially dissected integument is brought in contact with the nose, and the arm confined there until adhesion has taken place, which generally takes, I suppose, a week. This position I regard as more constrained than the one mentioned in this case.
Q. Is that ever attended with paralysis?
A. I have never known it to be.

[The witness was here interrupted to put Dr. Tunnicliffe on the stand, it being desired by the defense to take his testimony first.]

346   STATE PRISON INVESTIGATION.

DR. JOSEPH TUNNICLIFFE SWORN.
Examined by Mr. Conely:
Q. Where do you reside, doctor?
A. Jackson city.
Q. What is your business?
A. Physician and surgeon.
Q. How long have you been in practice?
A. Thirty-four years.
Q. Have you ever been prison physician?
A. Well, I was thinking about that this morning. I have been physician here eight or nine years of the time.
Q. Were you prison physician in November, 1870?
A. Yes, sir.
Q. In whose hand-writing are these entries of November 28th and subsequent entries for a considerable time in the hospital prescription record of the prison? [Shown a book.]
A. That is my hand-writing.
Q. I will call your attention to an entry under date of November 30th, 1870.
[The witness interpreted the entry that McDonald was prescribed for and ordered to go to work. The prescription consisted of iodide of potassium, to be taken once in three hours, for some difficulty which had escaped the doctor's memory. He thought McDonald needed an alterative or diuretic. He thought it might have been some trouble with his urinary organs, or some rheumatic complaint, but had no definite recollection about it.]
Q. Is iodide of potassium sometimes given for syphilitic complaints?
A. Yes, sir.
Q. But you cannot state for what particular complaint that was given?
A. I cannot.
Q. I read now from the check-book for labor which shows he worked half a day on November 30th. I would like to have you read the entry of December 7, 1870.
A. Well, in that case he had a cut thumb, and was simply ordered to the hospital.
Q. The check-book shows he was sick that day. I will call your attention to December 12.
A. "Wm. McDonald was prescribed for and ordered to work." Given some quinine and ipecac powders. I can't tell exactly what it was for now—perhaps a little cold, or something of that kind.
Q. I notice opposite some of the names the complaint is given.
A. Yes, where it is supposed to be of any consequence.
Q. The check-book of the same date shows that he worked. I will now call your attention to the 14th.
A. Well, that day he was ordered to work and a prescription of capsicum and ipecac given him.
Q. The 16th?
A. He was ordered to work, and put back on iodide of potassium for that old trouble, whatever it was, that he claimed he had.
Q. I will call your attention to January 19th, 1871?
A. Well, in this case he evidently came to me complaining that the kind of work he was engaged in was injuring him, and he prevailed upon me, at least for that day, to order a change in the labor. I don't remember now what that

STATE PRISON INVESTIGATION. 347

was for. It was a very common thing with some prisoners to be always dissatisfied with what they were doing, and wanting some different kind of labor. I think he must have persisted in that for some time, as I wouldn't have ordered it on a first complaint; but I indulged him that time by ordering a change in the kind of labor. I don't remember the particular case to-day.

Q. Now, on the next page, the 11th of January?

A. Well, he was put back on quinine and ipecac once in 3 hours, and ordered to work; claimed to have a cold or something, probably.

Q. Do you know how long you kept him on iodide of potassium?

A. No, I do not; I think he was taking it more or less along then for a month or two. At irregular periods he would take a bottle out there; but the directions were to use it continuously. I think he complained of some obscure rheumatic pains somewhere in his limbs; that is my recollection of it. I would remark here, that the last date, the 11th, shows that he worked in the shop. The check book shows that he was sick from the 12th to the 25th inclusive, being marked with the letter "S." Then on the 26th he was sick, and on the 27th worked half a day; on the 28th, 30th, and 31st, a full day's work each, making 13½ days during the month.

Q. Now, on the 13th, doctor, of that month, I wish you would read the record from the hospital record book.

A. Witness translated the entry to signify that McDonald was allowed to remain in the hospital that day, still continued upon alterative treatment, either iodide of potassium or alterative powders, consisting of pulverized chalk with calomel or some other mercurial preparation added and given as a gentle alterative or stimulant of the liver. It was understood at the hospital that that particular powder was made up for special use, and its use continued in all syphilitic affections and troubles of that character, especially in treating chronic cases where an alterative was needed.

Q. What was the treatment on the 16th and 17th?

A. On the 16th he was allowed to remain in the hospital and was given some quinine and a little whisky. On the 17th still in the hospital; given some oil and turpentine, followed with quinine and whisky. The turpentine was given as a diuretic, and as he had been taking alteratives, probably calomel, the oil was to secure an operation and clean out his system. We didn't always mark it down if they had syphilis, not unless they were very bad indeed; that is, we didn't put the name on the book, because we could not do that without thirty or forty of them knowing about it, and it would be known all over the yard among the convicts. Sometimes a man might have slight syphilis and we carried it right along blank and treated him to get it out of his system without his being known to have had the disease. On the 18th of January he remained in hospital and had some quinine and whisky. On the 19th was allowed to remain in the hospital again. For some cause or other I ordered him to his cell that day. Whether some complaint was made that he didn't behave himself in the hospital, I don't remember, but I marked him for the hospital and subsequently to go to his cell and stay there. In that case the probabilities are that some complaint was made to me of his conduct.

Mr. Webber:

Q. You speak now only from presumption from general practice?

A. That is all the guide I have.

Mr. Conely:

Q. Now, the 20th, doctor?

A. It was the same, in hospital, sent to his cell and allowed a little quinine and whisky.

Q. The 21st?

A. The same treatment, except we put him on alteratives again. He remained in his cell.

Q. The 24th?

A. The same thing, only he was to remain in his cell and was allowed some epsom salts as a physic.

Q. 25th?

A. Same prescription, in the cell, and had some more epsom salts.

Q. The 26th?

A. The same repeated again.

Q. 27th?

A. There I have marked down that it is rheumatism, and I didn't give him any medicine, and that shows that he had been claiming to me all the time that he had rheumatism. I ordered him to his work and didn't give him any medicine. This is the first day-light that has struck me in the book. I begin to comprehend it now. I was in doubt whether what he claimed was true or not, and I thought I would test him a little by sending him away.

Q. Are rheumatic pains sometimes accompaniments of syphilitic affections?

A. Oh, yes.

Q. It is common as a result of syphilis, is it?

A. Very common, very common.

Q. Does paralysis of one or more of the extremities sometimes follow syphilis?

A. Yes, sir.

Q. As a result of syphilis?

A. They do; I can scarcely think of any bad result but what may flow directly from syphilis, short of death, and even death itself; almost every possible form of disease: blindness, deafness, paralysis, and almost every conceivable form of calamity follow in the train of syphilis.

Q. What about insanity?

A. Well, that of course,—in, fact, I don't know of anything bad but what may flow from it.

Q. The labor book for February shows that he worked every day; the labor book for March shows that he was sick on the 16th of March, and worked for the other days; I would call the doctor's attention to his record book of the 6th of March to McDonald's entry.

A. Well, on the 6th of March I prescribed for him; he evidently came in complaining of some kind of pain somewhere, but I did not deem it sufficiently serious to justify keeping him in the hospital, and I ordered him back to his work and gave him a little gelseminum, ten drops, and ordered him back to his work.

Q. What is gelseminum given for?

A. Well, in this case it was probably given for pain; perhaps he complained of headache; it is often given for headache.

Q. March 16th?

A. On March 16th he came in again and claimed that something ailed him; I don't know exactly what; and I gave him some quinine and ipecac and sent him back to his work again; perhaps gave him two or three powders. Generally those were cases where they came in and claimed that they had a cold. We gave them quinine and ipecac.

Q. I wish you would look at the several entries to which your attention is now called without stating anything—March 21st, April 12th and April 25th. [Book examined by witness.] Can you state, doctor, from the entries which you have seen in this hospital prescription record, what the matter was with McDonald?

A. I am inclined to think he must have had some form of syphilitic trouble.

Q. You can't speak positively, I suppose?

A. I do not remember; I only judge from the form and persistence of a certain kind of prescription that I suspected something of that kind, and that induced me to give him so much of the remedies we are in the habit of giving for that kind of trouble.

Q. Who succeeded you as prison physician?

A. Doctor Smith, I think.

Q. John E. Smith?

A. Yes, sir.

Q. He was the homeopathist, I think, and lived on First street?

A. Yes, sir.

Q. Do you know Smith's hand-writing?

A. I do not.

Q. Is Dr. Smith residing in Jackson now?

A. No, sir.

Q. Do you know where he lives?

A. No, sir, I do not, only from hearsay.

Q. Well, where do you hear he lives?

A. In Nebraska.

Q. Do you know how long he remained at the prison as physician?

A. I think it was in the vicinity of a year, but that, of course, is uncertain, only a guess; his health gave out and he went west.

Q. I will call your attention to another book, doctor; what is this book, do you recognize it?

A. Yes, that is my writing in 1870.

Q. Is it the hospital prescription record for 1870?

A. Yes, sir.

Q. I will call your attention to the record on the last page of this book, refering to William McDonald and his treatment.

A. Yes, there is a prescription that would indicate trouble with his water works as far back as November; I gave him balsam of copaiva about that time, and that was evidently for trouble with his water works some way,—disease of his urinary organs.

Cross-examined by Senator Webber:

Q. Doctor, do you remember at what date your office as prison physician ceased in 1871?

A. No, sir.

Q. Can you tell by looking at that record?

A. [Looks] Yes, sir; it was May 20th.

Q. 1871?

A. 1871.

Q. In this record for prescriptions there is a column with a printed heading for the name of the complaint, is there not?

A. Yes, sir.

Q. Now, in the case of McDonald, you only find an entry in that column in the cases to which your attention has been called, in two cases, I think, or but one.

A. A cut thumb and rheumatism, and I don't remember anything more than that.

Q. I will give you a chance to explain; now in all the other cases to which your attention has been called it is left blank in that column.

A. Yes, sir.

Q. When you left that blank, knowing what your practice was, what did it indicate as to the seriousness of the disease or complaint?

A. I see the point; at sometimes the disease is mentioned back months previous, and then not mentioned at all for a long period of time; that may have been so in this case and may not, it would not be an absolute indication that the man had the disease necessarily very light, and yet it would rather indicate that the more active symptoms of the disease at that time were not prominent, that is, he had the worst form of the symptoms just at that time, or syphilis, or any other disease, whatever it was.

Q. When you speak of syphilis in connection with McDonald, I understand you speak of it only as a probability and not from any recollection on the subject.

A. I do not recollect distinctly, no, sir.

Q. From the character of the remedies prescribed from time to time, should you say his ailments were serious or otherwise?

A. Well, I evidently should not have made the prescription I did unless I had apprehended some serious ulterior results. I gave it to save him from worse results.

Q. When you ordered men to work it was because, in your judgment, they were competent to work.

A. It was because in my judgment it was better for them, even though they might be sick, to be out at work, in view of all the circumstances. We often did that with the men that were sick, and in some chronic troubles I know we thought it would be just as well if not better for them.

Q. Were such cases understood by the Agent, so that the men would not be punished if they should happen to fail in working a full task?

[Mr. Conely expressed a doubt whether that question was a proper one, because Dr. Tunnicliffe was not there when Mr. Morris was Agent.]

A. He was a part of the time.

Mr. Conely—Then the question might be confined to the time when Mr. Morris was Agent.

A. You mean in cases where men were ordered to work?

Q. You say men were ordered to work that were sick.

A. Well, if we ordered them to work, our instructions were to see that they worked. The physician takes the responsibility in these cases, and orders men to work half a day, or three-quarters, or full labor. If it is not qualified it is full labor. Of course, if the Agent sees fit to lessen the labor he can do so, but he is abundantly justified in seeing that the men work.

Q. Did you ever witness any punishments?

A. Yes, I was in the habit of witnessing punishments while prison physician.

Q. Did you know there was a regulation of the board of inspectors requiring the physician to be present to witness the punishment?

A. Yes; that was while I was physician there.

Q. That continued in force until you left?

STATE PRISON INVESTIGATION. 351

A. Yes, sir.
Q. State whether you ever knew of its being repealed?
A. I know nothing about it, sir.
Q. Know nothing about it after you left?
A. No, sir.
Q. Do you remember about what time it was adopted?
A. No; I don't think I could recall the period. It would only be a mere guess. It might have been six months or a year before I left. I was in here about two years the last period, and I think it was during the last year while Mr. Bingham was Agent.
By Mr. Bartow:
Q. What year was that?
A. 1870 and 1871. I am not certain about the time this rule was adopted. I know I had received a notice from the Agent to that effect.
By Mr. Webber:
Q. Now, do you know whether you were required to be present at punishments while you were acting as physician?
A. I do not know that I had any special instructions about it; I had my own ideas about it. I don't think I received any special instructions about it.
Q. What authority would you have felt at liberty, under the board as it then existed, to exercise on such an occasion?
A. The rule was that when I told them to stop they stopped, that was the rule, and they always left it to me.
Re-direct, by Mr. Conely:
Q. Do you remember whether that regulation of the board of inspectors was ever reduced to writing?
A. I think it was, but I have no recollection of any writing reaching me.
Q. Have you any recollection of being present at any punishment inflicted by Mr. Morris himself?
A. No, sir; I was not.
Q. Have you any recollection of Mr. Morris being present at any punishment and you present at the same time?
A. I have no recollection of it; I have no recollection of any man being punished after Mr. Morris came in, up to the time that I left; it may have been so, but I have no recollection of it.
By Mr. Bartow—You don't know whether that rule was reduced to writing or not?
A. I do not; I remember that Mr. Bingham said to me one day, "Doctor, the board of inspectors passed a resolution that you must be present every time a man is punished hereafter, and you must do so;" I said, "very well, sir," and afterwards they notified me, and I was present when they punished men.
By Mr. Mellen:
Q. Did they use the shower bath at that time?
A. I am not certain about that; what punishments I saw were with the whip, "cat," I think, entirely, except minor punishments, confining in the cell, or something of that kind.
By Mr. Webber:
Q. Let me ask you, doctor, while you were there, when punishments were inflicted by the whip or "cat," on what part of the body would the punishment be inflicted?
A. The intention was always to put it over the shoulders and back.

Q. Was it allowable in any case to strike so that the lash would wind around and bring the main blow on the abdomen.

A. I don't think it would have been justified, but would sometimes occur in spite of anything you could do ; some men are wonderful eel-like under such an infliction, and sometimes would present another part entirely, and when the whip came down it would hit there, no matter how they were tied up; we would always try to avoid anything like a blow there, but it would reach around once in a while in spite of all we could do.

DR. RANNEY RECALLED.

By Mr. Conely:

Q. You have heard the testimony of Dr. Tunnicliffe, Dr. Ranney?

A. Yes, sir.

Q. And the entries that have been produced in evidence from the hospital record?

A. I have; at least a portion of them.

Q. You have heard those that have been read while he has been testifying?

A. Yes, sir.

Q. Can you form any opinion from the treatment which that man received during the winter of 1870 and '71, as to the class or kind of diseases that he had at that time, probably?

A. It would be a general inference. I should infer very much as Dr. Tunnicliffe has. We give iodide of potassium frequently for rheumatism, more frequently for syphilis, or rheumatism resulting from syphilis. Quinine and ipecac are frequently given for colds and little aguish conditions, something of that kind.

Q. Would the giving of iodide of potassium indicate any disturbance of the nervous centres, or that there was any disease of the nerves, necessarily or probably?

A. I think as a rule the intelligent physician would prescribe iodide of potassium almost invariably in cases of syphilitic taint.

Q. I suppose it might be prescribed for other things too?

A. Yes; in a great variety of cases.

Q. Taking the testimony of Dr. Tunnicliffe and the hospital records, in connection with your own interview with the man, and the examination you have made of the arm, can you state whether there is any necessary or probable connection between the paralysis of the arm and the mental disturbances that are now indicated?

A. I do not know how necessary it may be; I know that paralysis follows as a result of lesion of the nerve centres.

Q. Does the lesion or injury to the nervous centres sometimes produce mental disturbance?

A. Yes, sir.

Q. Let me ask you, Doctor, may not both the paralysis of the arm and the mental disturbance be evidence of some original injury to the nervous centres?

A. Yes; the paralysis may be a step or symptom of a more serious disease, of which insanity is a manifestation.

Q. Taking into consideration, then, the symptoms indicated by the record and the treatment, together with the paralysis and the amount of disturbances, can you say whether the original injury that produced these things was recent or of long standing?

A. I should infer that it was of long standing.

Q. I don't know but I asked you when upon the stand before whether these disturbances sometimes followed as a consequence of syphilitic affections?

A. They do.

Q. You have had some experience in the army, I think you said?

A. Yes, sir.

Q. You have seen amputations performed?

A. Yes, sir.

Q. Does the amputation of a part of the arm produce paralysis of the portion which is left?

A. I never knew it to.

Q. Suppose, then, a person received an injury, a serious injury, upon the lower part of the arm near the wrist, what likelihood, in your opinion, would there be of it producing paralysis of the entire arm?

A. I don't think it would do it as an original cause. It might be the exciting cause, the same as lying on the arm at night.

Q. You mean it might develop an existing disease,—is that your idea?

A. It might develop an existing disease.

Q. What effect, if any, would non-use of one of the extremities have in bringing about paralysis of that extremity?

A. If protracted for a long time, it would produce an atrophy or wasting of the muscles. Any surgeon of experience in treating fractures by splint, is aware of the fact that non-use will produce an atrophy of the muscles.

Mr. *Webber*—I suggest that it would be quite sufficient to take the doctor's professional opinion without extending the record by elaborate questions and answers.

Mr. *Conely*—That is a matter about which there may be difference of opinion. We do not seek to extend the record beyond what is necessary to make a clear exhibit of all the facts.

Mr. *Webber*—Doctor, I would like to ask you one or two questions. Suppose a man has had an arm dislocated at the shoulder, and after it has become nearly healed—months afterwards—he should be placed upon the cross with arms extended, and kept there, say for nine or ten hours, would in your judgment there be any more danger of paralysis from such a punishment under such circumstances than there would be if there had been no previous dislocation?

A. I can conceive that the power of the arm to resist disease might be less than in the other arm.

Q. In case he should be placed upon the cross and a strap placed very tightly about his wrists, and left there in that condition for nine or ten hours, would you think ill results would be more likely to follow than if the strap were left loose?

A. I should from the point beyond the strap.

Q. Now, if a hand is affected from injuries in the wrist, by simple contact, may not the injury extend up the arm until a part at least of the arm may become involved in the same difficulty with the hand?

A. If the wound becomes poisonous the poison might be absorbed, and in that way injure the rest of the arm—in fact, the whole system.

Q. In case one were extended upon such a cross, with the arms so tightly stretched as not to permit the movement of the arm, and the wrist so tightly bound as not to permit the turning of the wrist, and kept there for nine or ten hours, would you anticipate any evil results from such a circumstance?

A. I could conceive, of course, that a man's arms might be drawn out of their sockets, and in this way permanently injured.

Q. But without any special traction, were the arm extended as far as one could extend it voluntarily, and there bound fast, would you anticipate any such injury?

A. Not in a healthy man.

Q. From the mere tightening of the strap or cord about the wrist, by putting it about twice and leaving it there for eight or nine hours, would you anticipate any injury?

A. I shouldn't expect a permanent injury to the arm above the point of ligation, but would below the point where the strap was on the wrist.

LEWIS H. WURTZ SWORN.

Examined by Mr. Conely:

Q. What is your business, Mr. Wurtz?
A. Physician and surgeon.
Q. Do you reside in Jackson?
A. Yes, sir.
Q. How long since you began to practice?
A. Last summer.
Q. Were you ever employed here in the prison?
A. Yes, sir.
Q. Under what contract?
A. I was superintendent of the cigar contract for several years.
Q. In the employment of Mr. Hollingsworth?
A. Yes, sir.
Q. Did you know the convict McDonald?
A. Yes, sir.
Q. Was he employed on that contract?
A. Yes, sir.
Q. Were you so employed in the summer of 1871.
A. Yes, sir.
Q. Do you remember hearing of the punishment of McDonald?
A. Yes, sir; I do remember the instance.
Q. Do you remember any circumstances connected with it?
A. Yes; I know he complained of being unwell—I think it was lameness of the shoulder—this has been in my mind ever since as the complaint he gave—but of course it was my duty to see that every man performed the work properly, and it was the keeper's duty to see that the work was performed.
Q. In the course of the performance of that duty, did you ever have occasion to notice to what extent this man complained?
A. I didn't; no, sir.
Q. Do you know who reported him at that time?
A. He had some difficulty with the keeper; Wing, I think, was the name.
Q. Have you seen him since?
A. McDonald? yes; I see him frequently; I saw him this morning, and spoke to him.
Q. How is his mental condition as compared with it at that time?
A. Well, I never considered his mental condition very good, and this morning I noticed quite a change for the worse.
Q. Did you talk with him about his sickness?

STATE PRISON INVESTIGATION. 355

A. I inquired of him concerning his recent sickness; I asked him his condition for the past few days; he said he heard that he was sick, but he didn't know, he waked up and was told that he had been sick.

Q What did he say, if anything, about his having been sick before the time he was punished?

A. Dr. Ranney was with me; he said he had never been sick before his punishment but once, and I think that was with the typhoid fever.

Q. What did he say about having been healthy up to the time the punishment was inflicted?

A. He said he was very healthy and sound.

Cross-examined by Senator Webber:

Q. That was this morning?

A. Yes, sir.

Q. I understood you to say you never considered him sound mentally?

A. I never did.

Q. What did you observe?

A. Well, there are certain peculiarities about some men's talk that don't sound rational to others, we can't exactly tell what it is.

DR. TUNNICLIFFE RECALLED.

Examined by Mr. Conely:

Q. Have you seen McDonald this morning?

A. I have.

Q. Have you seen his arm?

A. Yes, and talked with him some.

Q. Did you ever see the instrument that was one time used in the prison called the cross?

A. Well, I think I have seen it, but don't remember it distinctly; never saw any punishment on it.

Q. Suppose a person were tied to that cross, by the arms, and remained there a period of eight or ten hours, the ligature being about the lower part of the arm, about the wrist; what, in your opinion, is the probability of such a punishment producing the trouble there is in McDonald's arm?

A. Well, my own theory of the matter is, that paralysis could not possibly result as alone the effect of that position or punishment. I think it simply impossible. I don't think it would be done if you would tie him up there a week.

By Mr. Barlow:

Q. Suppose the ligature was drawn very tight, so as to stop circulation, what would be the effect of it?

A. That might injure the limb beyond the point ligated; he might lose his hand from interrupted circulation. Paralysis is not a disease, but a symptom of disease, and that disease is originally in the base of the brain, and probably some portion of the spinal column. The injury of the arm would be external to the disease entirely. An injury to the spinal column itself would be likely to produce paralysis. You have got to injure at the foundation where the nervous influence comes from. The original trouble in this case must have been in the spinal column.

Q What kind of paralysis do you call this?

A. Well, I am inclined to think it is syphilitic paralysis,—that is my honest judgment about it,—that it had its origin in syphilis.

By Mr. Webber:

Q. You consider this a clear case of paralysis of the arm?

A. I think it is, but don't know; the arm has the appearance of being paralyzed.

Q. Could such an arm be produced without paralysis?

A. Yes, sir; I think it could, exactly.

Q. How would you do it?

A. Just shut those fingers together and put the arm in this shape [showing], and keep it there long enough and it would become just such a thing as that, and no medical skill could tell how it was produced; I think it is quite probable that this man has just what he claims, a paralyzed arm, and yet there is a strong possibility of its being the other way, for he is a persistent and skillful worker at deception.

Q. Doctor, if this left arm had been dislocated and afterwards tied out there on that cross for nine or ten hours, with the ligature tied about the wrist, would you suppose that the combined effect of being on the cross and the former dislocation could produce any such effect as this?

A. No, sir; nothing like it, nothing like it at all, you can do that over and over and over again and it wouldn't produce paralysis; I asked him about that dislocation, and he says he was hung up by some wristlets (what do you call 'em?), handcuffs, and while he was suspended the shoulder slipped out; this may have injured him somewhat; he says he was treated three or four months for that shoulder; there might have been some little injury in the nerve there, but it would be only temporary.

Q. What distinction would you make between creeping paralysis and syphilitic paralysis?

[The doctor confessed that he was not clear as to the meaning of "creeping paralysis," and that it had been so long since he had read up in the books he could give no exact definition.]

PATRICK M'CRYSTAL SWORN.

Examined by Mr. Conely:

Q. You are a convict, McCrystal, I believe.

A. Yes, sir.

Q. When did you come here?

A. I was sentenced on the 3d day of November [the year lost]; I came here on the 19th of that month.

Q. For what was you sent?

A. I was sent on two charges; one charge taking a piece of a man's nose; the other, writing letters threatening to burn property.

Q. Where was you sent from?

A. Menominee county.

Q. Had you ever been here before?

A. Yes, sir.

Q. How long ago?

A. I was sent here on the 10th of October, 1868. I was sentenced for 18 months.

Q. What for?

A. For trying to steal a suit of clothes.

Q. Do you know the convict Wm. McDonald?

A. I do.

STATE PRISON INVESTIGATION. 357

Q. When you came to the prison the last time, McCrystal, was there anything the matter with your feet?
A. Yes, sir.
Q. What was it?
A. I had my feet froze.
Q. Were you confined to the hospital?
A. Yes, sir.
Q. During the winter of 1870 and 1871 and the early part of 1871, did you then know the convict William McDonald?
A. Yes, sir.
Q. Do you remember his being at the hospital at that time?
A. Yes, he was in the hospital with me at that time.
Q. Do you know what was the matter with him?
A. He had a lame arm and a lame breast.
Q. What was the matter with his arm?
A. He claimed he had the rheumatism in his arm.
Q. What was the matter with his breast?
A. He claimed to have an abscess in his breast.
Q. What time did you get out of the hospital?
A. I came out of the hospital on the 5th of June, 1871.

Cross-examined by Mr. Webber:
Q. How long had you been in the hospital before the fifth of June?
A. I went into the hospital on the 22d of November, 1870.
Q. Did you know more than one McDonald in the hospital at that time?
A. No, sir; only one.
Q. Do you know whether his first name was William or whether it was F. McDonald?
A. He went by the name of McDonald only in the hospital, but when I became acquainted with him he told me what his first name was and what he was sent for.
Q. What was the matter with you?
A. My feet was frozen, sir?
Q. You say you was discharged on the 5th of June?
A. On the 5th of June, 1871, I went off the doctor's list into the shoe shop and worked on the day's work on full time.
Q. Did you see whether he had any abscess on his breast?
A. He had a lame breast, and he told me that was his disease, and I saw him rubbing medicine on his breast.
Q. Did you see any sore?
A. Yes, sir.

By Mr. Conely:
Q. Was he the same McDonald that was around with the lame arm?
A. Yes, sir.

NAPOLEON LA MOUNTAIN, SWORN.

Examined by Mr. Conely:
Q. You are here under what charge?
A. Burglary and larceny.
Q. From where were you sent?
A. From Detroit, county of Wayne.
Q. Do you know the convict McDonald?
A. Yes, sir; William McDonald.

Q. When did you first know him?

A. I knew him last October; that is the first time I got personally acquainted with him.

Q. Did you ever have any conversation with him about his arm?

A. Yes, sir.

Q. What did he say about it?

A. He told me that he had made the sore on his arm with potash; he said that he first used pure potash, but afterwards dissolved it in a small vial, and applied the solution to his arm with a cloth.

Q. Did he say why he did it?

A. Yes, sir.

Q. What did he say about that?

A. He said he knew he was in danger of losing his arm, but if he had to serve here fifteen years his arm would be of very little consequence; he also told me of a man in the Wisconsin prison who had lost a hand through the carelessness of an officer compelling him to work on a circular saw, and he afterwards recovered thirty thousand dollars from the State, and said it was his intention to prosecute the State for the recovery of damage to his arm.

Q. Where did he tell you this?

A. In the hospital.

Q. Were you sick then?

A. Yes, sir.

Q. What was the matter?

A. General debility, diarrhea, and for a time I had the dumb ague; I don't know what the physician treated me for; I told him the disease.

Q. Were you brought before the Board of Inspectors a while ago in relation to this matter?

A. Yes, sir.

Q. And made your statement to them, did you?

A. Yes, sir.

Q. Have you had any talk with McDonald since that time?

Q. Yes, sir; he knew I had been before the board of inspectors, and as I had been punished before on several occasions, he thought I was there to state my troubles; and he asked me what I was up before the board for, and I told him for several reasons, and asked him what he was there for. He said he was there to show his arm; and I said "What did they think of it?" and he said "I guess I will make a pretty good thing out of it." I then asked him and said "Last fall you remember the directions you gave me, and I applied it to my body and it made a sore, but it healed very quick; what is the reason this didn't heal up so quick?" And he said "You remember me asking you for a piece of brass?" and I said "Yes;" and he said "I intended to tell you that you should take some tallow off your candle and melt it in this brass till it got green and apply it to the sore." I asked him if that was the way he done, and he said yes. At the time that he asked me for the piece of brass, he didn't have time to finish his story. This was between the State carpenter and the Cooley contract shops, on the corner of the sidewalk. The time he asked me for the piece of brass, before he could finish his conversation, there was a keeper by the name of Webster coming up the sidewalk and I walked away.

Q. Did you ever make any test with the potash on your body?

A. Yes, sir.

Q. On what part of your body?

A. On my side (shows a scar on right side).
Q. When did you do that?
A. It was about the 20th of October, I should think.
Q. Why did you do that?
A. I did it to make a sore on my breast, so that I might remain in the hospital. My reason for that was, I was aiming to make my escape. I was then making a key for the door of the center building, and had it very near accomplished. About the 5th of November I was detected at the door, seen by somebody, and a convict named Clark. The next day I was brought up and stripped to be punished, when Mr. Morris saw the sore on my side, and that put a stop to it.

Q. Have you, since this talk about the candle grease, with McDonald, had any further talk with him?
A. Yes, sir; I think it was the next day, Friday. He some way got wind that I had been before the board of inspectors and testified against him what he had told me. He said that he had found out in the yard that I had been before the board of inspectors and testified against him, and at the same time he dropped his broom that he was sweeping with, and walked up to me as close as he could, and stuck his hand in his pocket and walked along side of me, and I watched his hand and saw he was fumbling something. I didn't know whether he had anything or not. I thought I had better not provoke him. I asked him what he was talking about. Says he "you know what I am talking about." "Well," says I, "explain yourself; I don't know what you are talking about." Finally, he kept talking on that way until I got sick of him, and went into the bath-house and left him there.

Q What further did he say at that time?
A The last word was, says he, "I never spoke to you, except about that piece of brass." I never said anything more but walked away.

Cross-examined by Mr. Webber:

Q You were detected in your effort to escape?
A. Yes, sir.
Q Did you get your key nearly completed?
A. It was completed; but when I was detected at the door I was afraid of being searched, so I gave it to another man; and I suppose they meant to steal a march on me, and when they went to the door and tried to open it, instead of turning downwards they turned upwards, and broke the key in the door. It was made out of bad metal. I had opened the door myself with it, but they didn't understand it, and broke the key.
Q. You had opened the bolt but not the door?
A. Yes, sir; and then I gave the key to a man named St. Clair; and it appears that he afterwards gave it to a man named Proctor, who went to the door and afterwards broke it.
Q. You say you were called out and stripped to be punished?
A. Yes, sir.
Q For what punishment was you stripped?
A. Well, I guess Mr. Morris had a strap on a piece of stick that he calls the "bat."
Q. Have you ever been punished with that?
A. I have been punished with the whip.
Q. When Mr. Morris saw the sore on your side he let you go without punishment?
A. No, sir; it was like this: He brought me into the wing, and after I was

stripped he demanded an explanation and wanted to know. Says he, "What is it," says he, "LaMountain about this key business; I want you to tell me all about it?" Then Mr. Morris asked me, "What is that sore on your body?" Said I, "This is the effect of the whipping you gave me." Said he, "I know better than that." Said I, "If you know better, all right." Said I, "What would be my object in making those sores?" And he said, "You are so full of the devil no one would know what was your object." And he said, "No physician would say this was the result of the lash."

Q. You were whipped?
A. No, sir; I told him the circumstances of the key, what there was about it, and then he took me to the cell, searched the cell, and put a wire cage on me.
Q. How long did you have to wear that?
A. I wore it about three weeks; I should think about that time.
Q. Do you know whether St. Clair or the others were punished?
A. I understood they were.
Q. You didn't see them punished?
A. No, sir.

By Senator Mellen:
Q. Have you any other marks on your body?
A. Not from the effect of that.
Q. From the use of the whip?
A. No, sir.
[Witness dismissed.]

Senator Webber here took the hospital record book and read the entries concerning McDonald, which showed that he was in the hospital on the 15th, 16th, 17th and 18th of June, 1871, for rheumatism; on the 21st of June for catarrh; on the 22d and 23d of June for rheumatism; on the 25th, 27th, 28th, 29th and 30th of June for dysentery—also for dysentery on the 1st and 3d of July; and on the 7th of July still in hospital, prescription being "liniment." On the 8th of July McDonald was in his cell and treated with "acupuncture;" on the 11th, 12th and 13th in his cell, "acupuncture;" on the 14th and 17th of July, in his cell, and the complaint is recorded as paralysis; on the last day he was also treated to "acupuncture;" also on the 17th the complaint is marked "injury;" on the 18th, 19th and 21st in his cell; and on the 21st treated with "acupuncture," and the complaint said to be paralysis. The record shows him also in cell—complaint alleged as paralysis—on the 22d and 24th of July. It shows him in his cell on the 25th of July, and the complaint said to be "paralysis injury," and the treatment is "acupuncture." The record shows him in his cell on the 26th of July, and the complaint said to be paralysis; the same on the 28th, 29th and 31st. Records of the same character extend into and through August, with occasional treatment by "acupuncture" in August.

Mr. Conely—May 22, 1871, the hospital record shows that he was sick from "tobacco poisoning," and that he was in the shop and not in the hospital. The check book for labor shows that he worked every day in May, that he worked in June to the 14th, and was sick on the 15th, and worked half a day on the 17th.

WILLIAM HOLT SWORN.

Examined by Mr. Conely:
Q. Holt, what were you sent here for?
A. For murder in the first degree.

STATE PRISON INVESTIGATION. 361

Q. What is your sentence?
A. Solitary for life.
Q. When were you sent here?
A. On the 16th of May, 1865.
Q. Did you know the convict McDonald?
A. Yes, sir.
Q. Did you ever have any talk with him about his arm?
A. I had frequent talks with him about his arm.
Q. Did he ever say anything about applying lime or potash to his arm?
A. He never did to me.
Q. Were you employed in the hospital during a part of the time that McDonald had the lame arm?
A. Yes, sir.
Q. I wish you would state to this committee in what way his arm and hand were bandaged?
A. Well, his hand was bandaged tight, so as it would be in about that shape [showing]; my own arm was broken, and I used to bathe it; we had frequent talks in the wash-house about the way I fixed my arm to promote circulation in it; he had hurt himself in the shoulder by keeping it bandaged up, and when he let it down the flesh fell away like, and the hand was smaller; I asked him why he did it, and he said the State was good for his arm when he got out; I told him I thought he was foolish to cut off his nose in this way to spite his face; he would never bathe his arm in my presence; his arm kept growing smaller and smaller, until it got in the condition it now is; I have not seen it lately, probably not for a year or two.
Q. Did you ever have any talk about this punishment that he received in 1871?
A. Yes; we talked about that sometimes; almost every time we would meet we would talk about his arm; he told me half a dozen times if he had done what he was told to do he would not have been punished.
Q. Did he say what they wanted him to do?
A. No, sir; he did not tell me.

AFTERNOON SESSION.

[Mr. John R. Martin, called for defense, was next sworn and examined. Being sick, his testimony was taken at his house.]
By Mr. Conely:
Q. Mr Martin, you know the convict Wm. McDonald?
A. Yes, I know him very well.
Q. Do you remember his being punished on the cross in July, 1871?
A. Yes, I remember it.
Q. How many times was he put upon the cross?
A. Only once to my knowledge.
Q. Do you know of his being put upon the cross on two successive days?
A. I don't know that he was.
Q. Do you remember how long he remained on the cross?

A. As well as my recollection serves me he must have been there some six or eight hours.
Q. Who, if any one, assisted you in putting him on the cross?
A. If any one, it was Mr. Lane; I don't recollect that any one assisted me.
Q. What keeper reported him?
A. I cannot tell you.
Q. Do you remember whether he had worked on the cigar contract?
A. He had been at work on the cigar contract. The keeper's name has slipped my mind.
Q. Was it Wing?
A. I think it was Wing.
Q. What knowledge, if any, had Mr. Morris of that punishment?
A. I think,—I could not say positively what knowledge he had,—but my impression is it was ordered by Mr. Morris. Those things were usually ordered by Mr. Morris when done.
Q. Do you speak of it with reference to what was usual, or do you remember?
A. I do not remember.
Q. Do you know why no record was made of this punishment?
A. I can't tell you why it was not.
Q. Do you know of Mr. Morris' being present any of the time that punishment was going on?
A. I do not recollect that he was; I think he was not. Mr. Morris would order men to be punished and leave it to me to execute, frequently.
Q. You don't speak now of this particular case.
A. No, but what was usual.
Q. You don't recollect about this particular case?
A. I recollect of his being on the cross, but other particulars I do not recollect so distinctly about.

Cross-examined by Mr. Barlow:
Q. What was your occupation at the prison?
A. I was deputy keeper.
Q. What time did it commence and what time terminate?
A. As deputy keeper?
Q. Yes, sir.
A. My first commencement was in 1859.
Q. What time did it terminate?
A. It terminated in December, I think, of 1871.
Q. How long was you deputy keeper under Mr. Morris' administration?
A. I think about two years,—somewhere near that length of time.
Q. Did you witness punishments inflicted by Mr. Morris?
A. I do not recollect that I did; punishments were usually inflicted by myself when I was there.
Q. Do you remember what Mr. McDonald was punished for at the time you speak of?
A. I think, sir, it is a very strong impression,—that it was for refusing to do his work.
Q. Do you remember the day of the month that he was on the cross?
A. I do not. I could not state the day of the month.
Q. If there was any fault in Mr. Morris' administration, in what did you consider that fault was?

A. Well, I think the fault was more in his leniency towards the convicts than in anything else.

Q State whether Mr. Morris' punishments were uniform for the same class of offenses?

A. Well, I don't know; I couldn't answer that question. I think the punishments would be diff-rent with different individuals.

Q. Then you think Mr. Morris lacked in strict discipline?

A. I do, in consequence of his leniency towards the convicts. Such has always been my impression.

Q. State whether, during your observation, he treated all alike?

A. No; I don't think that could be done by any Agent, or any other man.

Q. Well, state whether he seemed to have some favorites with the convicts?

A. Well, I should rather think that some would be more favorites than others, in fact, it seems to me impossible for it to be otherwise. Where a man would come up and behave himself like a man, everything right, and square, and honest, and others right opposite to that, it seems to me it would be quite different.

Q. Now, state what you know, if anything, about a rule being adopted by the inspectors, that no punishment should be inflicted except in the presence of the physician?

A. I think there was a resolution of that kind passed when Mr. Bingham was Agent, that no man should be punished with the lash unless it was done in the presence of the physician. I think that resolution was adopted by the inspectors.

Q Do you think that was in writing?

A. I think it was reduced to writing; that is my impression, yet I would not swear it was s ; yet I think such is the case.

Q Do you know of that ever being repealed?

A. I do not know of its ever being repealed,—and in fact, I would not swear that it was adop'ed, but such is my impression, that it was adopted.

Q. Do you recollect that that was for some time the practice?

A. Well, not much, at any rate; I think, perhaps, for two or three times, under Mr Bingham it was practiced, but it is my impression that was the end of it; and I don't know that I ever saw the resolution on the book. My impression now is that Mr. Bingham told me that such was the case. I recollect two or three punishments was inflicted in the presence of the physician. I think Mr. Tunnicliffe was the physician. That had reference to the lash more particularly than anything else.

Q. What was the conduct of McDonald generally?

A. Well, sir, I think he was the meanest man I ever knew on earth,—contrary, ugly, lying,—you couldn't believe one word in twenty that he would say, and he was full of mean, contemptible tricks, getting other convicts into trouble, and I think I never knew so mean a man in that prison as he was.

Q. You knew Thurston there?

A. Yes ; I knew him well.

Q What was his general conduct?

A. Thurston's general conduct was pretty good while I was there ; I had to reprimand him two or three times, but never had to punish him while I was there,—got along without.

Q. What was Mr. Morris' habit in regard to seeing that the duties of his subordinates was performed?

A. Well, I thought Mr. Morris was pretty punctual about seeing that his subordinates were under duty.

Q. How many females were there in the prison,—about how many—when Mr. Morris' administration commenced?
A. My impression is there was eight.
Q. What work did they have to perform?
A. Oh, they used to make shirts for the male convicts, mend them, make stockings, etc.,—work of that kind.
Q. Where were they kept?
A. They were kept in what was called the female prison—the brick building now used for a hospital.
Q. Whose duty was it to take care of them?
A. It was the matron's duty.
Q. Whose duty was it to lock them up and see that they were unlocked?
A. The matron's.
Q. In the absence of the matron whose duty was it?
A. In the absence of the matron sometimes it was done by one of the female convicts in the presence of some officer; it has been done in my presence; and sometimes Mrs. Morris would go in occasionally and see it done, and sometimes Mr. Morris' daughter has been and seen that it was done.
Q. Do you remember an occasion, the 24th of October, 1872, when Mrs. Morris and the matron were gone from the prison?
A. Yes, sir; I remember it distinctly.
Q. State what you know about Susan Schultz being in her cell that night.
[Objected to on the ground that neither of the resolutions under which this committee was appointed has any bearing upon anything other than acts of cruelty, and upon the things stated in the Adrian Press, and things similar in character to those therein stated.]
A. I do not know that she was in her cell that night. She was not there in the morning; that is all I know about it.
Q. Give what you know of your own knowledge.
A. Well, there is very little I know about it. I came in in the morning. I was in the habit of going to the prison and fetching the girls out to the Agent's house to work. I went after Susan and she had n't been there. I went back to the house to find out,—went up, I think, into the Agent's house,—and met the Agent, and he told me he had taken Susan out to stay over night with his little girl, who was very nervous at something that occurred the day before, and he took her out to stay with his little girl over night. That was the sum and substance of it, and all I know about it.
Q. Where was she that morning when you made your search?
A. In the Agent's house, I should judge; I don't know; I didn't see her.
Mr. Conely:
Q. Mr. Martin, had this girl been in the habit of doing the kitchen work previous to that time?
A. Oh, yes.
Q. For how long a time?
A. I couldn't tell you how long a time, but for quite a number of months.
Mr. Bartow:
Q. She would be locked in her cell nights?
A. Yes, sir.
Mr. Conely:
Q. What time of night was she locked in her cell?
A. Usually, I think, about 8 o'clock; sometimes it might be 9.

STATE PRISON INVESTIGATION. 365

Q. Later than the other convicts?
A. Yes; she would get through her supper arrangements, wash the dishes, etc., before she would go to her cell; all these girls that worked for Mr. Morris staid later than others.
Q. They staid later than others, and when their work was done they were locked in their cells?
A. Yes, sir.

DOCTOR GORDON CHITTOCK SWORN.

Examined by Mr. Conely:
Q. You are a physician, I believe?
A. I am, sir.
Q. How long have you been engaged in the practice of medicine?
A. Nearly twenty-five years, sir.
Q. Where do you reside?
A. Jackson.
Q. Were you at the prison this morning?
A. I was.
Q. Did you se the convict McDonald?
A. I saw a convict that they called McDonald.
Q. A man with a lame arm?
A. I did, sir.
Q. Did you examine the arm?
A. I did.
Q. Did you talk with him?
A. I did.
Q. Were you present this morning during the taking of the testimony of Dr. Tunnicliffe?
A. I was.
Q. Did you hear the doctor state the manner in which that man had been treated, and some of the symptoms that were indicated while he was being treated in the early part of 1871?
A. Yes; that is, I heard the evidence he gave after I came into the room; I do not know whether he had been on the stand before or not; I heard all the evidence then.
Q. Did you come to any conclusion in reference to this man's arm?
A. Yes, sir.
Q. What conclusion did you come to?
A. My honest conviction was that there was an atrophy of the muscles, a wasting away of the tissues of the arm—not a very active member anyway. Some might call this paralysis. Paralysis may mean simply disuse long continued, till a limb will not obey the mandates of the will; another sense of the word would be loss of sensation. We have other causes for a member refusing to obey the mandates of the will besides paralysis, and I doubt whether the case under investigation was originally paralysis. An atrophy may be produced by other causes than paralysis. Disuse causes loss of function, and atrophy follows as a natural consequence. We may have loss of function, that is, of motion, without impaired sensibility. The sensibilities may remain as acute as before, even more so, and yet the muscles refuse to obey the mandate of the will. There are different causes which produce that condition. Confining a member in a particular position, where the muscles cannot be brought into use for a

long period, compresses and shuts off nutrition, and necessarily causes a wasting of the member, and this result may be caused by the exercise of the will without any original disease of the nerve centers. The same effect would follow disease of the roots of the spinal nerves. If a man had a wilful, malignant intent to destroy a member, he could accomplish that result, as in this case, and we could not tell with any certainty how the effect was produced. The indication in McDonald's case is that he has a withered, atrophied, distorted limb, not likely to be of any use to him. Of course I cannot detail the the means by which it was destroyed. Paralysis is a peculiar disease,— a disease that sometimes takes place very suddenly, supervening on no visible cause. An individual may go to bed at night in unusual health, and on attempting to rise in the morning, find himself unable to do so. Examine and you find it a case of hemiplegy. It may extend even to the muscles of one side of the face. It may contract the muscles of only one side of the body, and continue so while the individual lives; or there may be a wasting away of the tissue without any visible cause. It is a difficult matter to define the original cause of the disease. From McDonald's history, as given by his fellow-convicts, I should infer that in his case it was brought about by his own malign disposition, and I testify fearlessly, honestly, candidly, in regard to the matter.

Q. Suppose a man were compelled to stand upon his feet against a wooden structure in the form of a cross, with his arms extended horizontally at right angles to the trunk, say eight or ten hours, a ligature about the arm close to the wrist; would such a thing, in your judgment, produce the trouble that you see in this man's arm?

A. I should not think it would, sir. If the circulation were obstructed in the hand for ten hours, inflamation would probably set in, which might extend to the tissues and produce gangrene; but it would not be sufficient of itself to produce paralysis. This is produced by injury to the roots of the nerves or the nerve fiber itself, that passes from the spinal cord to and over the plexes from which the nerves take their origin, and are distributed to the sentient extremity. It may be produced by injuring the spinal cord itself, or the tunic of that cord.

Q. Doctor, I think you stated before that in your opinion the present trouble with that man's arm was atrophy?

A. Atrophy; yes, sir.

Q. Now you have also given it as your opinion that this condition may come simply from disuse.

A. That would be one of the causes.

Q. Suppose that in point of fact this man has not been guilty to any extent of bringing this about, might it not be brought about in him from some disturbance at the nerve centres?

A. Yes, sir.

Q. Would not the presence of syphilitic taint in the system have a tendency to increase or produce that difficulty?

A It might predispose to that condition.

Q. Did you have any conversation with him to-day at the prison?

A. I did, sir.

Q. What statement, if any, did he make to you in regard to his ever having had any venereal disorder?

A. I asked him that question, and he answered it in the affirmative.

Cross-examined by Mr. Webber:

Q. Doctor, from your interview with McDonald to-day do you regard him as sane or insane?

A. Well, sir, my acquaintance with the man was very short, and it is a very difficult thing to determine as to the sanity of an individual by seeing him for ten or fifteen minutes.

Q. You never saw him till to-day?

A. No, sir, and then only for ten or fifteen minutes. He answered my questions, and I considered answered them intelligently.

Q. Did his physical health seem to be fair?

A. For a man that has probably been in the condition he has, and considering the length of time he has been incarcerated, I should say it was. As I understand the testimony, he has been in there since 1861 or prior to that time. He told me it was 1861 the handcuffs were put on him and his shoulder hurt. That was in the Columbus State prison. Then he has been through another term here. I asked what ailed his arm and he said he had hurt his shoulder. I asked him how it was hurt, and he said in 1861 handcuffs were put on him and his hands brought up, and one hand being smaller than the other, it came out and gave him a jerk, and something gave way in his shoulder.

Q. Now, doctor, if his shoulder had been dislocated, and after it got nearly healed his arms should be extended horizontally or partially raised above a horizontal position and made fast, and the ligature making them fast should be so tight as to impede circulation, would that be a cause sufficient to produce the condition the hand is in?

A. That would depend upon the amount of violence and the length of time he was fastened there.

Q. Suppose he was kept there nine or ten hours?

A. The result would then depend on the amount of strangulation.

Q. Now, you spoke of this atrophy being produced by the position. Do I understand you to mean that the mere effect of the will would produce that result?

A. It is not merely an effect of the will—it takes a long time to accomplish it. I said I found the limb wasted away. Put a man's arm in a sling and keep it there long enough, and he would have atrophy of the muscles from disease; but if you bind a man's arm with a bandage and then put it in a sling you would facilitate that condition, because by tightening the bandage you would shut off nutrition from the part.

WM. L. SEATON SWORN.

Examined by Mr. Conely:

Q. You reside in Jackson?
A. Yes, sir.
Q. Postmaster here?
A. Yes, sir.
Q. Was formerly Agent at the prison?
A. Yes, sir.
Q. At what time?
A. I think it was from 1859 to 1865.
Q. Who succeeded you?
A. Mr. Winton.
Q. During the time you were Agent were there female convicts in the prison?
A. Yes, sir.
Q. Do you know whether, at any time, any of those female convicts were in the habit of sleeping in the Agent's house?
A. They were, sir, both before and while I was Agent.

Cross-examined by Mr. Webber:

Q. Was the Agent's house within the walls of the prison?

A. It is considered so by the Board. I think the resolution of the Board made it a part of the prison.

Q. Were there prison doors between the Agent's house and the outside streets?

A. Yes, sir.

Q. Were those doors locked every night?

A. One of them was locked every night; the other was kept guarded by the keeper.

Q. Then prisoners that were allowed to remain in the Agent's house were considered as in prison while in that house?

A. Yes, sir.

Q. State whether any particular ones were designated for that, and lodged there constantly, that is, right along, generally.

A. Yes, sir; particular ones that we could trust; I recollect one very distinctly that the former Agent, Mr. Hammond, thought he could trust, but she was not faithful to the trust, and ran away.

Q. While being lodged in the Agent's house she had the opportunity to get away?

A. Yes, sir.

Q. Was there any order of the inspectors that permitted an Agent to give these convicts an opportunity to escape in this manner?

A. No, sir; I don't think there was.

Q. The Agent did it on his own responsibility?

A. I think so; yes, sir; it was decided by the inspectors that the Agent's house should be considered a portion of the prison and that convicts at work in the Agent's house would be still confined in prison,

Q. Yes, sir; but they might work in the Agent's house and sleep in cells, might they not?

A. Yes, sir; most of them did; it was a matter of discretion with the Agent as to whom he could trust.

Mr. Conely—I will ask whether the ones who lodged in the house did the kitchen work?

A. They did.

[Some discussion was had as to the propriety of striking out that portion of Mr. Martin's testimony to which exceptions had been taken by the defense, but the committee decided to let it stand].

MR. MARTIN RECALLED.

[In the evening, Mr. Conely, Mr. Bartow, and the stenographer, went to the house of Mr. Martin, who was further examined as follows:]

By Mr. Conely:

Q. Mr. Martin I want to ask you who, in the fall of 1872, was in the habit of unlocking and locking the cells of the female convicts?

A. The Matron.

Q. Did Mr. Morris have anything to do with that?

A. Not to my knowledge,—he didn't.

Q. Now, in your testimony to-day, did you mean to be understood that Mr. Morris went to the cell of this woman, after she had been locked in for the night, and let her out?

A. No, sir.

STATE PRISON INVESTIGATION. 369

Q. Or did you mean to be understood that she remained out?

A. I didn't mean to be understood that after she was locked in the cell, he went and took her out, by any means. I don't know but the woman had been out all day, I can't tell about that; all I know was, the next morning I found her out, and think, perhaps, she had been out the day before. What I supposed was, she had been out the day previous. The probability is she staid out, and hadn't been to the prison at all that night, and had been at work the day previous.

Q. Did you mean to be understood as saying that Mr. Morris went to the cell and let her out?

A. I didn't mean to be understood that way at all. I don't know that Mr. Morris ever saw her unlocked, or was there when she was unlocked.

[Attention of the witness was here called to that part of his testimony given in the afternoon in which he relates a conversation with Mr. Morris about taking the girl out.]

Mr. Martin—The explanation is this: I don't think Mr. Morris said,—I don't wish to be understood as saying that he said he had taken her out,—but that he had kept her out; not that he had *taken* her out, but *kept* her out; that is, she hadn't been taken back to the female prison, but had staid at the Agent's house that night with his little girl.

Q. Did he state what was the matter with his little girl?

A. She was nervous from a fright at something that happened in the prison the day before.

Q. Did you ever know of Mr. Morris' locking the cells of the female convicts, or unlocking them?

A. I never did.

By Mr. Morris:

Q. Or conducting them any distance at all?

A. I never knew whether he went from the house to the female prison or some one else. I know I used to be in the habit of going there myself when I was with Mr. Bingham.

Cross-examined by Mr. Bartow:

Q. Was it the custom that this woman and the rest of the female convicts should be locked in their cells over night?

A. That was the custom, yet there was exceptions to it. They frequently staid out over night, but it was the custom to be locked in nights, but sometimes that custom was not carried out. Sometimes some of them staid out over night.

Mr. Bartow, on behalf of the committee, made the following admission: "It is admitted by the committee that the only object in asking Mr. Martin if Mrs. Schultz staid in the Agent's house all night was to show irregularities in the discipline and management of the prison."

FRIDAY EVENING, APRIL 23.

Committee met at Lansing Friday evening, April 23d, and resumed the investigation.

Present—Senators Nelson, Jones, Mellen, Webber; Representatives Morris, Bartow, Eggleston.

G. D. GRIDLEY, SWORN.

Examined by Mr. Conely:
Q. You reside at Jackson?
A. Yes, sir.
Q. What is your business?
A. Attorney at law.
Q. Do you know Mr. Perkins, who was a convict at the prison?
A. Perkins? yes, sir; I have known him for years.
Q. Where did he reside when you knew him?
A. At Jackson.
Q. What was his business at that time?
A. Practicing law.
Q. Were you acquainted with his reputation for truth and veracity?
A. I think I was.
Q. Was it good or bad?
A. Rather bad.

MARVIN DORRILL, SWORN.

Examined by Mr. Conely:
Q. Do you know Mr. Perkins?
A. I do.
Q. Did you know him when he resided at Jackson?
A. I did.
Q. Did you know his reputation for truth and veracity?
A. Yes, sir.
Q. Was it good or bad?
A. Bad, I think, sir.

AGENT MORRIS SWORN.

Examined by Mr. Conely:
Q. Mr. Morris, when did you first become connected with the prison, in any capacity?
A. I think, sir, that the first thing I had to do with the prison was in the year 1862, under an appointment as inspector from Governor Blair.
Q. How long did you have that position?
A. I left it in March, 1864.
Q. When did you become Agent?
A. I took up the reins as Agent March 17, 1874.
Q. I wish you would state to the committee what has been done in the way of experiment or otherwise as to various methods of punishment that have been tried there since you became Agent, showing, if you can, successively, what has been introduced, if any has been abolished, what was abolished, and why. State it in your own language, as plainly and as briefly as you can.
A. Well, sir, my first connection with the prison in 1862 led me to give the subject of prison management a good deal of attention. From that time until I went to the prison as agent I took more than a usual interest in everything that happened at the prison. While inspector I became acquainted with a good many persons throughout the country by correspondence. I was chairman of the board, and made two or three reports. I read everything that I saw in the papers and periodicals, everything published concerning prison management. Wrote now and then a little item myself. I had theories of my own for several years, differing somewhat from those in practice at the prison, more particu-

arly concerning discipline. I had no practical experience. I went there in full belief that some of my theories might be tried without any doubt of success. I had for years thought that the prison might be managed without corporal punishment, for one thing. I looked upon the prison as a large body of turbulent, ill-disposed, refractory men. I went there not only for the purpose of performing its business duties as Agent, but if possible to do some little good in the way of reforming these men, inducing them to lead better lives when they left the prison. That has been my sole aim ever since. I tried to preserve what little manhood a convict brought with him to the prison door, to keep it alive, if possible. I found very many of my theories which read very prettily were not practicable. The prison itself was in a very unfavorable condition for keeping good, healthy discipline, or good living in any way. The buildings, walls, fences, walks, barns, and sheds were in a dilapidated condition. I couldn't place my eye on anything that was complete. The means for living, cooking, and washing were of the most primitive kind. One of the first things I sought to do was to get acquainted with the men as fast and far as I could; to learn something of their history, to interest myself in their little wants. I was firm in the belief that I could manage that prison without resorting to any very severe punishments, particularly with the lash. I made no immediate change in my subordinates. The deputy had been there several years, and had a good deal of prison experience. I necessarily had to lean largely upon him. He was strongly in favor of the lash,—had used it for years. He did not indorse my view, and he sustained me very poorly in that direction all the time he was with me. Some of my other subordinates, some four or five of them, leading men in the prison, were with him more than with me. They didn't like my experiment. I found very good support in the board. I immediately saw very clearly that I wanted experience and observation. They counseled me to let the lash be used only when all other means were exhausted. This I tried for about four months.

Q. Now, state right here, what methods of punishment you sought to get along with in the early part of your administration without resorting to the lash ; what you first tried?

A. Well, sir, the first few weeks of my administration there I didn't try anything severe at all,—simply the bare cell, locking men up ; I found a good deal of embarrassment in this attempt ; the men there were all working on contracts ; locking a bad man in a bare cell, or any cell, for any length of time was likely to interfere seriously with the labor ; the men worked in gangs ; it often happens that only one or two men in a shop can run some particular little machine, and all the work done in a shop has to go through that machine ; take that man away from that machine for a considerable length of time and you interfere seriously with the interest of the contract ; if he is in good health they will hardly submit to it ; I found the discipline was relaxing ; scenes of violence were occurring almost every day, some of them very serious in their character, endangering life and limb ; I hadn't been in the prison thirty days before the former Agent, passing quietly through the shops, was seized by two or three rough men and thrown out into the yard ; men grew defiant and reckless ; I think I made the experiment of it consistently ; I never said to the prisoners that I had abandoned the whip, that no man would be punished ; but the bad men, the wild men, men of wild natures, seemed to take the idea that the whip was thrown out entirely, and took advantage of it ; keepers daily complained that they didn't think it safe to do their own duty in the prison ; for the want of any better means I finally took up the lash.

Q. Did you try some other things before resorting to the lash?
A. Yes, sir.
Q. What were they?
A. One of the first things was the construction of the cross.
Q. Was that finally thrown out?
A. Yes, sir; it was thrown out within less than two years afterwards.
Q. Why was it thrown out?
A. We didn't like it in many respects Not so much from its severity as from the impressions people obtained of it outside. The cross itself was not a severe penalty, not a severe punishment—simply a position of fatigue. I couldn't see anything in it calculated to injure a man's limbs or his health.
Q. Did you know any injurious results occasioned by it?
A. I never heard of any.
Q. Now, in this connection, I will ask you whether at the time of McDonald's punishment or before it you were apprised of it in any way?
A. I have no recollection of McDonald ever being punished on the cross or in any other way. If he was punished, it was of such a trifling character that I don't recollect it.
Q. Was he ever punished by your order, Mr. Morris?
A. Not that I recollect. I don't recollect ever ordering McDonald to be put on the cross. I might as well say right here, with due respect to Mr. Martin, who was my deputy, that there was always a contest for supremacy between us in that particular. He maintained his right as deputy of the prison to inflict punishment whenever he thought it was necessary and in the manner he thought best, without consulting me. He had to yield that position. I couldn't stand it after I got so I could say yes and no myself; but he never liked it. He said it was a privilege that had always been allowed him under the former Agent. I have nothing to warrant the truth of the assertion, however.
Q. That is, you don't know whether that privilege had been accorded him or not?
A. I do not know.
Q. What was your first recollection of McDonald?
A. Well, sir, I can't tell the first time that I knew who McDonald was; we always have quite a large body of men in prison who are defective in various ways from injuries and from disease; it takes a stranger quite a good while to get acquainted with all the men in the prison so that he knows who they are when he sees them; we have a good many men in prison to day, some of them using canes, others with defective hands and limbs, and it is impossible for me to tell to-night whether they were injured the year that I came there, or the year before, or two years since, in many instances.
Q. Does your recollection of McDonald reach back to a time prior to his injury, or prior to its being so manifest as to appear plainly that he had a lame arm?
A. I have seen McDonald for the last two and a half or three years with his hand done up in a bandage; there was something ailed it.
Q. Does your memory go far enough back to call him to mind when he hadn't his hand bound up?
A. It does not, sir.
Q. You have said, Mr. Morris, that the walls and buildings were of a kind that interfered to some extent with the discipline at the commencement of your term. I wish you would explain more clearly how that is?

A. If I recollect right, the Legislature appropriated thirty thousand dollars in 1871, for improving the wall. This work was commenced in about sixty days after I went to the prison. They removed the old wall and built a new one, commencing at the southeast corner of the east wing, and running east 185 feet; north 600 feet, and west 185 feet, where it joined with the old wall again.

Q. What was the height of the old wall?

A. The old wall averaged about 16 or 17 feet around the yard.

Q. What is the height of the new one.

A. The height of the new one is 24 feet.

Q. McDonald, in his statement, Mr. Morris, speaks of your coming into the solitary at a time when he was there on the cross,—have you any recollection of that?

A. I have no sort of recollection of seing McDonald undergoing any penalty for any prison misdemeanor.

Q. He also says he spoke to you about getting some liniment the next morning?

A. I say of that the same as of all the rest, that I have no recollection of it.

Q. Did he ever claim to you that the injury to his arm had been occasioned by any thing that occurred within the prison?

A. He never spoke to me of suffering at all, in any shape or manner, nor any one else connected with the prison.

Q. When were you first apprised that it was claimed that the trouble in his arm was occasioned by his treatment in the prison?

A. Very soon after the article appeared in the Adrian Press, charging me with suspending him.

Q. Had you any knowledge on that subject, or had any information been conveyed to you by any person that McDonald claimed that his injury occurred in consequence of punishment in the prison, prior to the publication in the Adrian paper?

A. I don't recollect of any person every alluding to or hinting such a thing to me. When I first read the article I searched the conduct records to see if McDonald ever had any difficulty, and couldn't find anything.

Q. Do you know of any reason why that didn't go upon the record?

A. I have no sort of reason to give. I have questioned Mr. Martin about it, and asked him to show his memorandum book, but he didn't know where his memorandum book was. He has been lying dangerously sick until within a few days. He said he would try to have his folks find it, but he never has.

Q. After the experiment was tried with the cross, what was the next method of punishment in order?

A. Well, before we abandoned the cross entirely, we commenced using what we termed the hose, as a matter of convenience. A little hydrant stood in the lower hall of the center building, and I conceived the idea that it would be a very convenient punishment, without incurring much danger. We commenced using it in moderate weather, first upon the feet, afterwards by removing the pants and playing upon the legs, and finally, upon the whole body.

Q. Ever about the face or mouth?

A About the face sometimes. It is impossible to play upon a man's mouth because he always has the freedom of his neck and person, except his hands, and can turn his head in any direction, and keep it out of his face or mouth.

Q. What else has been tried except the hose?

A. In cases of persistant efforts to escape I have used a light clog that was in use when I went there,—in a few instances, not many.

Q. The clog shown to the committee?

A. That was one of them; there were heavier ones; I never used the heavier ones.

Q. What other things have been used?

A. I saw the wire cap used in Auburn prison two years ago, and I came home and made a couple of them. I have used them in several instances, just to mark men.

Q. That was the same cap exhibited at Jackson.

A. Yes, sir; I have never had but two of them made.

Q. Were they alike in weight and style?

A. Nearly the same.

Q. Well, what other things in the way of punishment?

A. There are many little things almost as light as air in themselves in the way of deprivation of privileges. I might mention the strap right here as well as any time. It was introduced in order to get rid of the cross and of the apparent injurious effects of the lash. An old keeper from Joliet said he could prepare me a little thing that would not cut men at all; would not leave any scars. I told him to make one and we would see how it would work. He made one the same day that he spoke about it; it was laid away for several months, as we had no occasion to use it.

A. The strap shown to the committee; Marshal Fay made it, or had it made.

Q. Well, what was the next?

A. For minor offenses, such as talking, or any violations of the rules pertaining to correspondence or lights,—these things had been prohibited, taken away from them. A good many little things have been thrown in from time to time just upon the spur of the moment. Sometimes a man working on improvements would be right in the way—like enough talking or demoralizing the gang—and we would tell him to go and sit on the hydrant for an hour—a cast-iron hydrant standing in the yard. I have set them down on a stone. In two or three instances I think they have been required to get upon the wooden staging horse.

Q. Let me ask you about that horse, Mr. Morris,—is it one that was prepared for the purpose of punishment?

A. The horse happened to be standing there just at that time, used in the construction of the work going on. We did not hold it as a permanent thing in the prison at all as a means of punishing. There were men working on contracts—on the grindstones—that suffered as much every hour as men did on the wooden horse, and in various other places about the yard.

Q. Well, you finally came to the whip, did you?

A. Finally came to it.

Q. Yes, sir.

A. I came to the whip before I came to these articles; I come to the whip about four months after I came to the prison; took it up for a time; didn't like it, and abandoned it and substituted the strap in its place.

Q. Something has been said in the testimony about the whipping of the man Thurston, I think?

A. Yes, sir; I whipped him.

Q. Was the whipping in his case continued to any extent, and if so, to what extent, after he had yielded obedience?

A. Just as soon as Thurston's promises were full and complete, I stopped whipping him; Thurston had tried my patience for weeks and for months, and I had brought the censure of all the officers in the yard on myself by my forbearance with that man. One afternoon in June, a convict in whom I had considerable confidence as a man, came to me and told me that I must stand clear of it; that he had seen a dirk knife in his bosom that day, and he told him that he would strike me to the heart the first chance he got with it; he had repeatedly threatened a good many times before that. I called him in and found the convict's statement correct concerning the knife. I wish here to state that I have never meant to give any man more than fifty lashes; I punished Thurston as severely as any man in the prison, and I counted very carefully the number of lashes, and don't think I gave him more than one above.

Q. I wish now to call your attention to the whipping of Driscoll, and want to ask you why he was whipped?

A. I think Driscoll came to the prison in February, 1873, if my memory serves me; I know he came in February, in the winter, and he soon manifested considerable determination and defiance ; rumors kept coming to me every day of some scheme in which Driscoll was the leader ; some of them were quite alarming and serious, and caused us a good deal of misapprehension, and we used unusual caution for several months just on his account more than any body else's; he came there with another man from Saginaw, with a very bad reputation by the officers; it was quite usual for us to get some history of the men from the officers who brought them there. One of the first precautions we took on Driscoll's account was placing a large iron clasp on the outer gate, and stationing an extra guard there with weapons on Sunday morning while the men were marching to church, and during church service ; the reason for doing this on Sunday morning more than any other morning, was because there is usually quite a crowd of visitors come over from the city to church, and we feared he would take this opportunity to make a break, and lead men who were in plot with him; Driscoll did escape in quite a mysterious manner; I happened to be the first and leading man after him; I intercepted him about a mile and a half from the prison on the river bottoms, in a thick growth of underbrush and grass, where he had hid for a few moments; a colored man some fifty or sixty rods from his hiding place, informed me where he had just seen him, passing from one bunch of undergrowth to another; I went in the direction pointed by the colored man, and looking closely and sharply, I at last discovered him rising— well, he was fairly up when I first saw him, I should think about fifty or sixty feet from me in a thick growth of brush, starting to run; a single step would have taken him out of my sight, placed the bushes between me and him; I fired and happened to hit him—fired with a navy revolver; he exclaimed, "my God! what did you shoot me for?" I told him to throw up his hands and come to me —to put his hands over his head and come out of there.

Q. Why did you tell him that?

A. It was the week of the horse fair, and there had been a good many strange sporting men there visiting it, and I feared he might have a revolver or some weapon about him. I asked him if he was struck with the ball, and he said he was, but couldn't tell just where. I told him to hurry out to the railroad. It was, I should think, about twenty rods to where the track swept across the bottoms. When he reached the railroad track I told him to about face and tell me who helped him to get out of prison—who assisted him to escape. He said he would tell me all about it when he got up to the prison. I said something more to him about his wound, and he thought the ball had entered his lungs. I told him to step along lively and we would get home as quick as we could. I didn't see much signs of blood. He seemed to change his views before he had gone a great ways and kept looking about him from right to left, and he wouldn't put up his hands as I told him. But we finally reached the prison, and I sent him to the hospital and called a physician. Before the physician reached there we examined his wound and found it was just the slightest kind of a flesh wound in his back—nothing serious at all. The ball was removed and he was sent to the shop, where he had been at work, perhaps an hour before the bell at noon. Driscoll's escape produced quite a sensation in the yard. There is a sort of free-masonry in the prison yard, and a matter of that kind will spread very quick through the yard. The officers told me the convicts were all aware that Driscoll had left the yard and that I was alone and had better look out for him or I would not get him. After his wounds were dressed I saw that there was no sort of danger, and I told him to take his seat on the block till the bell rang when the men could all see him. He marched to dinner with the men at noon; took his dinner and worked in the afternoon. It was a very hot day. I was somewhat fatigued with the excitement and chase. Said nothing more to him that day. I made considerable effort to find out all the surroundings and all the circumstances of his escape, but got no clue to who his aid was. The next morning after breakfast I took him to the hall and asked him—I don't know but I asked him before I went to the hall. He was very defiant and insolent and wouldn't tell me a word about it. After considerable effort to persuade him to tell me something about it I had to pick up the whip. I think I gave him ten lashes. He told me the two men that helped him. One was a man named Seaton, and the other was Clark, who wrote the article on a piece of brown paper. Seaton denied everything, Clark admitted everything. Seaton was punished, Clark was not punished.

Q. Why was Driscoll whipped then? Was it for escaping or something else?

A. He was whipped because he wouldn't reveal the plot; I mistrusted the teamster very strongly of helping him; I didn't know that the wagon had stood in the yard over night; I supposed the teamster had gone in there with his team and helped load the hubs; the appearance was that the teamster must know something about it, and in that case it was highly important that I should know something about it.

Q. How large was Driscoll?

A. He measures 6 feet 2 inches in hight, and weighs 185 pounds.

Q. There was a man named McEvoy punished for something in relation to a pipe; was that pipe found, and if so, where?

A. The guard reported McEvoy several nights, I think, in succession for smoking; had smelt the smoke and saw it in his cell; still he persistently denied it; he was punished for smoking, and the pipe was afterwards found in a straw-bed.

Q. Betts,—what was he punished for?

A. Betts had been a wild, turbulent man from the day I went to the prison until the day he was punished; he had taken quite an active part in a number of rude scenes before that.

Q. Just give the circumstances that led to his punishment?

A. On the day that he was punished I punished another man, the first man that I whipped, Dave Smith; passing through the yard I was talking with Mr. Chase about it, and there were two or three convicts within hearing; I made some further allusion to the whip; we had purchased a whip and would use it after this rather than put up with any more such rough scenes as we had had; Betts looked up and laughed about it very sneeringly; I added some further reproof and left him; the same day he was reported for passing a letter to another convict in the shop; I took him in; I don't recollect how many lashes I gave him, but I think ten.

Q. Any ill result from this punishment?

A. No, sir; he went back to his work; he worked outside in the tar-bed (?) with three or four other men, and told them he had catched it.

Q. What knowledge have you ever had, Mr. Morris, in relation to any rule or supposed rule requiring the prison physician to be present at the administration of punishments?

A. Well, sir, I have no knowledge of any such rule; I have no knowledge to-day that any such rule is upon the records, except from information since the investigation commenced.

Q. When was the first you heard anything said about there having been any rule having any bearing upon that subject?

A. I don't recollect ever hearing any such rule until within the last thirty days.

Q. Something has been said by one of the witnesses in relation to favoritism to particular convicts or classes of convicts; to what extent, if any, have you permitted some convicts to be better dressed or have privileges which were not granted others?

A. Why, it is a necessity for the sake of decency and the appearance of the men in various positions about the yard that they should dress differently.

Q. Explain where that necessity is, that the committee may understand it?

A. We have to have convict help in the several offices of the prison, more or less, always; for instance, men caring for the sick in the hospital, or handling food in the dining-room or kitchen, a good deal more care has been exercised in their dress than with men who work at forges or in dirty places about the yard or shops.

Q. Has there been any distinction of dress except as it has been occasioned by such a necessity?

A. I never meant there should be any.

Q. Have the friends or relatives of convicts been permitted to bring in articles of clothing for the convicts to wear?

A. A few things, not many ; it has been my aim to keep the convicts almost wholly dependent upon the prison authorities for what they use, still, in some instances I have allowed handkerchiefs, tooth-brushes, and various little articles of ornament about the cells, that didn't interfere in any manner with the discipline of the prison ; sometimes they furnish underclothing ; sometimes they furnished a better article than we had, and I never objected to their furnishing anybody in this way if they chose.

Q. Have you had any complaints during the past winter, or at any other time, of any insufficiency of either clothing or bed-clothing?

A. The convicts frequently speak to me, wanting a great many things ; they are full of wants ; some of their wants are very reasonable ; in every such case I have tried to comply with them.

Q. Have you had any reason to suppose that at any time during the cold weather there has been an insufficiency of either bed-clothing or suitable garments for the men to wear?

A. Nothing that I could remedy at the time.

Q. Well, has there been anything that could not be remedied, and if so, why couldn't it be remedied?

A. The improvements have interfered largely with the prison discipline, with the heating of it for one thing. The central building was not fairly enclosed until the month of January, and its doors have been open. I had no control of that work at all.

Q. Under whose control was that?

A. That was under the control of the superintendent, Mr. Donough, and the exposure was unavoidable with him. The job was a large one and was hurried as fast as possible. The winter has been unusually severe. Great extremes of cold would come to us within ten or twelve hours; a single night often. My instructions to the engineer have been to keep the mercury at a degree not far from 65 degrees; but some of those extreme nights, when the mercury outside was down to 20 degrees below zero it ran down in the prison in the neighborhood of 50,—so I was told by the guards,—but I never had any serious complaints, no such as I expected to have. Those complaints always came from men in the lower cases of cells. Men in the upper part of the prison were usually warm enough.

Q. Was there any shortage of supplies?

A. In caring for such a large body of men you run short of supplies very often unavoidably. The hall master generally informs us if anything is wanted in that line. Sometimes he will discover that his supplies are short. I have ordered a number of bales of blankets from Detroit by telegraph just because the weather was so excessively cold, and they must come by the first train to meet our demands.

Q. Has there been any shortage of supply in the material out of which to make jackets or vests or pants,—anything for the body?

A. Yes, sir; the same exigencies arise occasionally in these supplies.

Q. To your knowledge has there been any deficiency in that regard.

A. We sometimes made a contract with the best men in the State and they fail to come to time, and it may be for good reasons. In one instance a year ago last fall we had completed a contract with the Constantine Mills for quite a large supply of cassimere. The goods were all in the loom being manufactured and before they were done the mill burned up. Of course such an exigency as that would leave us scant for several weeks perhaps, before we could make a turn and get goods from any other source. Last fall we got into quite an unpleasant fix through the failure of a manufacturer to fill a contract. The goods didn't answer the requirement. I refused to accept them and held off for a couple of weeks or so until the Board met. We were visited by some pretty cold weather during the interval, and needed the clothing very much.

Q. Have the materials of that sort been purchased within the State?

A. Always; I purchase everything I can in the State if I can find it at reasonable figures. I had always interpreted the law as requiring me to do it, until the other day.

Q. I called your attention to it.

A. Of course it has been the understanding of the board. I know I have never received any bids from any other State.

Q. It has been since this investigation begun that I called your attention to the fact that the law didn't require the goods to be purchased in this State.

STATE PRISON INVESTIGATION. 379

A. Yes, sir; I never received any complaints from the physician concerning clothing.

Q. From any other official source?

A. No, sir. Oh, the hall-master used sometimes to tell me that we needed more blankets.

Q. Some instances have occurred, Mr. Morris, it would seem, where punishments have been inflicted that have not gone upon the record. I wish you would explain as far as you can how that has happened; or if there is any reason within your knowledge why they have not gone upon the record, let the committee know it?

A. In all the cases that I know of where any omission has been made upon the record, it has been done to save the convict from an unjust loss of time. It sometimes occurs that the physician will pronounce a man entirely capable for work; he will refuse to work; in some instances men have been punished,—not hard. Where there is any doubt about it we make the punishment as light as possible. In some instances we have found out a man's complaints were just; no record has been made of it. In very infrequent cases the keepers will report a man for some apparent misdemeanor; the next day or a few days after it will appear that the convict was not to blame. Keepers sometimes admit themselves were at fault; in rare instances convicts have suffered punishment, and before the board met such a record would be cancelled.

Q. For what reason?

A. To save his time. I don't recollect any record ever being omitted from any other motive.

Q. Have you any knowledge of the omission from the record of any punishment for any other purpose than simply to save the convict's time to him?

A. I haven't any clear case to warrant me in such a statement, of my own knowledge, although I feel well satisfied it has been done.

Q. Has there been any case where you yourself have inflicted a punishment where the record has been kept so as to conceal the punishment, except for the purpose of benefiting the convict?

A. I do not recollect of any, sir.

Q. Have you, since your administration, Mr. Morris, been instrumental to any extent, in increasing the privileges of the convicts, in the matter of correspondence?

A. It has been my constant study to increase this privilege, as well as a great many others that would in no way conflict with the discipline of the prison. One reason why we have had to resort to severe punishments in the prison, has been that there were no privileges that we could deprive them of, that they must not indulge. If they were entitled to a large list of little things that we might deprive them of the use of, that might be used as a penalty. One little experiment I made which has proved more satisfactory, perhaps, than any other of the same importance, was correspondence with immediate friends. This was allowed once in three months when I went to the prison. I reduced it gradually to three weeks.

Q. To what extent have you been instrumental in introducing the lighter kinds of reading matter, magazines, and newspapers, to the convicts?

A. It has been my constant endeavor to keep a large supply in the prison all the time. When I went to the prison I found a sum not exceeding three hundred dollars had been invested in the year. I think the first year the prison board authorized me to expend five hundred dollars for books.

Q. Was that done at your request?

A. It was done with the approval of the board,—whether at my suggestion or not, I could not say.

Q. How about the introduction of newspapers or monthlies?

A. I found a very scanty supply of reading matter in the prison when I went there, and an immense supply of tobacco being used; six hundred and twenty-five men were drawing rations of tobacco every week, at quite a high price; in 1870 the sum expended for tobacco alone was two thousand dollars or more.

Q. Was that expenditure reduced?

A. Yes, sir.

Q. Do you remember to what extent?

A. I can't recollect how much the first year, but several hundred dollars; in July, 1871, I conceived the idea of changing tobacco for magazines; men were allowed lights only about five months in a year when I went to the prison; I gave every man a light who asked for one every night in the year until nine o'clock.

Q. What is the cost of the magazines that you substituted for the tobacco?

A. I made one purchase of over five hundred dollars; I think 175 men walked up, threw up the weed, and took the magazines in the year; papers were not allowed to come into the building for some time after that; when I went to the prison it was a difficult matter to find a scrap of paper in the prison.

Cross-examined by Senator Webber:

Q. Mr. Morris, as Agent of the prison, to what have you been in the habit of looking as the source of your authority in your official position?

A. Well, sir, my attention was first called to the statutes; after that to instructions, verbal and written, from the board.

Q. Speaking of punishments, were you aware of a statute which made it the duty of the keeper administering the punishment to make a written statement of the offense and the nature and extent of the punishment, such statement to be signed by him and handed in as early as the next day after the punishment was inflicted?

A. No, sir; I didn't know there was any such statute; I never saw it, in fact never heard that there was any such statute in the laws until I saw it in the new bill, and I heard then it was an old statute; I saw it in the first copy of the new bill which is before this House.

Q. Under your administration state whether it has been the practice to require any such report as the statue requires from those administering the punishment?

A. No, sir, it has not; I consider the whole thing fatal in the prison to allow a keeper to have anything to do with the penalties; I don't know a prison in the country that does do it.

Q. I don't care to argue with you as to the propriety of the practice; has it been your habit to administer the punishments adjudged by you with your own hands?

A. It has ever since my last deputy, or since Capt. Winans left the prison.

Q. What proportion of the corporal punishments inflicted under your administration has been resorted to as a means of inducing confession?

A. Mr. Webber, I could not give you the exact number; I have never computed it, but very few.

Q. Approximate one in ten?

A. Well, I should think not less than that.

STATE PRISON INVESTIGATION. 381

Q. When you obtained confessions from prisoners under punishment, what value did you attach to the confessions thus obtained?

A. Take the case of Driscoll. The circumstances of his escape showed positively that some one must have assisted him. It was of importance that I should know who did assist him, whether it was a freeman or a convict. He went out with a freeman's team. If he assisted a convict to escape it was important that I should know it. There had been other cases where the proof was clear beyond the possibility of a doubt. It depended largely upon the character of the confession, whatever it was.

Q. Did you ever consider such a confession, if it implicated other convicts, as sufficient evidence to justify you in administering corporal punishments on the convicts thus implicated?

A. No, sir; not unless other circumstances corroborated his testimony, or statement, or confession.

Q. You speak of keeping punishments from the record so as to save convicts their good time?

A. Yes, sir.

Q. If the record be made of the punishment, is it not in the discretion of the inspectors to allow the good time?

A. Yes, sir.

Q. Then why were these kept from the record when you could have entered with the record explanatory circumstances which the inspectors could have considered?

A. Well, sir, to be candid with you, I think that the better method; but we were not anticipating an investigation then. The motive was simply to avoid any misapprehension on the part of the board that might arise from the record. If I had the same thing to do over again, I don't think I should do it.

Q. Now, do you remember the case of that man Rusbing (?) that was punished by showering?

A. Yes, sir.

Q. Do you remember striking him with a cane?

A. Yes, sir; I tapped him three times with a small cane.

Q. Why didn't you put that on the record?

A. It was not a part of the punishment for the offense for which he was punished.

Q. Was the crying out which he indulged in under punishment an offense under the regulations?

A. Yes, sir; I should say it was; an outcry of any kind in the yard always produces quite a sensation with the men in hearing.

Q. Is it not customary for men to indulge in these outcries when undergoing punishments?

A. No, sir; it is considered a proud thing for a man to take his punishment without saying a word; still, some of the worst men we have in prison make the most fuss when you come to put them under the whip or any punishment.

Q. Do you recollect of kicking a man in the yard?

A. I never did, sir; I never could hear of that man except what Mr. Van Zandt said; I never could find anybody that did see him.

Q. Do you wish to be understood that you never did kick any one?

A. Yes, sir; I do most positively.

Q. Do you recollect slapping a colored boy's face in the dining room one Sunday?

A. Yes, sir.
Q. Was that entered of record?
A. No, sir; I don't think it was.
Q. Was it considered a punishment for a breach of discipline?
A. No, sir; I went to him and told him twice to sit around; he was sitting with his back towards some visitors and laughing, while a stranger was making a prayer in the morning, making merriment with some boys behind him; I tapped him lightly, so lightly that I didn't think it worth while to make any record of it; he was very penitent about it soon after, and asked my forgiveness.
Q. How long after McDonald was punished on the cross before the cross was destroyed?
A. The cross was destroyed in the spring of 1873, I think.
Q. 1873?
A. Yes, sir; but I didn't use it any for several months before. I don't think I used it any in the winter of 1873.
Q Do you know whether it was used at all in 1872?
A. I should think it was.
Q. You think it was?
A. Yes, sir; I know I made it within two or three months after I went to the prison, hoping it might prove a good substitute for the lash.
Q. Do you think the punishment upon the cross was not severe?
A. No, sir; I do not think it was.
Q. Would not its severity depend entirely upon the manner in which the convict would be attached to it?
A. He might be attached in a manner that would make it very severe, indeed, —on the cross, or anything else.
Q. When you administered punishment by whipping, did you always time your punishment?
A. I did n't time it, I always counted.
Q. You counted?
A. Yes, sir.
Q. Did you count the blows given Driscoll?
A. Yes, sir.
Q. How many did you give him?
A. I think I gave him ten; I don't know but fifteen.
Q. Did you always record the exact number that was given?
A. I did when I knew exactly.
Q. When you punished Thurston with the lash, did you count yourself the number that was given?
A. Yes, sir; I counted very closely.
Q. Did you record the number?
A. No, sir, not definitely; I said not less than fifty, and I meant by that it was about fifty I gave him for the first punishment.
Q. You gave that number for the first punishment; the record of the second punishment gives no number?
A, No, sir.
Q. When you punished by showering did you time the application of the water?
A. I always did where it exceeded more than a minute or two.
Q. Did you time it yourself, or have it done?

A. Yes, I always timed it myself ; in some cases I would order three or five minutes water ; that would be administered by the deputy.

Q. What proportion of the entries by showering stated the time of punishment?

A. I presume very many of them do not state it at all ; I know many of them do not.

Q. You have the Inspectors' record in your office?

A. Yes, sir.

Q. You are at liberty to examine it any time you please?

A. Yes, sir.

Q. Did you ever look over the record to see what rules and orders had been made by the Inspectors before you came there?

A. Yes, sir; I have to a great extent.

Q. Did you ever find that rule requiring the physician to be present when punishments are inflicted?

A. I never did, and never heard of it.

Q. Until when?

A. Until within the last ten days.

Q. Who first told you?

A. It was brought up in the investigation at the prison. I don't recollect how it occurred.

Q. Do you recollect the controversy with Dr. Tuttle about clothing for the prison?

A. I don't recollect it about clothing. He said in a report one morning something derogatory to the management about there not having been sufficient clothing in the prison for the comfort of the men. I wrote him a note, telling him that I never heard of his complaint until I saw it in his report, and I wished when he had any reports of that kind to make he would come to me.

Q. Do you remember that in the report of Dr. Smith, made in October, 1871, he called your attention to the importance of a more general use of flannel under clothing for the men during the cold season for the purpose of saving them from pulmonary diseases, rheumatism, etc.

A. Yes, sir.

Q. And as a matter of economy?

A. Yes, sir; and we have tried to pay attention to that. Two hundred men are wearing flannels in the prison to-day.

Q. Was it not a common thing during the cold weather for the convicts to complain of insufficient clothing?

A. No, sir, not a common thing.

Q. Were any such complaints made to you?

A. Very likely; it would be strange if there had not.

Q. In your opinion, was the clothing which the men wore during the past winter sufficient to make them comfortable, and keep them healthy?

A. It was, so far as I could control it or help it, or any one else about the prison.

Q. Was there any restriction placed upon your authority to furnish the quantity of clothing for the men?

A. No, sir; there was no restriction placed upon the clothing or upon the weather. The weather has been unusually severe, and I guess we have all felt the effect of it.

Q. Was there any restriction placed upon your authority to furnish clothing?

A. Nothing but good sense.

Q. In your judgment, were the men furnished with sufficient clothing to make them comfortable?

A. If I had to pass through another such a season, I should give them more than the past winter if we were in the same condition.

Q. I understand that you have reduced expenses somewhat by cutting off the tobacco ration. Do you think that has had any effect upon the discipline?

A. Yes, sir.

Q. In what way?

A. I think it is a useless, expensive habit, demoralizing in all its effects.

Q. You don't use it yourself?

A. Not if I can help it.

Q. What effect do you think cutting off the tobacco ration has had upon the discipline of the prison?

A. I think anything that increases the sanitary condition of the prison adds to its cleanliness and wholesomeness in every department,—helps its discipline.

Q. I am not speaking of theories.

A. I am speaking of practical things.

Q. Now, I ask you whether the men have been more or less quiet under it?

A. I think they have been fully as quiet; and, also, more quiet, the more I think of it.

Q. You have 125 men engaged on the cigar contract?

A. Yes, sir.

Q. And those men are, more or less of them, in the habit of using tobacco?

A. Very likely.

Q. And it is done with the knowledge of the keepers and the Agent?

A. No, sir; I don't allow them to use it; they do a great many things, but we can't always put our finger upon the men; it is a very common thing for us to stop a squad and search them from head to foot for tobacco.

Q. I don't speak of their stealing it and carrying it away, but isn't the use of it there an infraction of the rule?

A. Yes, sir.

Q. And the keepers are instructed to report men for its use?

A. Yes; they do report it.

Q. Are you aware that, as a rule, they don't report it?

A. I don't think I am aware that they don't report, as a rule; we shut men up in darkness, away from their friends, and take away their whisky, their ale, their tea, coffee, and all the comforts of society, and I don't see why we should give them tobacco because they are in prison.

By Mr. Bartow:

Q. Was your engagement at the prison from the year 1862 to the present time continuous?

A. No, sir.

Q. What time were you out?

A. I left the prison board in, I think, March, 1864, when Mr. Winton was appointed; I think the entire board resigned in one day.

Q. How long were you out of the prison?

A. I was out from March, 1864, to March, 1871.

Q. How long did you try to control the convicts without corporal punishment?

A. The first man I punished with the whip was in July after I went there; I don't remember the day; it was some time in July.

Q. Did you try other punishment during the period from March to July?

A. I don't recollect of anything that called for corporal punishment, except in wearing the clog.

Q. What punishments were in vogue at the time you took command of the Prison?

A. Well, sir, I am not able to tell you, as I know only from hearsay. Mr. Bingham told me himself that he hadn't punished a man with the whip for several months, I think three or four. Other punishments, perhaps, were the clog and the bare cell and confinement on short rations.

Q. What punishments did you institute that were new?

A. The first thing I tried was the cross instead of the whip.

Q. Any other?

A. Well, the next most prominent thing was the hose, and other little things sometimes for trifling offenses.

Q. How soon did you administer any corporal punishment after you commenced your administration?

A. In about four months I should think.

Q. Did you administer *any* corporal punishment?

A. What do you call corporal punishment? I don't recollect anything very serious, unless I might have tied a man up, perhaps, or something like that.

Q. What punishment did you find to be the most efficacious to subdue the convict?

A. What convict?

Q. Any convict.

A. I couldn't name any single punishment that seemed to be the most efficacious.

Q. You say you have tried some experiments?

A. It depends entirely upon the character of the man; I have seen men show as much chagrin and regret at being placed in a bare cell in five minutes as other men would endure under the whip.

Q. When was the cross abolished?

Q. I don't think the cross was used at all after the fall of 1872; I think the cross was used some eighteen or twenty months; it was an experiment; everything that I have tried, aside from the ———, has been an experiment. I never said I would not use the lash in any instance, and the board never said so.

Q. Is it a rule of the prison that any other person than yourself may administer punishment without your order?

A. There is a rule at the prison, made by myself, that has been repeated by myself, and I understand it to be a rule of the prison, that no man should be punished without my knowledge and approval.

Q. When was the first that you knew Mr. Martin had inflicted punishment without your order?

A. I couldn't give you the exact time; I know we found men locked up in several instances that I hadn't heard of—he hadn't reported them to me.

Q. How long was this before he left the prison?

A. It was at different intervals; he never would give up that idea entirely but what he had a right to punish without consulting me.

Q. Did you regard that as an infraction of your rights or of the rules of the prison?

A. Yes, sir, I did.
Q. Did you report it to the inspectors?
A. I couldn't say whether I did or not; I know I have talked with the Governor about it. I recollect finding one locked up one day when walking through the prison with Governor Baldwin that I didn't know had been locked up.
Q. How long now has McDonald been in the prison?
A. The records show that he has been there since 1869.
Q. Do you remember when he was not a cripple?
A. No, sir, I do not.
Q. Were you present the evening Martin's testimony was taken, when he said that he had examined his memorandum book that day?
A. No, sir; I didn't hear him say any such thing; I heard you ask him—if you want to know what I did hear—

[The inquiry concerning memorandum book was to refresh memory of witness, and was ordered not to be taken.—Reporter.]

Since Mr. Martin has been able to talk upon this question I have asked him several times if he couldn't produce his old memorandum book, and he told me he didn't know where it was, but he would have his folks see if they couldn't find it; I think I have asked him three times within the last ten days.

By Senator Jones:
Q. Have you asked him since the examination,—since he was sworn.
A. Yes, sir; I asked him to-day.

By Mr. Bartow:
Q. When was the strap substituted for the lash?
A. I can't give you the precise day, Mr. Bartow; it was in the latter part of 1873 sometime; periods lapse there where you have no occasion to use the whip or strap; sometimes it runs along for several months, and then we may have two or three occasions in one day.
Q. Now, when a prisoner is whipped with the lash or with the strap, was there any rule requiring the number of strokes to be kept or recorded?
A. I should think the rules embraced such a thing, to get down to the strict letter of it; but the number of strokes would not indicate the amount of punishment at all; they might be light or heavy; say whipped them severely and it would mean severely.
Q. Now, when the record says that Thurston was whipped with "not less than fifty lashes," what would that indicate,—that he was whipped with just that number?
A. Yes, sir.
Q. Which whipping was that?
A. That was the first one.
Q. How many lashes were administered the second whipping?
A. I know that I counted for a time; I didn't give him any that I didn't count, but was parleying with him to get him to make some solemn assurance that such a thing would not occur again.
Q. Is there any memorandum or anything within your knowledge that shows the number?
A. No record that I know of showing the number of lashes received the last time by Thurston. Mr. Cook was acting as deputy at that time, and simply mentioned the punishment without giving the number of lashes.
Q. I understood you to say in the direct examination that when you found Driscoll he started to run?

STATE PRISON INVESTIGATION. 387

A. Yes, sir.
Q. And that one step would have taken him out of your sight. Now why did you say he started to run?
A. Because his face was in a position to run. He had been lying down apparently, and jumped up.
Q. Do you remember making any demand upon him to halt before you shot him?
A. No, sir; I did not.
Q. Did you expect when you shot, that if it hit him it might kill him?
A. I hadn't any definite idea about it.
Q. Now, you say you supposed that some freeman had helped him to escape?
A. Circumstances indicated that very clearly.
Q. Did you investigate before the whipping to know whether that was so or not?
A. I did all day, and tried hard to find out.
Q. Did I understand you to say, that sometimes you didn't make a record of the punishment, because you found the convict was not to blame?
A. Yes, sir.
Q. What was your mode of cancelling the record of punishments?
A. Not copying from the deputy's memorandum, such record would be omitted.
Q. Do you remember a convict by the name of George Redwood?
A. Yes, sir.
Q. Do you remember of his asking for more underclothing, and didn't get it, when you had means in your hands to get it for him?
A. No, sir; I don't remember his ever having spoken about it,—he might have spoken about it a dozen times.
Q. Did you have means of his in your hands?
A. Of Redwood's?
Q. Yes, sir.
A. I could not say; the clerk would be the proper person to know that. It is not a customary thing, I would like to say right here in justice to everybody, to invest a convict's money for articles that should be furnished by the State.
Q. Do you remember a convict in the prison within the last two years, that was suffering from diarrhœa, and was placed in a tub of cold water, and soon after that died?
A. I never heard of a convict being placed in a tub of cold water with the diarrhœa or without it.

By Senator Webber:
Q. I would like to ask you if you remember the date when David Smith was first punished?
A. It was early in July, 1871.
Q. Did he afterwards become insane?
A. Well, I have never been able to decide as to how much insanity there is about Smith.
Q. What I mean is, was he sent to the insane department of the prison?
A. Not long; sometimes we send men who are noisy and boisterous. I don't recollect of his having to go to the asylum; he might have gone there for a short period.
Q. Where is he now?
A. He is at work in the blacksmith-shop on the wagon contract.

Q. You speak of copying from the Deputy's memorandum?

A. Yes, sir.

Q. Now, has it ever been the practice to copy the memorandum?

A. I don't mean to copy his memorandum; I mean make a record from such data as he had taken from punishments observed, and memoranda taken soon after the event.

Q. I understand the practice to be that the Deputy makes short notes by way of memoranda, sometimes only putting down the parties' names, to call attention to it, and then when the record is written up this is looked at, and you write up from your memory of the facts.

A. My own memory and from his. It has been a great misfortune in the prison that I never had a Deputy that seemed to be able to write up such a memoradum to suit me.

Re-direct by Mr. Conely:

Q. Under your administration had it been the custom for the assistant keepers to administer punishments?

A. We never allowed them to at all in any instance.

Q. How does the clothing, as to quantity, during the past winter, compare with the amount of clothing worn by convicts and used by them in their bedding during the time that you were inspector?

A. Well, sir, I consider the amount of clothing in use in the prison for the last year largely above that of any other period that I have ever known.

Q. How does the amount of clothing, bed-clothing and clothing to be worn, used during your administration, compare with what it has been during former periods?

A. I am not prepared to say definitely. I have never had the means of instituting a comparison.

Q. Compare it with the time you were inspector, if you can.

A. Mr. Conely, I could not say; I regarded the men then as having a sufficient quantity for health and comfort.

With this examination of Mr. Morris, the committee decided the investigation closed.

ENTRIES FOUND IN THE CONDUCT RECORD BOOK.

"FEB. 26, 1873.—John Dalton and James Dennis, reported by Mr. Hatch for combined and repeated failure to do their day's work of 24 pairs of shoes. They were allowed to continue their work from bell to bell, and the keeper was instructed to watch them and see that they worked diligently. Again they both failed. Locked in bare cell, without food or drink, for 60 hours, and have at this date, March 1st, finished their task early."

"MARCH 16, 1873.—David E. Gee, reported by Keeper Lewis for making noise like a cat while boys were marching to Sabbath-school. Kept in his cell for 24 hours, without food or water, and compelled to repeat his cat noise while being showered."

"MARCH 16, 1873.—Charles Simmons, reported by Keeper Lewis for making noise while boys were marching to Sabbath-school. Had been reported several times lately for general meanness, and a running account had been kept against him, until this morning the whole thing was balanced to date by the application of Holly water. Simmons is a 25-year convict, and has been notoriously ugly almost every day. Made solemn promises of better behavior."

"MARCH 18, 1873.—Leander Wood, reported by hall master, who found quite a quantity of fine leaf tobacco in his cell, stolen from cigar contract. Copious application of Holly."

"APRIL 3, 1873.—Philander Crane, reported by Keeper Perrine for general meanness and frequent disobedience, talking, etc., in the shop. Locked in bare cell 12 hours."

"APRIL 11, 1873.—Benjamin Sanford, reported by Keeper Lewis for talking in shop. Bare cell 24 hours."

"APRIL 19, 1873.—Anthony Sweeney, reported for general and continuous meanness by his keeper, has been sullen and defiant ever since he came, and frequently reported for petty meanness. Balanced up a long running account by watering him thoroughly from head to foot."

"MAY 3, 1873.—James Nichols, reported by Keeper Lewis for insolence; was talking, and when keeper told him to stop or the keeper would send for the deputy, said, 'Send for him; that is just what I want, and we will see what you make by it.' In bare cell, without food or drink, 36 hours."

"MAY 10, 1873.—Benjamin F. Coe was reported for making a noise like a crow, in his cell before he was unlocked,—cold water improves his dialect and he crows no more."

"MAY 10, 1873.—Philander Crane, reported by keeper Burkhart for going into another cell in the morning when coming down from gallery; stoutly denied it, and laid keeper Burkhart in a falsehood,—a lively application of cold water brought out the facts, which he admitted the same as keeper reported."

"MAY 12, 1873.—George Smalley, reported for general meanness and insolence.

Works in cigar shop and sits on a chair. After his day's work was done, keeper turns his chair around facing him, and Smalley turns it back again; keeper called him up and told him to stop his talking, but Smalley would not do it, and continued to talk all the way back to his seat,—tried to excuse his insolence on the ground that he was an Englishman, and that he had been ridiculed and made fun of in various ways by keeper. All of which had no sort of foundation."

"June 12, 1873 —David Harrison, by keeper Tift, for jumping from an open window in grinding room to gather refuse tobacco from rear of cigar shop,—bare cell 40 hours."

"June 19, 1873.—Charles Thompson, for looking out doors and when remonstrated with, told keeper Blair that he had no business to go to the door, and that his eyes were his own and he should do as he pleased with them,—bare cell 48 hours."

"June 23, 1873.—Martin Donahue, for talking in ranks, bare cell 48 hours."

"June 26, 1873.—James Kelly, *alias* Mulligan, refused to work when ordered by keeper Glasgow,—bare cell 48 hours. Has been on the beat always."

"June 30, 1873.—William McKirchy, refused to work as ordered by keeper. Bare cell 48 hours."

"July 1, 1873.—James Nichols, for talking in shop,—bare cell 48 hours."

"July 3, 1873—John Leyden, *alias* Smith, rose in dining room near the close of breakfast, and in a loud voice said, 'all who desire their freedom, follow me.' He was removed to cell, and said when talked to about it, said he was put up to it, and then feigned craziness; eight lashes brought to the center of conclusion that he had made a fool of himself, and that he knew better all the time.'"

"July 11, 1873—Benjamin Sanford, for having stolen tobacco from cigar shop in his cell, pretended that he found it under rear of cigar shop."

"July 17, 1873—Oren Hunter [life solitary] was seen by keeper to be tinkering at something, and when approached, refused to let keeper see what he was making, and afterwards threw the article away among some rubbish. Hunter has been somewhat desperate and lawless for a long time, and seemed to forget his real sentence. Bare cell three and one half hours."

"Oct. 14, 1873—Jeremiah Dowd, Ed. Rice, and William Robinson, all reported for talking in the dining room. No punishment but this record."

"Oct. 23, 1873—James McGlinn, for insolence and general meanness in words, tone, and action. Bare cell over night. McGlinn is one of those men who know too much to say anything, but can be contemptible."

"Oct. 28, 1873—James Warren was ordered by the foreman of the polishing shop to do something with a belt, and said he would not until it was cleaned. Foreman told him he would report him, and Warren said, 'report if you dare, and I will report you for giving boys tobacco.' Keeper told him to fix the belt; he replied, hotly, 'I have been told once.' Bare cell 48 hours. Warren has got his face sharp set for the lower end of the hall.'"

"Oct. 28, 1873—James Peck, for talking in the dining room, bare cell 36 hours."

"Nov. 5, 1873—Albert Fincham, for carrying large knife and threatening to fix Agent with it, 18 moderate lashes."

"Nov. 5, 1873—William Wilson, 73 west, took above knife from Fincham and sharpened it up to stab Agent with. Got ten lashes for his trouble."

"Nov. 7, 1873—John Welch, John Bylesma, and James Jackson, for talking and loafing outside near dry-kiln,—no punishment."

STATE PRISON INVESTIGATION. 391

"Nov. 9, 1873. James McGinnn, for talking in the shop and general bad conduct. No punishment, but a running account still open."

"Nov. 9, 1873. John Driscoll and Washington Pardee, for talking while in the gallery. Both owned the soft impeachment and were allowed to go"

"Nov. 17, 1873. John Madden and John Minor, for fighting in the shop. Madden was the aggressor again, and nothing but the lash seemed available in this case. Twelve lashes took all the belligerence out of him for that day. Minor showered."

"Nov. 24, 1873. William Van Sickle, for talking in the shop,—no punishment.

"JAN. 30, 1874. Milo Holcomb, Reason Webster, Willard Sanford, Benjamin F. Coe, and John S. Gage, all detected in smoking and dealing in cigars purloined from debris from cigar shop. All watered all over."

FEB. 2, 1874. John McMartin, for having in his possession stolen tobacco; James O'Neil, for passing the tobacco to McMartin; William Linch, for passing the tobacco to O'Neil; John Williams, for stealing said tobacco from contract; Charles Smith, for stealing tobacco from contract; James Manion, for having said tobacco in his possession. All six of the above named men stripped and showered."

In an entry of Feb. 4, 1874, a convict is spoken of as "A lazy, shiftless, impudent old liar and thief, and would not earn his dinner once a week of his own accord."

Punishments are often stated in the following terms : "Watered all over mildly." "Cold water from head to foot." "Cold water all over." "Watered from head to foot." "Showered from head to foot."

"JUNE 17, 1874.—John Driscoll, for turning his head and making motions and signals to another company; when ta ked to about the matter was very insolent. Deputy told him if he did not keep his head straight it would be straightened for him. He replied: "It takes a man to do that." He was in a bare cell two and one-half days, and became very mellow."

"JUNE 22, 1874.—George McKenzie, Edward Hutson, John Welch and John Stevenson, all reported for talking in ranks and in dining room. All suspended by the hand for one hour. Suspending is done by placing a cord around the wrists loosely, and drawing them up."

"JUNE 29, 1874.—Benjamin Hill is full of various little, mean tricks ; is thieving, lying, lazy, and contemptible ; was chalked in his own cell for talking ; in the afternoon of Sunday, while some rehearsals were taking place in the dining-room, he hallooed three times loudly, so as to be heard all over the prison, and even outside ; Agent heard him distinctly while sitting in the dining-room ; guard was right under his cell, and was sure he was right ; several convicts also corroborated guard ; Hill was strapped mildly for his cussedness."

"AUG. 3, 1874 —Albert Payne, Homer Mentor, Charles Jacobs, and J. Bajley, for talking in the ranks, ordered to bare cell all night, and reported by guard in the morning for talking, singing, and sneezing during the night ; tied up by their hands for one hour, when they dropped all their fun."

"JUNE 3, 1873.—Drayton Thurston for several months past has been under lock and key full half the time, for various mean, deceptive tricks, and has hung back about work, pretending to be sick, and would vomit when he pleased, like a turkey buzzard ; had been sent to the shop repeatedly, and promised doing better, but failed every time ; has violent and irritable temper, and tries to control it but little at times ; as a last effort to conciliate him, he was placed to work on the improvements, and said if he had any trouble down there the

Agent might punish him severely ; did very well for a few days and then commenced to shirk about work ; talked a good deal, and was constantly joking, and working up some scheme to escape,--in fact he was on the beat every moment ; the Superintendent, Mr. Donough, had noticed this disposition for several days, and more especially on this day ; he seemed to be only in the way ; he finally told him to go to another place and go to work, when he threw his pick to the bottom of the ditch, very contemptibly in manner and looks ; the attention of the deputy was called to his conduct, when he became very violent, and would not go to the hall, nor do a thing that he was bidden, only when a revolver was produced ; he went to the bare cell, and then could not be silent, and continued to make the most terrific, blasphemous threats to every one that came within his hearing ; the Agent allowed nothing to be said to him that afternoon, in the hope that his frantic spasm would pass off, but the next morning he seemed as turbulent and defiant as ever ; he seemed bent on some desperate row ; water was applied to him copiously in his cell, but with no effect only to increase his anger ; finally he was ordered to come out of his cell, but refused until a revolver was again placed on him by the Agent; he was taken to the lower end of the hall ; kept his tongue running constantly, and said, after his hands were tied, that he would take a knife out of the Agent's bowels within a week if he punished him ; not less than 50 lashes were given him, light and heavy, before he would yield and make any promises of better conduct ; he finally seemed to yield completely, and was let down and sent to his cell for rest and repairs, but was soon dancing in his cell, and showed but little evidence of any better intentions.

June 13.—Thurston had been allowed to work in the yard for the past week, while a close watch was kept on his movements, and from them the Agent became satisfied that he was still bent on mischief. Other convicts confidentially reported him as having a concealed weapon upon his person, with the design of executing his former wicked threat upon the Agent or any one else that might in any way interfere with him. He was again brought to the hall and sat for a few minutes upon a bench, and was seen to hide something in a spittoon near by. Upon the demand of the Agent he produced a keen, double-edged dirk; said it was made and prepared for him by Charles Simmons, a 25-year man upon the wagon contract. Simmons has always been very reckless and desperate since he came; has given the authorities much serious trouble in various ways, almost daily. The two men were punished severely with the whip until they made ample promises of correct behavior hereafter.

REPORT OF COMMITTEE TO THE LEGISLATURE.

The joint committee appointed by concurrent resolution of March 29, 1875, to investigate the charges which had been made in the Adrian Press of March 27th and 29th against John Morris, Agent, and his subordinates, in the management of the State Prison at Jackson, commenced taking testimony, and having examined the party making the charges without finding sufficient evidence to justify the pursuit of the inquiry relative to the truth of the specific charges named in the preamble and resolutions, asked for such increased power as would enable them to investigate generally as to the management of the prison under Mr. Morris' administration, which power was conferred by joint resolution of April 8, 1875. Under this authority an extended investigation has been had, and your committee beg leave to report as follows:

Your committee, entering upon the performance of their duties, found themselves embarrassed, from the fact that there was no one to act as prosecutor, whose business it would be to bring before the committee such evidence as would tend to throw light upon the subject under examination. Your committee has called a large number of witnesses, selecting such as it seemed most probable would be able to throw light upon the subject, and taken a large amount of testimony, some portions of which are found to be quite irrelevant and immaterial, while other portions furnish information concerning the matter in question. This testimony your committee has caused to be printed, and the same will be laid upon the tables of members with this report.

The inspectors of the State Prison were among the first witnesses examined, and from their testimony (which was confirmed by that taken subsequently), we find that while the statute requires that convicts should be punished for misconduct, in such manner and under such regulations as the Board of Inspectors should adopt, and also that a written memorandum of the punishment should be made and signed by the one inflicting the punishment, stating the offense committed and the kind and amount of punishment inflicted; yet the inspectors had not considered this statute a practicable one to be carried into effect, and the question of punishment was left almost, if not entirely, to the discretion of the Agent, such discretion being regulated only by oral advice, given from time to time by the Board of Inspectors. Any infraction of prison rules by a convict reported to the Agent was by him adjudged summarily, and in his discretion the convict was allowed to go unpunished, or be punished in such manner and to such extent as to him at the time seemed proper, and such record was made of it as met his approval; the general practice during the term of his administration having been to make merely a brief memorandum by the deputy, at or about the time the punishment was inflicted, and from such memorandum and from the recollection of the Agent and deputy, at the close of the month, the "conduct record" would be written up.

We find that some severe punishments have been inflicted of which no record has been made, and no sufficient reason given for the omission to make such record.

We find some very severe punishments have been inflicted for causes which do not seem to the committee to justify the infliction of punishment to such an extent, and which we do not think calculated to improve the discipline of the prison.

We find the following modes of punishment have, in the discretion of the Agent, been resorted to:

Locking in bare cell without provision, in some cases as long as forty-eight hours, but generally a shorter time; showering, usually upon the naked body, by water thrown from a hose; placing convicts upon a wooden horse; placing a wire cap, with an iron collar, around the head and about the neck of the convict, to be worn day and night continuously, in some cases as high as thirty days; tying up by the hands; punishment with the lash and with the strap; punishment upon the cross, and by placing clogs upon the ankles, as well as minor punishments, by deprivation of lights, reading matter, and good time.

We find from the testimony that there seems to have been a want of dignity on the part of the Agent in the treatment of convicts, and in imposing punishments and making a record thereof, the records of punishments in many cases being stated in a light, trifling manner, or with slang expressions which do not comport with a proper sense of the responsibility resting upon one occupying the position of Agent.

We find some cases of punishment which we can only account for by supposing that they were inflicted while in anger; as, for instance, the striking of the convict Rushing with a cane upon his naked person with such force as to keep him in the hospital from eight to ten days, as testified by Dr. Tuttle.

We find that a large percentage of the punishments grew out of the tobacco question. Mr. Morris having a theory that he could run the prison better without than with tobacco, adopted such a regulation as would prevent the bulk of the convicts from its use; and yet a hundred and twenty-five of them were kept at work upon the cigar contract with tobacco constantly in their hands and before them. Under such circumstances, of course it could not but be expected that infractions of the rule would occur.

We find that the punishment by the lash and upon the cross has been abandoned as not proper punishments for use; and yet there has been no rule or regulation, other than the discretion of the Agent, defining the character or amount of punishment. We do not believe that such a large discretion should be vested in any man.

These convicts being in the State prison, every presumption is against them. Their mouths are substantially closed; for, being under the will of the Agent, they are likely to remain silent under almost any infliction, rather than complain and take the risk of being visited with a severe punishment.

The employes, keepers, guards, etc., about the prison are forbidden by the rules adopted by the inspectors from speaking outside the walls of matters which transpire in the prison. We think it would be an improvement in the regulations if every keeper and guard were at liberty to report to the inspectors every act of the Agent which was an infraction of the general rules of the prison, and especially should this be the duty of the deputy.

As to the clothing of the convicts, we find that it is insufficient for cold weather, and that the prison physician called attention to this fact, but instead of meeting

STATE PRISON INVESTIGATION.   395.

the cordial co-operation of the Agent to remedy the deficiency, he was regarded as an intermeddler with that which was none of his business.

So far as we can learn, the duties of the chaplain and of the prison physician have been carefully, faithfully, and conscientiously performed.

We believe that the food of the convicts is ample and wholesome.

We have taken no testimony as to the sanitary condition of the cells, but we quote from the report made by Dr. Kedzie, dated Nov. 14, 1874, and found in the Report of the Secretary of the State Board of Health, on page 107, in which, after stating that the provision for ventilation was entirely insufficient, he says:

"At six o'clock in the morning, before the men had left their beds, I gathered specimens of air from four cells, widely separated from each other. The guards informed me that when the men all march out from their cells in the morning, each carrying his night bucket, the halls are filled with an overpowering odor. The air in every cell examined was loathsome and disgusting in the extreme. Analysis of this air gave the following results." He then gives the analysis of the four specimens, the purest of which contained 21.9 parts of carbonic acid, and he adds: "No comment is required."

It is the opinion of your committee that men who have lodged in such an atmosphere can hardly be regarded as in good condition for labor when they enter upon their day's duties in the shops; and we think the interest of the State would be promoted by adopting such means as will make the rest of the convicts in their cells a matter of invigoration, rather than of prostration.

As the Legislature at this session has passed a bill for the regulation of the State Prison, your committee will not enlarge this report by further particular recommendations. But we trust the testimony which has been taken by the committee will be carefully read by every member, and we believe that the investigation will not be without good results.

Your committee believe that those in charge of our State institutions should ever bear in mind that one man has no right over another except as given by law, and that if the Agent of the State Prison, or any other officer, exceeds that authority he puts himself outside the protection of law.

The law adjudges these convicts to imprisonment at hard labor for a given term. We regard it as the duty of the State, and all the officers chosen, to see its laws executed,—to enforce the law firmly, but kindly. We believe that convicts have a sense of justice which is outraged when punishments are inflicted without sufficient cause, or when gross breaches of discipline go unpunished, and that the best discipline can be attained only by a firm and wise administration of a *uniform* law; and we think there should be a law governing convicts in the prison as well as citizens generally.

We believe the inspectors to be good and true men, who have a sincere desire to promote the best interests of the State and of the convicts, but we think they have allowed too much discretion to the Agent, and from what we learn from them we are of opinion that they agree with us in this regard.

Your committee cannot close this report without expressing the opinion (deduced from the testimony and from an examination of the prison), that the good of the convicts and the interest of the State would be promoted if an arrangement could be made to keep the worst convicts, those most ungovernable, by themselves. A small percentage of the whole number, the most incorrigible, might be selected for some more rigorous labor and confinement, with a provision, say, that when they had conducted themselves in accordance with the requirements for a certain time they might be permitted to have the enlarged privileges of the others, and with the understanding that any serious infraction of the rules would subject others to the same rigorous treatment We believe some such arrangement would improve the discipline, and add to the productive labor of the prison.

Your committee regret that their appointment at so late a period and the large amount of testimony taken render it necessary to make their report at so late a day in the session; but the results of the investigation and the report are submitted as the best attainable under the circumstances.

CHAS. D. NELSON,
JOHN H. JONES,
JOHN N. MELLEN,
WM. L. WEBBER,
MOSES BARTOW,
CHAS. H. MORSE,
JAMES EGGLESTON.

INDEX.

	PAGE.
Entries in Record Book of Conduct	389
Preliminary proceedings	3
Report of Committee	393

LIST OF WITNESSES.

Name.	PAGE.
Allen, A. A.	98, 133
Ayers, Junius	175
Bliss, A. A.	56
Bannister, George	112
Bedford, John	135
Bennett, J. R.	274
Beebe, Calvin T.	288
Cook, George	30
Chase, B. W.	43
Clark, F. S.	259, 303, 333
Crawford, R. C.	272
Cole, Clark	300
Chittock, Dr. Gordon	365
Dorrill, Marvin	370
Foster, Ulysses	217
Gridley, G. D.	370
Hendee, S. H.	103
Hawley, A. E.	108, 110
Hickox, Chaplain Geo. H.	191
Hinkley, James D.	263, 293
Hunt, Sanford	290
Howard, J. H.	341
Holt, Wm.	360
King, Henry N.	26
Kirschgessner, Charles	335
Lovell, L. W.	18
Leavenworth, E.	131
Ladeau, Philip	334
Lane, David	336
La Mountain, Napoleon	357
Morris, John	340, 370
McCrystal, Patrick	356
McDonald, Wm.	304
Martin, John R.	361, 368
O'Neil, Patrick	248
Perry, E. S.	106
Perrine, Hulbert	228
Parmenter, Jessee	115, 190
Perkins, J. L.	153, 185
Ranney, Dr. G. E.	343, 352
Stearns, Willard	24
Stroud, David R.	94
Smith, Alexander	282

LIST OF WITNESSES—Continued.

Name.	Page.
Spaulding, Henry D.	335
Seaton, Wm. L.	367
Thorne, Ransom	53
Tuttle, Dr. J. B.	236
Tunnicliff, Dr. Joseph	346, 355
Van Zandt, Elisha	87
Wilcox, W. S.	4, 109, 221
Winans, George	67, 93
Wood, Socrates H.	200, 254
Webster, Wm.	212
Woodard, H. L.	261
Warner, Esaias	275
Welton, Charles H.	279
Wurtz, L. H.	354

Printed in Dunstable, United Kingdom